Life seems to have stood still in Tangier. It has grown old, it is true, but it has not grown wiser or better. Or rather it seems not as if it had grown old, but as if it had never been young. To an artist—and many artists visit Tangier—it must be an enchanting place; but it would disgust a thrifty farmer or an enterprising trader, and make every hair of an inspector of nuisances stand on end.

—AMELIA PERRIER, 1876

Antæus

THE FINAL ISSUE

EDITED BY

DANIEL HALPERN

NO. 75/76, AUTUMN, 1994

Founding Editor
PAUL BOWLES
Founding Publisher
DRUE HEINZ
Associate Publisher
JEANNE WILMOT CARTER
Managing Editor
ELLEN FOOS
Publicity & Marketing
WILLIAM CRAGER
LISA ANN WEISBROD
Production Manager
VINCENT JANOSKI
Assistant Editors
HEATHER WINTERER
CHRISTINA THOMPSON

Contributing Editors
ANDREAS BROWN   JOHN HAWKES
JOHN FOWLES   STANLEY KUNITZ
DONALD HALL   W.S. MERWIN
MARK STRAND

ANTÆUS *is published by The Ecco Press, 100 West Broad Street, Hopewell, NJ 08525.*
Distributed by W. W. Norton & Company, Inc., 500 Fifth Avenue, New York, NY 10110, Ingram
Periodicals, 347 Reedwood Drive, Nashville, TN 37217, and B. DeBoer, Inc., 113 East Centre St.,
Nutley, NJ 07110. Distributed in England & Europe by W. W. Norton & Company, Inc.

ANTÆUS
100 West Broad Street, Hopewell, NJ 08525
Back issues available—write for a complete listing

ISSN 0003-5319
ISBN 0-88001-392-3
Library of Congress Card Number: 70-612646
Copyright © 1995 by ANTÆUS, *Hopewell, NJ*
Cover art: Fresco from Giotto Chapel (detail)
Cover design: Lorraine Louie

"The Eternal Heartbreak" by Elizabeth Hardwick and "Without Regret" by May Sarton,
reprinted in Antæus *71/72: On Music, were originally published in* Opera News *Magazine.*

Publication of this magazine has been made possible in part by a grant
from the National Endowment for the Arts.
Logo: Ahmed Yacoubi

EDITORIAL NOTE: Certain pieces have been reprinted from earlier issues—these are the contributions by Paul Bowles, Italo Calvino, Bill Clinton, Hart Crane, F. Scott Fitzgerald, and Ernest Hemingway. Helen Vendler's essay "A Reviewer's Beginnings" was commissioned for the *Princeton University Library Chronicle*, Spring 1994.

CONTENTS

POETRY

DOCUMENTS

DANIEL HALPERN

Editor's Note for the Final Issue

*A*nt*æus* was conceived in the spring of 1968, when Paul Bowles and I took a walk around the outskirts of Tangier, where I was living at the time. He wanted to call our proposed publication *Atlas;* we settled on *Antæus*. The first issue, which I edited and Paul published, was assembled in the autumn of 1969 and actually appeared in the summer of 1970, when I moved to New York.

This autumn marks our twenty-fifth year, and the last year I will edit *Antæus*—seventy-six issues and a public education later. During these twenty-five years it's been my good fortune to read new work by many of the best writers around the world, to meet and publish in *Antæus* writers such as W. H. Auden—who asked if I would have recommended to my parents, had I been around to be consulted, that they marry each other; Muriel Rukeyser; Lawrence Durrell; Jorge Luis Borges—who quizzed me regarding the names in English of the female genitalia; Cyril Connolly—who related how he was asked by his first editor, after writing a book review for the newspaper, to avoid involving himself with the work of his girlfriends, in fact a book by [Paul] Valéry; Tennessee Williams; John Berryman; Italo Calvino—who gave my bride and me the wedding dinner after our marriage in the Campidoglio in Rome; Pablo Neruda; Robert Lowell; Elizabeth Bishop—who took me for a tour of the Unicorn Tapestries at the Met, each of her descriptions that day an unpublished Bishop poem; Christopher Isherwood—who spent most of an evening talking about meeting an amazingly winning young singer called Mick Jagger; Alberto Moravia; Julio Cortázar; Jane Bowles—who attempted to persuade me to help her end her life because she was no longer capable of writing; and Djuna Barnes—who asked me if I had read her play *The Antiphon,* and proceeded to tell me that Marianne Moore likened reading it to reading an unknown language in which you know all the words. Djuna did contribute a poem to the second issue, but then took it back when she decided I was a certain loathsome "Southern boy who thinks he's going to write my biography!" I believe she was thinking of someone else. I have listed only those writers no longer with us, because they are unable to question my failing memory.

So here is my last issue. It has been a pleasant task preparing this final number of *Antæus*. I have been the luckiest of editors, in that I have been able to publish what seemed (always at the time) most alive and moving to me; and so the decision to end the magazine—before it begins losing its hair, eyesight and hearing, and succumbing to other maladies of old age—is an easy and affirmative one.

The final issue is a large, representative anthology of new work by past contributors, as well as unpublished writing by a few writers who over the years slipped through our net. I want to thank our devoted readers for having been a part of it all—and for being here now, at the end.

MARGARET ATWOOD

Simple Murders

He had a thin rapacious moustache and very pointed shoes. She had green eyes and hair the color of flame. He had a silver cigarette case and large, brutal thumbs. She had a scar across her cheekbone and a bitter laugh. He had the guileless blue eyes of a cherub but the soulless smile of a fiend. She had a black hat. He had a black cat. Every single one of them was in disguise.

* * *

He was lying facedown on the priceless Oriental carpet, with the bejeweled handle of the dagger protruding from between his expensively suited shoulder blades. She was draped over the disheveled bed, in her red nylon negligee, with the livid marks of ten huge fingers standing out on her throat.

No. Let's start again.

He was sheathed in green plastic garbage bags, tied neatly all the way down with a row of his own festive neckties, and buried at the bottom of the garden. They never would have found him if the neighbor hadn't wanted to replace the fence. It was the wife who did it, with a frying pan. He'd been beating her up for years.

As for the other one, she was run through a meat grinder and frozen in little freezer baggies labeled *"Stew."* Her daughter wanted the old-age checks. I learned about all of this in a British Rail station, en route to Norwich, because my train was late. You can't make such things up.

* * *

It was because of the chocolate bars. It was because of the stars. It was because of a life behind bars. It was her hormones. It was the radiation from the wires and phones. It was his mother saying, *You'll never amount to a hill of beans.* It was because he was so all-fired mean. It was the sleeping pills. It was the frills, on the blouse, under the jacket, over the breasts. It was the blood tests. It was the sigh, the cry, the hand on the thigh. It was the hunger, it was the rage, it was the spirit of the age.

It was a coincidence. It was the wrong bottle. My hand slipped. How was I to know it was loaded?

It was the fear. It was the cold, cold voice of the frozen angel, the voice from the outer darkness, whispering in my ear.

*　*　*

Mr. Plum, in the conservatory, with the wrench. She saw the wrench and she said, *What's that wrench for?* And I thought she wanted sex. So I strangled her.

*　*　*

It was the dog hair on the back seat of the car. It was the bloodstain on the chandelier. It was the fingernail in the pail. It was the chalice with the palace. It was the chicken that did nothing in the nighttime. It was the one detail you always forget, and for that they will come to get you. *Aha,* they will say. *You thought you were so smart.* This is the worst part, just before you wake.

*　*　*

It was the heart, the too-small heart, the too-small devious heart, the lopsided heart, the impoverished heart, the heart someone dropped, the heart with a crack in it. It was the heart that thought it needed to kill. To show them all. To feel. To heal. To become whole.

PAUL AUSTER

Last Days

Mr. Bones knew that Willy wasn't long for this world. The cough had been inside him for over six months, and by now there wasn't a chance in hell he would ever get rid of it. Mr. Bones had been there from the start, and he'd tracked every shift and nuance of Willy's decline, from the first phlegm-filled rattle in the lungs on February third to the wheezy sputum-jigs and gobby convulsions of high summer. All that was bad enough, but in the past two weeks a new tonality had crept into the bronchial music—something tight and flinty and percussive—and the attacks came so often now as to be almost constant. Each time one of them started, Mr. Bones half expected Willy's chest to explode from the rockets of pressure bursting against his rib cage. He figured that blood would be the next step, and when that fatal moment finally occurred on Saturday afternoon, it was as if all the angels in heaven had opened their mouths and started to sing. Mr. Bones saw it happen with his own eyes, standing by the side of the road between Washington and Baltimore as Willy hawked up a few miserable clots of red matter into his handkerchief, and right then and there he knew that every ounce of hope was gone. The smell of death had settled upon Willy G. Christmas, and as surely as the sun was a lamp in the clouds that went off and on every day, the end was drawing near.

What was a poor dog to do? Mr. Bones had been with Willy since his earliest days as a pup, and to put it in plain and simple Ingloosh, it was next to impossible for him to imagine a world that did not have his master in it. Every thought, every memory, every particle of the earth and air was saturated with Willy's presence. Habits die hard, and no doubt there's some truth to the adage that you can't teach an old dog new tricks, but it was more than just love or devotion that caused Mr. Bones to dread what was coming. It was pure ontological terror. Subtract Willy from the world, and the odds were that the world itself would cease to exist.

Such was the quandary Mr. Bones faced that August morning as he shuffled through the streets of Baltimore with his ailing master. A dog alone was no better than a dead dog, and once Willy breathed his last, he'd have nothing to look forward to but his own imminent demise. Willy had been cautioning him about this for many days now, and Mr. Bones knew the drill by heart: how to avoid the dogcatchers and constables, the paddy wagons and unmarked cars, the hypocrites from the so-called humane societies. No matter how sweetly they talked to him, the word *shelter* meant trouble. It would begin with nets and tranquilizer guns, devolve into a nightmare of cages and fluorescent lights, and end with a lethal injection or a dose of poison gas. If Mr. Bones had belonged to some recognizable breed, he might have stood a chance in the daily beauty contests for prospective owners, but Willy's sidekick was a hodgepodge of genetic strains—part collie, part Labrador, part spaniel, part canine puzzle—and to make matters worse, there were burrs protruding from his ragged coat, bad smells emanating from his mouth, and a perpetual, bloodshot sadness lurking in his eyes. No one was going to want to rescue him. As the homeless bard was fond of putting it, the outcome was written in stone. Unless Mr. Bones found another master in one quick hurry, he was a pooch primed for oblivion.

"And if the stun guns don't get you," Willy continued, clinging to a lamppost that foggy morning in Baltimore to prevent himself from falling, "there's a thousand other things that will. I'm warning you, kemosabe. You get yourself some new gig, or your days are numbered. Just look around this dreary burg. There's a Chinese restaurant on every block, and if you think mouths won't water when you come strolling by, then you don't know the first thing about Oriental cuisine. They prize the taste of dog, friend. The chefs round up strays and slaughter them in the alley right behind the kitchen—ten, twenty, thirty dogs a week. They might pass them off as ducks and pigs on the menu, but the in-crowd knows what they're getting, the gourmets aren't fooled for a second. Unless you want to wind up in a platter of moo goo gai pan, you'll think twice before you wag your tail in front of one of those Chink beaneries. Do you catch my drift, Mr. Bones? Know thine enemy—and then keep a wide berth."

Mr. Bones understood. He always understood what Willy said to him. This had been the case for as long as he could remember, and by now his knowledge of Ingloosh was as good as any other immigrant who had spent seven years on American soil. It was his second language, of course, and quite different from the one his mother had taught him, but even though his pronunciation left something to be desired, he had thoroughly mastered the ins and outs of its grammar, syntax, and idioms. None of this should be seen as strange or unusual for a dog of Mr. Bones's intelligence. Most dogs acquire a good working knowledge of two-legged speech, but in Mr. Bones's case there was the advantage of being blessed with a master who did not treat him as an inferior. They had been boon companions from the start, and when you added in the fact that Mr. Bones was not just Willy's best friend but his only friend, and then further considered that Willy was a man in love with the sound of his own voice, a genuine, dyed-in-the-wool logomaniac who scarcely stopped talking from the instant he opened his eyes in the morning until he passed out drunk at night, it made perfect sense that Mr. Bones should have felt so at home in the native lingo. The only wonder, finally, was that he hadn't learned to talk better himself. It wasn't for lack of earnest effort, but biology was against him, and what with the configuration of muzzle, teeth, and tongue that fate had saddled him with, the best he could do was emit a series of yaps and yawns and yowls, a mooning, muddled sort of discourse. He was painfully aware of how far from fluency these noises were, but Willy always let him have his say, and in the end that was the only thing that mattered. Mr. Bones was free to put in his two cents, and whenever he did so his master would give him his full attention, and to look at Willy's face as he watched his friend struggle to make like a member of the human tribe, you would have sworn he was hanging on every word.

That gloomy Sunday in Baltimore, however, Mr. Bones kept his mouth shut. They were down to their last days together, perhaps even their last hours, and this was no time to indulge in caterwauling antics and loopy contortions, no time for the old shenanigans. Certain situations called for tact and discipline, and in their present dire straits it would be far better to hold his tongue and behave like a good, loyal dog. He let Willy snap the leash onto his collar without protest. He didn't whine about not having eaten in the past thirty-six hours; he didn't sniff the air for female scents; he didn't stop to pee on every lamppost and fire hydrant. He simply ambled along beside Willy, following his master as they searched the empty avenues for 316 Calvert Street.

Mr. Bones had nothing against Baltimore per se. It smelled no worse than any other city they'd camped in over the years, but even though he understood the purpose of the trip, it grieved him to think that a man could choose to spend his last moments on earth in a place he'd never been to before. A dog would never commit such a blunder. He would make his peace with the world and then see to it that he gave up the ghost on familiar ground. But Willy still had two things to accomplish before he died, and with typical stubbornness he'd gotten it into his head that there was only one person who could help him. The name of that person was Bea Swanson, and since said Bea Swanson was last known to be living in Baltimore, they had come to Baltimore to find her. All well and good, but unless Willy's plan did what it was supposed to do, Mr. Bones would be marooned in this city of crab cakes and marble steps, and what was he going to do then? A telephone call would have done the job in half a minute, but Willy had a philosophical aversion to using the phone for important business. He would rather walk for days on end than pick up one of those contraptions and talk to someone he couldn't see. So here they were, two hundred miles later, wandering around the streets of Baltimore without a map, looking for an address that might or might not exist.

Of the two things Willy still hoped to accomplish before he died, neither one took precedence over the other. Each was all-important to him, and since time had grown too short to think of tackling them separately, he had come up with what he referred to as the Chesapeake Gambit: an eleventh-hour ploy to kill both birds with one stone. The first has already been discussed in the previous paragraphs: to find new digs for his furry companion. The second was to wrap up his own affairs and make sure that his manuscripts were left in good hands. At the moment, his life's work was crammed into a rental locker at the Greyhound Bus terminal on Fayette Street, two and a half blocks north of where he and Mr. Bones were standing. The key was in his pocket, and unless he found someone worthy enough to entrust with that key, every word he had ever written would be destroyed, disposed of as so much unclaimed baggage.

In the twenty-three years since he'd taken on the surname of Christmas, Willy had filled the pages of seventy-four notebooks with his writings. These included poems, stories, essays, diary entries, epigrams, autobiographical musings, and the first eighteen hundred lines of an epic-in-progress, *Vagabond Days*. The majority of these works had been composed at the kitchen table of his mother's apartment in Brooklyn, but since her death four years ago he'd been forced to write in the open air, often battling the elements on park benches and in dusty alleyways as he struggled to get his thoughts down on paper. In his secret heart of hearts, Willy had no delusions about himself. He knew that he was a troubled soul and not fit for this world, but he also knew that much good work was buried in those notebooks and that on that score at least he could hold his head high. Maybe if he had been more scrupulous about taking his medication, or maybe if his body had been a bit stronger, or maybe if he hadn't been so fond of malts and spirits and the hubbub of bars, he might have done even more good work. That was perfectly possible, but it was too late to dwell on regrets and errors now. Willy had written the last sentence he would ever write, and there were no more than a few ticks left in the clock. The words in the locker were all he had to show for himself. If the words vanished, it would be as if he had never lived.

That was where Bea Swanson entered the picture. Willy knew it was a stab in the dark, but if and when he managed to find her, he was convinced that she would move heaven and earth to help him. Once upon a time, Mrs. Swanson had been his high school English teacher, and if not for her, it was doubtful he ever would have become a writer. He was still William Gurevitch back in those days, a scrawny sixteen-year-old boy with a passion for books and beebop jazz, and she had taken him under her wing and encouraged him to fly, lavishing his early work with praise that was so excessive, so far out of proportion to its true merit, that he began to think of himself as a budding genius, the next great hope of American literature. Whether she was right or wrong to do so is not the question, for results are less important at that stage than potential, and Mrs. Swanson had recognized his talent, she'd seen the spark in his young soul, and no one can ever amount to anything in this life without someone else to believe in him. That's a proven fact, and while the rest of the junior class at Midwood High School saw Mrs. Swanson as a squat, fortyish woman with blubbery arms that bounced and wiggled whenever she wrote on the blackboard, Willy thought she was beautiful, and over the course of that year he fell madly in love with her.

By the time school started again in the fall, however, Mrs. Swanson was gone. Her husband had been offered a new job down in Baltimore, and since Mrs. Swanson was not only a teacher but a wife, what choice did she have but to leave Brooklyn and go where Mr. Swanson went? It was a tough blow for Willy to absorb, but it could have been worse—for even though his mentor was far away, she did not forget him. Over the next several years, Mrs. Swanson kept up a lively correspondence with her young friend, continuing to read and comment on the manuscripts he sent her, to remember his birthday with gifts of old Charlie Parker records, and to suggest little magazines where he could begin submitting his work. The gushing, rhapsodic letter of recommendation she wrote for him in his senior year helped clinch a full scholarship for Willy at Columbia. Mrs. Swanson was his muse, his guardian angel, and good luck charm all rolled into one, and at that point in Willy's life, the sky was definitely the limit. But then came his breakdown, the schizo flipout of 1968, the mad fandango of truth or consequences on a high-voltage tension wire. They shut him up in a hospital, and after six months of shock treatment and psychopharmacological therapy, he was never, uh, never quite the same again. Willy had joined the ranks of the walking wounded, and even though he continued to churn out his poems and stories, to go on writing in both sickness and in health, he rarely got around to answering Mrs. Swanson's letters. The reasons were unimportant. Perhaps Willy was embarrassed to stay in touch with her. Perhaps he was distracted, preoccupied with other business. Perhaps he had lost faith in the U.S. Postal Service and no longer trusted the mail carriers not to snoop inside the letters they delivered. One way or the other, his once voluminous exchanges with Mrs. Swanson ebbed to almost nothing. For a year or two they consisted of the odd, desultory postcard, then the store-bought Christmas greeting, and then, by 1976, they had stopped altogether. Since that time, not one syllable of communication had passed between them.

Mr. Bones knew all this, and that was precisely what worried him. Seventeen years. Gerald Ford had been president back then, for Chrissakes, and he himself would not even be born for another decade. Who was Willy trying to kid? Think of all the things that can happen in that time. Think of the changes that can occur in seventeen hours or seventeen minutes, let alone in seventeen years. At the very least, Mrs. Swanson had probably moved to another address. The old girl would be pushing seventy by now, and if she wasn't senile or living in a trailer park in Florida, there was a better than even chance that she was dead. Willy had admitted as much when they hit the streets of Baltimore that evening, but what the fuck, he'd said, it was their one and only shot, and since life was a gamble anyway, why not go for broke?

RUSSELL BANKS

Canadians

I was lurking around at the Northcountry Mall up in Plattsburgh this
one night alone because the bikers at Russell's crib where I was crashed
in the livingroom had been wired on meth for three days straight until
finally they kicked me and Russell out for not having any weed. Russ
said he was going to his mom's to chill for a few days but no way I could
do the same, not with my mom and stepdad still hanging up on me because of when I got caught shoplifting and all. Russ said I couldn't
sleep in his car, he had it parked at his mom's and she was definitely
against that, so I didn't have any place to go which is why I decided to
hitch up to the mall even though I didn't have any money and no weed
to sell.

It was snowing and I caught a ride from this Air Force guy heading
back to the base and in the car I was like talking to myself, saying, Asshole, asshole, asshole, all the way from where he'd picked me up in
Ausable Forks. I really wanted to go home to my mom's but I didn't
know how to do it. The Air Force guy must've thought I was whacked
or something because he didn't once ask me what the matter was, just
dropped me like a turd at the exit off the Northway and booked.

I cruised a while and ended up hanging by the fountain at the center of the mall which is more or less a crossroad, looking for somebody I
could bum a smoke off of when I spotted this little girl who I figured was
lost. Her face was red like from crying although she was not at that moment crying, she was peering around the place searching for her mom
probably so I said, Hey, kid, how's it going? You lost or something? She
was maybe eight or nine, stringy blond hair, ratty red parka, and sneak-
ers with no socks. I noticed the no socks because it was cold and snowing out and it was unusual for a kid to be in a skimpy dress and almost
barefoot. She stood by the fountain looking back and forth like this little
alleycat caught in the middle of the road with cars whizzing past on
both sides and not sure whether to go ahead or go back.

C'mere, kid, I said and I got up and approached her a little too fast I guess because she jumped away from me. I'm not gonna hurt you, for chrissake, I said.

Then I felt the long arm of the law so to speak, a heavy black hand on my shoulder and when I turned around I saw the hand was connected to one of the security guys, this black dude named Bart who I once sold some weed to and who busted me anyhow for shoplifting when I was trying to do a little Christmas shopping to get back into my mom's good graces. He's ex-military from Rochester. Sort of a dim bulb.

Chappie, he says to me, what the hell are you doing here again? I told you to keep your little punk ass out of here.

Hey it's America, jerk-off. Remember? Land of the free home of the brave, man.

Don't give me no shit. You're loitering. Now g'wan, before I toss you out with the garbage.

Where you scoring for weed now, man? I ask him, just to remind him of the true nature of our relationship which he seems to want to forget. You still smoking them blunts? I say.

Chappie, he says to me, don't fuckin' antagonize the cops.

You're only a rent-a-cop, man. I'm waiting to meet somebody, I say.

Wait outside. Do it now, he says, and he spins me around with one hand which he can do because he's a sizeable dude and I'm small for my age anyhow. He says, That's a nice shearling jacket you got, Chappie. Who'd you rob it off?

I got it last year from my stepfather, asshole, I tell him, which happens to be true and I ease off in the general direction of Sears.

Yeah, sure, he says and laughs and heads slowly in the opposite direction. Walking his beat. He knows I'm only changing seats, moving to another crossing in the mall and he's not especially worried because it's kids like me that make his otherwise boring job interesting.

A few minutes later I was walking past Victoria's Secret which is this fancy ladies' nightgown and underwear store and which also happens to be where Bart busted me for shoplifting last month, so I look inside with a special interest in the place and I notice the same little girl in the red parka from before. Only this time she's with somebody, this pot-bellied dude with a big soft nose and cribbage-board skin and thin black strands of hair that he's combed sideways over his head like a barcode. He's got the kid by the hand like he's her uncle. Not her father. It's like they're supposed to be shopping for a present for somebody only I can't figure who. This guy was not the type who had a wife or a girl friend even, he was all rumpled and the buttons of his navy peacoat were crossed up.

I don't know what, but something about the guy held my attention, like I knew him from someplace else, although I didn't. I watched them through the glass and the guy bought what looked like ladies' pantyhose stockings, a whole bunch, six or seven packages of them, and while he blah-blahs the salesgirl in this over-friendly way the kid just stands there beside him like she's half-asleep or maybe stoned, but she's too young to be high, I think. I figure maybe they're traveling someplace, like from Canada, and she's tired. Must be Canadians, I think, and then when I start to move off they come out and the guy gives me this long stare like, What the hell are you? He doesn't say anything but it's like he's never seen a kid with a mohawk or nose-ring before, which is probably true for Canadians.

I don't know why I thought he was a Canadian. My stepdad is from Ontario but the guy didn't look anything like my stepdad who is this neat and trim sort of person, in perfect shape and all, a control freak with a crewcut and creases in his jeans who my mom thinks is God and I'm supposed to try and be just like him. Right. Naturally he thinks I'm a total loser, which is okay because his idea of a real man is Arnold Schwarzenegger or General Schwartzkopf or anybody with a name with Schwartz in it because he's basically a Nazi without the uniform is how I see him. What bums me is that my mom buys that crap and tells me I'm lucky to have him for my stepdad.

You got a problem? I say to the Canadian because of the way he looked at me and he smiles and says not at all and takes the little girl by the hand and walks off, real relaxed. I watched them for a minute wondering why they seemed so laid back and all, especially him, if they were traveling so far from home, because even if the border is only about an hour from here Canada is a huge place and they look definitely funky, like they've been on the road for a week and you'd think they'd want to get where they're going. Plus him buying the packages of pantyhose is strange, unless they can't get those in Canada.

Anyhow I didn't exactly have anything better to do that night so I followed them, keeping back a ways and out of sight. I guess I was only curious about the guy but also I was thinking maybe he has cigarettes. It was cold outside, I remember, and snowing. I thought, maybe he's driving one of those big RV's or a van that they're sleeping in and he's parked it out in the lot and he'll let me crash there till tomorrow or till the bikers run out of speed and Russ and I can get back into our crib over the Video Den in Ausable Forks. That's where Russ works nights. He's sixteen and older than me which is why he has a regular job and a car and I don't.

So I follow the guy and the little girl in and out of the Wiz and then the Foot Locker, where the guy actually buys the kid some socks which she puts on right there in the store while he waits and looks around and almost catches me watching, and after a while I realize that I'm all hyped up, I'm like peaking out at a million RPMs and my heart is hammering in my chest and my hands are all sweaty. I didn't know what was happening at the time but suddenly it was like I'm looking down this tunnel at the Canadian guy and the little girl, especially at the little girl who I was really worried about now, like some terrible thing was about to happen to her and she couldn't see it coming but I could. I wanted to tell her something important about people but I didn't want her to have to know it yet, she was too young still. It's no that, it's more complicated than that. It's the reverse. She was the one who knew something and I didn't want her to tell it.

It's weird but as long as I didn't look directly at her and watched the guy with her instead, her uncle or whatever, I didn't flip out, all I was into was maybe bumming a smoke from the guy. But the second I switched over to the kid it's like something terrible is about to happen, this huge heavy ugly grey thing shaped like a tyrannosaurus rex or the country of Canada on the map is hovering over the entire United States of America and is about to fall or break apart and avalanche down on me and cut off my breath, so I start to breathe in and out real fast like I remember once Willie the cat at my mom's house did when he had a hairball in his throat and got all humped over with his head down next to the livingroom carpet making these quick little gagging noises. My stepfather walked in from the kitchen and gave him a kick across the room because he was afraid Willie was going to make a mess on the carpet, so Willie threw up in my closet instead and I never told anyone. I just cleaned it up myself.

People don't know how kids think, I guess they forget. But when you're a kid it's like you're wearing these binoculars strapped to your eyes and you can't see anything except what's in the dead center of the lenses because you're too scared of everything else or else you don't understand it and people expect you to, so you feel stupid all the time. Mostly a lot of stuff just doesn't get registered. You're always fucking up and there's a lot that you don't even see that people expect you to see, like the time when I was still a kid and my grandmother asked me if I got the ten dollars and the birthday card she sent me. I said to her I don't know and she started dissing me to my mom and all but it was true, I really didn't know and I wasn't even into drugs then.

The little girl in the red parka was wearing binoculars over her eyes like I did when I was her age and she couldn't see that she was in danger any more than I could have seen it back then, only it was different for her now because she had me to help her and I didn't have anyone.

They went into the food court and I followed a little ways behind and when they stopped at the Mr. Pizza and ordered slices I suddenly got too hungry to hang back any more so I came up behind the guy and I go like, Yo, man, you got some spare change so I can buy me a slice, man? I haven't eaten all day, man, I tell him which is basically true except for some cold french fries in Russ's car this morning that he gave me.

The little girl had her slice in one hand and a Coke in the other and she was looking for a place to sit down. I smiled at her like we're pals from before but she didn't change her expression which was as serious as a dollar so I'm thinking what the hell, she's scared, she doesn't know friend from foe anymore, I can relate to that, when suddenly it's like a hot white light has been thrown on my face warming my cheeks and forehead and almost blinding me with the glare. The Canadian guy is looking at me, he's staring directly into my eyes almost which people never do with me, not even kids because of my mohawk I guess and my earrings and the nose-ring and plus I try to discourage that type of looking. But this caught me by surprise probably because I was distracted by the little girl when the guy hit me with all the attention and before I can shove it back at him he's already talking a mile a minute which is definitely not like any Canadian I ever met.

Hey, you poor kid, you really do look like you're starving, he says to me. He goes, I'm gonna buy you some supper, young man, I'm gonna buy you something solid to eat, something to get some meat on those bones, he says stepping back and taking a look at me and shaking his head, Tsk, tsk, tsk.

I must have made a mistake, I think. All that stuff about the little girl being in danger and this guy being some kind of Canadian weirdo was only in my head, a produce of my fevered imagination and I just thought it because of what I know about my stepfather who is from Ontario and what I remembered feeling when I was a little kid myself. The guy's just a normal American I think who happens to talk a lot. And he likes me. And he's real interesting too.

What would please you, my good man? he says to me. You're skinny as a rail underneath that jacket.

I told him anything and he ordered me a slice and a Coke, same as the girl which is not so much if I'm starving so I ask him for a smoke while we're waiting and it turns out he's carrying Camel Lights which sort of proved he was American. When my order came he carried it over to the table where the little girl was and introduced me to her saying her name was Froggy, a.k.a. Froggy the Gremlin.

Hi, I say and tell them my name. Froggy doesn't seem to register anything.

Me Buster, the guy says pointing to himself with his thumb and I laugh.

Buster! No shit. How come Buster?

He goes, Hi-ya, kids, hi-ya, hi-ya, hi-ya! My name's Buster Brown and I live in a shoe. And that's Froggy the Gremlin, he said waving a hand at the girl who was mainly ignoring the guy like she was used to this stuff. Look for her in there too, he says.

He talked like that, in circles basically and different voices while I ate my slice and smoked my cigarette and mostly didn't say anything. I noticed the little girl, Froggy, she didn't say anything either. She just kept her eyes on her food and chomped her way through to the end and then looked out at the people walking past in the mall.

I asked Buster if Froggy was his kid and he goes, More than my child, Chappie, and less. She's my protege. I have had dozens of proteges over the years and they keep me rising like a phoenix from the ashes of my past. My proteges are my once and future acting career.

Yeah? I say. What's a protege?

Those who can, do, Chappie, and those who can't, teach. I could once but I can't now, and thus I teach. I was an actor once, my boy, not a very famous actor but a success nonetheless. I had my share of film and TV roles. Now, he said, now I train young actresses and actors, I make proteges of young people like Froggy the Gremlin here and the process like a heart transplant prolongs my own life as an actor, extending into the indefinite future my own early gifts and training.

You probably can't understand any of that, he says offering me another cigarette. You're much too young.

I'm thinking no way this guy was an actor, not with those pock marks and a nose like a mushroom although when he was young with a full head of hair and no pot belly he might not have been too bad-looking. His way of talking was cool though. I liked listening to him and it didn't really matter to me whether he was telling the truth or not. When he talked he looked right at me and made me feel like there was this spotlight on me and I was standing in the middle of a stage and anything I said would be listened to carefully and treated with total respect.

He said back in 1967 when he was a very young man he had been in this movie with Jack Nicholson and Peter Fonda called *The Trip*, I guess some kind of travel movie but I had never heard of it although I had heard of Jack Nicholson from *Batman* so I was pretty impressed. He asked me, what about me, wouldn't I like to become a TV star in New York City and Hollywood but I said no way.

I knew he was only this old gay guy hitting on me which I didn't care about because he was so interesting to listen to but also because I felt like I was baking in the sun with all the attention he was paying to me and of course he was feeding me cigarettes and even bought another slice of pizza for me, this time with pepperoni. Plus I was thinking maybe he had a place where I could crash for the night.

I wasn't afraid of Buster, not for myself anyhow even though he was a lot bigger than me because usually with these guys you just tell them what you'll do and what you won't do and they go along more or less. But I didn't know what was the deal with little Froggy. She was like dreaming at the table with her eyes open and I figured the guy must've been dosing her with something, 'ludes maybe but if I could get him to switch off of her and on to me then somebody like Black Bart the security cop would probably come by and latch onto her and get her back to wherever the hell she came from.

It was like a plan from a movie or a TV show, I know but those shows are usually based on reality. Also I was really getting off on the guy Buster Brown and I was even starting to feel jealous of Froggy in a weird way so that if Black Bart didn't come along and find her and take her to the lost kid office or wherever, I didn't care as long as I could take her place with Buster. Which probably makes me sound like a sick puppy but that's how it goes when you're as fucked up as I was then.

So how come Froggy never talks? I asked Buster and he went off on this number about how frogs don't talk, they croak or they keep you up all night cheeping and peeping and then he was talking about all the different types of frogs there are until I practically forgot my question. That's how he handled questions. He constantly changed the subject but that kept things interesting and he talked about you yourself a lot and that kept you from thinking too hard about him or Froggy. It's funny, he was so ugly-looking he made you feel handsome which is normal but he was so smart he made you feel smart too instead of stupid like smart people usually make you feel, like my stepdad for instance and teachers I have had.

At one point while he was rapping away I noticed Froggy get up from the table and take her tray and paper trash over to the barrel. She dumped her stuff and set the tray onto the pile there and started walking, heading back down the mall toward the fountain where I'd first seen her. It wasn't like she was sneaking off or anything and Buster didn't seem to care one way or the other although I didn't think he actually saw her leave. He must've known that she was gone, once she was gone but it was more like after I came onto his scene the little girl didn't exist anymore so it didn't matter to him if she was gone or not. Which was fine with me for various reasons so I wasn't going to point out to him that she had split and ask him what he thought of that. I just moved in and took her place so to speak.

I was wondering if Buster was high, coke I figured because of how he talked and could I get a little taste, when he asked me did I want to do a screen test.

Sure, I said. When?

Oh anytime. Tonight if you want.

Sure, I said and got up from the table and dumped the trash in the barrel like Froggy had done and Buster and I went back into the mall and headed toward the exit down past Sears and J. C. Penney's, opposite the way Froggy had gone. I was feeling lucky because of how things were turning out after such a lousy start—me and Russell being kicked out of our crib by the bikers and Russ going back to his mom's which was not an option for me and the cold and the snow and no money and no drugs. Now as I walked past Sears with this cool dude Buster Brown it looked like all my problems were solved, at least temporarily.

If I'm going to your place, I said to him, you oughta give me some money. For the screen test and all, I say.

That depends.

On what? I say and I stop right there so he'll know I'm serious.

He's like, Well, various things, Chappie. It depends on how much the camera loves you, for instance. You may not be in the slightest photogenic, despite your beauty to the naked eye. That's why it's called a screen *test*, Chappie. You have to *pass* it.

I'm like, Gimme twenty bucks up front or find yourself another protege. Plus I don't do no sex with you. No fucking or sucking. Just the screen test.

Just the screen test, he says smiling and he pulls a twenty from his wallet and hands it to me. You drive a hard bargain, Chappie, he says.

Yeah, well, I had a good teacher you might say. I'm thinking at that moment of my stepfather, I'm like flashing on his face, the outline of his head in the dark really so not quite his face and his smell of booze and Brut and the sandpaper scratch of his chin on my shoulder and neck. I almost never think about that stuff anymore except when my mom tells me how lucky I am that he's my stepfather which she doesn't do since they kicked me out of the house for stealing and me being into drugs and all.

So how come you bought those pantyhoses? I ask Buster as we pass out the door by Sears into the parking lot. It was snowing fairly hard by now and there weren't many cars in the lot. A couple of plows were scraping away at the far end.

Pantyhose! What makes you think that's what I've got? he asked and he held up the Victoria's Secret bag and wagged it.

I seen you buy them, man.

Ah, you were tracking me, were you? Playing detective, eh? And now you're thinking you've *caught* me, he said. Only maybe instead I've caught you. He laughed at that like it was a big joke.

Whaddaya got, a girl friend or something? I was starting to think he was a Canadian again because of the pantyhose which I don't think they have in Canada. You see a lot of Canadians down here buying stuff they can't get at home.

You'd look pretty terrific in pantyhose, he tells me.

Yeah sure, I say. You can forget that. Forget all about it, man. I asked him where his car was and he said back alongside the J. C. Penney's building. Then I asked him where's his crib and he just said not far. Good, I said, because I ain't going to no Canada tonight.

He said, No problema, Chappie. No problema. Canada's not my cup of tea. All those *Canadians*!

Yeah sure, I say. We're walking side by side close to the building to stay out of the wind and snow and as we're passing the big J. C. Penney's windows I notice up ahead that there's a guy working inside on one of the window displays and he's got all these naked mannequins that he's moving around. When we get closer I see that the mannequins are like in pieces with their arms and hands lying on the floor and some of them don't even have any heads and the ones that do are bald. They have breasts and all but no nipples or public hair. It's like they're adults but they're really little kids. Then the guy who's setting them up disappears through a door into the store to get some clothes for them or something and I stop by the glass and look in at all the body parts.

C'mon, Chappie, Buster said. We've done our window-shopping for tonight.

Yeah wait a minute, I said. I had never seen mannequins like that before, all naked with their arms and heads looking like they were sliced off. There were these bright overhead lights inside the window that made it look like a dissecting room in a morgue or something. Definitely it was the grossest thing I'd ever seen, at least at that moment it was, which is strange I guess because I've seen lots of really gross things in my life.

C'mon, let's get out of here, Buster says like suddenly he's afraid someone'll see us.

I say, I don't think I want to do that screen test, man.

Cut the shit, Chappie. We have a deal.

No, I say and I back off a few steps. I still couldn't take my eyes off the mannequins. It was like I was in a dream and I didn't want to wake up and this guy Buster Brown was standing by my bed shaking me by the shoulder.

He goes like, There's the matter of my twenty bucks, kid.

That's when I turned and started running. I ran back the way we'd come, past the Sears toward the entrance to the mall and I hear Buster's feet slamming along behind me, him hollering, You little bastard! Give me back my money! Buster was definitely pissed and he ran pretty good for an old guy so when I go through the door he's only a few steps behind me.

Inside there was no one in sight except way in the distance by the fountain but I spotted a fire exit sign a little ways down the mall and a door I could maybe lock behind me once I got through. I raced over to it and yanked it open and went in and slammed it shut just as Buster got there. There was no way to lock it from the inside so I clamped onto the handle while Buster pulled on the other side until finally I couldn't hold it closed anymore and when I let go Buster went flying.

Before he could get up I pulled the door shut again and took off down this long narrow hallway. There were doors and other hallways running off the main hall like in a video-game maze and will all these fluorescent lights it was very bright but no people anywhere. At one point I stopped and peeked back around a corner and listened for Buster. I could hear footsteps in the distance, somebody running, but I couldn't tell if it was water dripping or him or if he was going in the other direction away from me or about to pounce on me from behind. I didn't even know how to get back to the mall where the people were.

This time when I start to run it's like I'm lost in a funhouse and panicking. I go down one hall, hang a left, come to a dead-end and make a U-turn back the same way I came. A second later I'm running along another hall and when I fly through a door with an exit sign on it I'm in a hall just like the one I left. I'm totally confused by now. It's like I've been taken off the planet earth and set down on this new planet where there's no people. I think I was almost crying by then.

Suddenly I smelled food cooking. There was a door ahead of me and when I pushed through it I almost knocked over a huge stainless steel counter with all kinds of steaming food in these big pans. I'm back in the mall but I've come out in the middle of the food court behind the counter of Wang's Pavilion the Chinese take-out place and these three Chinese guys and a tiny Chinese woman are staring at me very shocked. They all start jabbering in Chinese at once and waving their hands at me in this very pissed-off way.

I go, C'mon, man, chill out, willya fucking chill, for crissake, but it's like they don't understand English. It was late and there were no customers in the place anyhow but these people were acting like I'm some kind of mad bomber. I pull out Buster's twenty and go, Hey, man, I just want to buy some chopped suey, and they shut up for a second and stare suspiciously at the money like it's not American but then I glance over their heads into the food court and see Buster coming along.

I freeze, and the Chinese guys follow my eyes and slowly turn around and then they see him too and they must figure that he's the bad guy I'm running from because they don't say anything, they just go back to work cleaning out their pans and stacking trays and so on. Then I noticed that Buster had Froggy the Gremlin with him. He was holding her by the hand almost like she was a rag doll. She looked really tired now, like she was in a nod.

They walked slowly past Wang's and out of the food court on down the mall toward the exit to the parking lot and I watched them the whole time until they had disappeared from sight. I felt incredibly sad then. What was going to happen to her? I felt guilty too because of losing my courage when I saw those mannequins in the window and decided not to take her place.

What you want? the head Chinese guy said to me.

I pointed to a couple of green and brown things in the pans and he dished the stuff into a Styrofoam box and I paid and got my change. I was ready to book through the front when I spotted Black Bart cruising the food court looking spaced like he'd managed to score some weed. It was late, there was almost nobody left in the mall except the workers and Bart was making his nightly round-up of the last couple of kids still hanging out and the bums sleeping on the benches and so on, driving them with his stoned smile into the cold snowy night.

Not me though. I slipped through the door behind Wang's Pavilion with my box of food and returned to the maze of hallways out back where I wandered around until finally I found this janitor's closet I could sleep in and Bart didn't find out about me crashing back there every night until about two weeks later. By then everything was cool with the bikers again and Russ's mom had kicked him out for drinking all her booze one night and busting the place up so we went back to our old crib over the Video Den in Ausable Forks. Russ had his same room as before and I still had to sleep on the couch in the livingroom but I didn't mind, I knew then that as long as my stepdad was at my mom's I was never going back there.

ANN BEATTIE

The Infamous Fall of Howell the Clown

"It was 1954, and it just wasn't done. You didn't have an unsupervised birthday party for a seven-year-old, presided over only by a gentleman friend dressed up in a polka-dot jumpsuit with an organdy collar and red lipstick and blue eyeshadow, wearing beach sandals with pink socks. Well—go ahead and laugh. It turned into a disaster, didn't it?"

"How old was Cousin Charlie?"

"It was 1954. Charlie was seven, Steven was six. I should also add that your mother was twenty-five, but because women in those days wore almost as much makeup as the clown, she looked like a more mature woman than she was. She was only twenty-five, one year younger than your Aunt Sylvie, who had never been put on God's green earth to supervise the upbringing of children, so of course who did Sylvie marry but Parker Winkleman, the most irresponsible, pig-headed boy for miles around. Nine months from the day they married they had Charlie, and he was no more than brought home from the hospital than the two of them had the bassinette on the back porch and were out in the street riding their bicycles, telling anyone who asked that they were 'keeping an ear out for the baby.' Why, the woman who lived next door would have to go out on her front lawn and flag them down when she got too worried about the crying. There they'd be, riding in bigger and bigger circles, ringing their bells at each other like a couple of bears in the circus. No one could believe such irresponsibility. When she went in to have the second one, Sylvie's mother took her aside and told her, 'Tie your tubes.' She would never have listened, except that she had two babies, and suddenly Parker Winkleman had lost his job at the bank."

"And when he disappeared, no one went to look for him?"

"What do you think it was, the wild west? Somebody saddled up his horse and galloped from town to town, inquiring about mysterious strangers? Nobody could take time off from work. Private detectives weren't heard of in those days, or at least I never knew anyone who'd heard of them. We thought he'd find himself a job and send for the family. We certainly didn't think he'd disappear. Every time the phone rang, we'd all leap for it. Every occasion, we'd expect to see him return: somebody was always sure to announce a scenario in which he'd suddenly appear, with birthday presents for his child, or bringing flowers on their anniversary. You have to understand that we had no frame of reference for Parker Winkleman. Even Mrs. Winkleman never understood him. She raised him the same as his brother, but he threw spitballs in Sunday school and aimed his slingshot at songbirds, and when he married Sylvie, he had plans to move to Paris, France, and turn her into a fashion model, though how he thought having two children in two years would help her form, I don't know."

"How long was he gone before Sylvie started the affair with Howell?"

"First of all, I'm not walking along this street with you today saying that any such thing happened. At least, we never thought in terms of 'affairs.' Laugh if you want, but in those days, we thought two people could be friends. I don't have any stories about Howell creeping out of her house early in the morning, and no one ever so much as saw him put his arm around her shoulder, even when they stood at the funeral of Mrs. Winkleman. They behaved very properly. Friends of Sylvie's often went along if they went to the movies, or for a sundae. His father accompanied them, before he became so ill. I think, frankly, that a lot of men in the neighborhood felt sorry for the two boys left without a father and rallied to Sylvie's side. I don't know that they had an affair. Maybe he felt sympathetic toward her and the boys."

"Then why was it so wrong to leave him in charge of the birthday party?"

"You tell me, please, why Sylvie had to go shopping when she had a party full of children. For clothes, it was—not even groceries. Oh, I see your look. You think it was liberated of her to go off and do what she wanted. But think of the position it put poor Howell in: you can't be an adult doing your job of supervising when you're also disguised as a clown and going around making mischief. You can't be two things with children at one time, or they'll stop believing. Can you imagine Santa Claus placing presents under the tree and muttering, 'Where did the stains come from all of a sudden on this carpet?' The most important thing was to convince the children he was a clown—I think he had a curly, red wig and those bushy eyebrows attached to a big red nose, as well—anyway, if he hadn't had the bad reaction to the medicine the doctor had given him, he would have stayed put in his tree, but the medicine poisoned him, in combination with the glass of beer he had before he was in costume, when he and Sylvie were stringing crepe paper from tree to tree. He was not a drinker, and it turned into a very hot day, and he must have been twice as hot inside that clown suit, and then the penicillin he'd been given for his throat must have reacted with the beer, so that after he climbed up in the tree to pretend to be Juliet calling to Romeo, which is not something I'm very clear on, or ever was—from up in the tree, he just opened his arms like a big red-haired, red-nosed angel spreading its wings and Bam! He crashed down, and if it had not been for the birthday presents on the ground that cushioned his fall, Howell would have hit flat into the earth like a meteor. They think he fainted from the heat, and that he was a little delusional when he got into the tree because the medicine had already started to interact with the beer. Apparently he'd been frustrated because the children had never heard of Romeo and Juliet; that was going to ruin his clown routine, so he had to stand there in the hot sun, feeling sicker and sicker, explaining the story, and by the time he started to climb he was already sweating, and more than a little anxious, because he'd seen Sylvie's car pulling out of the driveway, and where was she going? Surely the poor man never in a million years thought his Juliet would open her arms and then black out and take a dive into boxes filled with animal toys and erector sets and Mr. Potato Heads. He fell with such force they found a baby manatee under an azalea bush outside the porch one week later, and some piece of the Mr. Potato Head stabbed his forehead, so he looked like the Frankenstein monster with its screw when they turned him over. We can only laugh because they fixed him at the hospital, but that day no one was laughing, and some of the children stayed so frightened they didn't even want to have birthday parties when their time came around. They started going to matinees with a few friends, seeing 'The King and I' over and over. I, personally, consider that a fate worse than death. I never could stand Yul Brynner, but I think that other bald actor, Sean Connery, is extremely handsome. Of course, it helped that he played James Bond, and didn't have to stalk around a palace singing, 'Et cetera, et cetera.'"

"And that night Steven's nightmares began?"

"Yes. Before Howell fell, he'd picked out Steven to be Romeo, and he was speaking directly to Steven when he hit the ground. You can see that would be traumatic for a child. All through school, every play by

Shakespeare made him terribly nervous. When they were the lesson, he wanted to stay home, whether it was 'All's Well That Ends Well' or 'Macbeth.'"

"Well," I said, "I thought he spoke beautifully at the service. Maybe in spite of that crazy day, years ago, Howell still inspired him to be an actor. When we were kids, he was always so shy. I didn't expect him to be so dynamic."

"If you're so curious, I don't know why you've never asked," Daphne said suddenly. "When we get to Steven's apartment, why don't you ask him before Sylvie shows up and stop bothering me about things I don't know the answer to."

"I'm not sure he or Charlie would tell me the truth. They were always a little distant. They always kept secrets from me, you know."

"You're a girl. I don't think they knew what to make of you. They were used to teasing girls, being attracted to them but trying to pretend they weren't. They saw you as their responsibility, but they weren't sure how to act toward you because you were also a family member. They were eleven and twelve when you went to live with them, and you were thirteen years old and acted much older. They both had crushes on you. Or at least Steven did."

"Daphne."

"I'm not saying he wanted to marry you. There are other kinds of crushes." She frowned at me. "You were always too hard on Steven. Do you realize that? When you were little children, playing together, you'd sometimes explain to people who came into the room that Steven was just there because he was tired of playing outside. You'd find some way to explain that he didn't really want to be with you, it was just the lesser of two evils. Why have you always been so hard on Steven?"

"I'm not hard on him. Didn't I say he was the best speaker at Howell's memorial service?"

"Oh," Daphne said, "it's so hard to believe. Howell was doing fine until he went for that new treatment, and it poisoned him just like the beer and the penicillin did. He never had a strong constitution. I hope he was her lover, you know. Because if he wasn't her lover, I don't think he would have been anyone's. At least, not much of one, spending all his free time with Sylvie and you and the boys, and the rest of the time living at home with that cranky old father."

As we talked, we had walked from the church up Sixth Avenue to Sixteenth Street. A few tulips had poked up in the tree boxes, but either someone had picked the blooms or they had not blossomed: the anemic green leaves, dust-speckled, curled like banana peels as they drooped to the ground; a single marigold bloomed in a squiggle of foliage. Next to it lay a baby's pacifier. Further up the street, we saw one high heel. It was spring in New York, the trees budding, pollen like yellow chalk dust on the steps of the brownstones, vibrant red tulips in a vase offering proof that indoors, at least, tulips prospered. We both saw them through the iron bars of someone's ground-floor window. I had once lived in the Village behind similar bars and screens—lived far enough downtown that Sixteenth Street seemed like uptown, which it did not seem at the moment. Compared to 54th Street, where the hotel I was staying in was located, this was still quiet, pastoral New York.

I had come into the city the night before from Pennsylvania for Howell's memorial service, meeting Daphne in the morning as she got off the Metroliner from Washington at Penn Station. There she had stood, five feet tall, carrying an overnight bag patterned with roses, her good George Jensen pin, a stylized, sterling silver maple leaf, pinning her scarf to her wool jacket. She was as alert as a bird, bright-eyed, at-tuned to the roar of the trains, the noise of the p.a. system, the crowd. But she had never understood New York. She didn't know if Penn Station was uptown or downtown, and furthermore, she couldn't re-member where uptown became dangerous or at what point downtown turned into Wall Street. She understood, in theory, how the avenues ran, but alone, she would turn a corner and find herself on another ave-nue, not a cross street, and how was that possible? She understood there was some mysterious benefit to crossing a street to catch a cab much of the time, but when those times were, or which streets ran uptown or downtown, she could never remember.

Now she hopped along at my side, her practical, leather, laced shoes stuffed with two layers of Dr. Scholl's cushion inserts, part of her money folded in a slip pouch, other money pinned inside her bra, a crisp twenty dollar bill and all her change in her wallet, in case someone demanded her purse. In the last few years, she had begun coloring her hair, which had not become predominantly grey until well after her six-tieth birthday. Whoever was doing the dyeing was good: a few streaks of grey were left, waving away from her temples; it gave her hair a look of motion, made it look as if the wind had uncovered unexpected ripples of grey.

Daphne had always been my mother's best friend, as far back as I could remember. The two of them had spent so much time together, they had often come to use the same expressions, accompanied by

many of the same gestures as they spoke. But the way I had been supposed to see it, my mother had been a practical, down-to-earth person,
Daphne something of a dreamer. My mother was the organized, determined woman who had looked adversity in the face and triumphed over
it, becoming a dental hygienist when my father divorced her, whereas
Daphne talked about going to college but never enrolled, even though
the handwriting was on the wall about her husband's job. Whether my
mother had meant to present this concept of Daphne deliberately or
not, I have no idea, but she had consistently planted seeds of doubt
about whether Daphne was, at all, a practical person. Since they told
each other almost every thought and desire, and since my mother repeated many of those things to me, there were always a lot of things to
hope, or even to pray for, on Daphne's behalf, whether it be that she
find her missing cat, Bugle Boy, or that her husband get a much-needed
raise, or that she be selected to sing a solo in the church choir. My
mother gave me to understand that Daphne always wanted things—the
implication was that she was constantly at odds with the way things
were, that she was sadly dissatisfied—and while my mother would say
to me that she wished all Daphne's dreams could come true (finding the
cat or singing a solo were, equally, "dreams"), that was not very likely
for Daphne, or for anyone. What I think now is that my mother, so dissatisfied and disappointed by life after her divorce, which forced her to
get a job she hated ("Another day of carving the pumpkins," she would
say in the morning, opening her mouth wide and jutting out her jaw as
she examined her own teeth in the bathroom mirror), needed someone
she could consider more troubled and insecure than she. In her resolute
but world-weary disparagement of Daphne, my mother rose to more
heroic heights, the way a person reading a fairy tale will nod knowingly
and cue a child to anticipate disaster from the moment the wolf appears
in Grandma's bed.

When I was young, like every other child, I accepted my mother's
version of everything; then, of course, I saw that she did not predict
things perfectly, that her sister—my Aunt Sylvie—took something of
the same attitude toward her that my mother took toward Daphne. Perhaps because back then people did not often directly contradict others,
as is common now, people relied more on gestures, such as an upward
roll of the eye or a raised eyebrow. Throughout my childhood, I began
to observe a domino effect of skepticism that tipped so gently it did not
knock the person down but nevertheless passed like an electric current
from my grandmother to her oldest daughter, from the oldest to the

youngest, from the youngest to her best friend. And no doubt part of the reason I was so fascinated was because the falling dominoes did not extend to me; though I was next in line, I was displaced by Daphne. Unwittingly, just because of her constant presence and because of the place she occupied in my mother's affections, Daphne became the recipient of my mother's *sotto voce* concern, the person we of course wished well, though her ideas were quite unlikely to materialize.

What a shocking thing it must have been for my mother when she realized she, herself, was dying—that the cancer Daphne had assured her would stay in remission had recurred, that she would in all probability be leaving her beloved only child to the care of none other than Daphne, a woman who adhered to predictions from psychics, who believed doctors did not pay enough attention to exceptions—to those few patients who inevitably survived unlikely odds. Over coffee, when I was present, my mother gave Daphne the bad news. The wolf just sat in the bed and stared. Whatever Daphne thought, in its own good time, the wolf was simply going to devour its prey, my mother would die, and that, and only that, would now be the end of the story. Of course, my mother had a sort of love-hate relationship with Daphne— she was the voice of my mother's own hopeful, unspoken optimism; how could she not be?—so, toward the end, my mother complicated matters by arranging for Sylvie to take me, though she made Daphne swear that she would oversee my upbringing, made Sylvie promise that Daphne would be a second mother to me, made the two of them all but promise that they would bake alternating layers for my birthday cakes and sing to me in unison.

Fortunately, Sylvie did not dislike Daphne or resent her intrusion. She had seen so much of her through the years, she considered her a member of the family. It was also a rather lonely life, difficult enough economically and emotionally before I joined her household of two increasingly wild boys—and because I withdrew so completely after my mother's death, Sylvie was no doubt happy to have someone else shoulder part of the burden: someone to share the task of driving me twice a week to the psychologist's office; another person to confer with about her decision to take out a loan and settle me, eventually, in another school; someone to confer with as she tried to learn the proper but always shifting signals of when to approach me and when to leave me alone.

Though Daphne was married, I have only the sketchiest memory of her husband, who worked a night shift and slept most of the day, so that even when my mother was alive, he rarely appeared in our lives. Also, by that time, something had happened and it had been decided— or had it simply turned out?—that Howell Jenkins would not join Sylvie's household. He stayed with his parents, nursing first his mother, then his father, through long illnesses. When I first went to live with Sylvie his mother was very ill, and in part because of guilt (his mother was very ill, but my mother was dead), because of the numbing grief we had in common, and because there was such turmoil when I first tried to settle in with Sylvie and the boys, Howell began to visit infrequently. A few times Daphne came to stay at Sylvie's house on the weekend to take care of the three of us while—we were told—Sylvie stayed at the Jenkins' house. Or maybe she didn't: maybe he left his parents to fend for themselves, and he and Sylvie went to a motel and had wild sex for two days. Maybe they watched *Casablanca* on TV and ordered steaks from room service and drank champagne and planned their future in the happier times sure to come. They could have, because somewhere along the way Sylvie had gotten divorced from her runaway husband, eventually Howell's mother died, and in the last year of his life, Howell's father was moved to a nursing home when Howell could no longer lift him, so finally Howell had the house to himself. Then she could have gone there anytime, snuck over in the afternoon during her lunch break from work, detoured there on her way back to her house after work. . . . All my information about Sylvie's divorce, and about Howell's parents, I found out in bits and pieces from Daphne, when we were shopping for new school clothes or eating lunch at a downtown tea room or—those times the psychic guaranteed Daphne would not break any bones—ice skating together in the evening, at Parker's pond. Daphne didn't suggest the romantic scenarios; I thought of them myself, admiring my grown-up imagination, sure that some day I, too, would operate deviously and complexly, leading whatever secret life was necessary to fulfill my every desire.

When I was the age my mother was when she married, eighteen, I was living in the East Village with a drug-dealing cabdriver who was married to a woman in Mexico City. That summer I left him, left New York for Vermont, though that may have been a preemptive strike, because he'd begun missing his wife in Mexico. When I was twenty, the age my mother was when she had me, I had dropped out of school and was working as a waitress, proud of myself, in those years of pinwheel eyes and paranoid, incantatory fixations, for not using anything stronger than grass. I was mugged on Avenue A by two teenagers who said, "Peace and love" as they jumped my back, got arrested for shoplifting, applied for a student loan and went to another college which I flunked out of at the end of spring semester, had an abortion, wrote half a novel, was arrested for rioting, finished the novel and abandoned it, dramatically, on the IRT, hitched to California, went with a man to London, broke my ankle dancing in a nightclub, and through it all— though I can't picture it and I don't want to remember the particulars —I apparently wrote letters to Sylvie and to Daphne, as well as called Daphne, drunk, from a pub in Wales, asking that she send me my blue jacket which, as I described it, she realized was a jacket I'd had when I was eight or nine years old. A boy I'd broken up with maliciously called Sylvie and said I'd o.d.'d and was dead. During that same period, Daphne phoned a friend in London and asked her to come to my flat and take me to dinner, and when the woman got there, though I'd been hungry and therefore receptive to her proposal on the phone, I refused to go to the door and told my boyfriend to tell her I'd left London that afternoon. I think she saw me in there, behind him, sitting in one of the two canvas butterfly chairs, smoking a joint, listening to the Rolling Stones. I think I remember her going on tiptoes and waving at the same time I was waving a cloud of marijuana smoke away from my watering eyes. But that's pretty much the story of my generation. Maybe a little different in the particulars, but similar in content to so many other people's lives. Sort of the counterpart of Daphne's: *"It was 1954, and it just wasn't done."* It was 1967, and it was done every day.

The big surprise, once we were inside Steven's loft, was that Charlie had rushed to the airport, hoping to make it back to Boston before his wife gave birth. He called her at the end of the service, and the outgoing message on their answering machine said, "Charlie, come home. I've gone into labor. It's 12:30 and I'm leaving for the hospital."

"Gracious!" Daphne said. "I suppose that was the sensible thing to do, but I can still remember when a woman never referred to her condition. Women stayed inside the last months of their pregnancy. They certainly wouldn't have broadcast the news to the world."

"We all need a drink," Steven said, steering us toward the front of the loft. "A friend from work's tending bar. Tell him what you want, and have something to eat. He's brought beautiful things to eat." He pointed toward his friend and the few people who had preceded us, so strongly backlit they'd become shadows.

"Even I need a drink," Daphne said, as I helped our out of her coat.

"How are you, sweetheart?" Steven said to me, kissing the side of my head.

Damian, Steven's assistant, was sitting on a stool, leaning on the drawing table, propped on one elbow. Though he had on a suit at the service, he had changed into jeans and a pullover. "Because there's a reception here now following a memorial service," Damian said, speaking into the phone in his thick English accent. "What do you think—we should let you test the security system and maybe at the same time we could turn on the radio and hope for a test of the emergency broadcasting system? Maybe run the Kentucky Derby through while we're at it?"

"They're very officious," Steven said apologetically, as if we were on the receiving end of Damian's sarcasm. "It's about my new security system," he said. "They want to test it right this minute. It's no time to do it, is the point."

"The point is," Damian echoed, "this is not the time."

"So *officious*," Steven hissed to the ceiling.

"Love, can you understand what I'm telling you? We don't want to activate the cross-beams because people are standing all over the place. Grieving people. We're here mourning the dead," Damian enunciated slowly.

This was when it occurred to me that we were not. We were shaking off our coats, anticipating socializing with one another in a more private setting out of the church, relieved that the service was over: annoyance at life's absurdities began creeping in; hunger was gnawing.

"Security system?" Daphne was saying to no one in particular, as I put my arm around her shoulder and moved her toward the far end of the loft. "I hope he hasn't been robbed," she said. "I guess it's just a precaution." Then, "I couldn't live like this."

"How are you?" Steven's friend from work said warmly, reaching across the table to shake Daphne's hand, then mine. "We met briefly last Christmas," he said to Daphne. "I was going out as you were coming in."

"Oh, yes. You had your dog, on a leash."

"Didn't seem proper to bring him today," the man said. "I usually take him everywhere. They started a day-care center where we work, you know, and now I drop the dog at the daycare. He loves children. They said that if one more person wanted to bring a dog, I'd have to leave mine at home. But do you know what? Nobody wants to. Or they have cats. I'm just lucky. The dog and I got lucky."

"A dog in daycare," Daphne said. She didn't seem surprised. Perhaps it might have surprised her if she hadn't already had her quotient of surprises hearing about the way Charlie found out his wife had gone into labor and learning that a security company wanted to conduct a test which would catch all of us in a klieg light of sound. Somewhere down below, a car alarm was set off, whirring a repetitive, mechanical shriek, as though the woman on the phone had exacted revenge, haunting us with the possibility that obnoxious sounds might yet move closer. As Daphne requested a Bloody Mary, I looked past Steven's friend who was bartending, seeing the sky darkening with rain clouds, the wall of sand-colored buildings facing our building from across the street. In the high shine on Steven's floors I could see shadows of the clouds reflected, and for a minute it reminded me of Parker's pond, the blurrily indistinct shapes cast by one's legs and feet and skates. When I looked up, Steven's friend was holding out two glasses: one a wineglass, one a glass filled with ice, silently offering me two possibilities. "White wine, thanks," I said, but my interest was in the stack of cubes in the other glass. Like the world in miniature, they reminded me of the surface of the pond, the pond on which Daphne had been promised she would not slip, one of the many places I followed her, believing that if she was safe from harm, of course I was safe. Now, through the years, things had changed. It had begun to work the other way, so that Daphne followed me: uptown, downtown, a silent accomplice in the mysterious ritual of how to get a cab that would take off in the right direction.

When Sylvie came in, she was wet from the rain. With her hair plastered to her head, she looked like a woebegone little girl, though the mist on her face had enlivened her cheeks, at least . . . she had been so pale in the church. She blew us a kiss and—shoes slipped off—hurried into the bathroom, probably to towel-dry her hair, reapply lipstick. What could it be like, to lose someone you had such a close relationship with for forty years? What would it be like to go to that person's memorial service and hear people praise the person's unfailingly unique virtues, allude to intimacies, offer gentle jokes the deceased would presumably smile to hear? So many private thoughts in public places.

What would Sylvie's private thoughts have been? Why didn't he marry her? Or was the answer clear, and only outsiders didn't intuit it?

I looked around the room. The people were family friends—or they were Steven's friends, like the man tending bar, like Damian—people who barely knew Howell. Though many of Howell's friends had been at the memorial service, as I looked around the room I saw that only two people who seemed to be Howell's personal friends had come to Steven's loft. And those two, a man about Howell's age, wearing a too-closely-fitted dark suit he looked uncomfortable in, and a younger man with badly dyed blond hair and nervously hunched shoulders, who either did not have, or who was deliberately not wearing, the sort of clothes everyone else had on—even those two, I realized, were gay. There had been such an assortment of people in the church—people he'd worked with, people from organizations he'd given his time to, neighbors—that until the core group assembled, the obvious never occurred to me. As much as this gathering was for Sylvie—for her children, her niece, her sister's onetime best friend—as much as it was Steven's gesture toward his mother, it was also his gesture toward the two men, who seemed hardly to know one another, yet who stood close together, silently, awkwardly, the younger man finally helping the older man off with his jacket and adding it to a pile of coats on the chair by the entranceway, exchanging a few pleasantries with Damian, the older man so contrite it was almost possible to read his mind, to understand that what he really wanted was to bolt. Then the younger man went back to his side and gestured toward the table set up by the front window. I had been staring at them—I hadn't meant to, but when my thoughts locked, my eyes must have, also—so of course as they came nearer they pretended not to notice me, or my stare. The older man walked right past me, but as the younger man passed, he turned, then walked back to where I stood, his shoulders hunched, as if he were trying to fold into himself. "Ladies," he said, ducking his head and raising it again. It was the first time in what seemed like hours that I realized Daphne was at my side, that she was all but clinging to me, her glass empty, her expression slightly worried as she looked in the direction of the still-closed bathroom door.

"You don't know who I am," the man said as he approached, "but Howell often spoke of you. My name is Justin DeKalb. The surprising thing is, I would have recognized you anywhere, because I used to skate at Parker's pond. Howell described you both to me many times, but the minute I walked in, I realized I actually knew you. Not exactly that I know you, but I used to be there when you were. At Parker's pond." As he said this, he clasped Daphne's hand, smiling at her and then—more tenuously, it pained me to see—at me. How long had I been staring at this man? How long had I been rooted to the spot, oblivious of Daphne, of Sylvie's long disappearance, of the men's discomfort? With the floor gleaming around us, I had the giddy feeling we were, all three of us, back there—back at the big pond Mr. Parker had dredged one winter on his front fifty acres that had seemed to all of us the most miraculous thing, the most wonderful gift. The memory made me spontaneously reach out to take Justin DeKalb's hand, the way so many of us had locked fingers on those winter nights, at times to tease someone who was skating too slowly into action, or to coax someone into being our partner, or simply for the fun of making contact, seeing if fingers could communicate an idea: figure eights, or a race, or a conga line.

"I can't believe it," Daphne was saying. "That crowd of people, and you remember the two of us? Well, I guess that says something, but I don't know that I want to know what." She smiled, her eyes glittering.

"I liked the way you skated together," he said. "You were beautiful skaters."

"I never was," Daphne said, though she did not protest too strongly. "I was scared to death," Daphne said, still gaily, but lowering her voice. "Scared silly, and you'll laugh, but I always paid a psychic before I got out on the ice to tell me if I was going to make it. One time she advised against it, and I didn't go. I pretended to be sick. Here's something I never confessed until now: I pretended to have a terrible stomachache—you may even remember," she said to me, "because you were so disappointed. I knew you'd be angry at me if I told you we couldn't go because the person you called 'Madame Money' said the ice might crack." She turned to Justin DeKalb. "Then I felt terrible, because it was always a way to get her out of herself, because she was so hopelessly sad her mother had died, and none of us who loved her knew what to do. Skating always did the trick, but that time I just lost my courage. Now I look back and wish we'd never missed one night at Parker's pond."

This heartfelt confession so surprised me that I just stood there. As Daphne was talking, Justin DeKalb had let go of my hand, and I looked at it, as if perplexed by the emptiness of my own hand. Because as she talked—up until almost the end of her confession—I had been on Parker's pond. I had felt that freedom again, the exhilarating, numbing cold, and the sensation had cleared something in my head. Without

Daphne—without the approval of anyone else—I could, and should, simply proceed with my life.

"Yes," Justin DeKalb said, nodding his head. "It was a tragedy that your mother died so young. My condolences."

"And mine, of course, about the death of Howell," I said.

"Oh, God, we have got to get more cheerful," Daphne said. "At the very least, I need another drink to bolster myself."

"You were scared?" I said suddenly. "Every time?"

"I was," she said, "but it was a good kind of scared. I only feel bad that I let you down that one time. Sylvie was—" she looked toward the closed bathroom door "—considering the things that had happened in her life, of course she was traumatized, but she always took her responsibilities very seriously. She wouldn't skate herself, you know, and she refused to let you go there without adult supervision. So I just got so I'd hold my breath and do it. After the first few minutes, it wasn't so bad." She smiled. "And look," she said. "We survived."

Sylvie left on the last shuttle for Boston. "Off to the birthing room!" Steven said to his mother. "Straight life is so hectic," he sighed, hailing a cab. Sylvie embraced us: first me, then Steven, not caring that the cabdriver had started the meter when he stopped, or that he was looking impatiently out the window. As she got into the cab, I thought how much Sylvie looked like my mother. The rain had twirled her hair into soft curls. Like my mother, she was wearing a heavy coat of lipstick that glowed the unnatural pink-purple of phlox, though she wore no other makeup. In the cab she looked as small as Daphne, like someone who could also use a little protection in the big city, though I knew she knew where she was going, and also that the news from Boston had been a sort of exciting ending to a difficult day. I was still not sure if she had lost a friend or a lover, though it began to seem strange even to me that I was still fixated on that. Maybe I had just wanted to live vicariously; maybe, like most other adolescents, I had wanted to think her totally in my control, while at the same time I had an urge for her to have escaped me, to have a secret life. And perhaps she had, though she probably did not silently contain the conventional secret I had suspected it would be.

"What was it Tiny Tim said?" Sylvie said, rolling down the window as the driver waited to move into traffic. "'God bless us, each and every one?'"

"I think Tiny Tim *sang* it," Steven said. "I think he sang it, and it was, 'Tiptoe through the tulips.'"

She sniffed, with a look of mock exasperation. As the cab pulled away, Steven stood at the curb, playing air music, strumming an imaginary ukelele close to his chest, looking as wild-eyed as he could. The rain had also made his hair curly, which helped. That, and his shirt hanging out of his pants, the dark circles under his eyes at the end of this long day. "To the gaaaaaarden wall," he was singing in falsetto as the cab pulled away.

"That's 'LaGuardia,'" I said to him.

"Good one," he said.

"You're not going to believe this, but it wasn't until tonight that I realized Howell was gay," I said to Steven.

"What did you think?" he said.

I said, "I didn't think anything."

"But you know what was interesting?" he said, opening the inside door with a key, walking toward the elevator. "What was interesting was that he knew about me before I did. Remember that party when he got drunk and fell out of the tree? Don't even bother to answer, because I know you remember. A perfectly ordinary accident, and it's become family lore. Somebody got a little out of control, and nobody's ever recovered from it. Think about it: divorces are never mentioned, my father took off and was never heard from again, but all Howell did was get a little tipsy and take a tumble, and for all eternity, everybody's been fixated on his bizarre behavior. The infamous fall of Howell the clown. I'd bet money that even though nobody brought it up at the memorial service, it was on a lot of people's minds. I look back now, and do you know what? I'm still the only one who understands why it happened. That stuff about Romeo and Juliet. His playing Juliet to my Romeo. He knew then that I was gay, and I didn't."

"Steven—weren't you six years old or something?"

We got onto the elevator. He pushed 5. "Seven, wasn't I?" he said.

"He never—"

"Jesus," he said. "Of course not."

"What about Sylvie and Howell?" I blurted out.

"That's an interesting question. My guess?"

I nodded.

"My guess would be that when Dad took off and when your mother died, when Sylvie had to get that job she always hated, and when—don't take this wrong—you came to live with us and for so long you were so goddamn inconsolable, by that time Sylvie felt like she'd pretty much seen it all come and go. I think for most of his life, Howell couldn't *wait* to see it go so he could get on with his life, but that somewhere in between his wish for things to change and her certainty about how life was going to be, they got attached to each other. That if there was no going forward, there wasn't any going back, either."

The elevator doors opened. What he'd said was very astute, but I wasn't fully concentrating. What he'd said had just reminded me of something. It had reminded me of years ago, the first of the many times I'd left New York, when I'd been living with the man in Alphabetland. He said the only way out of New York was to make a run for it, because if you thought about it, you'd be like everybody else who was trapped; you'd weigh the pros and cons, and the bottom line would be that you'd never get out. It made me wonder, now, if it was easier to leave a lover or to leave a city—though of course so many times the two are so interconnected you can't be sure what you're turning your back on. Or maybe you do find out, but not until you're really out there, on the road. Then, if it feels like the road's stretching toward something, you find out you've still got horizons, but if all you can see, in all that space, is a person, that person's no mirage. He won't recede. You just have to turn around and find him again.

I was thinking these thoughts not so much because of the man I ran away from when I was eighteen, but because at the moment I was, for all intents and purposes, in limbo, the labyrinthine yet familiar limbo of New York. It wasn't my home in Allentown, and it wasn't whatever I'd go toward next. The day before Howell's memorial service, my husband had said there was no use in pretending, no point in his going to a memorial service and sitting at my side as if we shared a life; we were going to separate, and it was only a question of time before one of us was gone.

As soon as Steven turned his key in the lock and opened the door, I glided past everyone, hurrying across the huge expanse of shiny floorboards to the windows, the big glass windows that fronted on lower Fifth Avenue, and stared outside with such concentration, tears rose in my unblinking eyes. There were stars in the sky; I could see them where the rain clouds drifted apart, and though there were only a few, they still seemed as wonderful as they had seemed scattered everywhere, long ago, above Parker's pond. There were the stars and, far below, there was steam blanching the night, rising from below ground, where, on the subways, distances were being traversed, people were in transit. I saw through to that. I saw it as clearly as Daphne had seen inside Sylvie's mind earlier in the evening, and as clearly as I had seen into Howell's gentleman friend's mind when he stood in Steven's apartment and hoped to disappear in a crowd that was not crowded enough, having no idea whether it would be more painful to be acknowledged or to go unnoticed. I suddenly felt as though I could see through anything, much the way Madame Money had claimed to Daphne she could see the future. Like her, I knew at the very least how to make an educated guess. Keep pressing your luck and eventually your luck won't hold: ice will crack, subway cars collide. At some point, accommodate fear, because otherwise fear will subsume you. But it was difficult to think cynically that minute. Across Steven's loft, Daphne was talking with Damian, a fresh drink in her hand, and the man with yellow, yellow hair was waiting on the fringes, eager to approach. At Howell's memorial service, and at the reception afterwards, Daphne was flirting, cocking her head in mock disbelief at whatever Damian was saying to shock her, and as strange a feeling as it was to have, I envied her. I envied her because in all probability she was playing a game she did not even know she was playing. The farther I moved away from the glass, the more clearly they were reflected, though because I knew them so well, because I cared for them or sympathized with them or just because I appreciated their good intentions in difficult circumstances, they couldn't hold my attention long.

Eventually I moved forward, almost nose-to-the-glass close, so I felt the outside coldness through the window almost as an ache. Then I simply stood there to spy on the world that had nothing to do with them. As I looked down to the wide, open spaces of the city—though it's true those spaces existed primarily as corridors between buildings—I could have been Howell in the tree, intentionally myopic, a little dazed, wishing to be a little daring, but unlike Howell I had braced myself to stand firm, taking in everything that was not the life inside this room, this claustrophobic room that had become a repository for people's good intentions, for their attempts at understanding, this loft high above Fifth Avenue that most of them would never stand in again, which had suddenly become the place where they could understand what was not understandable, where they could have a drink, meet the people they'd always wanted to encounter, where they could forgive at the same time they were forgetting. Though I looked at Daphne reflexively for my love to be beamed back, I knew I had already begun a journey outside her parameters. Nose and fingers to the glass—because who was watching, who cared?—there was all of New York. Outside there seemed, amid steam and stars, to be nothing but space.

PAUL BOWLES

Afternoon with Antæus

You wanted to see me? They told you right. That's my name. Ntiuz. The African Giant's what they've called me ever since I started fighting. What can I do for you? Have you seen the town? It isn't such a bad wind that comes through here. But without it the sun's too hot. Argos? Never heard of it. I've never been over to the other side.

A man named Kherakli? Yes, yes, he was here. It was a long time ago. I remember him. We even put on a fight together.

Killed me! Is that what he told them back there? I see. And when you got here you heard I was still around, and so you wanted to meet me? I understand.

Why don't we sit here? There's a spring in the courtyard that has the coldest water in town. You asked about Kherakli. No, he had no trouble here, except losing his fight. Why would anyone bother him? A man alone. You never saw him before. You let him go on his way. You don't bother him. Only savages attack a stranger walking alone. They kill him and fight over his loincloth. We let people go through without a word. They come in on one side and go out on the other. That's the way we like it. Peaceful and friendly with everyone. We have a saying: Never hit a man unless you know you can kill him, and then kill him fast. Up where I come from we're rougher than they are down here on the coast. We have a harder life, but we're healthier. Look at me, and I could almost be your father. If I'd lived down here on the coast all my life I wouldn't be like this now. And still I'm nothing to what I was twenty years ago. In those days I went to every festival and put on shows for the people. I'd lift a bull with one hand and hit him between the horns with the other, so he'd fall dead. People like to see that. Sometimes I broke beams with my head. That was popular, too, but the bull was religious, of course, so it was the one people wanted to see most. There was nobody who didn't know about me.

Have some nuts? I eat them all day. I get them up in the forest. There are trees up there bigger than any you ever saw.

It was at least twenty years ago he came through here, but I remember him, all right. Not because he was any good as a fighter, but because he was so crazy. You can't help remembering a man as crazy as Kherakli.

Have some more. I've got a whole sack full. That's true, the flavor's not quite like anything else. I don't suppose you have them over on the other side.

I'll be only too glad to take you up to the forest, if you'd like to see it. It's not far. You don't mind climbing a little?

Of course he didn't make any friends here, but a man like that can't have friends. He was so full of great ideas about himself that he didn't even see us. He thought we were all savages, ready to swallow his stories. Even before the fight everybody was laughing at him. Strong, yes, but not a good fighter. An awful boaster and a terrible liar. And ignorant.

We'll turn here and go up this path. He talked all the time. If you believed him, there was nothing he couldn't do, and do it better than anybody else.

You'll get a fine view on the way. The edge of the world. How does it feel, when you're used to being in the middle, to be out here at the end? It must be a different feeling.

Kherakli came into town without anyone noticing him. He must have had a little money with him, because he began to meet two or three men I knew every day and pay for their drinks. They told me about him, and I went along one day just to see what he looked like, not to meet him. Right away I knew he was no good. No good as a fighter, no good as a man. I didn't even take him seriously enough to challenge him. How can you take a man seriously when he has a beard that looks like the wool on a sheep?

He stayed around town awhile and saw me kill a few bulls. I fought a match or two, too, while he was here, and it seems he came each time to watch me. The next thing I knew, he'd challenged me. It was he who wanted the match. It was hard to believe. And what's more, they told me he held it against me that I hadn't been the one who challenged him. It just never entered my mind.

All this land you see up here is mine. This and the forest up ahead. I keep everybody out. I like to walk, and I don't want to meet people when I'm walking. It makes me nervous. I used to fight every man I met. At least, in the beginning.

When I was a small boy in my village I liked to go late in the after-noon to a big rock. I'd sit on it and look down the valley and pretend enemies were coming. I'd let them get to a certain point, and then I'd start a boulder rolling down the mountain to hit them. I killed them every time. My father caught me and I got punished. I might have hit sheep or goats, or even men down there.

But I'm not dead, as you can see, no matter what Kherakli may be saying. I want you to look at my trees. Look at the size of the trunk of that one. Follow it up, up, up, to where the first branches begin. Have you ever seen trees this big anywhere?

When I got a little older I learned how to throw a calf, and later a bull. By that time I was fighting. I always won. Never lost yet. They forgot my name was Ntiuz and began to call me The Giant. Not because of my size, of course. I'm not so big. But because nobody could beat me in a match. They came from all around, and afterwards from far away. You know how they do when they hear of a fighter who's never lost. They can't believe that somehow or other they won't manage to get him down. That was the way with your Kherakli. I didn't meet him until the fight, but I'd heard all about him from my friends. He told them he'd studied me, and he knew how to beat me. He didn't say how he was going to do it. And I never even found out what he thought he was going to do until after the fight.

No, I'm not dead. I'm still the champion. Anybody here can tell you. It's too bad you never met Kherakli yourself. You wouldn't be so surprised. You'd understand that whatever he said when he got back home was what he wanted to tell and nothing more. He couldn't tell the truth if he wanted to.

Are you tired? It's a steep climb if you're not used to it. The fight itself? It didn't last long. He was so busy trying to use the system he'd worked out. He'd back away, and then come up to me and just stand there with his hands on me. I couldn't understand what he was trying to do. The crowd was jeering. For a minute I thought: He's the kind that gets his pleasure this way, running his hands over a man's chest and squeezing his waist. He didn't like it because I laughed and shouted to the crowd. He was very serious the whole time. And I was wrong anyway. Are we going too fast? And you're carrying that heavy pouch at your waist. We can go as slowly as you want to. There's no hurry.

That's a good idea. Why don't we sit a minute and rest? Do you feel all right? No. Nothing. I thought you looked a little pale. It may be the light. The sun never gets down in here.

It was only after the fight that one of my friends told me what

Kherakli wanted to do. Instead of trying to throw me, the crazy fool was trying to lift me off the ground and hold me up there. It's hard to believe, isn't it? But that's what he had in his mind. That was his great system. Why? Don't ask me. I'm an African. I don't know what goes on in the heads of the men of your country.

Have some more nuts. No, no, they couldn't have hurt you. It's the air. Our climate doesn't suit people from the other side. While he was trying to make up his mind how to lift me I finished him. They had to drag him out.

Shall we go on? Or would you rather wait awhile? Are you still out of breath? There's no air here in the forest.

Don't you think we ought to wait awhile? Of course, if you want to go. We can walk slowly. Let me help you up. It's too bad we couldn't have gone further. The biggest trees are up that way.

Yes, they dragged him out, and he stayed three days lying on a mat before he left here. Finally he limped out of town like a dog, with everybody laughing at him along the way. Hang on to me. I won't let you fall. You're walking all right. Just keep going. He didn't look left or right on his way out of town. Must have been glad to get into the mountains.

Relax. First one foot, then the other foot. I don't know where he went. I'm afraid there's no water here. We'll get some as soon as we get to town. You'll be all right. I suppose he went back where he came from. We never saw him again here, in any case.

Does it seem like such a long time that we've been walking? It's only a few minutes. You recognize the path but you don't know where you are? Why should you know where you are? It's not your forest. Relax. Step. Step. Step.

You're right. It's the same rock where we were sitting a few minutes ago. I wondered if you'd notice. Of course I know my way! I thought you'd better rest again before we started into town. That's right, you just lie back there. You'll be fine as soon as you've had a little sleep. It's very quiet here.

No, you haven't been asleep so long. How do you feel now? Good. I knew a little sleep would do it. You're not used to the air here. A pouch? I don't think you were carrying anything.

There's no need to make a face like that. You don't think I took it, do you?

I thought we were friends. I treated you like a friend. And now you pay me back.

I'm not going to take you anywhere. Get down to the town by yourself. I'm going the other way.

Go on back to your country and tell them about me. You can walk all right.

Just keep going.

And get out of the forest fast!

SANDRA CISNEROS

I Would Love You Like a Jacaranda

He said, *Muñeca. Muñeca.* Just that single word. He said it casually. He said it to all the women he made love to, indifferently. Sorry and too late. Her past blossomed like a branch of flaming jacaranda. Like an umbrella. Oh my god. Said that one word, and like open sesame, the magic pronouncement summoned more than she could explain. How do you say? In neither English nor Spanish. There was no word for what he was doing to her. Like Houdini pulling a thousand silk scarves from a thimble. Voilà! She wanted to say Daddy, but she didn't have to, did she?

So you see, this man, hovering like a hummingbird, this one, was like that for her. And somehow she could not see nor explain it. Except that he opened something, a memory she didn't know she had.

What? What was it? What bright eureka? What missing Rosetta Stone? Where? And how and who? It made no sense. A sliver of the Snow Queen's mirror lodged in the heart for generations, a tender spot that hurt only when you breathed. But where was it? Where in the psyche? In what vital organ? What liver? What spleen? In what sheen between waking and dream?

The little key. The keystone. The Achilles' heel. The hammer that set the trigger. The missing link. The raw sinkhole of the infant's skull. In each of us, the tragic flaw, the King Tut's tomb, the propensity, sweet predilection. An arrow flint. A thorn. The ouija needle of the heart. Hello. Goodbye.

Oh the body! That blabbermouth. When you hunkered down to love, did you have any idea? You trying to be so cool, so debonair. And the body yak-yakketing. Guess how many beans are in the jar? Spilling your 5,746 secrets, your greedy, pathetic need.

DON DeLILLO

Videotape

It shows a man driving a car. It is the simplest sort of family video. You see a man at the wheel of a medium Dodge.

It is just a kid aiming her camera through the rear window of the family car at the windshield of the car behind her.

You know about families and their video cameras. You know how kids get involved, how the camera shows them that every subject is potentially charged, a million things they never see with the unaided eye. They investigate the meaning of inert objects and dumb pets and they poke at family privacy. They learn to see things twice.

It is the kid's own privacy that is being protected here. She is twelve years old and her name is being withheld even though she is neither the victim nor the perpetrator of the crime but only the means of recording it.

It shows a man in a sport shirt at the wheel of his car. There is nothing else to see. The car approaches briefly, then falls back.

You know how children with cameras learn to work the exposed moments that define the family cluster. They break every trust, spy out the undefended space, catching Mom coming out of the bathroom in her cumbrous robe and turbaned towel, looking bloodless and plucked. It is not a joke. They will shoot you sitting on the pot if they can manage a suitable vantage.

The tape has the jostled sort of noneventness that marks the family product. Of course the man in this case is not a member of the family but a stranger in a car, a random figure, someone who has happened along in the slow lane.

It shows a man in his forties wearing a pale shirt open at the throat, the image washed by reflections and sunglint, with many jostled moments.

It is not just another video homicide. It is a homicide recorded by a child who thought she was doing something simple and maybe halfway clever, shooting some tape of a man in a car.

He sees the girl and waves briefly, wagging a hand without taking it off the wheel—an underplayed reaction that makes you like him.

It is unrelenting footage that rolls on and on. It has an aimless determination, a persistence that lives outside the subject matter. You are looking into the mind of home video. It is innocent, it is aimless, it is determined, it is real.

He is bald up the middle of his head, a nice guy in his forties whose whole life seems open to the hand-held camera.

But there is also an element of suspense. You keep on looking not because you know something is going to happen—of course you do know something is going to happen and you do look for that reason but you might also keep on looking if you came across this footage for the first time without knowing the outcome. There is a crude power operating here. You keep on looking because things combine to hold you fast—a sense of the random, the amateurish, the accidental, the impending. You don't think of the tape as boring or interesting. It is crude, it is blunt, it is relentless. It is the jostled part of your mind, the film that runs through your hotel brain under all the thoughts you know you're thinking.

The world is lurking in the camera, already framed, waiting for the boy or girl who will come along and take up the device, learn the instrument, shooting old Granddad at breakfast, all stroked out so his nostrils gape, the cereal spoon baby-gripped in his pale fist.

It shows a man alone in a medium Dodge. It seems to go on forever.

There's something about the nature of the tape, the grain of the image, the sputtering black-and-white tones, the starkness—you think this is more real, truer-to-life than anything around you. The things around you have a rehearsed and layered and cosmetic look. The tape is superreal, or maybe underreal is the way you want to put it. It is what lies at the scraped bottom of all the layers you have added. And this is another reason why you keep on looking. The tape has a searing realness.

It shows him giving an abbreviated wave, stiff-palmed, like a signal flag at a siding.

You know how families make up games. This is just another game in which the child invents the rules as she goes along. She likes the idea of videotaping a man in his car. She has probably never done it before and she sees no reason to vary the format or terminate early or pan to another car. This is her game and she is learning it and playing it at the same time. She feels halfway clever and inventive and maybe slightly intrusive as well, a little bit of brazenness that spices any game.

And you keep on looking. You look because this is the nature of the footage, to make a channeled path through time, to give things a shape and a destiny.

Of course if she had panned to another car, the right car at the precise time, she would have caught the gunman as he fired.

The chance quality of the encounter. The victim, the killer, and the child with a camera. Random energies that approach a common point. There's something here that speaks to you directly, saying terrible things about forces beyond your control, lines of intersection that cut through history and logic and every reasonable layer of human expectation.

She wandered into it. The girl got lost and wandered clear-eyed into horror. This is a children's story about straying too far from home. But it isn't the family car that serves as the instrument of the child's curiosity, her inclination to explore. It is the camera that puts her in the tale.

You know about holidays and family celebrations and how somebody shows up with a camcorder and the relatives stand around and barely react because they're numbingly accustomed to the process of being taped and decked and shown on the VCR with the coffee and cake.

He is hit soon after. If you've seen the tape many times you know from the handwave exactly when he will be hit. It is something, naturally, that you wait for. You say to your wife, if you're at home and she is there, Now here is where he gets it. You say, Janet, hurry up, this is where it happens.

Now here is where he gets it. You see him jolted, sort of wire-shocked—then he seizes up and falls toward the door or maybe leans or slides into the door is the proper way to put it. It is awful and unremarkable at the same time. The car stays in the slow lane. It approaches briefly, then falls back.

You don't usually call your wife over to the TV set. She has her programs, you have yours. But there's a certain urgency here. You want her to see how it looks. The tape has been running forever and now the thing is finally going to happen and you want her to be here when he's shot.

Here it comes, all right. He is shot, head-shot, and the camera reacts, the child reacts—there is a jolting movement but she keeps on taping, there is a sympathetic response, a nerve response, her heart is beating faster but she keeps the camera trained on the subject as he slides into the door and even as you see him die you're thinking of the girl. At some level the girl has to be present here, watching what you're watching, unprepared—the girl is seeing this cold and you have to marvel at the fact that she keeps the tape rolling.

It shows something awful and unaccompanied. You want your wife to see it because it is real this time, not fancy movie violence—the realness beneath the layers of cosmetic perception. Hurry up, Janet, here it comes. He dies so fast. There is no accompaniment of any kind. It is very stripped. You want to tell her it is realer than real but then she will ask what that means.

The way the camera reacts to the gunshot—a startle reaction that brings pity and terror into the frame, the girl's own shock, the girl's identification with the victim.

You don't see the blood, which is probably trickling behind his ear and down the back of his neck. The way his head is twisted away from the door, the twist of the head gives you only a partial profile and it's the wrong side, it's not the side where he was hit.

And maybe you're being a little aggressive here, practically forcing your wife to watch. Why? What are you telling her? Are you making a little statement? Like I'm going to ruin your day out of ordinary spite. Or a big statement? Like this is the risk of existing. Either way you're rubbing her face in this tape and you don't know why.

It shows the car drifting toward the guardrail and then there's a jostling sense of two other lanes and part of another car, a split-second blur, and the tape ends here, either because the girl stopped shooting or because some central authority, the police or the district attorney or the TV station, decided there was nothing else you had to see.

This is either the tenth or eleventh homicide committed by the Texas Highway Killer. The number is uncertain because the police believe that one of the shootings may have been a copycat crime.

And there is something about videotape, isn't there, and this particular kind of serial crime? This is a crime designed for random taping and immediate playing. You sit there and wonder if this kind of crime became more possible when the means of taping and playing an event— playing it immediately after the taping—became part of the culture. The principal doesn't necessarily commit the sequence of crimes in order to see them taped and played. He commits the crimes as if they were a form of taped-and-played event. The crimes are inseparable from the idea of taping and playing. You sit there thinking that this is a crime that has found its medium, or vice versa—cheap mass production, the sequence of repeated images and victims, stark and glary and more or less unremarkable.

It shows very little in the end. It is a famous murder because it is on tape and because the murderer has done it many times and because the crime was recorded by a child. So the child is involved, the Video Kid as she is sometimes called because they have to call her something. The tape is famous and so is she. She is famous in the modern manner of people whose names are strategically withheld. They are famous without names or faces, spirits living apart from their bodies, the victims and witnesses, the underage criminals, out there somewhere at the edges of perception.

Seeing someone at the moment he dies, dying unexpectedly. This is reason alone to stay fixed to the screen. It is instructional, watching a man shot dead as he drives along on a sunny day. It demonstrates an elemental truth, that every breath you take has two possible endings. And that's another thing. There's a joke locked away here, a note of cruel slapstick that you are completely willing to appreciate. Maybe the victim's a chump, a dope, classically unlucky. He had it coming, in a way, like an innocent fool in a silent movie.

You don't want Janet to give you any crap about it's on all the time, they show it a thousand times a day. They show it because it exists, because they have to show it, because this is why they're out there. The horror freezes your soul but this doesn't mean that you want them to stop.

RICHARD FORD

Middlewest

For a brief time after my return from France I signed up for a job as a quality control inspector for a company that certified motels and restaurants across the nation, a job that simply required me to drive a rented Plymouth around a four-state area (mine turned out to be Wyoming, Nebraska, North and South Dakota) assessing whether the motels and eateries there were sticking to their agreement that entitled them to advertise the company's "Recommended" plaque—a gold liberty bell hung from a little wooden belfry—in their plate glass windows and on their lighted *No Vacancy* marquees. "Analysts," which is what we inspectors were called, were chosen from geographical areas far from the locales where we did our anonymous snooping, and on my training trip from Williston, N. D., eastwards toward spiritless Minot, I was accompanied by a company instructor named Vic Moynahan, from the home office in Itasca.

Vic Moynahan was a former Chicago cop, a big, pinkish jolly fatboy type whose flat-top, smooth skin and pudgy digits made him look much younger and a whole world less sinister than he actually was. Vic had gone to Viet Nam in the sixties (when I was lounging around like a young pasha in Ann Arbor) and when he'd come back he'd gone into "police work," in the Windy City, only to go bouncing out ten years later because of some unauthorized gunplay and a series of cracked heads that even further tarnished the police department's image. Vic had gone to work after that for the Freedom Travel Club (Liberty Bell's parent company), first on the security side, rattling door locks and staring night after night at pale TV screens showing empty alleyways and closed back stairwells. Though little by little he'd worked his way out of his glass cage (almost certainly via his apparently jolly demeanor) and up to the department that doled out the Liberty Bell certificates—first as an analyst himself, and later when his boiled cabbage face and overstuffed profile became familiar to every motel clerk and waitress in America, on to a supervisor's job showing new analysts the rules of the road, a job he relished.

Analysts had a relatively brief effective-life-span. The time on the road alone in remote, underpopulated, eventless sections of America drove most qualified people straight out of their wits in two weeks. Plus, the motels and restaurants were far from excellent. They were motels with names like The Thunderbird, The Ivanho, The Wrangler, which possibly were attractive, top-notch places forty years ago because they were strung along the old red-sign business routes in towns like Laramie and Fargo, had big brightly-lit red, yellow and green flashing neon marquees and could offer double beds, air conditioning, direct dial phones, and primitive color TV all before the Interstate turned them into over-priced, out-of-the-way dumps you only checked into when all the newer places had their "No" signs illuminated, or when you needed a motel in a hurry and wanted to be sure no one you knew would see you. The restaurants were more or less the same.

Anybody, of course, could do an analyst's work, but middle-aged men like myself turned out to be best at it. We lasted longest and supposedly got more satisfaction from the job. And we were less recognizable, Vic Moynahan explained on my maiden voyage from Williston, N. D., north and east out along the lesser state highways through the towns of Lignite, Bowbells, Coteau, Niobe, and Donnbrook. "Guyz-r-age all sort of look alike, if you know what I mean," Vic said, a fat 50¢ cigar in his moist mouth, holding the steering wheel of our rented Polaris at arm's length so as to squeeze his Milwaukee goiter in under the arc. He wore big maroon Bermudas and a bright green luau shirt, with just his regular black police brogans and a pair of black over-the-calf socks. He looked more like a man on a cut-rate vacation (it was August and hot as Niger) than a business man on a training trip. "When you get to be late forties, early fifties, people tend not to notice us anymore. Particularly women," he said, smiling buoyantly. This seemed to make him happy, though I couldn't understand why. "We're just part of the overall landscape. Not worth a closer look. Plus, most of us have been married so goddamned long we can put up with anything." He extracted his cigar and stared down at the dark part he'd just been grinding on, raised his pink brows, said "Ummhh," then licked his lips agreeably, cranked the window down and flipped the stogie out. "So," he said, "What's your deal, Frank?" The window went up. "You a vet? You married? Got kids? Divorced?"

"Divorced," I said, happy to be asked, though I didn't like the picture of Vic and me as look-alikes or the thought that I was helplessly disappearing from view. "I wasn't in Viet Nam," I said good-naturedly and less loud. "I joined the Marines but I got hepatitis and got out...."

"Well, you lucked out there. That was boring," Vic said, driving and still seeming pleased. "Though I was at the '68 convention in Chicago and we kicked some draft-resister ass back there I want to tell you." Vic said "Chicago" like a native, with the middle 'a' sounding like a grunted 'u.' "I was in police work then, of course."

"I watched it on TV." It was, in fact, the year my former wife and I were married.

"How'd I look?" Vic said, beaming at the thought of himself busily whonking his fellow Americans in the head while his police badge was stowed safely in his pocket.

"It seemed pretty rough to me."

"Spirited independence, in whatever form, scares the shit out of some people, I guess."

I had no earthly idea of what he meant, but I eyed him sidewise to be sure he wasn't making a monkey out of me.

"I thought that night was probably the beginning of the end of the next twenty years in American life," I said.

"Possibly," Vic said, the serene look still spread across his pink, fleshy map. "You might well be right."

"Does it make you happy?"

"Well, nobody's perfect yet." Then he added cheerfully, "Though everybody *wants* to be." He was feeling for another cigar under the visor. "All these motels out here in Shitsville, they don't *want* to be fleabags—except the ones the Pakistanis own. They just are. So?" he said and forgot about his cigar when he couldn't find one. He plunged his hand into his green shirt pocket, took out a package of spearmint, put a little gray slab into his mouth, extended the package to me, and I did likewise. And then for a while we sat silently facing forward in our Polaris, spinning over the summer wheat prairie, while I chewed and oddly enjoyed the sweet flavor in the auto-air. "A time comes," Vic said as if he'd been chewing over what he'd said, "when it dawns on you you probably won't advance much closer to perfection than you have already, and you have to be satisfied with your small achievements." He nodded his head and raised his fat chin slightly so that from my side his face looked like a young Alfred Hitchcock. "That's as close as I get to Orientalism."

"Do you forgive yourself for beating the stuffing out of a bunch of innocent people?"

"I was just acknowledging myself, Frank," Vic said amiably. "And I forgive me. Do you forgive me?" He sidled his skint head over and smiled a big convivial smile.

"I guess not," I said, then *almost* said, "but that doesn't necessarily mean I don't like you," only instead said, "But that doesn't mean anything."

"Same difference," Vic said, installing another Wrigley in his mouth and blinking at the road to Minot as if ours was the fast lane to paradise.

Vic Moynahan, of course, wasn't just any disgraced cop/Vietvet. He'd grown up in an affluent far north Chicago suburb, to parents who were both Unitarian ministers, gone to Kenyon on a football scholarship in the early sixties, steered off the path into hallucinogens, and eventually steered himself off the team, out of school, out of his deferment and whack into Viet Nam at the age of nineteen (not an unusual story of my generation). And in the better version of the story, he would've come back from Nam, brooding but wiser, finished his degree going nights at Chicago Circle, taken a cop job while attending law school at Roosevelt, read *Atlas Shrugged,* seen through to its flaw of inhumanity, married, had kids, lost weight, divorced, gotten involved in veterans affairs, quit the force and joined the public defender's office, where he'd have made some people stand up and notice him. Later he'd have run for Congress as a Republican with unexpressed moderate tendencies, lost, then bucked the tide and won his district as a Democrat with staunch conservative leanings, and right now would have a solid seat on the Foreign Affairs Committee and be living out a bright future in the service of his country.

Instead, Vic was working for Freedom Travel, was fat as a Holstein and happy as a skylark just to be teaching people like me to hand out gold and brown stickers to put on shitty motel windows. Who was I to argue with him?

It turned out Vic liked nothing better, after a day of driving and inspecting, than swaying on into some dark cowboy or plow-jockey bar, shouting out scathing, salacious remarks that usually involved barnyard animals and somebody's wife or girlfriend, then laughing like hell so that the whole place turned against him, after which he tossed people around the room like chairs.

"Any of you women want to go home with me tonight?" Vic said very loudly at closing time in a place called the El Reno Club on the strip in Minot. "That includes you men, too. I'm not choosy. Anybody's wife, I'll take her, as long as she's not too fat and doesn't stink like a fucking pig. I hate pigs, but I wouldn't even be in this shit-burg if I was particular, would I? Haw, haw, haw, haw, haw. What's say, Frank? Anybody here look good enough to fuck besides the bartender? I know it's dark. Haw, haw, haw, haw, haw, haw. How 'bout that one over there?" Vic pointed to a tiny, bubble-haired blond woman sitting with a long-haired, lizard-looking guy with tattoos and a cowboy hat and his jeans tucked in his boots. "Come on over here sweetheart and give ole Vic a nice rim-job," he shouted. He'd been drinking sloe gin for three hours and seemed happy to get killed.

After a couple more remarks like the first, the tattoo-lizard guy got up reluctantly and came toward Vic, clearly hoping to murder him with his hands. But Vic just clouted him once across the side of the head with his big fist, worked some tricky police hold that involved turning the cowboy around and knuckling him under his ear in something like the old "sleeper" hold the wrestlers used when I was a kid, after which the guy fell instantly limp—all while I watched, well out of the way.

Later, there was another fight in the Trail's End Bar, and this time Vic got cracked with a pool cue, though he went on to win in the same manner—paralyzing some poor cowboy with a punch then putting him to "sleep." The police, however, were called and Vic was finally led away laughing in cuffs and taken to jail, though he was out in less than an hour. The police, he said, always gave you a play if you showed them your Benevolent card and promised to be out of town the next morning and hadn't killed anybody, hurt a cop, or stolen something valuable. Driving back to our motel, The Stagecoach, he told me he missed the old days "out in the field," and that nights like tonight were practically the only way he could "visualize" who he was. He said he never did any of these things at home and had never disfigured anybody, which he seemed to think was the most you could hope for in a long and complicated life from which we were gradually disappearing.

Next morning I drove Vic out to the Minot airport. He had a thick, red welt across the side of his cheek, and a butterfly bandage over his cut eyebrow. He was wearing his maroon Bermudas and a new bright yellow luau shirt and carrying a black plastic gladstone. As we drove out along the margins of the wheat prairie where a modest industrial park had recently risen beyond the runway and a river lay out to the east like a glistening carpet in the morning sun, Vic grew pensive (conceivably in reaction to his injuries). The little finger on his plump right hand, where he wore the tiniest of gold signet rings, was dark and swollen to half again its normal size, and Vic kept it clutched like a weiner in the other hand as though it hurt like the dickens.　＼

"My sense is you'll do fine at this work, Frank." Vic nodded, staring piggy-eyed at the approaching modern airport buildings and the red tail fin of a Northwest jet already arrived at the gate. Telling me this was what he was supposed to do, I understood, part of his training. But he hadn't asked me more than three questions in two days and hadn't listened to the answers, and knew nothing about me. He was not a man interested in the lives of others. "Just use common sense like you used last night when you didn't get in those biffs with me. Because you wouldn't have gotten out of jail back there, then I'd have had to fire you and leave you out here. We wouldn't take responsibility."

"I got scared and froze," I said, "it didn't really take brains."

"Same difference," Vic said and seemed preoccupied—I couldn't imagine by precisely what. "Somebody should've shot me by now or beat me to death or stabbed me or blown my car up with me in it, or something. That's a mystery." He took a deep breath and let it out in tiny little bursts. "I'm not prudent anymore."

"You sure seem to like your life, though."

"Absolutely love it," he said. "It frees you." Vic looked at me with his pink, bloodshot blue eyes, one slightly swollen and purpled. He seemed to want me to consider this as profound.

"What does?" I said.

"Not being tied down by a bunch of responsibilities or talents. Just doing what's easy." Then he sort of muttered, "I need my independence."

"I can tell," I said, and I steered us on in under the concrete awning at Minot International.

A scattering of North Dakotans were outside the terminal beside their cars, struggling suitcases and some big cardboard boxes in toward the double doors, looking anxious about their one-hour flight to "The Cities," but extremely eager to get the hell out of Minot. Vic just sat in his seat, staring at the fields sailing off beyond the airport parking lot toward the indistinct horizon, his puffy digits joined on top of his plastic gladstone like two stiff cow's udders.

"Do you know where you going to be buried yet?" he said.

"No!" I said. "Why should I? Do you?"

"Oh, you bet."

"Where?" I shoved the gearshift up and half-turned to look at him.

"Down in Tennessee. North of Goodlettsville."

"What the hell for?"

"Well," he said softly, "I was just riding through there one morning last April, doing just what we're doing this week. And I passed by this place where a river opened out into a big, wide reservoir. A man-made lake, kind of. And people were fishing out there. Somebody was jet-skiing, and there were two or three party barges floating around with people having drinks. And I saw this cemetery, one of the places with no headstones or fences, just some flowers and a few flags. And I thought: what a great place. No one would ever know you were here. I went over to the little toolshed and got a number off the door and called up. And pretty soon I had a plot. It looks right down on the reservoir."

"What did your wife say about it?" Vic was beginning to struggle himself free of the car.

"Oh, she thought it was okay. Her parents are Polacks, and she wants to be buried in Hamtramck. I wouldn't like that. So, I made a decision to be buried in Tennessee, where I don't know anybody. Seemed smart." He was on his feet outside the car, moving as if he was a little stiff from the poleaxings he'd given out and received the night before. I couldn't see his face, just the big seat of his maroon shorts.

"I hope it makes you happy," I said, and stuck my hand out to Vic before he could even see it.

"Oh yeah," Vic said distractedly. He reached in and took my hand in his less tender left mitt and gave it a queer little wiggle, standing there in his yellow shirt and his pale, fat, hairless legs. "Don't get too involved in the job, and you'll be great at it."

"I'll do the best I can, Vic. Thanks."

Vic didn't say goodbye. He just slammed the door back hard and started away as if he'd pulled up in a cab driven by a complete stranger.

* * *

The job, of course, did not work out. It lasted in fact only two more days, though if I'd stayed in it (or, worse than worst, *had* to stay in it) I'd have been in the bughouse in two weeks.

The Freedom Travel people had given me a complete list of Liberty Bell motels and restaurants to visit on my drive from Minot over to Grand Forks, after which I could just head home to New Jersey and wait for them to call and send me out again. I had a sheaf of triplicate, tricolor report forms to fill at each location, a job I performed by checking boxes the same way anyone would who ate lunch in some franchise eatery, and decided to fill out a "We'd Like Your Input" card and dropped it in the box by the cash register (a box which of course the manager empties into the garbage at closing time, after sitting around in a back booth with the waitresses and the fry-cooks, smoking cigarettes and reading the "comments" out loud and laughing their asses off about what morons their customers are for thinking anyone could give a shit about their opinions on anything).

My assignment wasn't to visit every accredited Liberty Bell location between Minot and Grand Forks (surprisingly, there were quite a few), but to do "randoms" from my list of businesses that hadn't been "analyzed" in the last four years—the length of time the accreditation lasted—and to send my reports in to Itasca at the end of every day (why every day, I never knew other than it prevented you from later rethinking your opinions, something I couldn't have imagined ever doing). During these two days I checked into as many as nine motels and visited at least an equal number of restaurants, sometimes only having a-cup-and-a-slice, but sometimes going the full four courses which meant warm tomato juice, a complimentary cold relish tray plus marshmallow and green jello desert.

My job was to do nothing more than to see how good the food was, whether the waitresses wore underwear (something, Vic said, that drove the older customers crazy), pay heed to whether the silverware, chairs, linen and floors were clean, if there was hardened gum under the tables, note down how long I waited for my order, how long food stayed under the warmer, whether the restrooms (I could usually only get into the men's) smelled like a donkey barn and had French Tickler machines (a low grade), if there was a no-smoking section, whether diagrams were posted for saving choking diners, and in general estimate the percentage "value-for-the-dollar" of the whole experience (a total judgment call, though 70 percent was considered high).

The motels were more or less graded the same: cleanliness, how I was treated by the room clerk, how firm the beds were, were there odd smells, was there at least one premium channel among the cable offerings (no smut channels). I scouted out the presence of working smoke alarms, a lighted parking lot, whether pets were "welcome" (they were supposed to be), working a/c, two-towel minimum, adequate soap and hot water, direct-dial phone, working door locks with night chains, and whether the office stayed open until midnight. A small "Comments" section was designed to give me a latitude to express personal observations—if I saw evidence of prostitution, if truckers were parking their rigs in the lot and letting them rumble and fume all night, if unadvertised "day-rates" were available (also graded down), or any suspicious goings-on that might alarm guests and make them feel like they were going to be robbed or murdered or have their vacations ruined.

By the time I reached Devil's Lake, N. D., at the end of the first day (though only 120 miles) I had gained almost six pounds, checked in and out of nineteen motels, was queasy in the stomach and jittery and sleepless from too much coffee, and was becoming fearful about the rest of the trip to Grand Forks (another eight motels and ten or fifteen more meals).

Every place I'd checked into had rated out fine—enough skimpy towels and smoke alarms and reasonably clear TV pictures. The restaurants all seemed to have purchased their food from the same large, institutional kitchen in the middle of the continent—though there was nothing wrong with it, nothing to make you nauseated or that didn't taste like something you might've gotten someplace else and been unable to remember what you'd eaten forty-five minutes later—crunchy English peas, too-soft-and-saltless succotash, thin cream corn, green beans out of a can, frozen apple crisp; ditto the ribs, the broasted chicken, the beef bourguignon, the baked "halibut." It all could've been made with papier-mâché or dog shit and painted with acrylics by fourth graders, and been just as likable to the average Mr. and Ms. Overland Traveler suffering from hemorrhoids, colitis, cystitis, high blood pressure, diabetes or Crohn's disease. Who *expects* to get a home-cooked meal away from home? I thought. It was why there were such things as homes! (Freedom Travel, of course, assumed no liability for food-poisoned customers, or people jeopardized by microwave use, or for overnight guests going psycho because a slaughterhouse or a stamping plant was operating just over the fence and sleep was at a premium.)

My only two bad experiences were that in a little steak joint in Rugby, two elderly waitresses got into a screaming fist fight, which ended when one hit the other with a tubular counter stool and knocked her cold. (I was having the French Dip in the main dining room and barely noticed a disturbance.) The other, down in Denbigh, was at The Wrangler Motel, when an Indian woman entered my room wearing a red peignoir and bedroom slippers, and went to sleep while I was gorked out watching the Cubs in the other twin—a case of mistaken identity the Wrangler management could hardly be held accountable for since I hadn't chained my door (though I did "comment" they should probably install doors that opened with a key).

Everything else was a long pale horizon before a cloudy sky on which little rose of notice and where I was lonely as a ghost.

What I might've thought I was getting into, I can't know now. It's true, and directly relatable to what Vic said, that unmarried, unemployed men in their mid-to-late forties lack a crucial credibility and can even attract unwholesome attention, in tightly knit, relatively conservative suburban communities such as I lived in in Haddam, New Jersey. In Haddam, I'd realized in my then-dormant state, I was in jeopardy of becoming the personage I least wanted to be, and in the three years since my divorce, most coldly feared: "the suspicious bachelor," the man whose life, while still visible, had no mystery; the graying, slightly jowly, slightly too-tanned-and-trim middle-lifer, cruising the town streets in a cheesy '58 Chevy ragtop (polished to a squeak), always alone on balmy summer nights, wearing a faded yellow polo shirt and green suntans, elbow over the window top, listening to Fifties tapes and pretending to have everything under control.

Beyond that, on the day I got divorced, sitting alone in my big empty house in the late afternoon gloom, wailing like an Arab over "my loss," I finally collected myself enough to promise never to complain about life again. (I didn't promise not to regret it or occasionally muse on it to distraction.) And I'd done pretty damn well in the years since, given that there's just so much you can do to better your lot, that life has the unnerving capacity to make us think we ought to be a lot happier than we are; and that the standard American impulse as life goes on is toward isolation in the personal sector (though all isolation really means is that fewer and fewer people agree with you, at the same time that you become increasingly determined to believe what you believe no matter what the hell).

But possibly I might've felt that a few weeks of driving around in the middle of asshole nowhere would help me locate what was "central to my being" and save me from these fates I feared—becoming a nonentity, becoming a complainer. Maybe, too, I was afraid if I didn't use my life, use it even in some outlandishly preposterous way, I'd lose it (the thing boys used to say about their dicks when I was a kid). Or maybe (and this is more like it) I had the telepathy that I was entering a "phase" and leaving a "phase," and wanted to head out to where I could run up the pennant on a new quadrant of life, unnoticed and unprotested. (The other possibility, of course, was that I did it for no good reason except that I could, and supposed I'd figure out a smart reason later—which I'm sure was what Vic Moynahan did and called "independence.")

* * *

When I made it finally to Grand Forks, I checked into four or five motels, stopped in at six or seven restaurants, filling out my evaluation sheets right at the table, in full view of waitresses and anybody else who cared to watch. At one place I had a soft drink and a sticky bun, at another a cuppa joe, at another a lamb pastie (the house specialty) and by eight o'clock I was done with my "randoms," had grown bleak with indigestion and solitude, and was ready to fly home to New Jersey in the morning and never think about the whole business another minute. I was, I felt, not temperamentally suited to be an analyst.

Later, at about ten, after a nap, a shower and some Gelusils in front of the TV, I walked out into the evening and across Highway 2 from the little Sacajawea Lodge, where I had checked in to stay, and wandered into a little cinder block bar called the "Low Down" which was not far from the University of North Dakota campus. And to my surprise—it was a Friday—the bar was barely a third full, though the few people inside (mostly squarehead Norskies and pie-faced Finns) were all standing around a harshly lit little stage, listening to four young Negroes play jazz—a running, hustling, melodious, swirly type that I found to be surprisingly sweet and lyrical and that was produced by a soprano sax, an electric guitar, a double bass and a drummer. All the jazzmen were young, skinny, tall and studious-looking and wearing horn-rimmed glasses, which I took to be a trademark. They wore black, sheeny-looking shirts and baggy hipster pants, and they were playing a lot of the great Thelonious Monk and Dizzy Gillespie arrangements from the fifties, interleaved with some unruly compositions of their own—which featured much more bumptious, atonal virtuoso solos—all with titles (announced by the sax guy in a soft but deeply ironic voice) like "The Present Tense De-personified," and "Histofactionalysis," names that meant nothing to us white listeners (which was probably the idea) but that represented involuted, multi-layered racial in-jokes that continually made all four musicians roll their eyes and snort back big belly laughs when the songs were announced, and that were intended to make the crowd feel like rubes, but didn't because most of what was said into the microphone wasn't intelligible, and all anybody cared about anyway was the music.

I drifted over to the bar, ordered a double gin, which I felt I deserved after my five-motel day, then stood blissfully leaning on my elbow among the young, modern North Dakotans, listening to the music. Many of the men had longish but well-kept hair, neatly trimmed beards, were dressed in suits and ties, and were in the company of big, young wholesome looking girls in dresses and stockings or slacks, all of whom seemed to be fans of the quartet and conceivably had followed them up from Omaha, where the musicians called home. There were also a scattering of older types—my age and on—women and men wearing sandals and beat-up jeans and T-shirts and dark glasses, who were parked quietly at peripheral tables in the dark, nursing small drinks and taking in the music as intensely as they could, rarely speaking, rarely getting up to get another drink or go to the bathroom—just listening. Between tunes they would smile and talk quietly, seeming to agree about most things, then grow silent as soon as the next number was announced.

I realized almost immediately that I was among a segment of the population almost exactly like myself; people in decent, nondescript lives, many of whom had gone to land grant colleges, who had unremarkable fascinations, ordinary intensities and GPAs, and who had ventured briefly out into the populous world unheralded, vaguely wary, but in quest of something unusual and possibly good—after which, with it or without it, they'd retreat back to their diurnal affairs of running record stores, teaching in high schools or sitting home quietly watching TV. And it made me feel better, almost happy, even though I didn't know the first thing about these folks or much about jazz and in fact usually got bored when the improvisation took leave of the melody, and always quit listening in the drum solo when the other musicians put down their instruments and started making eye contact with women in the audience.

I sidled comfortably away from the bar and squeezed in closer between the standing listeners until I was very near the band members, who were going to town vigorously on their various instruments, over which they held undisputed mastery. Eventually I moved farther to the left in the crowd and around to the edge, so that I was only two or three feet from the drummer, who was a tall athletic-looking bean pole, wearing a goatee, buzzed-short hair, thick sunglasses, and a pair of black knee-length shorts that weren't much different from Vic Moynahan's, and had to bend his long legs awkwardly to fit in behind his drums. Though when he played, all his parts operated in perfectly syncopated yet independent movements: his big feet thumping, his long head nodding, his two hands dervishing their sticks around in different but complementary bims, bams and pings on the cymbals and rims, while he sat straight and seemed to vibrate on his stool at a frequency that had seemingly nothing, but everything, to do with what the others were playing—some corn belt-inspired transubstantiation of "Take The A-Train," or so I conceived from the few notes I recognized.

And I admired the hell out of him. He was doing something, in whatever trance he'd pitched himself, that I couldn't begin to do, though he was half a life younger and probably just a hayseed from the wrong side of the tracks. Vic Moynahan would've given him a once-over and determined it either wasn't very hard to play drums or else it wasn't worth it to be in a jazzy quartet and to apply oneself to the nuts and bolts of paradiddles, rolls, drop-beats. "Just do what's easy, Buck." But he'd have been dead wrong! Possibly I *could've* done some of the mechanical things (with years of practice): cymbal flutters with the brushes, roll the snare, bang one foot at one speed while tapping the other at a different one. But I couldn't do any of it together, couldn't know when to do one and when to do something else, couldn't know when to *quit* playing—could never know the whole gist of playing a seven skin kit behind three other guys who were only seeming to play "Take The A-Train." (Later, as I was leaving, I heard the sax player say they were actually playing a Togoan tribal chant, and that Billy Strayhorn, who had written "Take The A-Train" had stolen it from Africa and made unjust millions with it.)

But what made this man a drummer (I wished fat-boy Vic *had* been there; he might've been won over, even though he wasn't crazy about Negroes) was not only that he knew *how* to hit the drums, and *when,* but also *why*—a spiritual impulse having nothing to do with rhythm or race but with the vital hum of the human spirit. And it didn't matter that the only place anybody listened to him and admired him for this spirit and command was in Grand Forks, N. D., because there was still a rakish splendor to him and his talents that transcended all time and place.

I, on the other hand (in the way that admiration can be the guilty father of despair, suddenly making me feel wretched and gully heart-sick), *I* knew nothing; was accomplished at nothing. I could truthfully not think of one thing I could put into practice at that moment for any-one's spirit and good except possibly breathing out and in more or less on cue if somebody in the crowd were to need CPR. Or, if somebody needed to know the quality of a blueberry pancake on a scale of one to five, while noting if a place offered the de-caf option without having to be asked; or if some joint in Lignite had a wheelchair stall in the crap-per, or a sprinkler system over the deep-fry trough so customers could consume their sorry-ass meals without suffering the anxiety that they might suddenly be sizzled like bacon strips in a disaster for which no one was going to prove liable—*then,* I was your man. F. Bascombe. Analyst.

If the drummer in the quartet had suddenly turned to me and won-dered, basso profundo, "Yo, Frank, my man, whassup?" I'd have been stuck for a goddamn answer, would've had to say, "Well, tell the truth Tyrone, nothing's up. But if you're awake at three a.m. and hungry as a horse, you don't have to go very far to find the best fried egg sandwich west of the Twin Cities, served anytime with all the java you can stom-ach: that'd be Larry's Rotisserie out on Route 2. Tell 'em Frank sent you. It doesn't even matter that you're a Negro."

I wasn't even at risk of going off the deep end; of becoming the Bas-combe family eccentric, the cousin who works the "strange job" he's not eager to discuss, in behalf of maintaining his collection of Limoges figurines representing all the characters in Dickens. No, I was in jeopardy of disappearing into the shallow end, of letting independence become not cushy invisibility but inanition: one day the suspicious bachelor drives his cherry Chevy to the outskirts of town, takes a last nostalgic look over his shoulder and just drives away—though later he's found at home, or no farther than one town away doing pretty much the same things, his car all shined, his tan slightly faded.

I stood on the sidelines by the jazz band for a little while longer, feeling remarkably and increasingly destitute. I drank two more gins so that my eyes started to go goofy and feel cushioned in their sockets, and until I had the sensation that the NoDaks all around me actually *couldn't* see me. Several big guys, in fact, with their big, neatly dressed wives—bumped right into me trying to get nearer to the stage and the music. People began to look at me with long, indifferent looks so that it seemed they must've been looking at someone behind me, like one of the ghosts in "Topper." I tried to strike up some purposefully elliptical afficianado chatter with a couple of somber-looking, bearded men at the bar (jazz buffs of my own vintage), but in each case they just looked my way, said nothing and walked off, as if they were hearing whispered, unbodily voices.

Eventually, I began grinding my teeth like an ape, my jaw began cramping and my body gradually began to constrict and bend inwards (people who enter fast-food restaurants and open up with AK 47s on innocent teens are reported to feel this way moments before they do their desperate deeds). I suddenly needed, I realized, to get out of there and in a hurry. So out a side door I went, into the bland and softened summer somnolence of Grand Forks nighttime, my heart unexpectedly booming like the drumhead, my teeth clinched tight, my head in a whirl of gin and dismay.

Instantly, sleek towny cars full of guys and gals in love were slowly dragging the wide, brightly lit and noisy western street in front of me, their youthful drivers staring longingly and narrow-eyed at the row of bright motels with their gaudy signage strung out to the brink of dark wheat fields over which I could make out only a blinking, tiny light high above the invisible horizon. "Why me? Why *not* me?" the drivers said. But as I stood at the curb outside the Low Down trying to breathe in calm from the hot nitrogenated air, readying myself to venture back across the busy Route 2 to the Sacajawea—which I'd already certified as "A-OK," "good as they come," "reasonable rates"—a big red Cadillac Brougham veered right over out of the traffic and stopped in front of me. Four Japanese men, business types all in their thirties, wearing suits and white shirts, all with big enthusiastic smiles, short haircuts, and leather briefcases piled between them in the seats, peered up and out of the two side windows.

"We're very sorry to bother you," the driver said and the three others bent forward, beaming out at me. "Can you tell where is the good places to stay in Grand Forks? We don't know anything." Everyone in the dark car—which had a yellow Hertz sticker on its back window—laughed riotously, and I realized they were all drunk, could even smell whiskey coming out of the car. "You can say that again," I heard one of the men say, then the others laughed, including the driver. Then one of them said, "You can say that again," again.

"It's seems pretty busy in town tonight," I said, and looked beyond their car roof to the Sacajawea, which was a little red-brick tourist court with "Welcome Boy's 4-Ball State Champ" and "FREE CUNT B'FAST" on its yellow sign alongside the Liberty Bell insignia. All the car slots were full. Lights were on in all the units.

"They're holding the boys' state four-ball tourney this week," I said, glib as a native.

"Four-ball," the Japanese driver said. The men in the back all said it too. "Four-ball, four-ball, four-ball."

"We have four-ball," the driver said with a smile of possible condescension.

"A room'll be hard to come by is all I mean," I said. "Which way you headed?"

"Which way we headed?" the driver said and looked baffled.

"West," someone said, then laughed raucously.

"West," the driver said forthrightly and too loud. "We're going fishing in a big lake. Tomorrow."

"I bet you'll have a wonderful time," I said, thinking I could probably recommend a motel up in Devil's Lake—the Sioux Teepee Courts, which I was sure had plenty of rooms, soft towels and door locks. "I wish I could go with you," I said. I was still drunk myself, but visible now.

"You can go!" the driver said and grinned at me. "Everything's arranged. We have guide. Just no place to sleep. And we're drunk. Snafu." Everybody inside howled at that idea.

"I'm staying across over there," I said. "But I'm afraid it's full up."

They all suddenly turned inside the Cadillac and looked across the busy street at the little lighted office which indeed had a hand-written sign on the door bluntly stating, "No," though no such sign was on the yellow marquee. It still said "Yes."

"Shit out of luck," the Japanese driver said and shook his head as though to get his eyes to focus.

"Maybe we ask the police," one of his cohorts mumbled, and the two others burst out laughing again. They had a bottle of Black and White scotch in the back seat, a long tube of plastic cups, a bag of ice cubes and some big bottles of ginger ale.

"I'd steer clear of the police," I said. "They'll give you a place to stay, but they wouldn't let you go fishing."

"Exactly!" the driver said and laughed abruptly. "Avoid the police. We'll find someplace good that's better than here."

"I'll drink to that," the back seat said.

"Exactly!" the driver said and smiled regally, dropping the Caddie down into gear.

"Wait a minute," I said. "I've got one idea. It may not work," (though of course I knew it would).

There's not much use of going on with this, since it must be obvious. I simply directed the four Japanese fishermen to turn into the Sacajawea while I woozily crossed the wide street and walked up to the glass office door and knocked until the owner came out in his pajamas, scowling and squinty and pasty-mouthed. (It was midnight.) I explained to him that four Japanese industrialists were in danger of getting put in the pokey for drunk driving and that they would pay a premium price for a decent room, and that I was an analyst of the Freedom Travel Club and could pretty well promise him a "Distinguished Host" citation plaque plus a feature story in the Liberty newsletter if he could see his way to finding a room with four beds our foreign friends could fall safely to sleep in (both of these promises I made up on the spot).

And of course the owner saw the wisdom of this scheme in a twinkling. He in fact had a room "around back" (for just such desperate, well-heeled out-of-staters, rich Texans or Jewish bankers from faraway), though its old Fedders only ran half-speed, and the Japanese had to sleep two to a bed, and the TV was a black-and-white Crosley table model with tin-foiled rabbit ears, and both the table lamps lacked bulbs. The manager said he was planning a big remodelling project once the tourist season was over and was going to fix up some of the original rooms, of which this was one. It was quiet, though, and all for $200, which the Japanese giggled about as they paid cash.

In an hour we were all of us crowded in their tiny room, finishing off the scotch and ordering a pizza, while the Japanese, who were actually all in the dental supply business, smoked cigarettes in their T-shirts and talked a mile a minute about new dental market opportunities and laughed about the TV (they had never seen black and white *or* rabbit ears). And after a while I said good-bye, declined their offer to go fishing and mosied up the bug-strewn, yellow-lit concrete walk back to my own room, where my new a/c hummed and the TV shown out clear and crisp and in full-color with fifty-six channels, plus a paid dirty channel I hadn't mentioned in my report. I had no one to direct dial at that hour, though just for the hell of it, I called a woman in New York City whom I had not talked to in a while and listened to her recorded message but didn't feel the urge to leave one of my own. And when I went to bed I felt much better. I concluded, in the face of all, even in Grand Forks, I was not completely out of ideas since I had used my small skills and brought the day to a slightly better end than it had started for four strangers and myself, something of a promising accomplishment in anyone's life—a defeat of inanition and a defeat of invisibility, if not an actual victory over middle life itself. I hoped it would be a harbinger of better things to come.

GARY GILDNER

Pavol Hudák, the Poet, Is Talking

"Pavol is drinking hard cider for breakfast. You would not guess this, but he is a very good pickpocket. He travels to pretty Levoča, a prosperous town. I could make a fine living here, he thinks. Rich merchants, doctors, foreign tourists. I can slip money from their coats and trousers like a magician. So this is what I do, I move here. You yourself, Gary, can see how successful I am as I drink cider for breakfast while others slave away.

"One morning in the Main Square I observe a beautiful woman walking toward me. She is such a wonderful sight, my eyes go weak as she approaches. I can only look at her face a few moments, then I must look down, at her basket of flowers. I am suddenly bashful, like a boy. I even stumble as we pass each other. I am in the clouds, a confused and lucky leaf. I touch my chest to calm my heart. Wait. Breathe slowly, Pavol. What is this? My purse is not in my shirt here, where I always keep it. I'm certain I brought it with me when I left my room only moments ago. I stopped nowhere, saw no one—no one except the beauty. Is it possible *she* took it? I am ashamed and astounded at this thought, and curious too. Very curious.

"I turn, I run after her. My heart is beating. I say to her, 'Excuse me, please. I must ask you a stupid question.' Her eyes are a glory to look at. 'I am only Pavol, a poet and, to tell the truth, a pickpocket. I ran after you because I am curious. Did you by any chance take my purse? Please, you can relax, I won't tell the police if you did.'

"She looks at me a long moment. Up and down. I tell you her eyes are the color of grass and sky. Impossible, I know, but that's the truth. Finally she says, 'Yes, in fact I did.'

"We talk. I want to say a poem to her, but this other news, of her great gift, as good as my own, is what we discuss. In short, I suggest we work together. We can be fantastic! So this is what we do, Gary. We become a team. We make so much money we buy a house. We become lovers, of course, it is inevitable. And one day we decide to marry. Why not? We can have children. We can teach them what we know. We can retire into a nice old age and let our kids do the work.

"So Slavka becomes pregnant. It is amazing how this new condition makes her an even better pickpocket. Because she doesn't seem the type, does she? She can get closer to people. They trust her, offer their arms, and so forth.

"Then the baby is ready. I run for the midwife. The best one. She brings out from Slavka a boy, Pavol, named after me. He is fine looking, has those beautiful eyes of his mother, and is healthy except for one thing. He holds his left arm close to his chest. I try very gently to pull it away, but he resists. He will reach up to me with his right hand, but his left he keeps to himself, clutched in a fist beside his heart.

"Time, I think, will fix things. Perhaps his coming into the world during winter was too shocking, too cold, although the midwife took care to bundle him quickly and hold him close. I watched, so I know.

"Thus we wait, doing all we can to encourage little Pavol to relax his arm, open his hand. We bathe him, caress him, sing to him. Not even my best poems, whispered in his ear, will help. The doctors (some whose pockets I once picked) all tell us the same thing: do not worry, nothing physically is wrong, after all, he is only an infant. But I am impatient—Slavka too—and we take Pavol to a woman in the country who is said by some to have old wisdom. Some even call her a witch. In truth, she looked like one, her hair all stuck out, no teeth.

"She gazed at Pavol a long time. She started to touch him but pulled her hand back. This made me nervous. I was ready to leave. She said, 'No—wait.' She tossed some sticks on her fire. Then she threw a handful of grain into the flames. 'Give me money,' she said, 'and I will tell you what to do. Give me money now.' I paid her. She counted it, the witch. Then she said to go home and tie a small piece of gold on a string and dangle it over the baby.

"We followed her instructions. We tied one of Slavka's gold earrings on a string and I held it like this. I could see him look at it. He raised his right hand. I moved the earring closer to his left hand. Slowly, very slowly, the little hand came away from his chest. The little fingers began to open. They opened so slowly I thought a week went by—and this is why, Gary: he was already holding something! Something very shiny! Do you know what it was? In his little palm he was holding the midwife's wedding ring!"

Pavol the poet looked into his own left palm, then he looked at me and winked.

I raised my glass. "Very good," I said.

"Do you think so?"

"Absolutely."

"Will it make me rich?"

"Don't you mean richer?"

"Of course!"

He clinked his glass against mine, gave me another wink, and said, "To happiness!" He finished his cider in one gulp. Then, lifting his face toward the sky, eyes closed, he recited the following poem:

Really. You saw a hawk there
swooping without mercy
on yellow hens . . .

That's life
diving
head down
on to childhood.

NADINE GORDIMER

Visiting Oupa

Mrs. Stark returned to her office on Monday morning and was told Oupa was back in hospital. It was early, the story vague. Only the receptionist at his desk: Oupa had sat about "in a funny way" last week, he was bent and couldn't breathe properly. Then he went to the doctor and didn't return. Someone phoned the doctor and was told he'd been sent to hospital. And then? What did the doctor say was the matter?

No further sense to be got out of a young man who didn't pay attention to what he heard, was incapable of reporting anything accurately. No wonder messages received at the Foundation were often garbled; irritation with the Foundation's indulgence of incompetence distracted her attention as she called the doctor's paging number. She reached him at the hospital. Slow internal bleeding, the lung. Well, it was difficult to say why, it seemed there was an undetected injury sustained when the bullet penetrated, perhaps a cracked rib, and some strenuous effort on the part of the patient had caused a fracture to penetrate the lung. It was being drained. The condition was stable.

At lunchtime Mrs. Stark and Lazar Feldman went to visit their colleague. What should they take him? They stopped on the way to buy fruit. At the hospital they were directed to the Intensive Care Unit. Whites habitually misspell African names. Mrs. Stark repeated Oupa's: wasn't there some mistake? The direction was confirmed. As they walked shining corridors in a procession of stretchers pushed by masked attendants, old men bearing wheeled standards from which hung bags containing urine draining from tubes attached under their gowns, messengers skidding past with beribboned baskets of flowers, unease grew. The community of noise and surrounding activity fell away as they reached the last corridor, only the squelch of Lazar's rubber soles accompanied a solemnity that imposes itself on even the most skeptical of unbelievers when approaching a shrine where unknown rites are practised. She shook her head and shrugged to Lazar: what would Oupa, his bullet in a cigarette pack, recovered from what had happened to him and her on the road, be there for as she pictured him, sitting up in bed ready to tell the story to his visitors?

At the double doors there was a bell under a No Entry sign. They rang and nobody came, so Vera walked in with Lazar lifting his feet carefully and placing them quietly behind her. Cells were open to a wide central area with a counter, telephones, a bank of graphs and charts, a row of white gowns pegged on the wall. A young black nurse in toweling slippers went to call the sister in charge.

Was the place empty?

Is there nobody here?

The wait filled with a silence neither could recognize; the presence of unconscious people.

The sister in charge came out of one of the doorways pulling a mask away from nostrils pink as the scrubbed skin pleated on her knuckles. —Ward Three? We're pleased with him today, gave us a smile this morning.— The nurse was signaled to take the packet of fruit from Lazar. —Nothing by mouth.— They robed themselves in the gowns.

On a high bed a man lay naked except for a cloth between the thighs, a body black against the sheets. Tubes connected this body to machines and plastic bags, one amber with urine, another dark with blood. The sister checked the flow of a saline drip as if twitching a displaced flower back into place in a vase. The man had his back to them, they moved slowly round to the other side of the bed to find him.

Oupa. A naked man is always another man, known only to a lover or the team under the shower after a match. Friendship, an office coterie, identifies only by heads and hands. The body is for after hours. Even in the intimacy of the injured, on the road, bodies retain their secrecy. Oupa. His fuzzy lashes on closed eyes, the particular settle of his scooped round nostrils against his cheek, his mouth, the dominant feature in a black face, recognized as such in this race as in no other with an aesthetic emphasis created by highly developed function, since we speak and sing through the mouth as well as kiss and ingest by it—his mouth, bold lips parted, fluttering slightly with uneven breaths.

—He's asleep, we'll come back later.—

The sister stood displaying him.

—No. Unconscious. It's the high fever we're trying to get down. Speak to him, maybe if he knows your voices they'll rouse him. Sometimes it works. Go on. Speak to him.—

With these gentle calls you bring a child back from a nightmare or wake a lover who has overslept.

Oupa, Oupa, it's Lazar.

Oupa, it's Lazar and Vera, here. Oupa, it's Vera.

She took the hand that was resting near his face. It felt to the touch like a rubber glove filled to bursting point with hot air. His eyelids showed the movement of the orbs beneath the skin. They talked at him chivvyingly, what do you think you're doing here, who said you could take leave, man, my desk's a mess, we need you. . . . Oupa, it's Lazar, it's Vera. . . . And his head stirred or they imagined it, under the concentration they held on his face.

—There, he hears you. You see? Now nurse's going to give him a nice cool sponge-down.—

In the reception area Vera waylaid the woman as she strode away. —Why is he in a fever like this—what's the reason for the high temperature?—

—Septicaemia . . . the blood leaked into the body's cavity, you see.— The lowered tone of confidential gossip. —Of course, he should have had himself admitted the moment he had symptoms. Dosed himself with brandy instead. . . . But I'm telling you, at least he hasn't gone down, he's fighting, we're pleased with him.—

The nurse came to Lazar with the packet of fruit. It had become evidence of their foolish ignorance, his and Mrs. Stark's, of the nature of the anteroom in life to which they had been directed, of this retreat for those upon whom violence has been done, where their colleague had entered as one enters an order under vows of silence and submission. By contrast, the uninitiated are clumsy and intrusive and have only the useless to offer. —Oh no, keep it, won't you.—

A giggle of pleasure. —Oh thanks, ay. Lovely grapes!—

There was an official roster of Foundation colleagues taking turns to visit the hospital every working day. At weekends others felt they had a right to disappear into their private lives; Mrs. Stark was older, there were surely no urgencies of family demands, love entanglements, waiting to be taken up, for a woman like her. She joined the trooping crowds of relatives and friends who filled the hospital on Saturday and Sunday. Out-of-works, beggars and staggering meths drinkers officiously directed cars and minibuses searching for parking, sleeping children were slung round the necks of fathers, there were girls adorned and made up to remind male patients of their sexuality, Afrikaner aunts in church-going hats, bored young men gathered outside for a smoke, Indian grandmothers sitting in their wide-swathed bulk like buddhas, popcorn packets and soft drink cartons stuck behind the pots of snake plant and philodendron intended to distract people from bleak asepsis, the smells and sights of suffering, the same plants that stand about in banks to distract queues from their anxiety in the power of money.

The first Saturday and Sunday, and the second. Oupa, the body that was Oupa identified by the mute face, lay as he was placed, on this side or that, sometimes on his back. And that was something to stop the intruder where she stood, entering the cell that was always open. No privacy for that body. On his back, totally exposed. Once she asked if there could be a sheet to cover him and was dismissed with impatience at ignorant interference: he was kept naked because every bodily change, every function had to be monitored all the time, nurses coming in to observe him every fifteen minutes; he was kept naked to fan away the heat of infection raging in there, see the flush in his face, the purplish red mounting under the black. When she was alone—with him but alone—she carefully (he must never know, even if he were to be aware of the need for the small gesture it would humiliate him) drew the piece of cloth between his legs over the genitals that lolled out, ignored by nurses. Sometimes he seemed asleep as well as unconscious. The breathing changed; the men she had slept with breathed like that deep in the night. She wanted to tell him she—at least someone—was there yet it was a violation to touch him when he seemed so doubly, utterly removed. At other times she stood with her hand over his; it was the gesture she knew from other circumstances. She fell back upon it for want of any other because nobody knew what he might need or want, they believed he had no thirst because salt water dripped into his veins, they believed he did not feel vulnerable in his nakedness because fever glowed in him like coal. Whether or not the people he shared One-Twenty-One with came to see him she did not know. And moving away from the black townships he had lost touch with neighbours and friends there, most did not know where he lived, now, in a building among whites. Very likely they would not have been allowed in to see him if they had come; the sister in charge made it clear that visits were to be restricted to his employer since it seemed he had no family.

Of course he has a family—but who knew how to get in touch with the plump young woman sitting among all the women who are left behind in veld houses put together as igloos are constructed from what the environment affords, snow or mud. No one had an address; as an employee and as a patient Oupa had given his permanent residence as

One-Twenty-One Delville Wood. The only way to reach her was to re-trace the journey from the turn-off at the eucalyptus trees—could some-one from the Foundation be spared to drive there? Mrs. Stark knew the way but her husband, supported by her son out from London on a visit, absolutely forbade her to revive the trauma of the attack in this way.

During the week Lazar Feldman and others tiptoed in and stood a few minutes, afraid of closeness to what the familiar young-man-about-the-office had become, the grotesque miracle of his metamorphosis. One of the clerks who had meekly suffered because she was too plain to attract him, wept. They went away and some found excuses not to come again: what did visits help a man, said to be Oupa, who did not know there was anyone present, did not know that he himself was present.

Vera glanced at her watch and set herself the endurance of twenty minutes. But she forgot to look at the dial again. What was a presence? Must consciousness be receptive, cognitive, responsive, for there to be a presence? Didn't the flesh have a consciousness of its own, the body sig-naling its presence through the lungs struggling to breathe with the help of some machine, the kidneys producing urine trickling into a bag, the stool forming in the bowels.

An insect settles on a leaf and slowly moves its wings.

She sat and watched.

The fat nurse and the thin one, the Chinese and the Black (nurses are known by rank and the most obvious features, they seem to have no names) came and went, marking the passing of time as ritually as the tongue of a church bell striking against its palate where traffic is not yet heavy enough to break the sound waves. How ignorant, how far away from this. She had been curious: *what's it like. This* is what it's like; an anatomical demonstration that spares nothing. When, in church be-tween her mother and father, she heard about that moral division, the soul and the body, and grew up unable to believe in the invisible, what the priest really was talking about and didn't know it, was this: what he called soul was absence, the body was presence. It was swollen now, not only the hands: one day when she walked in there was the young man's flat belly blown up, the skin taut and shiny, a version in a fun-fair dis-torting mirror. To look for identity in the face was to be confronted by an oxygen mask. The Chinese gave it a touch to make it what she judged would be more comfortable, if one could feel. The Black one used a little blood-sucking device to draw specimens from a huge toe pierced again and again. The Fat one cleaned the leaking anus. If one could feel? The dumb creature that is the body cannot tell. It is an effigy of life ritually, meticulously attended. Outside, in between times, the acolytes eat grapes, arrange on the counter flowers left behind by dead patients, and whisper forbidden telephone calls to children home from school and boyfriends at work.

Vera no longer imagined the plump young woman down the turn-off from the eucalyptus trees and phrased what she ought to be saying to her. Ivan, back at the house where he was conceived, disappeared from her awareness as if he were still in England. The wheeze and click of machines that now breathed for the body and eliminated its waste chattered over its silence. Remote from her, within that awe, a final contemplation was taking place—isn't that what it is—what it's like?—the years on the Island, night study to be a lawyer in what the politicians promise to be a new day, freedom the dimensions of a flat in a white suburb, a box-cart pulled through the dust by children—who knew what the final contemplation must be? In that silence she saw that the certainty she had had of death, Zeph Rapulana's death among nine at Odensville, when he was, in fact, to appear before her alive, was merely a mis-sort in time, a letter first delivered to the wrong address: the certainty belonged to her where it reached her now, in this place, in this presence.

Among the casualties of violence listed in the newspaper is a clerk in the employ of the Legal Foundation, Oupa Sejake, who has died of complications resulting from an injury received when the Foundation's vehicle was hijacked.

SHIRLEY HAZZARD

Longing

The gale had blown all week from the Pole, raising foam on the sea and grit in the city. On Friday, it faltered. And then the town, which had been obscured by dust and by the visible force with which dust was driven, reassembled into roofs of red iron and walls of buff weatherboard and stocky modern buildings from before the war. By Saturday morning, the wind was felt only in those salt gusts usual at corners and crossroads of Wellington; and it was said again, by way of conversation, that the slow spring of 1949 would turn to summer by Christmas.

Invited for the day by a friend in her French class, Julia Bogle crossed the town on an early tram to take the bus for the bays, which left from a shed near the station. On Saturday mornings, offices and shops were open; and the tram rocked, a rattling shepherd, behind a flock of Morris Minors and bicycles—striking, with ancient bell, its note of the past as it rounded the curve at the Hotel St. George and listed into Willis Street. Here, it passed by the shops, close to their tin awnings on dented poles; close enough to see stained linoleum in the tea room and glazed buns beneath a celluloid dome, and to read the titles of books in South's window.

At one o'clock, such mild clamor would relapse, not into a holiday release of spirits but rather, and gratefully, into extinction. Meantime, it was silver morning in the potholed streets and among those small buildings, inward and unlovely, that could, without effort, neutralize radiance. From intersections, you could see beyond the quays to a blue harbor, and to the far mountains whose incommunicable grandeur might, for all the town cared, have hung there on a calendar. Remoteness had generated timidity and a fear of occasion. The populace clung to its small concerns—as their British forebears had clung to these islands, greeting them as rafts and spars in the wild ocean, rather than as destination. They had left their destination behind them—the home for which they never ceased to hanker—and could only re-create, here, its lesser emblems and stratagems. Audacity had been exhausted in arriving at the uttermost end of earth. They wished above all to pretend that nothing had happened.

Something of this the girl Julia noted, as she set out to visit her friend Barbara Baillie. There was the dated way in which people looked, lorn, from windows, conjuring some gesture from the external world.

Parted from her best thoughts and her great love, she was at a loss, on such a morning, to account for her own light spirits.

Described by Barbara as no great shakes, the bus for the bays proved quite the contrary, as it struck out wildly for the curve of Lower Hutt: passengers felt their organs leap and flutter inside the casing of a body slung on bones. Years since, asphalt had been poured slapdash; had flowed headlong before running off into wayside reeds. The old motor labored in a nearly animal effort to do its bit as it scrambled over rises or pulled up, gasping, to let on, let off: Ar, step aside there, give the bloke a charnce. Aboard, there was a Noah's Ark of caps and cardigans, skirts and shirts, and all the woollen coverings, paired and indistinct, of season and region. There was the mixture of sandy and saturnine, and a stalwart symbolic couple with Maori blood. There was the fat child, content as yet to be smothered in Mum's embrace, while the baby lay awhimper in Granny's arms. A man of thirty-odd had lost a hand—at Anzio, or Monte Cassino—and held his newspaper with a device of metal and black leather. The rustle could be heard whenever, with a glint of steel, he turned a page.

Weathered suburbs straggled, fence rails suggested countryside. The bus for the bays trundled into graveled depressions and swept with petrol breath the encroaching scrub. The passengers, who at first had stared ahead, unbudging, now glanced about, on one pretext or another, hoping to catch someone out in a manifestation of life. Like pupils in a class, they wished for unseemly diversion if others would provide it. Hills were bristled by gorse with which the nostalgic founders of the nation had reinvented Scotland: introduced for sentiment, it had come to dominate. It was ineradicable; and when it flowered, late in the year, no one would say Gorgeous—the subversion being resented as if the plant itself had shown duplicity. In this way, however, it supplied a topic irreproachable as weather or the latest seismic tremor, and there was always someone to speak up for the common grievance.

Next to Julia, there sat a grim little passenger—a woman, not old, but overworked as to face, shoulders, and hands, and burdened with bundles. This figure made a wry and wiry contrast with the fresh girl beside her: a cautionary picture of youth and age. They were both of small, slight build, although the woman's slimness had been put through the wringer. The woman's hair, fringed out under the dusty brim of a small felt hat, kept some glint of its first fairness; her unblinking eyes were gray. What had been stripped away—not youth alone, but all bloom, charm, hope, and receptivity—was only what time and circumstances might take from anybody. It was the comparison that made impression. And now she said, not loudly but addressing, as it were, the laboring bus rather than any person present: "Ye can no' be rid o' it. Break it, burn it, back it comes the stronger. They could ha' known it." A downward settling of lips made clear that blame was a habitual means of registering.

The public words stood in air, like skywriting. And it seemed that no one would exorcise them with reply. Until, across the aisle, a man with plentiful white hair half-turned his stout body in the metal seat and said, "It was the longing." Gingered tweed was buttoned to creaking-point. "They were longing for their home."

This was personal. And there was worse to come—for he was tilting his head back, as people do when preparing to quote:

"Heard on Lavernia Scargill's whispering trees,
And pined by Arno for my lovelier Tees."

All highflown utterance was to be deplored, but poetry was alarming as nakedness. As to the speaker, it was unclear whether he had distinguished or disgraced himself—nor did he appear to care, smiling with rather fleshy lips and with eyes of a clear blue unsuited to his age. Something carnal was not incompatible with spirituality. The local women would have said he was rather, well, you know what I mean. He knew this to be so, and might even have enjoyed it.

Before long, he got off at a crossroad. From her bleared window, Julia watched him walk away on a dirt track, smiling abstractedly and slightly swinging a string bag of small packages wrapped in newsprint. Even so, there was the antipodean touch of desolation: the path indistinguishable from ten thousand others, the wayside leaves flanneled with dust, the net bag; the walking into oblivion.

The girl felt that, banished to the Arno, she would not have repined.

At a tin shelter that served as terminus, Barbara was waiting.

When she stepped into sunlight, tall, smiling, and dressed in blue, people could not help admiring. Julia thought, She should be meeting a lover; and so should I.

The two young women touched hands. They walked off, on the Baillies' earthy path, speaking and laughing not quite naturally, for they could not help being pleased by the attention of dispersing passengers and by their own nearly meritorious youth. Here too, the scrub soon closed in, but they were near to a rise of sweet-smelling beech and firs, and, on their right, to sun and sea. Along the track there were marks of tiny animals, of paws and claws; and small sounds flickered out from clumps of fern.

"A man on the bus quoted poetry."

"No, really? Out loud?"

"Well, audibly. Obviously." Julia added, "Only a line or two"—meaning, This man was not a maniac.

"What was it?"

"Macaulay."

"They must have had a fit."

"They went rigid." Julia recalled the man's pink, sensual face, the white, excessive hair and brows, the incommensurate bright eyes. Elsewhere, indeed, he might have been a danger to young girls. But here the bush had swallowed him.

And now there was no one to see how pleasant these women looked in their soft clothes; and how, passing there, they enhanced, for their instant, the immemorial scene. They felt it themselves: the waste.

The Baillie house was backed by trees, and faced a short, pale beach. At the far end of the cove, there was one other house, smaller but similar; and that too was wooden, two-storeyed, and painted "cream." Both had been built by the Baillie grandfather, architect also of a family house in the town, and whiskered subject of an incompetent portrait in a civic hall in Tinakori Road. The profession lingered in Barbara's father, who was a building contractor—an easygoing, ruddy-faced chap who drank a bit, made good money, and was proud of his three slim, articulate daughters. Bruce Baillie would have been, elsewhere, a plain good sort; but the great south wound was on him, as it was on all men of the place. And his eyes, when he laughed, remained dark and glassy, like those of a teddy bear.

Barbara's mother, born in Timaru, was distantly if emphatically connected to a signatory of the Treaty of Waitangi. Pale and heavy-lidded, with grooved almond mouth, she sloped into sad shoulders and attenuated limbs, and wore floral frocks that appeared faded even when new. Any youthful glow had long since been consumed in the obsessive gentility that, without ever blazing, shrivels all. Though not close, husband and wife were never quite distinct: the shared error of their marriage had become a bond.

Too cautious to detest, Mrs. Baillie did, however, and with some regularity, not quite like. Mrs. Baillie did not quite like Barbara's friendship with the Bogle girl. Julia Bogle had been overseas, though not in quite the right places; and was said to be enamored of an older man, some person of consequence, met in India or Ceylon. On all counts, this sounded like presumption. To be in love was itself not quite desirable, was not at all the same as announcing the engagement and having one's photograph—pensive and misted in tulle—in the *Dominion*. In Featherston Street, behind the Government Life Insurance Building, there was a nice shop displaying fruit plates in Crown Worcester, and a tea service with roses, and table mats, backed with cork, reproducing English county scenes by Rowland Hilder. Standing one day with Julia before this shrine, Mrs. Baillie had said, "I do feel that Barbara should begin to gather a few such things together." And the girl's silence had displeased her. Sharpening her argument, the mother had later remarked that French was all very well in its way, but that it would do nothing for Barbara in the life to come. This observation referred neither to love nor religion, but to domesticity.

By now, the two girls had crossed the wooden verandah at the bay and were entering a grotto of limp cretonne, flowered papers, rugs of gray peonies, and rose-painted tin trays. Fronds of real Dorothy Perkins, intruding through open windows, partook of indoor dust. Reproductions of "The Blue Boy" and "The Laughing Cavalier" called for alignment. For entertainment, an old wireless teetered on cabriole legs, and folders of sallow songs were stacked on an upright piano. Books, in their single mesh-fronted case, came from the lachrymose or costumed past: *Anthony Adverse, Lorna Doone, The Prisoner of Zenda, The Viper of Milan*. Wild outdoor smells of shrubbery and shore were no match for odors of humid linen in warped cupboards, pipe tobacco, mutton and potatoes, camphor, mildewed bread, and a slight leak of gas. The arrival of Barbara's parents at nightfall would scarcely inspirit these rooms, which had already had the worst of it from family associations. Only the presence of the three pretty sisters, all of them together, might have let in light.

In the kitchen, Barbara put milk in an enamel saucepan and

spooned coffee from a canister. They took turns to watch and stir. Drops fell on linoleum. A window above the sink overlooked a fenced clearing between house and woods where spring planting was set out in rich, turned earth, and bulbs were coming through. This yard ended in tangled shrubbery and in the twin peaks of a compost heap and kitchen midden.

When the milk puckered, Barbara took a sieve, poured the mixture into mugs, and tipped out the grounds in the sink. Julia had the better mug—uncracked and marked CORONATION DAY, August 9th, 1902, showing the royal pair in red and yellow: Alexandra in pearl collar and satin bodice, Edward incorrigible in ermine.

"Like a bikkie?"

Listlessness was an effect of the house.

There they stood, sipping, munching: intelligent, charming, and immensely remote from all sources of charm and stimulus. As far as the world was concerned, they might stand thus forever, here or in similar kitchens. Of that danger, both were mortally aware.

In the living room, light entered through diamond panes. Here they would read their French lesson. Each took a book in hand and began to turn pages. But Barbara Baillie, extending her legs on a sofa and imagining herself some third party, wondered whether she or Julia might be considered the more attractive. Decency did not permit an immediate decision in her own favor. While appreciating her delicate length of body, she tried to calculate a more difficult measure of beauty. Julia's case was curious: so small as to be insignificant, yet so sweetly made, and with strokes of salient interest—the eyes and hands, the short nose and pink, uncolored lips; and being, as to wrists and ankles, what the French call *aux fines attaches*. The eyes, in particular, were quite strangely delineated, like those of a Husky or a Holbein. Some broad, clumsy man might take her smallness under protection—for men were, and wished to be, deluded by mere evidence.

It could not be said of Julia that her condition, of being in love, had conferred the reputed luminosity. Rather, such inexpressible desire, such passionate absorption inspired pity, and some fearfulness. It was in forgetting her predicament and calling up her powers that Julia appeared enchanting, vivid, and destined truly for other lands and lovely times.

They began to read aloud what Barbara called "the famous passage," because their teacher thus referred to it: "the celebrated passage of the thrush." They opened their books laughing but soon were decently engrossed.

"Hier au soir, je me promenais seul; le ciel ressemblait
à un ciel d'automne; un vent froid soufflait par intervalles."

Julia's voice was low and without contrivance. The past and its sublime expression were hers by right of affinity. Declaiming those phrases in so far a place, the two girls became not provincials but exiles.

"Transporté subitement dans le passé—"

They continued to read, by turns for that magic—which, on Barbara Baillie, worked less consistently, the mood and convictions being to her mind odder and less congenial. Aware of the discrepancy, she weighed its implications, as she had earlier compared her own good looks and Julia's. Nor could she help—even while raising her voice to words now stately, now crystalline—some thoughts about a pink twin-set, in lamb's wool, seen in a window on Lambton Quay, and a possible trip to the Bay of Islands if summer ever settled in. Digressions that could not seem culpable since, in their agglomerations, they must ultimately pass for a semblance of purpose, and show of acquiescence, in most young women of the town. And if not that, then what? Some spinsterly good works, or inexorable effort of ideas: boredom, or the precipice.

Of serious transgression, such a girl had no conception. For her and her companions, love was above all a release of tenderness, of which they had far more than almost any man could stand. At all events, in New Zealand, there was nowhere to throw over the traces.

Julia herself was not immune to the allure of a Pringle twin-set, but had little money for clothes, and even for the books that she did, or could not, buy. On Friday evenings, she and Barbara sometimes went together to bookshops, which were few but fairly serious. Apart from South's, there was the place in Cuba Street, the large bookseller on Lambton Quay, and, near the wooden rick of the parliament buildings, a slot of a shop where, from slim volumes ranked on white shelves, Faber poets rushed forward like hussars. While Julia, eyes swimming with desire, touched and even sniffed at broadcloth bindings and sewn pages, Barbara would buy a novel in orange paper or a book of blue British history—and, once, a collection of writings on rural England by "Alpha of the Plough."

For three years now, Barbara's father had annually promised to set his work aside and take the family to England: three months on the sea for the round-trip, and three months to make sense of the blinking place. He did not expect to enjoy himself, but knew what was due to his position and, more obscurely, to existence itself; they'd have achieved that much, at any rate. However, again and again, disinclination prevailed. And when, in the third year, he renewed excuses, Barbara had asked—not, in that moment, a daughter, but speaking levelly as one person to another—"Won't we go then, ever?" He had shifted, shuffled, then mumbled, "Course we'll go. Yair." Had stood looking at nearby air and from time to time taking a palmful of dried fruit—raisins and scraps of apricot—from a bowl on the sideboard. The girl was sorry for him, knew he would be concerned for expense and ill at ease abroad; even that he dreaded the entire enterprise. But she said, "I'd like to have the chance," without acknowledging or even comprehending all that this implied. Still examining vacancy, the father had replied, "Yair. Ar well. Next year she'll be right," and could not stave off a pang as he focused on his girl at last and met her eager, pleading eyes. He thought, The trip, that's one thing. But in the end she'll have to knuckle under. His wife herself, however she queened it, had knuckled under along with the rest, raising the kiddies and pitching into the drudgery, the ironing and baking and mending, the lot. He feared for her too, on the great round-trip, among glacial persons with whom Waitangi and Timaru, and the whole bloody Canterbury Bight, might cut no ice. He said to himself, Poor cow, withering a bit by now, and never any capacity for a laugh but still, as you could see, with some fancies tucked away, mulled over in silence with moist eyes. He himself, after a few drinks, sometimes felt a lack, you couldn't put it stronger than that.

With the women, though, moping was a big thing. Disappointment could take the place of experience.

At the world's far end, two girls lolled among dank cushions; swung a foot, twirled a lock of hair. On a low table, the mugs were derelict with stains and leavings. Putting Chateaubriand aside, Barbara said, "No man here would stand for it"—meaning, such ponderings, such poetry.

"They could not bear the power." They would not bear it, that thinking and feeling should make a man strong; that there should be contemplation without helplessness—without that same helplessness in which their women wallowed: as if, by being alive at all, one had become a victim. Then Julia thought, in him—in him—it is that same power that enthralls me.

They read next from an anthology of wartime verse on wartime paper, lines from unhappy France that passed like spasms over the indifferent room. When, in its turn, this too was put away, Barbara swung down her legs, saying that it was time to walk on the beach. The morning had passed, as mornings did pass there, with a bit of this and that, and with wishing oneself away. Later, there would be sandwiches and ginger beer.

Outside, the gale was returning in grainy gusts that hurt the throat and eyes and set hair flying at one moment forward and then streaming behind. Speech also was swept away—so that they spoke, if at all, in expendable words about the strong sea and the rough passage of the Picton ferry, each thinking of what had been said and read, and recalling the words of rhymed but passionate love. When they came to a sheltered place near trees, Barbara asked, "Have you ever met a man who might talk that way—*'toi seule existes,'* all that?"

Julia answered at once, "No," as if it were not a bold question to put to a girl in love.

"Here, they wouldn't have the energy."

"They wouldn't have the words."

"D'you think, though, that such men exist elsewhere? Or is it only in books?"

Julia stood under the trees, both hands to her blown hair. "Oh, I would like to find out." Defying not only those hope chests, coffins of defunct aspirations, but also the huge accident of geography, and even the Pacific Ocean—which might have promised marvelous departures but instead was rolling landward in cruel evocation of distance. The sea had risen so high on the horizon that those watching might imagine themselves diminutive, or even prostrate on the shore. In an intolerable instant of her life, Julia summoned the beloved image, wondering in what fine street, on the other, centuried side of earth, the passersby glanced at his face and form: he who was more present to her than this harbor, and more to her than all the beautiful splayed islands of the great south land.

He who had never said, to her or anyone, "You alone exist."

They had stopped in their tracks near the farther house, at the end of the cove.

"That house belongs to us, but it's rented. I don't want them to think, you know, that we're hanging round." Barbara said, "My grandfather built it for his children, so that he'd have the family within coo-ee. Then the oldest son was killed in the Dardanelles, and Grandpa died. And so on."

"It looks closed up."

The house needed painting. There was a break in the balustrade of the verandah, and the front plot of garden was unweeded. You could practically feel the splinters in the steps.

"Still, someone might be there." Barbara turned back, scrunching in canvas shoes over the glittering rubbish—of weeds, shells, tiny cara-paces, and chips of colored glass—marooned there. As they walked away, she said, "We let it for the summer to those Fairfax boys."

Two English brothers were at Wellington to await the return of their father from the Antarctic. Explorer-father had set out months pre-viously from Invercargill, leading an expedition, and would reappear at summer's end. The older son was of an age to have served in the war; the younger was possibly twenty. They would linger here, like figures in some legend, until the ice melted and released their father: that was their nearly primal condition. The elder, Jonas or Joshua, was writing a dissertation—of which no one had thought to ask the theme, being suffi-ciently impressed by the mere concept. It was not known how the younger—Geoffrey or Jeremy—passed his time. Rarely seen singly, they made a fine pair on the uneven pavements of the capital: not tall, but well formed and well turned out, light-eyed and fair. Barbara's mother had declared, Two princelings. The ladies of the town openly doted; their menfolk, though resentful, were cowed by the degree of self-possession—and by that very composure they mocked in surly asides. Above all, by the reality of the ice-bound father, whose polar tradition had been sanctified, at Lyttelton in 1910, by the fateful departure of Captain Robert Falcon Scott.

Julia would have liked to know what books the explorer had taken with him to the ice floes, and by what light they were read. She would have been interested to smell the reek of whale oil, and to learn whether, in winter, the sun rose at all. Her thoughts were ready to sail in all direc-tions, seeking escape.

She had seen the two brothers one evening at the Majestic, in Wil-lis Street, where dances were held in a big, blank room, cheaply red and annexed to the cinema. And had considered the question as to whether, in their own land, they would have appeared as princelings or merely as a couple of tow-headed and overly impassive youths. She had noticed them, that evening, seated in a small party of British people from the High Commissioner's office, and, with these matters in mind and her elbow on the viscous crimson tablecloth, had watched them refuse dry sandwiches and swallow thin coffee in heavy cups and rise civilly to dance in turn with the women of their party. Julia's own coffee was meanwhile cooling. And when her partner—Terence, from the Department of External Affairs—had asked her to dance the hokey-pokey, he placed the white saucer over the cup to keep it warm.

On the dance floor, she then lost sight of the Fairfaxes in the crowd that waggled and chanted:

"You put your left foot in,
  You put your left foot out,
  You put your left foot in,
  And you shake it all about—"

She might have been interested to see if they too, under the tyranny of obligingness, had waggled and chanted with the rest.

Terence had said, What fun.

Now, on the sandy shore, Barbara was ranting a bit.

"It's so obvious. They made a vow, coming here, not to saddle themselves with local girls. Not to run the risk of life sentences to colonial connections." She picked up a pebble, as if to throw, and instead examined its markings. "What I mind is, their imagining we don't see it. What I mind is, they think we're as stupid as they are." She laughed then, rolling the stone in her hand. "Oh well. If one of them did ask me out, I'd probably go. Wouldn't you?"

"I might. But from curiosity, from boredom." After the evening with Terence, anything. "And because they're personable."

"How funny you are. You talk as if you yourself would be invisible." Barbara went on, "Anyway, when they came to see the house, my mother had them to tea. Of course, it was only polite, but looked so pointed. Janet wouldn't show herself. Flora and I sat and smiled. Afterwards, the sides of our faces ached from smiling. And Mummy actually wore a hat, the big white hat she got at Kirks. In her own house. As if it were Windsor Castle."

The hat from Kirkaldie and Staines—flat and circular—was suited to Mrs. Baillie's inanition: as if a saucer had been placed on a tepid cup to impede further cooling.

"They haven't asked us back. They've been lent a flat in town, and are mostly there."

"Whose flat?"

"I don't know. I daresay, someone with daughters. It's in Buckle Street, near the museum." Barbara disclosed the stone in her palm, then dropped it. "Out of exclusivity, they've become mysterious and desirable. Rather as women are supposed to be."

Julia thought of the women of the town, of all the world, clamoring to be wed; mysterious only in their subsequent regrets. "But is mystery becoming to men? For them, the ideal—so we're told—is forthrightness." Whereas women are formed for concealment. That is the germ of our supposed mystery, the hoarded revelation.

Even so, if Barbara were to wed a Fairfax, it would be she who supplied spontaneity and candor. Thinking this, Julia drew nearer to her friend and, in imagination, embraced her.

Indoors, returning to the sink, they spread mustard and hacked at corned beef. Barbara had brought from town the remains of cabinet pudding and a dod of meringue, and they ate these in the living room, on a seat by leaded windows. Otherwise, in such a room, afternoon might seem like night. If they did not go back to their books, it was from indolence, or because some effect of the morning's reading, and of words exchanged, had not yet run its course.

Barbara carried the dishes to the kitchen, where she picked, also, at seeds of passion fruit lodged between her teeth. She splashed water over the plates in the slate sink, and into the Coronation mug: ENTHRONED IN THE HEARTS OF THEIR PEOPLE. She looked from the window at the tumbled yard, which had been this way ever since she could remember. Often, she had a physical desire for movement. She would have liked to rush, to run—not as mere escape and not aimlessly, but like the girl in a poem they had read that morning, who ran to meet her lover in the street, under the rain. Sluicing cold water round and round in the mug, she said aloud, *"Épanouie ravie ruisselante."* The same pent-up life was in her, but without release.

She could not remember whether, for his part, the lover ran also.

Julia, too, would run to such a meeting. But—for now and perhaps forever—to the lover who stood waiting.

When it was time to take the bus, Barbara closed the house against the wind, which had begun to swirl curtains and slap at blinds. Along the sand, the sea fell heavily; and rose again, thundering, and fell. Gusts disturbed the trees and bedeviled the furze. At the end of the beach, the small house of the princelings was preparing to yield more of its matchstick decoration. Sandy, solitary, it did for the moment suggest the last retreat of some monarch no longer enthroned in the hearts of his people. One might envisage the historic photograph. Unlikely places of the kind lie in wait for the deposed.

Barbara was recalling unhappily how her father's brother, staying there with all his family on a visit from Auckland, had broken the verandah rail during a balancing act. The girl liked her Uncle Alec, who was funny and kind, and did not want to see him disconcerted. There had been other damage, including a broken toaster, and the holiday had ended badly. When they were all gone, her mother had said, "That's Auckland for you."

The bus was waiting, and taking on passengers. Julia found a seat to the rear. When the motor started, she and Barbara mouthed farewells and raised their hands in an orthodox show of good cheer. It is difficult to convey sincerity through unclean glass. When Julia looked round from the bend of the road, Barbara was still there, not watching the bus but lowering her head and holding down her skirt against the gale.

Julia was retrieving the solitude that never left her. She was able to think of how, among the day's sensations, they had read about a past so full of desires and dreams that the whole world might seem charged with human wishing.

There was sand in her hair and shoes. Aboard the bus, all were unkempt from the wind that was also, as one could see, playing merry hell with the landscape. She recognized, among the passengers, the elder of the Fairfax brothers, alone and reading. The back of his head, and of his neck in particular, did not appear invulnerable; and he might have been misjudged. Like the rest of them, he would sometimes raise his eyes to the window, to be reminded of his surroundings, and perhaps of his existence. By the roadside, where lone figures were walking bravely against the wind, and within the bus itself, there was that same balked impetus of human hopes. The isolation of this land had bred endless yearning: it was the nation's sole enormity.

The girl remembered the drive out, in the bright morning; and how the white-haired man had spoken up on behalf of longing, and had gone away smiling for himself alone.

WILLIAM HOFFMAN

Trophy

She was a precious thing, Beth Anne, but she got no eyes for me. I could be a fence post or rock at the roadside. I'd wait for her to pass Arbuckle's Store, and I'd smile and tip my cap. She'd smile too, but she wasn't seeing me. I coulda been an empty bean can in the ditch.

The Boomer twins, their mother Pearl claimed, fought in her belly. They punched, kicked, and brawled before they ever saw the light of day. They grew up fighting despite their father taking straps to them till he wore the leather out. "I'd just as soon put whippings on wildcats," he said.

They fought so bad during grade school, Superintendent Hooper bussed Henry to Shawnee Central and John to Diamond Consolidated. Even preaching needed to be split, Pearl sending John to Healing Springs Baptist and Henry to Beautiful Zion Methodist. At Vacation Bible School, the twins got into an argument over a chicken leg, rassled against a tent pole, and brought canvas sagging down over the table set for graduation, causing Miss Hattie Bottom to holler she was suffocating and the strawberry ice cream to spill on the ground to be eat by hound dogs.

During high school, John was captain of the Shawnee team, Henry of Diamond. When they played, even bigtime West Virginia newspapers like the *Charleston Gazette* and the *Huntington Advertiser* sent reporters down to Bear Paw, neutral territory, to write up the game. It was like war. Grunting, cussing, screaming, slugging, whistles blowing, bottles tossed, bandages all over the field. Two years in a row they tied. The third year, Shawnee won by three points. John, whooping and tightrope-walking a rail, fell off the iron bridge across Poor Man's Creek. Henry got so drunk glooming, he toppled into a deep well and was bit by snakes.

There was never no chance they could live in the same house. While their daddy served time up at Moundsville for running liquor, Pearl separated them, making John find himself a patch of ground in the north end of the county at Big Fork and Henry settle south near

Deer Gap. She drew a line across an Amoco road map and ordered each to keep to his side.

The Boomer boys went into coal hauling and stripping. They was good workers, strong, never looking at a watch when a job had to be done or a dollar could be picked up. Step between a dollar and a Boomer and you'd think you'd been run over by an eighteen-wheeler hauling a load of bricks.

When Pearl kicked off from pee-numonia, the boys kept to the map awhile, respecting her death wish. She was smoking cigarettes in the bed the very evening she died. She made them promise, took a last deep drag from a Lucky, and closed her eyes. Smoke curled from her mouth with her last breath like the spirit rising to the Heavenly Gates.

Henry and John made good money. If they happened to be in the same place at the same time, they spoke but mostly steered clear of drinking together. When they met on the road, they couldn't help racing them fancy trucks a little. They ran Clyde Sharp into the ditch as he was returning from Slab Fork. Both got a reckless ticket from Trooper Giglio but was good-natured about it and paid to fix Clyde up good as new and gave him a Mason jar of first-run popskull to boot.

The peace held despite the hell-raising in they blood. Both had them trucks they kept gleaming, big snarling Detroit diesel engines, chrome exhausts blowing smoke, and triple-barrel air horns that would shake the dead in the grave. The boys didn't attend preaching, yet was popular with all the gals, particularly those that hung around Dewey's Dip down by the Tug River, a honky-tonk whose tarpaper sides puffed out like a blowtoad when the jukebox pumped music. Dewey's Dip was a house of sin.

The Boomers attended the football games, each sitting on opposite sides, and here come Beth Anne strutting and twirling down the field. She was a Gold Hawkette and wore tasseled white boots, a butter yeller jacket and skirt, and a tall white hat that had a gilt plastic hawk on it. Golden Hawks was Bear Paw's team name. Every Saturday night during intermission, she and the other Hawkettes tossed their silver batons up to spin in the lights and hipped side to side so those little skirts rode their thighs. All was pretty, but Beth Anne stood out like a pear in a peck of potatoes.

"Them Boomer boys got eyes for Beth Anne," Amos Arbuckle said, his store just east of the old C&O tracks that ran down the valley from Diamond to Bear Paw, now long abandoned, thistles and dandelions growing between rotted ties. His granddaddy Isaiah built the store in days when the coal market was red hot and clanking hopper cars passing through town didn't cause hound dogs even to raise their heads, though they'd still take a lazy swipe at fleas and flies.

"And Beth Anne got eyes for them," Flower Arbuckle said, she Amos' wife, eighty years old, her back still straight as a hoe handle. She never moved far from the cash register. The store was a two-story frame building Amos kept painted. At one time you could get your hair cut, shower, and rent a room upstairs. Now all that had closed down, and Amos had long ago quit carrying carbide, blasting powder, squibs, and chest augers. He sold general merchandise, sodas, and hunting licenses. He did still take scrip in payment. Mostly you waited on yourself, and he moved only to relieve you of your money and spit out the door.

"She a pretty thing," I said. I thought of them tasseled boots. My name was Otis Angley, and I had me a county paper route. I got it after Bartholomew Gilley gave it up after some lowdown rascal—I'm not mentioning names—slipped lump sugar in Bartholomew's gas tank during the black of night and ruint his engine. Every morning before sunup I met the bus at Diamond to count my papers and load them in my Dodge pickup. Some deliveries I had to four-wheel it up sides of hills goats wouldn't climb.

"You a nice man with a powerful preaching voice," Gardenia Eubank said when I laid the paper at her door. She was bent and white-haired. She kept cats and had a shack with a leaky tin roof. "I thank you for troubling to bring the paper."

"Though it costs more to run up here than I can clear, I like to treat everybody the way I'd want them to treat me," I said. She had nobody much to talk to except me and didn't know I charged her an extra ten cents held out from the company each time I drove to her door.

"The Lord bless you and keep you," she said and baked me biscuits that crumbled hot on the tongue.

I figured if the Lord didn't, nobody would. I wasn't a big man. I'd been hatched slight and with a twisted left leg. The only thing given me was my goodness with which I won people over. I sometimes preached at the Burning Bush Tabernacle. "Jesus, Jesus, come down and take the sting of sin out of your poor people!" I pleaded with God. I told sinners if they was fair with God, God would be fair to them.

I lived alone on a piece of scrubland hardly big enough to turn sideways on. The Lord in His wisdom and mysterious ways saw it fit to make me an orphan by drowning my parents when the dam gave way at Indian Lick, washing them downstream into the Big Sandy. My older sister Ida Jewel clung to a sycamore with one hand and to me with the other. She raised me till I was fourteen and she got in trouble about the peculiar weed. It wasn't her fault. She didn't know who'd planted it on the slope behind our cabin. She drove away in an old Mercury with a bad muffler and a rattling tailpipe. I never heard from her to this day.

A preacher named Stillwater kept me up through high school. He lived in Diamond. I tended furnaces at his house and the church. His wife taught me to play the piano for Sunday school. She was speaking at Christian Endeavor the night he snuck to my upstairs room, unbuttoned his pants to finger out his swollen sacred protruder, and laid a new dollar bill across it.

"Play your cards right, that dollar's yours," he said and grinned like a possum with a mouthful of yams.

"I'm going to the law about you," I said.

"That was your happy hemp, not Ida Jewel's," he said, retreating. "You was selling to kids at school."

"I'll tell the sheriff what you do to the little children," I said.

"Little sonofabitch," he said but backed off and never again invited me to dine at the sinners' table.

"I will try to forgive you," I said and got that new dollar bill anyhow.

I believed in forgiving everybody. I'd let a dog bite 'fore I'd kick him. I forgave Bartholomew Gilley. He suspicioned I'd dropped that lump sugar in his gas tank. When he spit on me in front of Arbuckle's store, I turned the other cheek.

I had me a brother named Grover. Before my mother died, she wrote us all down on a list in a shoebox. Me, Grover, and a cousin named Lyle owned us a old Mustang. Each put up money for a third. Then Grover wanted to go to Charleston and work for Union Carbide and Lyle was thinking of drywalling in Florida. I was against gambling, but we flipped for the car, odd man take it.

"You didn't show till after we did," Grover accused me. He'd inherited all size in the family. Almost as large as a Boomer.

"I showed soon as I could," I said. "I'm not as fast as you boys."

"You coulda seen us first," Lyle said. He wasn't much bigger than me but carried a buck knife he kept sharp.

"It ain't right of you to pick on and take advantage of a cripple," I said, and that's when Grover hit and Lyle kicked me. I hollered so loud lying there on the street that Deputy Hanks came arunning. He stuck Grover and Lyle in the Diamond jail for the night. I drove the Mustang away. I forgave Lyle and Grover what they did to me. I traded that Mustang for the Dodge pickup.

I finished my paper route in time to see Beth Anne each afternoon when she left Bear Paw High. I loved watching her quick, prissy step as she carried books hugged against her little titties. She smiled at everybody and whistled the Golden Hawks Fight Song:

Knock 'em up, Knock 'em down,
Knock 'em, knock 'em all around!

I knew county folks figured me too old to be seeing her, but I hosed mud off the Dodge, buttoned on my black preaching suit, and went acalling. It was a warming May Saturday afternoon, fresh after a rain, the creeks running full.

She lived with her daddy in a doublewide on the steep hillside above Bear Paw. Her daddy had worked at the Red Man Mines till the coal-cutter blade busted a sprocket and lopped off his right arm. He sat most of the time on the porch he'd built one-handed at the front of the doublewide, rocking and slapping at flies. He had his pension from the UMWA.

His wife Louisa Price gave up the ghost in church while singing "Beautiful, Beautiful Promise," just lowered her hymnbook, sat, and died as if meaning to rest a spell. Turned out to be a long rest. Beth Anne had to take care of her daddy.

"I know who you are," he said to me. He'd gained weight from sitting, his belly hanging over his belt with its Confederate buckle. He needed shaving. He'd kicked off his shoes and wore white socks Beth Anne kept washed for him. His mouth tightened to gum snuff. He held the swatter handy to whack at flies favoring that ugly stump of his. "I don't read papers. Hear lies enough over the radio."

"I come to see Beth Anne," I said. I'd washed my hair and slapped on a handful of Lilac Vegetal from a bottle bought at Arbuckle's. The bottle was dusty, probably been setting on the shelf ten years, but Amos still made me pay full price. Beth Anne's mother had once planted petunias in painted gallon cans set along the edge of the porch. Now the cans was empty.

"Question is, does she care to see a puny thing like you," Beth Anne's father said. He was a mean man, union, a drinker, and had served time for braining a scab with a chunk of coal during the walkout at Red Man. How Beth Anne could be so precious with him as a father was just another of life's multiple mysteries.

"I know I'm not a handsome sight to behold," I said. "But liquor has never touched my lips, and I have always striven to be a man of love and peace."

"Piece of what?" he asked and spit at the blue tomcat slinking along the porch. The cat hissed, jumped a foot in the air, glared, and licked a hind leg.

"It don't behoove you to make fun of a man who has come to your door in well-meaning good faith," I said.

"Step aside before I puke," he said.

Beth Anne pushed out the screen door, she all fresh in a pink dress with a white collar. Her straight yellow hair lay across her back. She wore stockings and black slippers. Charm bracelets jingled on both wrists. She was a tiny gal, maybe five one, her skin fair as fresh-shucked corn, eyes pale blue, like wild gentians up Blind Sheep Ridge. She had a dimple in her little chin. I thought of them white boots.

"Guess we could take a walk," she said. Her father hocked up an oyster and spit at the blue tomcat. It humped, hissed, and jumped off the porch. He was a mean man, but I forgave him.

We walked down the wooden steps from the doublewide to the holler. There'd once been railroad tracks to the Black Jack Mine, but they was crowbarred up and hauled away. Broken equipment rusted among ditch weeds. We stopped at Poor Man Creek. Beth Anne skimmed flat pebbles across the water. She held her tongue in the corner of her mouth each time she wound up and pitched. Her dress spun around her clean, fuzzy white legs. I thought of them tasseled boots she wore at the games. I thought of some other parts of her that weren't showing too. But them white boots was the light of my life.

"I was hoping maybe you'd drive over to Diamond with me and worship at the Revival Jubilee," I said. The Jubilee came through Shawnee County every spring and held a weeklong camp meeting. I handed out programs, took up collections, and prayed over the PA system. "We could have us a time on Sing Song Night. They serving pork barbecue and punch."

"Otis, I'd like to worst thing, but though I like you fine, you nice, I have to tell I got eyes for somebody else. It wouldn't be fair to lead you to believe different."

"It's them Boomers, ain't it?" I asked.

"I don't care to name names," she said, yet blushed and skipped another stone across the muddy water.

"I got to tell you them boys is trouble," I said.

"I appreciate you worrying about me," she said. "I don't know why people talk bad about you the way they do."

A pity for her is what it was. Those Boomers were two of the carousenist citizens of our county, big redheaded boys, each heavy of bone, strong, both hogging the road with those big Peterbilt trucks whose gleaming chrome they kept shined. Never saved a nickel the first day of their lives. When the boys came roaring through Bear Paw, every house and building shook, and you had to clap your hands over your ears to keep from getting headaches.

I had to admit they worked daylight to dark, but were rowdies too and of a Saturday night busted a man-sized hole through Dewey's Dip down by the river by punching Democrats against the wall during a political discussion. Judge McClintic over at the Diamond courthouse gave them ten days in jail and damages. You could see where Dewey patched the batten siding with painted-over Budweiser signs.

I hated to think of Beth Anne's getting mixed up with the Boomers. They drank and hell-raised even on Sundays. Me, I was a regular at the Burning Bush. When I got red hot and going good up at the altar, I sank sinners to their knees begging for God's mercy and grace. Spring Revival I brought eighteen to the Lord and laid my hand upon their heads. "Jehovah will forgive your willful wicked ways," I shouted. "Just give yourself over to Him!"

I wasn't certain the Lord would forgive the Boomer boys. Women might find them handsome. They wore western hats, leather vests, and buckle-strap engineer boots. They had big, flashing teeth. When they crossed a floor, their weight came through the boards. They blew them air horns as if playing a tune up and down hollers and yelled from their truck windows at everbody they passed. They could dance too, a Devil's device that'd never snared me even if my leg affliction hadn't denied me the choice.

The Boomers sometimes cooked liquor like their father before them. He'd kept a pet bear in a fenced-in lot behind his house and would bet anyone twenty-five dollars they couldn't rassle his bear to a fall. He made lots of money off that animal till the boys came along. They for the funning roughnecked it to a frazzle. Got so the bear wouldn't get off the ground even when people walked right up and poked him with a stick.

The old man had been a Republican. When Franklin D. Roosevelt drove through Shawnee County on the way to the Rhododendron Festival, people lined Creek Street, but that old man turned his back and crossed his arms. He had, he bragged, never sat at a table and broke bread with a Democrat.

Halloween it was when I had my trouble with the Boomer boys. I'd been to preaching, and they waited hid down at the head of the holler wearing sheets, hooting like spooks, and jumping out from pawpaws at people. I knowed it was the Boomers even with them sheets on. They'd been drinking and already put the bull in the schoolhouse. They demanded everybody passing by to declare they politics. "We got us a mule lover," they said when they grabbed me and shucked me out of my breeches. They used a roofing brush to slap red deck enamel on my sacred parts.

"Now you a real jackass!" they hollered and run me off trying to hold my pants up, my sacred parts burning from turpentine. I squatted in Dead Man Creek to cool the fire.

That's when Beth Anne seen. She rode by in the bus with the Gold Hawkettes. Headlights glared all over me before I could hide. I caught sight of faces as I jerked at my breeches. I heard cheers, a bugle, laughter, and a drumbeat. She had to be on that bus, seen, and remembered how I was that night. No way she could not.

The Boomers got lawed. They painted up half a dozen Democrats. Judge McClintic sentenced them to thirty days in jail and damages for what the bull did in the schoolhouse and clothes ruined by the deck paint. I don't guess he could do anything about my sacred parts. I forgave them.

"You've caused enough mischief around Bear Paw," the judge said. He had slicked white hair and a face like chipped flint. "I'm tired of writing warrants on you. If I have any more trouble with Boomers, they going to be spending a long vacation at the state hotel up Moundsville way."

How could Beth Anne care for fellows like that? I'd seen her at the Shawnee County Fair and the pig catching. Set loose among contestants was a shoat greased with crankcase oil. He ran squealing among legs, jumped the fence around the ring, and upset an apple butter exhibit. Those Boomer boys chased after him and rolled with him in the dirt. Laughing, calling to the girls, they brought him back to claim the fifty-dollar prize, both of them scratched and miry, yet clowning. Beth Anne looked at them as if she'd seen Jesus instead of just watching two carousers carry spread-eagled a wiggling, shrieking shoat.

After she won the Miss Shawnee County contest, Henry was first to take Beth Anne out. At least I believed he was. Telling Boomers apart was hard except you got close enough to see a little sickle-shaped scar on Henry's forehead where he'd been hit with a chunk of stove wood when him and John were boys and fighting over who discovered a stand of chinkapins.

Beth Anne's father was strict and allowed her to go out only on Saturdays, when she had to be in by ten. No drinking or stopping by Dewey's Dip. "I got me but one arm," he said, "yet it's fingered at the end and knows how to shoot a pistol. I own a .38 police special. Catch my meaning?"

When John too started courting her, there had to be bad and jealous feelings between the twins. Beth Anne was happy to let them take turns squiring. Henry drove her to the clogging over at High Rock. Then John took her to the Fiddler's Fandango in Diamond. I hid behind the sycamore tree at the bottom of the holler and saw them come driving out with her in they trucks, she sitting high and pleased in the big cabs they'd polished up for her, those air horns tooting like highballing locomotives each time they turned onto the highway. I am a patient man but got so I hated the sounds of them horns.

Lots of talk along the valley about her being seen with the Boomers. I thought of visiting her daddy and telling him he was making a mistake letting her go out with those boys. They had sin in their blood, I would've said. They bound to come to a no-good end. But her daddy wasn't partial to me. Wouldn't even take the paper when I offered him a copy free. "Make a timber rattler choke on a bite of you," he said.

Henry was setting new points on his Ford parked in front of his daddy's old trailer, he ducking down inside the engine well, at times just his legs and boots sticking out. He had on a CAT cap, a greasy T-shirt, and Levi's. Sweat shined him.

"You lost?" he asked. There was car and truck parts all over the yard. From a steel beam stuck between crotches of two shelly bark hickory trees hung a chain hoist and an engine carcass.

"Just passing, brother, and thought to say howdy," I said. "God blesses the working man."

"God ain't never yet changed points on a V-8," Henry said.

"I'd like you to know I forgive you for what you done to me with the paint," I said. "I am a forgiving man. Any way I can help you here."

"Not 'less you got a timer in your pocket," Henry said and dipped again into the engine well.

"Shame Henry don't help none," I said. "Guess he got Beth Anne on his mind. Him probably on hers too."

Now I knew I was talking to Henry. I saw the scar just at the edge of his hairline. He come up out of that truck like a fish bobber from river water. He squinted. He believed I'd mistaken which twin he was.

"You saying you think Beth Anne likes Henry better than me?" he asked, wiping his hands on the tail end of his pants.

"How she eyes Henry she got a tingle for him sure," I said. "Waved to him from Arbuckle's, and he stopped his rig to buy her an Big Orange."

"Stopping and buying a gal a soda don't mean nothing," he said, yet scowled and spit.

"She had a loving look on her face," I said. "Like he was Hershey bar candy. Well, nice to see you, John."

Later the same June afternoon I drove out to see John. He was waiting his turn to pull his truck up under the grinding, dust-swirling tipple where they was stripping near Panther Branch. Reared back, he'd dropped ashes on his brown coveralls from the cigar he was smoking. His buckle-strapped boots was hiked up to the dash of that black, shiny Peterbilt.

"I been hoping I could get you to sing at the Burning Bush," I told him. "We need us some big voices. Like yours, Henry."

"You thinking of me singing at the tabernacle?" he asked, staring down from the cab and believing I didn't know the difference between him and Henry. He laughed so loud men turned from the tipple. "Hellfire, tree toads make more music than me."

"Guess I'll have to ask John then," I said. "Course he's got Beth Anne on his mind. I believe she's sweet on him too. The way she was clogging down at High Rock. Looked at him like cherry pie and peach ice cream. If you won't sing, wish you'd attend revival. Sinners saved nightly."

"Wish you'd step in a deep hole," he said and bit down on that cigar so hard he had to spit the butt end out the window.

I didn't believe in telling stories on people but had to think of Beth Anne. The worst thing in the world was for a precious thing like her to get mixed up with rowdies. So it wasn't lies I was telling but words spoke to save her.

I had plenty of places to tell it as I delivered papers around the county. I'd take my time and tarry with people along the route. I'd let it be known one place that Henry was courting Beth Anne secretly and they'd been seen past dark down by the river willows. It was for her own good. Just like at another delivery I said John had parked his rig with her up on top Blind Sheep Ridge after she slipped out the house while her daddy was snoring off his pension check visit to the man in the moon.

I passed word that Henry said John might better be watching where he walked nights. And that John said Henry had best keep his eye on rock slides along the road down the mountain. They was dry tinder anyhow. All you needed was to strike a match.

I passed time with Auntie Perdue. Auntie worked in the Bear Paw post office. She was the Bear Paw post office, located in a cinder-block building at the north end of Creek Street, next to the barbershop. In her sixties, she sat evenings swinging and knitting on her porch. Because of sore feet from standing all day at the post office, she wore tennis shoes. She loved gossip better than greens and gizzards.

"Heard tell those boys been making brags about Beth Anne," I said. "Down at Dewey's Dip. Got bets on which of them's going to show a trophy."

"Trophy?" Auntie asked, and her knitting needles stopped clicking. She wore a brown wig but had gray eyebrows.

"Don't know it for a fact, but I heard tell they got a wager who can bring in evidence they has violated yet another of God's commandments. Guess you can figure out which."

"Why I have never in all my life heard the likes!" she said, and those knitting needles clicked like a telegraph. She'd spread the story around town from the post office just as surely as if it was on the radio. The story would multiply like mice.

No way it'd track to me, either. All you had to do was drop a word or two like bean seeds in a furrow, and gossipers would raise the crop. Just terrible what people will believe. It was their sinful nature. Gossip was the Devil's brew.

Beth Anne's daddy's ears got wind of details I'd never provided. He forbade her to see the Boomers. When Henry, envious of John, first, and then John, envious of Henry, appeared at the doublewide, he answered the door pistol in belt. He tossed painted petunia cans off the porch and quick-drawed to shoot holes through them in the air. The Boomers drove off fast.

Next I got the item. Over in Bluestone. I strolled along the mountain-shaded streets among frame row houses. Women still had wash hung. When I spotted what I needed, I waited till full dark before I slipped in a back gate and picked it off the line. Why buy when you can borrow is my motto.

Back in Bear Paw I sneaked to the school yard and pulled down the flag-pole rope. I attached the item to a clip and sent it skimming up the pole. In the morning there was the brassiere flapping in the warm southern breeze. By the time Edgar Dooley, the principal, snatched it down and hustled it inside, enough people had seen to catch the story on fire and send it blazing like wild grass on a north slope in a high wind.

It made no difference Beth Anne hadn't been out the house, that her daddy had been watching her like a prize heifer. People will do with stories what they want. Those in the south end of the county was telling one thing to Henry about John, and those in the north telling John other things about Henry.

That July Friday evening after work, both boys happened to park their rigs by Dewey's Dip, first Henry entering and sitting at the counter to order himself a cold one. He knew people was eyeing him. Knew there was talk. Might have seen that flapping brassiere.

Then John swaggered in, only he didn't sit at the counter but walked to a wooden booth at the far end of Dewey's. He ordered himself two beers, a bottle for each hand. He drank and stared at Henry. A long time he stared.

"Hear you been speaking my name," he said finally.

"Do polecats have names?" Henry asked. Skinny Dewey Skaggs, who owned the place, swallowed and looked scared.

"I reckon you ought to know that, being one," John said.

Henry was just reaching for his second bottle of Bud. Instead of waiting for Dewey to prize the cap off, Henry used his teeth, spit the cap on the floor, walked to John, and poured the beer over his head.

"You look like you can use a cooling on a hot day," he said.

John sat without moving while Henry walked back to the counter stool. John then licked at beer running down his face, wiped the back of a hand across his mouth, and crossed to the counter carrying a Bud. He poured it over Henry.

"Might help kill the skunk stink," John said.

Henry turned slow, beer curling around his ears, dripping off his nose, and snaking down his neck into the collar of his blue sweaty work shirt. The drops was tinted red from the buzzing neon BEER sign in the window.

"John, you done the wrong thing there," Henry said.

"Henry, you is the wrong thing," John said.

They swung at the same time. They was both left-handed and each knocked the other stumbling back. "Get the sheriff!" Dewey hollered. But the sheriff and Oliver Bottom, Bear Paw's deputy, was on the road carrying a felon from Diamond to Welch. When John and Henry got balanced, they went at it toe to toe for real.

People outside Dewey's Dip said they saw and heard the building rumbling and quaking as if elephants was stampeding inside. John and Henry pounded one another back and forth across the room. They knocked over the booths and chairs. They got serious ugly and snatched up bottles to throw. They lifted benches and tossed them. Customers hid under tables and behind the counter. They ran outside. John bulled Henry the length of the café and knocked him through that patched hole in the wall. Dewey was peeking up from behind the counter and wailing.

Henry butted John down the weedy bank to the river, where they sunk under and fought hip dip in the flowing water. They climbed out slipping, spitting, and growling. They again started swinging. They climbed the bank hitting and fought down the road along the tracks. They rolled, kicked, and bit. They was smeared with blood and cinders. They called time and heaved for breath awhile sitting on a rusty rail. Dark dust settled around them.

"It'd be smart of you to quit," Henry said and spit out a lower incisor.

"Smart ain't nothing you'd know much about," John said and put a hand to his ear which had been about half chewed off.

They sighed at the same time, stood, and hit their way down Creek Street. They was a crowd by then. People and hound dogs followed the fight. The hound dogs barked, people cheered sides and made bets, though nobody could no longer be sure who was who. The Boomers was too smudged and bloody. At Arbuckle's Store, they dropped their arms and staggered inside, where each of them sucked up a Big Orange. Flower lifted an axe handle. "Not in here, boys," she said. They wobbled out and fought till they sat down in the dirt in front of the store.

"You look like you been dropped out a meat grinder," Henry said, honking for breath.

"You best be careful buzzards don't take you for a run-over cat in the road," John said, his voice sounding like it was coming wheezy from somewhere way off.

They worked to they feet and fought their way past the barbershop to the post office. Auntie Perdue locked the door. At the old Hub Furniture Store, which was empty, they toppled through the dirty plate-glass window. Starlings that had been roosting in rafters flew away squawking. John and Henry tumbled out and rolled under Wesley Hawthorne's Chevy dump truck. They banged up against the side of the Fire House. They broke a wood post of the overhang at Pluto's Gas & Garage.

At dark they was still fighting. Us and the hound dogs followed along Creek Street. People carried flashlights. When Sheriff Whitlow came rolling into Bear Paw with his siren screaming and his blue lights flashing, John and Henry lay in front of Jeannette's Ritz Beauty Saloon. They was crawling on their bellies, slinging dust, and snapping at each other like alligators. The sheriff and Deputy Bottom lifted and loaded them in the cruiser to haul to Diamond.

Judge McClintic had endured all the stomaching of Boomers he could tolerate. Soon as John and Henry got let loose from the Emergency Room at the Miners' Hospital, he stood them before his high black bench.

"We have got us a war across the water," the judge said. "The military needs fighting men. You demolished enough property up and down Bear Paw to be put away for a year and a day. But I hate to see fighting go to waste. If you were to sell your trucks, pay out damages, and talk to the recruiter, the law would be disposed to show mercy. Otherwise you become honored guests of the state at our finest high-security accommodation."

The army was glad to have them. Viet Kong was calling. John and Henry sold they trucks, paid they debts, and rode off on the morning bus to Fort Benning. That was late July. John came back in February during a winter rain. Henry arrived in early May when gentians bloomed on mountain slopes and ramps was tasty. The boys was laid side by side flanking Pearl in the End of the Trail cemetery. An honor guard shot rifles over the caskets, scaring ravens on the ridge. Oh, it was sad. Everybody weeping and blowing noses. Judge McClintic wiped his eyes. I cried myself.

Most all the people in Bear Paw and half of Shawnee County attended the funeral. Not Beth Anne and her daddy. She had been shamed, and her daddy wouldn't let her leave the house. I waited till he took sick with a bad batch of radiator run and lay twitching in the bed. I patted on a good handful of Lilac Vegetal and carried Beth Anne a box of chocolate-covered cherries from Arbuckle's. We sat on her porch among those empty painted petunia cans. She looked pale, thin, and sad staring down over the hill into the holler. She looked like she'd been weeping every night for a year. The dimple was gone from her chin. I wondered if she still had them white boots.

"I come to comfort you," I told her as I reached and took her little hand in mine, which was the truth if I ever spoke it.

EDMUND KEELEY

Macedonia: Days of 1944

I begin this journal, dear Lotte, on the first day of spring, a bleak day for us in northern Greece but maybe no better for you at home. In our dormitory and mess hall we hear daily of new bombings of cities in Germany—Berlin, Leipzig, Frankfurt am Main—in return for our bombing of England. We also hear that the Russians have reached the borders of Romania and that our enemies in Italy have established a dangerous beachhead not far from Rome. It will not be long before this wretched war is over. One sign of how serious our situation has become is this morning's announcement that we can no longer expect regular mail deliveries in either direction. And along with that comes a ridiculous warning that even so we must be especially careful from now on about what we write our loved ones and others at home. In any case, it seems foolish to think that the letters I would want to write you would get past the censor even if they proved lucky enough to travel safely north as far as Austria. At the same time, I can't bear to speak through a veil, to hide the truth in what I write so as to make sure that it passes through the hands of those in control of the disaster ahead of us. That is why I have chosen this way, writing you when I can in this notebook, with no assurance that you will ever see what I have written but with some hope that I will survive to hand this to you when the right time comes.

The truth, dear Lotte, is that we have lost our soul. I don't know how to explain this so you understand that I'm no longer speaking simply as an Austrian soldier, or even as a citizen of the new Germany that swallowed our country, but as an ordinary man of flesh and blood. I turned twenty-three last month, which is young enough, but you are so much younger, even if only six years separate us, that I sense the need to protect you. Or maybe it is that I've become so old in this war that I see myself now more as a father to you than the friend who has felt as close to you as I could have been to any brother or sister by blood and more concerned for your well-being than my own. I suppose I've felt that way almost from the day your family moved in next to mine so many years ago.

When I say we've lost our soul I don't mean we've simply lost our direction in this war and with it everything that we were led to believe was our purpose. I mean we've gone over to the side of the devil. And when I say that, I'm not talking in the language of religion, which in any case has never been my language, though, as you know, for a while I studied our great philosophers in preparation for the university and was once moved by them. I speak about something quite down to earth: in our arrogance we have thought ourselves better than all others on this planet, and believing that, we have made enemies of all others, including our own allies and those of our own people who belong to another race.

I can be specific now that I am sure nobody will read what I say here until I pass this on to you in person someday. The allies I refer to are the Italians and what we did to them after their surrender last September. Nothing of this is official. For obvious reasons, there are no records in the files of what we did. But the stories came to us in the mess hall from eyewitnesses. It was of course the noncommissioned officers who talked. And this is what we learned. The Italians were supposed to turn over their arms to our people and prepare themselves to be transported back to Italy. Some of those who were slow to turn over their arms were simply shot where they stood. The rest were then told to give up everything they owned to be stacked in piles, including the uniforms they were wearing, which meant that they were made to stand naked through the night and the next day until it became simpler to give them back a uniform, anybody's uniform, rather than attempt to find another kind of clothing for them to wear. They looked ridiculous after that, we were told, comic figures, ill-fitted and now bowed down with humiliation, no longer soldiers worthy of the name. And then they were sent to the cattle cars, fifty or sixty to a car, for transportation not to Italy as they had been told but first to Vienna and then to camps for forced labor, I suppose in Germany, Poland, God knows where. And to keep them healthy during this journey into the unfamiliar northern autumn, pieces of bread made up mostly of wood shavings were thrown into the cars for those strong and hungry enough to fight over them.

I am truly sorry, dear Lotte, that this season brings me thoughts of this kind for what should be thoughts to please you. I would much rather tell you about the beauty of this place and the change in the fields that we have begun to see out of our dormitory window, the tall grass speckled now with red poppies and the daisies spread over the hillside behind us where sheep once grazed. It's almost enough to make one think that peace has returned to this land that we have desecrated for three years now. But peace has not returned. And it will not return until the devil in us has been defeated and the price has been paid for our arrogance. What, my dear Lotte, will the cost be for you and me, who were too young and ignorant to know what was waiting for us when it all began and who would not have wanted any of this had we known?

But I am avoiding what has moved me most to take up this way of speaking to you. It is a thing that happened to me some days ago, a thing that I hesitate to write down even in this secret way. But telling you my most personal thoughts, giving you an honest account of my days here may be the only way I have of keeping sane while an unspoken insanity surrounds me everywhere. In any case, I will write what I feel I have to and decide later when the time has come to show you what I've written—if that time is ever given me.

The point is, I met a woman, a woman who has moved me as no other has during my years away from home in this war. She is a Greek woman, somewhat younger than me but not much, one of those from the village of Arsaklí who work at our headquarters. This is how I met her. Oberleutnant Hertzel, the pinch-faced supervisor of my daytime life, had accused me of going beyond my duties as medical orderly and playing the doctor whenever I get the chance. He has now forbidden me from offering anything other than emergency first aid without first consulting him, whether or not I can find him. Also, since he caught me trying to read books in English from the library of the former American school that is serving as our home, he has been watching me more closely than usual, I suppose for some sign of further misconduct that he considers treasonable. In any case, on the day in question, he came to my dispensary for an unannounced inspection. "Really, Corporal Schonfeld," he said as he opened one of my wall cabinets, "is it necessary to pile so many packages of gauze on top of each other? What if they were to topple over and spill on the floor? Wouldn't that be dangerously unhygienic, given the condition of your floor?"

So I stayed late that afternoon to scrub the floor yet again, and while I was reorganizing the delinquent wall cabinet, a group of the village women came chattering down the corridor to deliver one of their group, clearly the youngest, who had somehow cut the middle fingers of her left hand almost to the bone. Of course I had no way of finding out exactly how this had happened since I wasn't able to understand what the women were saying, even if I could have quieted them down enough to get them to talk one at a time. The injured woman was the only one who was really calm, and this despite her pain.

She was not entirely a stranger to me. I had seen her once before that I remember, when I was called to a dormitory on the far side of our enclosure to deal with a villager whose donkeycart had been brushed off the road by one of our armored cars. I had put splints on one ankle and a forearm, and this woman, this girl, was among those who had come to see what was going on. I remember her because of what was in her eyes when I looked up and saw her watching me work on the injured man— an intensity, a directness that was unafraid, and behind that a darkness that I can't describe. And I recognized her now because she watched me work on her hand with the same intensity, as though it was a thing to study for what I was doing to it rather than a thing she could feel. This was the first thing that impressed me about her. I threw off the dirty dish towel that somebody had used to bind her hand, and in place of that I wound gauze tightly around her fingers to stop the flow of blood. Not a murmur came out of her. While she sat there quietly, entirely in control of herself, I managed somehow to make the other woman see that she would be all right and that it would be best if they were to wait for her in the corridor so that she was not disturbed by their sighing and exclaiming and so that I had some peace to work in.

The second thing that impressed me about this girl was the way she looked at me the minute we were alone—open, unashamed, as though I was neither a stranger to her nor an enemy, as though she had enough pride and courage to face me, a German soldier, the way she might any other man, any other man who touched the woman in her. It was not exactly a lover's look, but there was something of that in it. At the same time, it made me feel that some of the pride in it was meant to show me how unworthy I was to meet her look with the same openness. In any case, I didn't. I gave all my attention to the injured hand as I removed the gauze, holding her fingers tightly so that the cuts stayed closed when the bleeding started again. She had her eyes shut now. I asked her in German—how else could I ask her?—whether I was hurting her too much. She didn't answer me. Instead, she opened her eyes and touched my face with her fingertips, and her look now had a sweet sadness in it that I found more unbearable than the bit of pride I'd seen there earlier.

I finished treating the hand when the bleeding stopped, cleaning the wounds gently with hydrogen peroxide and binding the fingers again and then the whole hand with new gauze. She was very brave. And to show her that I understood that, I brought the bandaged hand to my lips quickly when I was finished and stood up to see her out. She didn't move from her chair. She sat there looking at me as she had at first. I smiled and gestured toward the door with my hand, and that made her stand up. Then I realized that I couldn't just send her off like that without telling her to come back the next evening so that I could check on her wound to make sure there was no infection and change the bandage, especially now that I had taken charge of her injury in a way that Oberleutnant Hertzel would no doubt consider a defiance of his rule against my playing doctor, ordinary though the woman's injury was. But how was I to tell her what I wanted? I had no way of talking to her, though I tried my best in German, rather stupidly. And then I found the way. I took a piece of paper from my desk and drew a picture of a clock, setting the hands at seven.

I have to say, dear Lotte, that there is something else about this woman that is striking: she is unusually bright compared to most of the village women who work for us. As soon as I had drawn the clock, she not only understood the drawing, but in a manner of speaking corrected it. That is to say, she took my pencil and drew a horizontal line under my clock and then a circle above her line with an arrow beside it pointing up and another pointing down. It took me longer to understand her drawing than it had taken her to understand mine, but I finally recognized her circle as a sun and her arrows as a way of showing me that I had not told her whether I meant seven in the morning or seven in the evening. I circled the arrow pointing down. As she hurried out, it came to me that we had discovered a way to talk to each other, but why that thought both pleased and frightened me didn't bear further thinking, at least not at that moment.

When she returned exactly at seven the next evening, there was only another cleaning woman in the building as far as I knew, on the floor above, but I made a point of keeping the door to the dispensary open. Suppose I was making more of what had happened between the two of us than what was truly there. What did I know of the customs in her country, the significance—or lack of it—that went into talking with the eyes?

I decided I had to be very careful. But when she came into the dispensary that evening and sat down, I had more time than I needed to see how beautiful she was. Not as beautiful as you will be at her age, maybe as you are already—it's been so long since I've seen you, dear Lotte—but with eyes that reminded me of yours. In any case, I was no longer sure as she sat there that I could be careful enough.

I wish there weren't more to tell you, but I'm afraid that is not so. I worked on her hand with full concentration and as skillfully as I could, removing the old gauze with its dried blood and bathing her wounded fingers until they were absolutely clean so that I could touch them quickly with iodine and bind them up again. Her bravery astounded me, not a sound, though she held her breath when I applied the iodine. I studied her, then let go of her wounded hand, then took up her free hand—I don't know why, I can't explain it—and put it to my face, and when she didn't take it back, I moved it so her fingers brushed against my lips. When I let the hand go, I knew that I had now crossed over to the enemy, and it was clear from her look that I was welcome there.

The following evening we met, despite the danger for both of us. We met in a place that has been my secret retreat since the school library was closed to me, a place where I can read as I please—and now write—beyond the watchful eye of Oberleutnant Hertzel. It is a shed that is used for storing wood in the winter, on the lower edge of our barbed-wire enclosure, with a sliding door on one side but no windows, and one reaches it by way of an old broken road that no longer leads anywhere. When the door of the shed is shut, it smells of thyme and aging wood, and it's a place of the sweetest darkness that no catastrophe can reach. I now live in that darkness when the sun begins to get low, and when it sets, I live in the recollection of where I've been until the sun comes up again.

In that shed without windows, where the only light that touches us comes from the cracks between the wallboards, the language we have is the language of our eyes and hands and the rhythm of what we make each other feel. Nothing enters our privacy from beyond that partial light, and the only words we can use to speak the pleasure we know is to say each other's name. How long, dear Lotte, can this purity of feeling last? And what is it in me that makes me ask you, my spiritual sister, the innocent one, a thing you cannot possibly tell me? Will you understand when I say that my enemy has now become what I am, and that I feel I would die for that enemy if I had to, just as I would die for you, my dearest friend?

*   *   *

This spring it will be the turn of the occupiers, our turn, to wait for transport to another country, the closest to the north. The difference, of course, is that unlike the Italian soldiers, we will decide when we leave, and we will know where we are going, at least on this earth. The only uncertainty is how long we will have to wait to pay for what we have done.

STEPHEN KING

Blind Willie

6:15 A.M.

He wakes to music, always to music; the shrill *beep-beep-beep* of the clock-radio's alarm is too much for his mind to cope with during those first blurry moments of the day. It sounds like a dump truck backing up. The radio is bad enough at this time of year, though; the easy-listening station he keeps the clock-radio tuned to is wall-to-wall Christmas carols, and this morning he wakes up to one of the two or three on his Most Hated List, something full of breathy voices and phony wonder. The Hare Krishna Chorale or the Andy Williams Singers or some such. Do you hear what I hear, the breathy voices sing as he sits up in bed, blinking groggily, hair sticking out in every direction. Do you see what I see, they sing as he swings his legs out, grimaces his way across the cold floor to the radio, and bangs the button that turns it off. When he turns around, Sharon has assumed her customary defensive posture—pillow folded over her head, nothing showing but the creamy curve of one shoulder, a lacy nightgown strap, and a fluff of blonde hair.

He goes into the bathroom, closes the door, slips off the pajama bottoms he sleeps in, drops them into the hamper, clicks on his electric razor. As he runs it over his face he thinks, Why not run through the rest of the sensory catalogue while you're at it, boys? Do you smell what I smell, do you taste what I taste, do you feel what I feel. I mean, hey, go for it.

"Humbug," he says as he turns on the shower. "All humbug."

Twenty minutes later, while he's dressing (the dark grey suit from Paul Stuart this morning, plus his favorite Sulka tie), Sharon wakes up a little. Not enough for him to fully understand what she's telling him, though.

"Come again?" he asks. "I got eggnog, but the rest was just ugga-wugga."

"I asked if you'd pick up two quarts of eggnog on your way home," she says. "We've got the Allens and the Dubrays coming over tonight, remember?"

"Christmas," he says, checking his hair carefully in the mirror. He no longer looks like the glaring, bewildered man who sits up in bed to the sound of music five mornings a week—sometimes six. Now he looks like all the other people who will ride into New York with him on the 7:40, and that is just what he wants.

"What about Christmas?" she asks with a sleepy smile. "Humbug, right?"

"Right," he agrees. "All humbug."

"If you remember, get some cinnamon too—"

"Okay."

"—but if you forget the eggnog, I'll *slaughter* you, Bill."

"I'll remember."

"I know. You're very dependable. Look nice too."

"Thanks."

She flops back down, then props herself up on one elbow as he makes a final minute adjustment to the tie, which is a dark blue. He has never worn a red tie in his life, and hopes he can go to his grave untouched by that particular virus. "I got the tinsel you wanted," she says.

"Mmmm?"

"The *tinsel*," she says. "It's on the kitchen table."

"Oh." Now he remembers. "Thanks."

"Sure." She's back down and already starting to drift off again. He doesn't envy the fact that she can stay in bed until nine—hell, until eleven, if she wants—but he envies that ability of hers to wake up, talk, then drift off again. She says something else, but now she's back to ugga-wugga. He knows what it is just the same, though: have a good day, hon.

"Thanks," he says, kissing her cheek. "I will."

"Look very nice," she mumbles again, although her eyes are closed. "Love you, Bill."

"Love you, too," he says and goes out.

His briefcase—Mark Cross, not quite top of the line but almost—is standing in the front hall, by the coat tree where his topcoat (from Barney's, on Madison) hangs. He grabs the case on his way by and takes it into the kitchen. The coffee is all made—God bless solid state electronics and microchips—and he pours himself a cup. He opens the briefcase, which is entirely empty, and picks up the ball of tinsel on the kitchen table. He holds it up for a moment, watching the way it sparkles under the light of the kitchen fluorescents, then puts it in his briefcase.

"Do you hear what I hear," he says to no one at all and snaps the briefcase shut.

*   *   *

8:15 A.M.

Outside the dirty window to his left, he can see the city drawing closer. The grime on the glass makes it look like some filthy, gargantuan ruin—Atlantis, maybe, just heaved back to the surface. It's a grey day with a load of snow caught in its throat, but that doesn't worry him much; it is just eight days until Christmas, and business will be good.

The car reeks of morning coffee, morning deodorant, morning aftershave, morning perfume, and morning stomachs. There is a tie in almost every seat—even the women wear them these days, it seems. The faces have that puffy eight o'clock look, the eyes both introspective and defenseless, the conversations halfhearted. This is the hour at which even people who don't drink look hung over. Most people just stick to their newspapers. He himself has the *Times* crossword open in front of him, and although he's filled in a few squares, it's mostly a defensive measure. He doesn't like to talk to people on the train, doesn't like loose conversation of any sort, and the last thing in the world he wants is a commuter buddy. When he starts seeing the same faces in any given car, when people start to nod to him or say "How you doin today?" as they go to their seats, he changes cars. It's not that hard to remain unknown, just another commuter, one who is conspicuous only in his adamant refusal to wear a red tie. Not that hard at all.

"All ready for Christmas?" the man in the aisle seat asks him.

He looks up, almost frowning, then decides it's not a substantive remark, but only the sort of empty time-passer some people seem to feel compelled to make. The man beside him is fat and will undoubtedly stink by noon no matter how much Speed Stik he used this morning . . . but he's hardly even looking at his seatmate, so that's all right.

"Yes, well, you know," he says, looking down at the briefcase between his shoes—the briefcase that contains a ball of tinsel and nothing else. "I'm getting in the spirit, little by little."

8:40 A.M.

He comes out of Penn Station with a thousand other topcoated commuters and commuterettes, mid-level executives for the most part, sleek gerbils who will be running full tilt on their exercise wheels by noon. He stands still for a moment, breathing deep of the cold grey air. Madison Square Garden has been tricked out with greenery and Christmas lights, and a little distance away a Santa Claus who looks Puerto Rican is ringing a bell. He's got a pot for contributions with an easel set up beside it. HELP THE HOMELESS THIS CHRISTMAS, the sign on the easel says, and the man in the blue tie thinks, How about a little truth in advertising, Santa? How about a sign that says, HELP ME SUPPORT MY CRACK HABIT THIS CHRISTMAS? Nevertheless, he drops a couple of dollar bills into the pot as he walks past. He has a good feeling about today. He's glad Sharon remembered the tinsel—he would have forgotten, himself; he always forgets stuff like that, the grace notes.

He walks five short blocks and then comes to his building. Standing outside the door is a young black man—a youth, actually, surely no more than seventeen—wearing black jeans and a dirty red sweater with a hood. He jives from foot to foot, blowing puffs of steam out of his mouth, smiling frequently, showing a gold tooth. In one hand he holds a partly crushed Styrofoam coffee cup. There's some change in it, which he rattles constantly.

"Spare a little?" he asks the passersby as they stream toward the revolving doors. "Spare a little, sir? Spare a little, ma'am? Just tryin to get a lil spot of breffus. Thank you, gobless you, merry Christmas. Spare a little, sir? Quarter, maybe? Thank you. Spare a little, ma'am?"

As he passes, Bill drops a nickel and two dimes into the young black man's cup.

"Thank you, sir, gobless, merry Christmas."

"You, too," he says.

The woman next to him frowns. "You shouldn't encourage them," she says.

He gives her a shrug and a small, shamefaced smile. "It's hard for me to say no to anyone at Christmas," he tells her.

He enters the lobby with a stream of others, stares briefly after the opinionated bitch as she heads for the newsstand, then goes to the elevators with their old-fashioned floor dials and their art deco numbers. Here several people nod to him, and he exchanges a few words with a couple of them as they wait—it's not like the train, after all, where you can change cars. Plus, the building is an old one, only fifteen stories high, and the elevators are cranky.

"How's the wife, Bill?" a scrawny, constantly grinning man from the fifth floor asks.

"Andi? She's fine."

"Kids?"

"Both good." He has no kids, of course—he wants kids about as much as he wants a hiatal hernia—and his wife's name isn't Andi, but those are things the scrawny, constantly grinning man will never know.

"Bet they can't wait for the big day," the scrawny man says, his grin widening and becoming something unspeakable. Now he looks like an editorial cartoonist's conception of Famine, all big eyes and huge teeth and shiny skin.

"That's right," he says, "but I think Sarah's getting kind of suspicious about the guy in the red suit." Hurry up, elevator, he thinks, Jesus, hurry up and save me from these stupidities.

"Yeah, yeah, it happens," the scrawny man says. His grin fades for a moment, as if they are discussing cancer instead of Santa. "How old's she now?"

"Eight."

"Boy, the time sure flies when you're having fun, doesn't it? Seems like she was just born a year or two ago."

"You can say that again," he says, fervently hoping the scrawny man *won't* say it again. At that moment one of the four elevators finally gasps open its doors and they herd themselves inside.

Bill and the scrawny man walk a little way down the fifth floor together, and then the scrawny man stops in front of a set of old-fashioned double doors with the words CONSOLIDATED INSURANCE written on one frosted-glass panel and ADJUSTORS OF AMERICA on the other. From behind these doors comes the muted clickety-click of computer keyboards and the slightly louder sound of ringing phones.

"Have a good day, Bill."

"You too."

The scrawny man lets himself into his office, and for a moment Bill sees a big wreath hung on the far side of the room. Also, the windows have been decorated with the kind of snow that comes in a spray can. He shudders and thinks, God save us, every one.

9:05 A.M.

His office—one of two he keeps in this building—is at the far end of the hall. The two offices up from it are dark and vacant, a situation that has held for the last six months and one he likes just fine. Printed on the frosted glass of his own office door are the words WESTERN STATES LAND ANALYSTS. There are three locks on the door: the one that was on it when he moved into the building nine years ago, plus two he has put on himself. He lets himself in, closes the door, turns the bolt, then engages the police lock.

A desk stands in the center of the room, and it is cluttered with papers, but none of them mean anything; they are simply window dressing for the cleaning service. Every so often he throws them all out and redistributes a fresh batch. In the center of the desk is a telephone on which he makes occasional random calls so that the phone company won't register the line as totally inactive. Last year he purchased a fax, and it looks very businesslike over in its corner by the door to the office's little second room, but it has never been used.

"Do you hear what I hear, do you smell what I smell, do you taste what I taste," he murmurs, and crosses to the door leading to the second room. Inside are shelves stacked high with more meaningless paper, two large file cabinets (there is a Walkman on top of one, his excuse on the few occasions when someone knocks on the locked door and gets no answer), a chair, and a stepladder.

Bill takes the stepladder back to the main room and unfolds it to the left of the desk. He puts his briefcase on top of it. Then he mounts the first three steps of the ladder, reaches up (the bottom half of his coat bells out around his legs as he does), and carefully moves aside one of the suspended ceiling panels.

Above is a dark area which cannot quite be called a utility space, although a few pipes and wires do run through it. There's no dust up here, at least not in this immediate area, and no rodent droppings, either—he uses D-Con Mouseprufe once a month. He wants to keep his clothes nice as he goes back and forth, of course, but that's not really the important part. The important part is to respect your work and your field. This he learned in the Marines, and he sometimes thinks it is the most important thing he did learn there. He stayed alive, of course, but he thinks now that was probably more luck than learning. Still, a person who respect his work and his field—the place where the work is done, the tools with which it is done—has a leg up in life. No doubt about that.

Above this narrow space (a ghostly, gentle wind hoots endlessly through it, bringing a smell of dust and the groan of the elevators) is the bottom of the sixth floor, and here is a square trap door about thirty inches on a side. Bill installed it himself; he's handy with tools, which is one of the things Sharon most appreciates about him.

He flips the trap door up, letting in muted light from above, then grabs his briefcase by the handle. As he sticks his head into the space between the floors, water rushes gustily down the fat bathroom conduit twenty or thirty feet north of his present position. An hour from now, when the people in the building start their coffee breaks, that sound will be as constant and as rhythmic as waves breaking on a beach. Bill hardly notices this or any of the other interfloor sounds; he's used to them.

He climbs carefully to the top of the stepladder, then boosts himself through into his sixth floor office, leaving Bill down on five. Up here he is Willie. This office has a workshop look, with coils and motors and vents stacked neatly on metal shelves and what looks like a filter of some kind squatting on one corner of the desk. It *is* an office, however; there's a computer terminal, an IN/OUT basket full of papers (also window dressing, which he periodically rotates like a farmer rotating crops), and file cabinets. On one wall is a framed Norman Rockwell print showing a family praying over Thanksgiving dinner. Next to it is a blowup of his honorable discharge from the Marines, also framed; the name on the sheet is William Teale, and his decorations, including the Bronze Star, are duly noted. On another wall is a poster from the sixties. It shows the peace sign. Below it, in red, white, and blue, is this punchline: TRACK OF THE GREAT AMERICAN CHICKEN.

Willie puts Bill's briefcase on the desk, then lies down on his stomach. He pokes his head and arms into the windy, oil-smelling darkness between the floors and replaces the ceiling panel of the fifth-floor office. It's locked up tight, he doesn't expect anyone anyway (he never does;

Western States Land Analysts has never had a single customer), but it's better to be safe. Always safe, never sorry.

With his fifth floor office set to rights, Willie lowers the trapdoor in this one. Up here the trap is hidden by a small rug which is Superglued to the wood, so it can go up and down without too much flopping or sliding around.

He gets to his feet, dusts off his hands, then turns to the briefcase and opens it. He takes out the ball of tinsel and puts it on top of the laser printer which stands next to the computer terminal.

"Good one," he says, thinking again that Sharon can be a real peach when she sets her mind to it . . . and she often does. He relatches the briefcase and then begins to undress, doing it carefully and methodically, reversing the steps he took at six-thirty, running the film backward. He strips off everything, even his undershorts and his black, knee-high socks. Naked, he hangs his topcoat, suit jacket, and shirt carefully in the closet where only one other item hangs—a bulky red jacket, not quite thick enough to be termed a parka. Below it is a boxlike thing, a little too bulky to be termed a briefcase. Willie puts his Mark Cross case next to it, then places his slacks in the pants press, taking pains with the crease. The tie goes on the rack screwed to the back of the closet door, where it hangs all by itself like a long blue tongue.

He pads barefoot-naked across to one of the file cabinets. On top of it is an ashtray embossed with a pissed-off-looking eagle and the Marine motto. In it are a pair of dogtags on a chain. Willie slips the chain over his head, then slides out the bottom drawer of the cabinet stack. Inside are underclothes. Neatly folded on top are a pair of khaki boxer shorts. He slips them on. Next come white athletic socks, followed by a white cotton T-shirt—roundneck, not strappy. The shapes of his dogtags stand out against it, as do his biceps and quads. They aren't as good as they were in '67, under the triple canopy, but they aren't bad. As he slides the drawer back in and opens the next, he begins to hum under his breath—not "Do You Hear What I Hear" but the Doors, the one about how the day destroys the night, the night divides the day.

He slips on a plain blue chambray shirt, then a pair of fatigue pants. He rolls this middle drawer back in and opens the top one. Here there is a pair of black boots, polished to a high sheen and looking as if they might last until the trump of judgment. Maybe even longer. They aren't standard Marine issue, not these—these are jumpboots, 101st Airborne stuff. But that's all right. He isn't actually trying to dress like a soldier. If he wanted to dress like a soldier, he would.

Still, there is no more reason to look sloppy than there is to allow dust to collect in the pass-through, and he's careful about the way he dresses. He does not tuck his pants into his boots, of course—he's headed for Fifth Avenue in December, not the Mekong in August—but he intends to look squared away. Looking good is as important to him as it is to Bill, maybe even more important. Respecting one's work and one's field begins, after all, with respecting one's self.

The last two items are in the back of the top drawer: a tube of makeup and a jar of hair gel. He squeezes some of the makeup into the palm of his left hand, then begins applying it, working from forehead to the base of his neck. He moves with the unconcerned speed of long experience, giving himself a moderate tan. With that done, he works some of the gel into his hair and then recombs it, getting rid of the part and sweeping it straight back from his forehead. It is the last touch, the smallest touch, and perhaps the most telling touch. There is no trace of the commuter who walked out of Penn Station an hour ago; the man in the mirror mounted on the back of the door to the small storage annex looks like a washed-up mercenary. There is a kind of silent, half-humbled pride in the tanned face, something people won't look at too long. It hurts them if they do. Willie knows this is so; he has seen it. He doesn't ask why it should be so. He has made himself a life pretty much without questions, and that's the way he likes it.

"All right," he says, closing the door to the storage room. "Lookin good, trooper."

He goes back to the closet for the red jacket, which is the reversible type, and the boxy case. He slips the jacket over his desk chair for the time being and puts the case on the desk. He unlatches it and swings the top up on sturdy hinges; now it looks a little like the cases the street salesmen use to display their cheap watches and costume jewelry. There are only a few items in Willie's, one of them broken down into two pieces so it will fit. He takes out a pair of gloves (he will want them today, no doubt about that), and then a sign on a length of stout cord. The cord has been knotted through holes in the cardboard at either side, so Willie can hang the sign over his neck. He closes the case again, not bothering to latch it, and puts the sign on top of it—the desk is so cluttery, it's the only good surface he has to work on.

Humming (we chased our pleasures here, dug our treasures there), he opens the wide drawer above the kneehole, paws past the pencils and Chapsticks and paper clips and memo pads, and finally finds his stapler. He then unrolls the ball of tinsel, places it carefully around the rectangle of his sign, snips off the extra, and staples the shiny stuff firmly into place. He holds it up for a moment, first assessing the effect, then admiring it.

"Perfect!" he says. "Wonderful! Sharon, you're a geni—"

The telephone rings and he stiffens, turning to look at it with eyes which are suddenly very small and hard and totally alert. One ring. Two. Three. On the fourth, the machine kicks in, answering in his voice—the version of it that goes with this office, anyway.

"Hi, you've reached Midtown Heating and Cooling," Willie Teale says. "No one can take your call right now, so leave a message at the beep."

Bee-eep.

He listens tensely, standing over his just-decorated sign with his hands balled into fists.

"Hi, this is Ed, from the Nynex Yellow Pages," the voice from the machine says, and Willie lets out breath he hasn't known he was holding. His hands begin to loosen. "Please have your company rep call me at 555-1000 for information on how you can increase your ad space in both versions of the Yellow Pages, and at the same time save big money on your yearly bill. Thanks."

Click.

Willie looks at the answering machine a moment longer, almost as if he expects it to speak again—to threaten him, perhaps, or to accuse him of some crime—but nothing happens.

"Squared away," he murmurs, putting the decorated sign back into the case. This time when he closes it, he latches it. Across the front is a bumper sticker, its message flanked by small American flags. I WAS PROUD TO SERVE, it reads. And below that: SEMPER FI.

"Squared away, baby, you better believe it."

He leaves the office, closing the door with MIDTOWN HEATING AND COOLING printed on the frosted-glass panel behind him, and turning all three of the locks.

* * *

9:40 A.M.

Halfway down the hall, he sees Ralph Williamson, one of the tubby accountants from Garowicz Financial Planning (all the accountants at Garowicz are tubby, from what Willie has been able to observe). There's a key chained to an old wooden paddle in one of Ralph's pink hands, and from this Willie deduces that he is looking at an accountant in need of a wee. Key on a paddle, just like in grade school, he thinks, and you know what? That's probably a comfort to him.

"Hey, Ralphie, what's doin?"

Ralph turns, sees Willie, brightens. "Hey, hi, merry Christmas!"

Willie grins at the look in Ralph's eyes. Tubby little fucker worships him, and why not? Just why the fuck not? If I were Ralph, I'd worship me too. Last of the fucking pioneers.

"Same to you, bro." He holds out his hand (now gloved, so he doesn't have to worry about it not matching his face), palm up. "Gimme five!"

Smiling shyly, Ralph does.

"Gimme ten!"

Ralph turns his pink, pudgy hand over and allows Willie to slap it.

"So goddamn good I gotta do it again!" Willie exclaims, and gives Ralph five more. "Got your Christmas shopping done, Ralphie?"

"Almost," Ralph says, grinning and jingling the bathroom key. "Yes, almost. How about you, Willie?"

Willie tips him a wink. "Oh, you know how it is, brother-man; I got two-three women, and I just let each of em buy me a little keepsake."

Ralph's admiring smile suggests he does not, in fact, know how it is, but rather wishes he did. "Got a service call?"

"A whole day's worth," Willie says. "'Tis the season, you know."

"Seems like it's always the season for you. Business must be good. You're hardly ever in your office."

"That's why God gave us answering machines, Ralphie-baby. Believe it. You better go on, now, or you're gonna be dealin with a wet spot on your best gabardine slacks."

Laughing (blushing a little, too), Ralph heads for the men's room.

Willie goes on down to the elevators, carrying his case in one hand and checking to make sure his glasses are still in his jacket pocket with the other. They are. The envelope is in there, too, thick and crackling with twenty-dollar bills. Fifteen of them. It's time for a little visit from Officer Wheelock; Willie expected him yesterday. Maybe he won't show until tomorrow, but Willie is betting on today . . . not that he likes it. He knows it's the way of the world, you have to grease the wheels if you want your wagon to roll, but he still has a resentment. There are lots of days when he thinks about how pleasant it would be to put a bullet in Jasper Wheelock's head. Rip his tongue out as a trophy, too, maybe—he could hang it in the closet next to Bill Teale's tie.

When the elevator comes, Willie gets in with a smile.

It doesn't stop on five, but the thought of that happening no longer makes him nervous. He has ridden down to the lobby many times with people who work on the same floor as Bill Teale—including the scrawny drink of water from Consolidated Insurance—and they don't recognize him. They should, he knows they *should,* but they don't. He used to think it was the change of clothes and the makeup, then he decided it was the hair, but in his heart he knows that none of those things can account for it. Not even their droning, numb-hearted insensitivity to the world they live in can account for it. What he's doing just isn't that radical—fatigue pants, billyhop boots, and a little brown makeup don't make a disguise. No way do they make a disguise. He doesn't know exactly how to explain it, and so mostly leaves it alone. He learned this technique, as he learned so many other things, in the Nam.

The young black man is still standing outside the lobby door (he's flipped up the hood of his grungy old sweater now), and he shakes his crumpled Styrofoam cup at Willie. He sees that the dude carrying the Mr. Repairman case in one hand is smiling, and so his own smile widens.

"Spare a little?" he asks Mr. Repairman. "What do you say, my man?"

"Get the fuck out of my way, you worthless, lazy dickhead, that's what I say," Willie tells him, still smiling. The young man falls back a step, the Styrofoam cup still at last, looking at Willie with shocked, wide eyes. Before he can think of anything to say, Mr. Repairman is halfway down the block and almost lost in the throngs of shoppers, his big, blocky case swinging from one gloved hand.

9:55 A.M.

He goes into the Whitmore Hotel, crosses the lobby, and takes the escalator up to the mezzanine, where the public restrooms are. This is the only part of the day he ever feels nervous about, and he can't say why; certainly nothing has ever happened before, during, or after one of his hotel bathroom stops (he rotates among roughly two dozen of them in the midtown area), but he is somehow certain that if things ever *do* turn dinky-dau on him, it will happen in a hotel shithouse. Because it's not like transforming from Bill Teale to Willie Teale; that feels clean and perfectly normal. The workday's final transformation, however—from Willie Teale to Blind Willie—has never felt that way. The last morph always feels murky and furtive, and until it's done and he's back on the street again, tapping his white cane in front of him, he feels as a snake must feel after it has shed its old skin and before the new one has grown back.

He looks around and sees the restroom is empty except for a pair of feet under the door of the second stall in a long row of them—a dozen in all. A throat clears softly. A newspaper rattles. There is the *ffft* sound of a polite little midtown fart.

Willie goes all the way down the line to the last stall. He puts down his case, latches the door shut, and takes off his red jacket. He turns it inside-out as he does so, reversing it. The other side is olive green. It has become an old soldier's field jacket with a single pull of the arms. Sharon, who really does have a touch of genius, bought this side of his coat in an army surplus store and tore out the lining so she could sew it easily into the red jacket. Before sewing, however, she put a staff sergeant's stripes on it, plus black strips of cloth where the name-and-unit slugs would have gone. She then washed the garment thirty or forty times. The stripes and the rest are gone, now, of course, but the places where they were stand out clearly—the cloth is greener on the sleeves and the left breast, fresher in patterns any veteran of the armed services must recognize at once.

Willie hangs the coat on the hook, drops trou, sits, then picks up his case and settles it on his thighs. He opens it, takes out the two pieces of his cane, and quickly screws them together. Holding it far down the shaft, he reaches up from his sitting position and hooks the handle over the top of his jacket. Then he relatches the case, pulls a little paper off the roll in order to create the proper business-is-finished sound effect (probably unnecessary, but always safe, never sorry), and flushes the john.

Before stepping out of the stall he takes the glasses from the jacket pocket which also holds the payoff envelope. They're big wraparounds, retro shades he associates with lava lamps and outlaw biker movies starring Peter Fonda. They're good for business, though, partly because they somehow say veteran to people, and partly because no one can peek in at his eyes, even from the sides.

Willie Teale stays behind in the mezzanine restroom of the Whitmore just as Bill Teale stays behind in the fifty-floor office of Western States Land Analysts. The man who comes out—a man wearing an old fatigue jacket, shades, and tapping a white cane lightly before him—is Blind Willie, a Fifth Avenue fixture since Reagan's first term.

As he crosses the smaller upstairs lobby toward the stairs (unaccompanied blind men never use escalators), he sees a woman in a red blazer coming toward him. With the heavily tinted lenses between them, she looks like some sort of exotic fish swimming in muddy water. And of course it is not just the glasses; he is Blind Willie now, and by two this afternoon he really *will* be blind, just as he was blind when he and Bernard Hogan, his best friend, were medivacked out of the DMZ back in '67. Only then he had been damned near deaf too. I'm blind, he kept telling the guy who was kneeling between him and Bernard. He could hear himself talking, but faintly, as if his mind had come loose from his head and blown like a balloon into another room while his stupid mouth just went on quacking. I'm blind, oh Christ, kid, the whole world blew up in our fucking faces and now I'm blind. The kid had smelled of pot and Old Spice, he remembers that. He patted Willie's cheek. You look okay around the eyes to me, he said. If you're lucky, maybe it's just concussion blindness. And that was what it turned out to be, although it hadn't worn off for nearly a week (well, three days, but he'd never let on until he was back in the States). Bernard hadn't been so lucky. Bernard had died, and so far as Willie knows, that doesn't wear off.

"Can I help you, sir?" the woman in the red blazer asks him.

"No, ma'am," Blind Willie says. The ceaselessly moving cane stops tapping floor and quests over emptiness. It pendulums back and forth, tapping the sides of the staircase. Blind Willie nods, then moves carefully but confidently forward until he can touch the railing with the hand which holds the bulky case. He switches the case to his cane-hand so he can grasp the railing, then turns toward the woman. He's careful not to smile directly at her but a little to her left. "No, thank you—I'm fine."

He starts downstairs, tapping ahead of him as he goes, big case held easily in spite of the cane—it's light, almost empty. Later, of course, it will be a different story.

* * *

Fifth Avenue is dressed up and decked out for the holiday season—glitter and finery he can only see dimly. Streetlamps wear garlands of holly. Trump Tower has become a garish Christmas package, complete with gigantic red bow. A wreath which must be forty feet across graces the staid grey facade of Bonwit Teller. Lights twinkle in show windows. In the Warner Brothers store, the Tasmanian Devil which usually sits astride the Harley-Davidson has been temporarily replaced by a Santa Claus in a black leather jacket. Bells jingle. Somewhere nearby, carolers are singing "Silent Night," not exactly Blind Willie's favorite tune, but a good deal better than "Do You Hear What I Hear."

He stops where he always stops, in front of St. Patrick's, across the street from Saks, allowing the package-laden shoppers to flood past in front of him. His movements now are simple and dignified. His discomfort in the men's room—that feeling of gawky and undignified nakedness about to be exposed—has passed. Now he feels like a man in the heart of some ritual, a private mass for both the living and the dead.

He squats, unlatches the case, and turns it so those approaching from uptown will be able to read the sticker on the top. He takes out the sign with its brave skirting of tinsel, and ducks under the string. The sign comes to rest against the front of his field jacket.

S/SGT WILLIAM J. TEALE, USMC RET.

SERVED DMZ, 1966–1967

LOST MY SIGHT CON THIEN, 1967

ROBBED OF BENEFITS BY A GRATEFUL GOVERNMENT, 1979

LOST HOME, 1985

ASHAMED TO BEG BUT HAVE A SON IN SCHOOL

THINK WELL OF ME IF YOU CAN

He raises his head so that the white light of this cold, almost-ready-to-snow day slides across the blind bulbs of his dark glasses. Now the work begins, and it is harder work than anyone will ever know. There is a way to stand, not quite the military posture which is called parade rest, but close to it. The head must stay up, looking both at and through the people who pass back and forth in their thousands and tens of thousands. The hands must hang straight down in their black gloves, never fiddling with the sign or with the fabric of his pants or with each other. The feeling he projects must continue to be that sense of hurt and humbled pride. There must be no cringing, no sense of shame or shaming, and most of all no taint of insanity. He never speaks unless spoken to, and only then when he is spoken to in kindness. He does not respond to people who ask him angrily why he doesn't get a real job, or ask him what he means about being robbed of his benefits, or accuse him of faking, or want to know what kind of son allows his father to put him through school by begging on a street corner. He remembers breaking this ironclad rule only once, on a sweltering summer afternoon in 1990. What school does your son go to? a woman asked him angrily. He doesn't know what she looked like, by then it was almost four and he had been as blind as a bat for three hours, but he had felt anger exploding out of her in all directions, like bedbugs exiting an old mattress. Tell me which one, I want to mail him a dog turd. Don't bother, he replied, turning toward the sound of her voice. If you've got a dog turd you want to mail somewhere, send it to LBJ. Federal Express must deliver to hell, they deliver everyplace else.

"God bless you, man," a guy in a cashmere overcoat says, and his voice trembles with surprising emotion. Except Blind Willie is not surprised. He's heard it all, he reckons, and if he hasn't, he soon will. The guy in the cashmere coat drops a bill into the open case. A five. The workday has begun.

* * *

10:45 A.M.

So far, so good. He lays his cane down carefully behind the case, drops to one knee, and sweeps a hand back and forth through the bills, although he can still see them pretty well. He picks them up—there's four or five hundred dollars in all, which puts him on the way to a three-thousand-dollar day, not great for this time of year, but not bad, either—then rolls them up and slips a rubber band around them. He then pushes a button on the inside of the case, and the false bottom drops down on springs, dumping the load of change all the way to the bottom. He adds the roll of bills, making no attempt to hide what he's doing, but feeling no qualms about it, either; in all the years he has been doing this, his case has never been stolen. God help the asshole who ever tries.

He lets go of the button, allowing the false bottom to snap back into place, and stands up. A hand immediately presses into the small of his back.

"Merry Christmas, Willie," the owner of the hand says. Blind Willie recognizes him by the smell of his cologne.

"Merry Christmas, Officer Wheelock," Willie responds. His head remains tilted upward in a faintly questioning posture; his hands hang at his sides; his feet in their brightly polished jumpboots remain apart in a stance not quite wide enough to be parade rest but nowhere near tight enough to pass as attention. "How are you today, sir?"

"In the pink, motherfucker," Wheelock says. "You know me, always in the pink."

Here comes a man in a topcoat hanging open over a bright red ski sweater. His hair is short, black on top, gray on the sides. His face has got a stern, carved look Blind Willie recognizes at once. He's got a couple of handle-top bags—one from Saks, one from Bally—in his hands. He stops and reads the sign.

"Con Thien?" he asks suddenly, speaking not as a man does when naming a place but as one does when recognizing an old acquaintance on a busy street.

"Yes, sir," Blind Willie says.

"Who was your CO?"

"Lieutenant Bob Grissum—with a 'u,' not an 'o'—and above him, Colonel Andrew Shelf, sir."

"I heard of Shelf," says the man in the open coat. His face suddenly looks different. As he walked toward the man on the corner, it looked as if it belonged on Fifth Avenue. Now it doesn't. "Never met him, though."

Blind Willie says nothing. He can smell Wheelock's cologne, though, stronger than ever, and the man is practically panting in his ear, sounding like a horny kid at the end of a hot date. Wheelock has never bought his act, and although Blind Willie pays for the privilege of being left alone on this corner, and quite handsomely by going rates, he knows that part of Wheelock is still cop enough to hope he'll fuck up. Part of Wheelock is actively rooting for that. But what the Wheelocks of the world never understand is that what looks fake isn't always fake. Sometimes the issues are a little more complicated than they look at first glance. That was something else the Nam had to teach him, back in the years before it became a political joke and a crutch for hack filmwriters.

"Sixty-seven was a hard year," the gray-haired man says. He speaks in a slow, heavy voice. "I was at Loc Ninh when the regulars tried to overrun the place. Up by the 'Bodian border. Do you remember Loc Ninh?"

"Ah, yes, sir," Blind Willie says. "I lost two friends on Tory Hill."

"Tory Hill," the man in the open coat says, and all at once he looks a thousand years old, the bright red ski sweater an obscenity, like something hung on a museum mummy by vandals who believe they are exhibiting a sense of humor. His eyes are off over a hundred horizons. Then they come back here, to this street where a nearby carillion is playing the one that goes I hear those sleighbells jingling, ring-ting-tingling too. He sets his bags down between his expensive shoes and takes a pigskin wallet out from an inner pocket. He opens it, riffles through a neat thickness of bills.

"Son all right, Teale?" he asks. "Making good grades?"

"Yes, sir."

"How old?"

"Twenty-one, sir."

"God willing, he'll never know what it's like to see his friends die and then get spit on in an airport concourse," the man in the open top-coat says. He takes a bill out of his wallet. Blind Willie feels as well as hears Wheelock's little gasp and hardly has to look at the bill to know it is a hundred.

"Yes, sir, God willing, sir."

The man in the topcoat touches Willie's hand with the bill, looks surprised when the gloved hand pulls back, as if it were bare and had been touched by something hot.

"Put it in my case, sir, if you would," Blind Willie says.

The man in the topcoat looks at him for a moment, eyebrows raised, frowning slightly, then seems to understand. He stoops, puts the bill in the case, then reaches into his front pocket and brings out a small handful of change. This he scatters across the face of old Ben Franklin, in order to hold the bill down. Then he stands up. His eyes are wet and bloodshot.

"Do you any good to give you my card?" he asks Blind Willie. "I can put you in touch with several veterans' organizations."

"Thank you, sir, I'm sure you could, but I must respectfully decline."

"Tried most of them?"

"Tried some, yes, sir."

"Where'd you V.A.?"

"San Francisco, sir." He hesitates, then adds, "The Pussy Palace, sir."

The man in the topcoat laughs heartily at this, and when his face crinkles, the tears which have been standing in his eyes run down his weathered cheeks. "Pussy Palace!" he cries. "I haven't heard that in fifteen years! Christ! A bedpan in every bed and a naked nurse to hold it in place, right? Except for the lovebeads, which they left on."

"Yes, sir, that about covers it, sir."

"Or uncovers it. Merry Christmas, soldier." The man in the topcoat ticks off a little one-finger salute.

"Merry Christmas to you, sir."

The man in the topcoat picks up his bags again and walks off. He doesn't look back. Blind Willie would not have seen him do so if he had; his vision is now down to ghosts and shadows.

"That was beautiful," Wheelock murmurs. The feeling of Wheelock's freshly used air puffing into the cup of his ear is hateful to Blind Willie—gruesome, in fact—but he will not give the man the pleasure of moving his head so much as an inch. "The old fuck was actually *crying*. As I'm sure you saw. But you can talk the talk, Willie, I'll give you that much."

Willie said nothing.

"Some V.A. hospital called the Pussy Palace, huh?" Wheelock asks. "Sounds like my kind of place. Where'd you read about it, *Soldier of Fortune*?"

The shadow of a woman, a dark shape in a darkening day, bends over the open case and drops something in. A gloved hand touches Willie's gloved hand and squeezes briefly. "God bless you," she says.

"Thank you, ma'am."

The shadow moves off. The little puffs of breath in Blind Willie's ear do not.

"You got something for me, pal?" Wheelock asks.

Blind Willie reaches into his jacket pocket. He brings out the envelope and holds it out, jabbing the chilly, unseen air with it. It is snatched from his fingers as soon as Wheelock can track it down and get hold of it.

"You asshole!" There's a touch of panic as well as anger in the cop's voice. "How many times have I told you, palm it, *palm* it!"

Blind Willie says a lot more nothing—he is giving a sermon of silence this morning.

"How much?" Wheelock asks after a moment.

"Three hundred," Blind Willie says. "Three hundred dollars, Officer Wheelock."

This is greeted by a little thinking silence, but he takes a step back from Blind Willie, and the puffs of breath in his ear diffuse a little. Blind Willie is grateful for small favors.

"That's okay," Wheelock says at last. "*This* time. But a new year's coming, pal, and your friend Jasper the Police-Smurf has a piece of land in upstate New York that he wants to build a little cabaña on. You understand? The price of poker is going up."

Blind Willie says nothing, but he is listening very, very carefully now. If this were all, all would be well. But Wheelock's voice suggests it isn't all.

"Actually, the cabaña isn't the important part," Wheelock goes on, confirming Blind Willie's assessment of the situation. "The important thing is I need a little better compensation if I have to deal with a lowlife fuck like you." Genuine anger is creeping into his voice. "How you can do this every day—even at *Christmas*—man, I don't know. People who beg, that's one thing, but a guy like you . . . you're no more blind than I am."

Oh, you're *lots* blinder than me, Blind Willie thinks, but still he holds his peace.

"And you're doing okay, aren't you? Probably not as good as that PTL fuck they busted and sent to the *callabozo*, but you must clear . . . what? A grand a day, this time a year? Two grand?'"

He is way low, but Blind Willie does not, of course, correct him. The miscalculation is actually music to his ears. It means that his silent partner is not watching him too closely or too frequently . . . not yet, anyway. But he doesn't like the anger in Wheelock's voice. Anger is like a wild card in a poker game.

"And you're no more blind than I am," Wheelock repeats. Apparently this is the part that really gets him. "Hey, pal, you know what? I ought to follow you some night when you get off work, you know? See what you do." He pauses. "Who you turn into."

For a moment Blind Willie actually stops breathing . . . then he starts again.

"You wouldn't want to do that, Officer Wheelock," he says.

"I wouldn't, huh? Why not, Willie? Why not? You lookin out for my welfare, is that it? Afraid I might kill the shitass who lays the golden turds? Hey, thirty-six hundred a year ain't all that much when you weigh it against a commendation, maybe a promotion." He pauses.

When he speaks again, his voice has a dreamy quality which Willie finds especially alarming. "I could be in the *Post*. HERO COP BUSTS HEARTLESS SCAM ARTIST ON FIFTH AVENUE."

"You'd be in the *Post*, all right, but there wouldn't be any commendation," Blind Willie says. "No promotion, either. In fact, you'd be out on the street, Officer Wheelock, looking for a job. You could skip applying for one with the security companies, though—a man who'll take a payoff can't be bonded."

It is Wheelock's turn to stop breathing. When he starts again, the puffs of breath in Blind Willie's ear have become a hurricane; the cop's moving mouth is almost on his skin. "What do you mean?" he whispers. A hand settles on the arm of Blind Willie's field jacket. "You just tell me what the fuck you mean."

But Blind Willie is silent, hands at his sides, head slightly raised, looking attentively into the darkness that will not clear until daylight is almost gone, and on his face is that lack of expression which so many passersby read as ruined pride, bruised grace, courage brought low but still somehow intact. It is that, not the sign or the dark glasses, which has allowed him to do so well over the years . . . and Wheelock is wrong: he *is* blind. They both are blind.

The hand on his arm shakes him slightly. It is almost a claw now. "You got a friend? Is that it, you son of a bitch? Is that why you hold the envelope out that way half the damned time? You got a friend taking my picture? Is that it?"

Blind Willie says nothing, has to say nothing. People like Jasper Wheelock will always think the worst if you let them. You only have to give them time to do it.

"You don't want to fuck with me, pal," Wheelock says viciously, but there is a subtle undertone of worry in his voice, and the hand on Blind Willie's jacket loosens. "We're going up to four hundred a month starting next week, and if you try playing any games with me, I'm going to show you where the real playground is. You understand me?"

Blind Willie says nothing. The puffs of air stop hitting his ear, and he knows Wheelock is going. But not yet; the nasty little puffs come back.

"You'll burn in hell for what you're doing," Wheelock tells him. He speaks with great, almost fervent, sincerity. "What I'm doing when I take your dirty money is a venial sin—I asked the priest, so I'm sure— but yours is mortal. You're going to hell, see how many handouts you get down there."

He walks away then, and Willie's thought—that he is glad to see him go—causes a rare smile to touch his face. It comes and goes like an errant ray of sunshine on a cloudy day.

1:40 P.M.

Three times he has banded the bills into rolls and dumped the change into the bottom of the case (this is really a storage function, and not an effort at concealment), now working completely by touch. He can no longer see the money, doesn't know a one from a hundred, but he senses he is having a very good day, indeed. There is no pleasure in the knowledge, however. There's never much, pleasure is not what Blind Willie is about, but even the sense of accomplishment he might have felt on another day has been muted by his conversation with Officer Wheelock.

At quarter to twelve, a young woman with a pretty voice—to Blind Willie she sounds like Whitney Houston—comes out of Saks and gives him a cup of hot coffee, as she does most days at this time. At quarter past, another woman—this one not so young, and probably white— brings him a cup of steaming chicken noodle soup. He thanks them both. The white lady kisses his cheek, calls him Will instead of Willie, and wishes him the merriest of merry Christmases.

There is a counterbalancing side to the day, though; there almost always is. Around one o'clock a teenage kid with his unseen posse laughing and joking and skylarking all around him speaks out of the darkness to Blind Willie's left, says he is one ugly motherfuck, then asks if he wears those gloves because he burned his fingers off trying to read the waffle iron. He and his friends charge off, howling with laughter at this ancient jape. Fifteen minutes or so later, someone kicks him, although that might have been an accident. Every time he bends over to the case, however, the case is right there. It is a city of hustlers, muggers, and thieves, but the case is right there, just as it has always been right there.

And through it all, he thinks about Wheelock.

The cop before Wheelock was easy; the one who comes when Wheelock either quits the force or gets moved out of Midtown North may also be easy. Wheelock will not last forever—something else he has learned in the Nam—and in the meantime, he, Blind Willie, must bend like a reed in a windstorm. Except that sometimes even the reed that bends is broken . . . if the wind blows hard enough.

Wheelock wants more money, but that isn't what bothers the man in the dark glasses and the army coat. Sooner or later they *all* want more money: when he started on this corner, he paid Officer Hanratty a hundred and a quarter, and although Hanratty was easy, he had Blind Willie up to two hundred a month by the time he retired in 1989. But Wheelock was angry this morning, *angry,* and Wheelock talked about having consulted a priest. These things worry him, but what worries him most of all is what Wheelock said about following him. *See what you do. Who you turn into.*

It would be easy, God knows—what could be simpler than shadowing a blind man, or even one who can see little more than shadows? Watching him turn into some hotel (one on the uptown side, this time), watching him go into the public men's room, watching him go into a stall? Watching him change from Blind Willie into plain old Willie, maybe even from Willie into Bill?

Thinking this brings back his morning jitters, his feeling of being a snake between skins. The fear that he has been photographed taking a bribe will hold Wheelock for a while, but if he is angry enough, there is no predicting what he may do. And that is scary.

"God love you, soldier," says a voice out of the darkness. "I wish I could do a few bucks more."

"Not necessary, sir," Blind Willie says, but his mind is still on Jasper Wheelock, who smells of cheap cologne and talked to a priest about the blind man with the sign, the blind man who is not, Wheelock thinks, blind at all. What had he said? *You're going to hell, see how many handouts you get down there.* "Have a very merry Christmas, sir, thank you for helping me."

And the day goes on.

4:25 P.M.

His sight has started to resurface—dim, distant, but there. It is his cue to pack up and go.

He kneels, back ramrod stiff, and lays his cane behind the case again. He bands the last of the bills, dumps them and the last coins into the bottom of the case one more time, then puts the tinsel-decorated sign inside. He latches the case and stands up, holding his cane in the other hand. Now the case is heavy, dragging at his arm with the deadweight of well-meant metal. There is a heavy rattling crunch as the coins avalanche into a new position, and then they are as still as ore plugged deep in the ground.

He sets off down Fifth, dangling the case at the end of his left arm like an anchor (after all these years he's used to the weight of it, could carry it much further than he'll need to this afternoon, if circumstances demanded), holding the cane in his right hand and tapping it delicately on the paving in front of him. The cane is magic, opening a pocket of empty space before him on the crowded, jostling sidewalk in a teardrop-shaped wave. By the time he gets to Fifth and Forty-third, he can actually see this space. He can also see the DON'T WALK sign at Forty-second stop flashing and hold solid, but he keeps walking anyway, letting a well-dressed man with long hair and gold chains reach out and grasp his shoulder to stop him.

"Watch it, big fella," the longhair says. "Traffic in a sec."

"Thank you, sir," Blind Willie says.

"Don't mention it—merry Christmas."

Blind Willie crosses, goes down two more blocks, then turns toward Broadway. No one accosts him; no one has loitered, watching him collect all day long, and then followed, waiting for the opportunity to bag the case and run (not that many thieves *could* run with it, not *this* case). Once, back in the summer of '91, two or three young guys, maybe black (he couldn't say for sure; they *sounded* black, but his vision had been slow coming back that day, it was always slower in warm weather, when the days stayed bright longer), had accosted him and began talking to him in a way he didn't quite like. It wasn't like the kids this afternoon, with their jokes about reading the waffle iron and what does a *Playboy* centerfold look like in braille. It was softer than that, and in some weird fashion almost kind—questions about how much he took in by St. Pat's back there, and would he perchance be generous enough to make a contribution to something called the Polo Recreational League, and did he want a little protection getting to his bus stop or train station or whatever. One, perhaps a budding sexologist, had asked if he liked a little young pussy once in a while. "It pep you up," the voice on his left said softly, almost longingly. "Yessir, you must believe *that* shit."

He had felt the way he imagined a mouse must feel when the cat is still just pawing at it, claws not out yet, curious about what the mouse will do, and how fast it can run, and what sorts of noises it will make as its terror grows. Blind Willie had not been terrified, however. He is *never* terrified. That is his advantage, and it had been their mistake. He had simply raised his voice, speaking as a man might speak to a large room filled with old friends. "Say!" he had exclaimed to the shadowy phantoms all around him on the sidewalk. "Say, does anyone see a policeman? I believe these young fellows here mean to take me off." And that did it, easy as pulling a segment off a peeled orange; the fellows who had been bracketing him were suddenly gone like a cool breeze.

He only wishes he could solve the problem of Officer Wheelock that easily.

4:40 P.M.

The Sheraton Gotham, at Fortieth and Broadway, is one of the largest first-class hotels in the world, and in the cave of its lobby thousands of people school back and forth beneath the gigantic chandelier. They chase their pleasures here and dig their treasures there, oblivious of the Christmas music flowing from the speakers, of the chatter from three different restaurants and five bars, of the scenic elevators sliding up and down in their notched shafts like pistons powering some exotic glass engine . . . and of the blind man who taps among them, working his way toward a public men's room almost the size of a subway station. He walks with the sticker on the case turned inward now, and he is as anonymous as a blind man can be. In this city, that's very anonymous.

Still, he thinks as he enters one of the stalls and takes off his jacket, turning it inside-out as he does so, how is it that in all these years no one has *ever* followed me? No one has *ever* noticed that the blind man who goes in and the sighted man who comes out are the same size, and carrying the same case?

Well, in New York, hardly anyone notices anything that isn't his or her own business—in their own way, they are all as blind as Blind Willie. Out of their offices, flooding down the sidewalks, thronging in the subway stations and cheap restaurants, there is something both repulsive and sad about them; they are like nests of moles turned up by a farmer's harrow. He has seen this blindness over and over again, and he knows that is one reason for his success . . . but surely not the only reason. They are not *all* moles, and he has been rolling the dice for a long time now. He takes precautions, of course he does, many of them, but there are still those moments (like now, sitting here with his pants down, unscrewing the white cane and stowing it back in his case) when he would be easy to catch, easy to rob . . . easy to expose. Wheelock is right about the *Post;* they would love him. The *News* would too. They would hang him higher than Haman, higher than O.J. Simpson. They would never understand, never even *want* to understand, or hear his side of it. *What* side?

He leaves the stall, leaves the bathroom, leaves the echoing confusion of the Sheraton Gotham, and no one walks up to him and says, "Excuse me, sir, but weren't you just blind?" No one looks at him twice as he walks out into the street, carrying the bulky case as if it weighed twenty pounds instead of a hundred. It has started to snow.

He walks slowly, Willie Teale again now, switching the case frequently from hand to hand, just one more tired guy at the end of the day. He continues to think about his inexplicable success as he goes. There's a verse from the Book of Matthew which he has committed to memory. They be blind leaders of the blind, it goes. And if the blind lead the blind, both shall fall into the ditch. Then there's the old saw that says that in the kingdom of the blind, the one-eyed man is king. Is *he* the one-eyed man? Has that been the secret of his success all these years?

He doesn't think so. In his heart of hearts he believes he has been protected. Not by God, exactly (he doesn't think he quite believes in God, certainly not the one advertised by the church in front of which he stands most days), but maybe by some half-sentient force that has *always* seen him as Blind Willie. Fate, you could call it that if you liked, or you could call it a higher power—Generic Brand God—as the alkies do. Or maybe it's only blind justice, balancing her scales. Most likely it doesn't matter. All he knows for sure is that he never consciously decided to become Blind Willie, and he has never been caught or taken off.

Of course, there has never been a Jasper Wheelock in his life, either.

Maybe I ought to follow you some night, Officer Wheelock whispers in his ear as Willie shifts the increasingly heavy case from one hand to the other. Both arms ache now; he will be glad to reach his building. *See what you do. See who you turn into.*

What, exactly, was he going to do about Officer Wheelock? What *could* he do?

He doesn't know.

* * *

The young panhandler in the dirty red sweatshirt is long gone. His place taken by yet another streetcorner Santa. Willie has no trouble recognizing the tubby young fellow currently dropping a dollar into Santa's pot.

"Hey, Ralphie!" he cries.

Ralph Williamson turns, and his face lights up when he sees Willie, and he raises one gloved hand. It's snowing harder now; with the bright lights around him and Santa Claus beside him, Ralph looks suspiciously like the central figure in a holiday greeting card. Or maybe a modern-day Bob Cratchet.

"Hey, Willie! How's it goin?"

"Goin like a house afire," he says, approaching the other man with an easy grin on his face. He sets his case down with a grunt, feels in his pants pocket, and finds a buck for Santa's pot. Probably just another crook, and he looks like shit, but what the hell.

"What you got in there?" Ralph asks, looking down at Willie's case as he fiddles with his scarf. "Sounds like you busted open some little kid's piggy bank."

"Nah, just heating coils," Willie says. "'Bout a damn thousand of 'em."

"You working right up until Christmas?"

"Yeah," he says, and suddenly knows what he is going to do about Wheelock. Not how, not yet, but that's okay; how is just a technicality. What is where the creative work is done. There's no burst of revelation, no feeling of eureka; it is as if part of him knew all along. He supposes part of him did. "Yeah, right up until Christmas. No rest for the wicked, you know."

Ralph's wide and pleasant face creases in a smile. "I doubt if you're very wicked, though."

Willie smiles back. "You don't know what evil lurks in the heart of the heatin-n-coolin man, that's all. I'll probably take a few days off after Christmas, though. I'm thinking that might be a really good idea."

"Go south?"

"South?" Willie looks startled, then laughs. "Oh, no," he says. "Not *this* kid. Plenty to do around my house, you know. A person's got to keep their house in order, Ralphie. Else it might just come down around their ears some day."

"I suppose." Ralph bundles the scarf higher around his ears. "See you tomorrow?"

"You bet," Willie says and holds out his gloved hand. "Gimme five."

Ralphie gives him five, then turns his hand over. His smile is shy but eager. "Give me ten, Willie."

Willie gives him ten. "How good is that, Ralphie-baby?"

The man's shy smile becomes a gleeful boy's grin. "So goddamn good I gotta do it again!" he cries, and slaps Willie's hand with real authority.

Willie laughs. "You the man, Ralph."

"You the man, too, Willie," Ralph replies, speaking with a prissy earnestness that's really sort of funny. "Merry Christmas."

"Right back atcha."

He stands where he is for a moment, watching Ralph trudge off into the snow. Beside him, the streetcorner Santa rings his bell monotonously. Willie picks up his case and starts for the door of his building. Then something catches his eye, and he pauses.

"Your beard's on crooked," he says to the Santa. "If you want people to believe in you, fix your goddamn beard."

He goes inside.

5:25 P.M.

There's a big carton in the storage annex of Midtown Heating and Cooling. It is full of the cloth bags, the sort banks use to hold loose coins. Such bags usually have various banks' names printed on them, but these don't—Willie orders them direct from the company in Moundsville, West Virginia, that makes them.

He opens the case, quickly sets aside the rolls of bills (these he will carry home in his Mark Cross briefcase), then fills four bags with coins. In a far corner of the storage room is a battered old metal cabinet simply marked PARTS. Willie swings it open—there is no lock to contend with—and reveals another two or three hundred coin-stuffed bags. A dozen times a year he and Sharon tour the midtown churches, pushing these bags through the contribution slots where they will fit, simply leaving them by the door where they won't. The lion's share always goes to St. Pat's, the vast church in front of which Blind Willie can be found most days, wearing his dark glasses and his sign.

But not *every* day, he thinks, I don't have to be there *every* day, and he thinks again that maybe both Blind Willie and Willie Teale will take the week after Christmas off. There might be work for Bill, though, and why not? Bill has it easy, as a rule. He wakes up to the clock radio, shaves, dresses, goes into the city . . . and then disappears until it's time to go home. Maybe it's time for Bill to do a little work, pitch in and do his share. There is stuff he could do in the week or so before New Year's Eve, when he and Sharon will once more tour the churches, leaving off the coins that are too bulky and troublesome to deal with.

I ought to follow you some night . . . see what you do. Who you turn into.

But maybe, he thinks, taking off Willie and putting on Bill (Paul Stuart, J. Press, Mark Cross, Sulka, Bally), maybe it's I who ought to follow *you,* Officer Wheelock. The part of me you'd never recognize in a million years, any more than Ralph Williamson would recognize Bill . . . or Blind Willie, for that matter. Maybe Bill needs to follow *you,* see what *you* do, who *you* turn into when you go home and take off your day along with your uniform.

Yes, I could do that, Bill thinks. He's used cold cream to remove his makeup and now steps carefully through the trap door and finds his footing on top of the stepladder. He takes the handle of his briefcase and pulls it through. He descends to the third step, then lowers the trap door into place and slides the ceiling panel back where it belongs. Yes, I could do that very easily. And . . .

Well, accidents sometimes happen. Sad but true. Even to big, brave fellows like Jasper the Police-Smurf, accidents sometimes happen.

"Do you hear what I hear," he sings softly as he folds the stepladder and puts it back, "do you smell what I smell, do you taste what I taste?"

Five minutes later he closes the door of Western States Land Analysts firmly behind him and triple locks it. Then he goes down the hallway. When the elevator comes and he steps in, he thinks, Eggnog. Don't forget. The Allens and the Dubrays.

"Also cinnamon," he says out loud. The three people in the elevator car with him look around, and Bill Teale grins self-consciously.

Outside, he turns toward Penn Station, registering only one thought as the snow beats full into his face and he flips up his coat collar: the Santa outside the building has fixed his beard.

*   *   *

"Share?"

"Hmmmm?"

Her voice is sleepy, distant. They have made long, slow love after the Dubrays finally left at eleven o'clock, and now she is drifting away. That's all right, though; he is drifting too. He has a feeling that all of his problems are solving themselves...or that the higher power upon whom he sometimes speculates, that savior of temporarily skinless snakes, is solving them for him.

"I may take a week or so off after Christmas. Do some inventory. Poke around some new sites. I'm thinking about changing locations." There is no need for her to know about what he may really be doing in the week before New Year's, he reasons; she couldn't do anything but worry and—perhaps, perhaps not, he sees no reason to find out for sure—feel guilty.

"Good," she says. "See a few movies while you're at it, why don't you?" Her hand gropes out of the dark and touches his arm briefly. "You work so hard." Pause. "Also, you remembered the eggnog. I really didn't think you would. I'm very pleased with you."

He grins in the dark at that, helpless not to. It is so perfectly Sharon.

"The Allens are all right, but the Dubrays are boring, aren't they?" she asks.

"A little," he allows.

"If that dress of hers had been cut any lower, she could have gotten a job in a topless bar."

He says nothing to that, but grins again.

"It was good tonight, wasn't it?" she asks him. It's not their little party that she's talking about.

"Yes, excellent."

"Did you have a good day? I didn't have a chance to ask."

"Fine day, Share."

"I love you, Bill."

"Love you, too."

"Goodnight."

"Goodnight."

He lies on his side, drifting into sleep while thinking about the man in the open topcoat and the bright red ski sweater. He crosses over without knowing it, thought melting effortlessly into dream. "Sixty-seven was a hard year," the man in the red sweater says. "I was at Loc Ninh, you know. Tory Hill. We lost a lot of good men." Then he brightens. "But I got this." From the lefthand pocket of his topcoat he takes a white beard hanging on a string. "And this." From the righthand pocket he takes a crumpled Styrofoam cup, which he shakes. A few loose coins rattle in the bottom like teeth. "So you see," he says, fading now, "there are compensations to even the blindest life."

Then the dream fades and he sleeps deeply until 6:15 the next morning, when the clock-radio wakes him to the sound of "The Little Drummer Boy."

COLLEEN McCULLOUGH

Oft in the Stilly Night

When he awoke it was to strangeness; he lay quietly with his eyes widening to encompass the darkness, blinking and calm. Panic was alien to him now, he had left it behind somewhere amid the lost feelings of other days. He seemed to have nothing save lassitude, a soft and passive tranquility, and as he lay without moving it came to him that to feel so was soothing, restful.

It was very dark, but as the seconds continued to tick away he began to take an interest in his surroundings, began to distinguish shadows and dim outlines. The same world, he thought, it's the same world. Only the place is strange. To one side of his head and slightly higher was the squat black bulk of a bureau or cupboard, and recognizing it for what it was made him more secure, less alone. Turning a little on the pillow, he watched the cupboard's top fixedly.

The seconds were ticking off hurriedly from somewhere near at hand, but it was not the feeble beating of his heart giving them their congé. He could see his grandfather's watch, which was almost level with his eyes, gleaming fitfully gold as its chased case gathered the light to itself jealously.

Behind the watch was a water glass, rounded like a little fishbowl, and in it swam a set of dentures. The impulse to chew immediately was instinctive; he moved his jaws up and down slowly, and ruminated on blunt, bare gums. His teeth they were, then. But what were his teeth doing cruising in the restricted ocean of a water glass, and why was his grandfather's watch so far from his heart?

A noise was emanating out of the darkness, someone retching and whimpering, and a reassuring murmur overrode it. More noises intruded: rhythmic clanks, stifled weak snores, the crunch of intolerably starched linen, wet and bubbling breathing, muffled footsteps, and away in the far distance the hiss of steam. So it was a hospital. I am in a hospital, he thought without much interest, watching his teeth archly smiling like the last remnant of a Cheshire skull. Yes, it was a hospital. No doubt of that. One by one, his faltering senses dragged the information in, sights and sounds and odors and indefinable convictions. A puff of air brought the cheesy smell of vomit with it and his sheets smelled too clean, too wrung out and pressure dried; everything was smothered under a pall of stunning cleanliness.

Light broke upon his eyes like a thunderclap and he winced, withdrawing his gaze from the sudden, glowing holocaust of the water glass and reflexively closing his eyes. When he opened them someone was bending over him; a faint, radiant halo surrounded the gauzy white veil of a nun, but her head was lost in darkness and he could not see her face.

"Awake, Mr. Johnson?"

He nodded wordlessly.

"How do you feel?"

"Did they bring me here to die?" he managed to say, one restless, listless hand plucking at the sheets.

"Of course they didn't! You're not going to die, Mr. Johnson. You'll be up and around and out of here in a very few days, you wait and see."

It was a soft, kind voice, and it made him want to weep. How long the years since anyone has spoken to me like that, he reflected dreamily, his lips parting in the ghost of a gummy smile. How long the years . . .

The flashlight she carried focused on his face, but as kindly now as her voice had come to him, reduced to a ruby-red glow with three black lines across it because she had shielded it with her fingers.

"Oh, I'm glad they brought me to die where there are people," he said. "I was sure I would die in my room with no one there. . . ."

"You're not going to die, Mr. Johnson," the voice insisted.

"I don't mind dying," he went on in a reedy old whisper. "I really don't mind dying. It was only being on my own that I minded. . . ."

A young, warm hand touched his forehead fleetingly, in an exquisite understanding. "Don't worry now, Mr. Johnson," the voice belonging to the hand crooned. "Try to sleep, then in the morning you'll feel so much better. There's a little button under your pillow, and if you want anything at all you just have to push it. I'll come back to see how you're doing from time to time, so you mustn't worry, please. I'm here, and it's all right. You are not alone, my dear."

My dear, my dear . . . On the words she was gone, off into the faintly glittering night with her thin, short white veil dancing round her head like a clouded prism. My dear, my dear . . . Was there anything in all the world more welcome than that? When the moment comes for going it should be rightly so, he thought. It should come humanly like that, echoing my dear.

Like a five-antennaed snail, his hand crept upward to the locker's top, and the knotted old fingers groped after his grandfather's watch, pushing it to the edge. He caught it as it fell and clasped it against his heart, with the long gold chain straying through the outer rim of his clenched fist and dropping sparkling into the abyss beyond the side of the bed. My dear, my dear . . . He stared at the teeth wavering in the water glass with the bland, milk-fed calm of a baby. My dear, my dear . . .

By the time she managed to get back to the bed a second time his eyes were closed; her hand went seeking a carotid pulse, her other hand pressed against the swelling bosom of her white apron where she kept her watch on a big safety pin along with the ward keys. Her sigh was only half a sigh, dimmed and unprotesting. She blessed herself, pulled the faded curtains around the bed and switched on the light.

"Gone?" another voice asked.

She turned her head. "Yes, poor old boy. Just out like a candle. I think he was glad to go."

"Probably. History says semi-destitute, no living relatives. You know the sort. Eking out an existence on the pension in some poky wee room down Darlo way, I suppose. I often wonder how they live to be so old. Nothing and nobody."

"Oh, *poor* old boy!"

They said their prayers above him, prayers for the dead, then together they began to strip away covers and clothing from the still, wasted figure in the bed, working swiftly but with a curious delicacy: a touch compounded of easy familiarity and tender respect.

"Oh, the poor old boy," she said again. "I thank Our Lord I won't have to go like that, all alone and only us to grieve."

"So do we all, Sister, so do we all. Stay with him while I get the mortuary pack."

And while she waited she combed the sparse threads of hair across the waxen skull; his grandfather's watch was still clutched tightly in his hand, and she prized his fingers away from it one by one until it was free and the long gold chain dangled from her own hand. Back onto the locker's top it went, next to the water glass. She fished the pink and white denture from its antisepticky bath and inserted it deftly, smoothing the pinched lines out of his upper lip until the mouth smiled at her faintly.

"There, old boy, does that feel better?" she asked, smiling back at him. She put her hand on his scraggy chest, and the skin slid across his bones as if it were separate, wrapping paper sloppily applied. "Heaven is less lonely than this earth, Mr. Johnson. I'll bet you were a *nice* old boy!"

MARY MORRIS

The People Next Door

Shortly after we bought our house on Third Street, the people next door disappeared. They got up in the middle of a summer's evening, locked the door, and never came back again. We didn't see them leave, but the Jensens who live on the other side did. The Jensens said they waved as if they were going out for ice cream and left with only the clothes on their backs. Budd and Shirlee were their names and it is twenty years this summer since they've been gone.

I had only seen them a few times before they left. Not that often, really. I saw them sitting in their yard, having a drink on the patio, or coming in with groceries. Shirlee welcomed us when we moved in. She was a feisty, small woman, a little on the stout side with coppery hair, and Budd was a large man—not fat, but large. Big eaters and probably drinkers. They looked like the kind of people who would eat a side of beef and thick slices of pie.

Though we'd never been over there, Budd and Shirlee were always pleasant and cordial. Once their sprinkler watered our deck, but after we told them, it never happened again. We live on a designated landmark block of brownstones and our house abuts theirs. We share a fire wall and low wooden fence. So even if we had never been over there, sometimes it seemed as if we had. Once they invited us for a drink. I wanted to go. I like seeing the inside of other people's houses. How they live. The things they have. But Roy Jr. got the chicken pox and then he gave it to Sara and by the time the kids were well, Budd and Shirlee were gone.

At first we just thought they'd left for the summer. People in our neighborhood do that sometimes. But then summer turned to fall. Fall to winter. Gas inspectors stood shivering on their front stoop. Notices pinned to their front door fluttered and blew down the street. The mail and newspapers piled up until the Jensens took it in. By Thanksgiving everything stopped.

When the first snow fell I said to Roy, "They aren't coming back."

"Who?" he asked, as if he'd forgotten.

"Budd and Shirlee. The people next door. They're gone."

"I know they're gone."

"I mean they're gone for good."

We learned to live with it. First to wonder at it, then to accept it. We worried over vermin, break-ins, squatters inhabiting the abandoned house. We watched the garden overrun—thick vines that inched their way month by month, season by season, climbing fences, slowly making their way on to our side. We fought them back with sharp pruning shears, trying to keep the wild growth away from our house. We watched as ivy slowly spread itself over their windows, dust settled inside the panes of glass, wasps and squirrels burrowed nests under eaves, cobwebs grew, and the house next door and its yard became a desolate, unattended place.

Sometimes the kids jumped over the fence to retrieve a lost ball or to play Tarzan and Jane. Once I caught them, half-naked, swinging on the wisteria vine that under its own weight had tumbled off the trellis. I told them not to play there, but soon they grew wary of it themselves because of the bees and wasps that had infested the small yard and because of the stories they heard at school about the house next door to ours and what might have happened there. And so the house just stood, the vines climbing unchecked, the windows darkened, soundless, without the clatter of dishes, the pierce of an alarm clock, or the murmur of goodnights, without a light ever going on or off. It just became the house of the people next door—the ones who went away.

Over the years I have wondered about what made them go. I cannot walk past their house and not think about it. I have various theories, as do others on the block. That they were involved in a criminal activity is the prevalent view. Swindling. Absconding with funds. Or perhaps the mob. My sister who lives in Seattle told me about a travel agent she knows whose partner took off with their secretary and all the company assets. The secretary left her three small children behind, if you can imagine that. Or maybe, it's occurred to me, Budd and Shirlee are dead. Or maybe they escaped by the skin of their teeth.

At night I'd sit up and try to talk to Roy about what happened to them. I worried about it so much that a few years after they left, Roy came home and said he had been looking into the house next door. He said it in a way that startled me, for I envisioned him peering into empty rooms, staring at the sofa with its impression of bodies long ago risen, at a jacket still draped over the bannister, a briefcase of dated documents on the stairs. But then he said, "No, Lily. I've been looking into it legally. Because after all, it is a brownstone that abuts our house and there are issues to consider. Things to think about. What if, for example, the bank repossesses it and the city puts a methadone clinic in?"

That actually happened to my college roommate in Cleveland. She bought a beautiful house in Shaker Heights (her husband is a very successful corporate lawyer, though they are now estranged) and the state bought the house behind theirs which had been tied up in probate forever. They turned it into a halfway house for mentally ill men, some of whom she speculates have Tourette's syndrome. She says she has men standing in her backyard shouting, "Shut the fuck up" all day long.

But Roy was pleased with his discoveries. He told me not to worry. There is no cause for concern. Because someone pays the taxes on the house. Someone takes care of the mortgage. Who, I asked? But Roy, who is a lawyer and a prosecutor for the state, couldn't find out, though I'd thought he'd have more pull.

Roy and I have been together since high school, and we have known one another since the fifth grade. In his mother's family album, there is actually a picture of us trick-or-treating. He is the Lone Ranger and I am a Mouseketeer. I wear a black wig, black ears, to match Annette, and am curtsying dumbly. Roy stands in his mask, gun raised, his lips parted for his "Heigh Ho Silver." I have no recollection of him then or of that Halloween, but I've joked that this is pretty much the way things have been for the last thirty years, but he says that isn't so.

Roy hasn't given much thought to the people next door beyond how it impacts on our property values. But I think about them all the time. I think about them especially at night when I cannot sleep. I try to imagine what it would be like not to care if your roof leaks or your bills are paid. Just to walk away from your life. It has been years that I cannot sleep, almost as many years, it seems, since they went away. I think about where they might have gone and names like Christmas Island, Paraguay, and Corfu pop into my mind. Once I woke Roy in the middle of the night and said, "Maybe they went to Madagascar. There are beautiful birds there." And he said, "You're crazy, Lily, go back to sleep." But for years I have stayed up at night and mostly, I suppose, I am listening. For voices, an angry word, an impassioned cry. For something coming from the other side of the wall, the sound that someone has come home.

Roy hasn't been himself lately. He has a large caseload for which he is poorly paid. He has been working longer and longer hours and getting up earlier. He seems happy when he's shaving. Happy while he puts on his cologne. In fact he seems happiest when he's leaving the house. I know I shouldn't be thinking this way, but I think about it a lot. I wish it were as simple as another woman—something concrete that I could see. But it's not like that. When you've been married as long as I have—when you knew your husband while you still walked in the neighborhood in Halloween costumes—you know that a marriage lives in its details. Last week we had dinner with the Jensens. We went to a restaurant in the neighborhood, and after dinner Roy passed me the cream and sugar for my coffee. I just stared at him and said, "I take it black."

For a long time I've wanted to move away to Tucson or Florida. Two years ago, Roy Jr. moved out somewhere near Tucson—a place he says he loves—where he plans to stay. He lives with a girlfriend named Linda who gets on the phone—or he makes her get on the phone—and says, "Hello, Mrs. Riordan, how are you today?" as if she's trying to sell me a new line of cosmetics. They both do something with mutual funds. Roy Jr. says he has bought a house with a swimming pool and Linda has a little shed out back where she grows her own orchids. We have not been invited out yet, but Roy Jr. comes home at Christmas. I hope what he's doing is legal. Our daughter Sara is a psychologist (Roy says shrink). She is a pretty girl, though she could dress better, and she dates from time to time. But nothing seems to stick.

They don't remember Budd and Shirlee. Roy Jr. claims he has a dim recollection of people living next door. He says he can remember laughter. Bawdy, raucous laughter, the kind when someone sits down on a whoopee cushion. Once he says his ball went over the fence and a man who didn't seem angry or annoyed, just indifferent, tossed it back.

Sara, who is five years younger than Roy Jr., doesn't remember a thing about the house next door except its emptiness. She doesn't remember laughter or fights. All she remembers is no one there. A few times when she was little she had nightmares about the house. Her bedroom was next to their wall, and she says that when she slept she dreamed the things that could have happened to the people next door. That in truth they had never left but had been locked inside. The only thing Sara remembers, though she says she is not certain if it is a real memory or just what I have told her is worth remembering, is the garden filled with colored lanterns. Chinese lanterns in red and blue and gold, and the garden filled with the light of these lanterns while people milled about, drinks in hand. Strangers danced on the other side of our fence and there were bursts of laughter in the night.

A few years ago, boys began to hang out on the front stoop. Black boys, I have to say. They smoked cigarettes and dangled from the branches of the linden tree which shades the sidewalk between our house and Budd and Shirlee's. I asked the boys to go away and they did, but before they left they threw a stone through the parlor-floor window of the people next door.

This presented a problem. It wasn't our window, but since it was smashed, someone could go through their house and come out into the back where we are exposed. We thought of boarding it up, but Roy said—and he was right—that this would make the house a target. So we decided to have a new window put in; we kept the invoice just in case we ever had anyone to send it to. The day before we had the window put in, I went next door and climbed up their front steps as if I were going to borrow something. I peered through the hole in the glass and saw that the front rooms were full of stuff. Things. The accumulation of a lifetime. Bicycles, tennis racquets, the signs of a leisurely life. Dishes, books, magazines, debris that somebody really needed to clean out.

After we replaced the window, I ordered window boxes for the people next door. I thought I may as well make the front look prettier, less derelict. I planted geraniums and impatiens. Roy didn't notice, though he said that the front looked nicer than it had.

On the twentieth anniversary of the night Budd and Shirlee went away, Roy comes home very late. He has a new case—mob-related—and he won't talk about it. He's got witnesses on the witness protection program and says, "I don't need my wife under protective custody as well." It is true that Roy has put wealthy, successful New Yorkers to work in convenience stores in the Pacific Northwest. Maybe that's what happened to Budd and Shirlee, I suggest. A witness protection program. "They didn't have them twenty years ago," Roy says.

"It's their anniversary," I tell Roy. "Maybe we should open some champagne."

"What?"

"It's twenty years tonight that they are gone."

"How can you remember such things?"

That night as we lie in bed, I try to curl up close to him, but Roy is fast asleep. He is a waking-the-dead kind of sleeper. A gun could go off next to his ear and I don't think he'd budge. But I am a listener. It is just something I do. Now as I am lying there next to him I hear the voices. Whispers coming from the other side of the wall, voices speaking low as if they don't want to disturb us.

The next day when Roy goes to work, I sit in the garden, sipping coffee. It is a lovely day and I look at our garden—a perennial garden that we have worked on for years. A perfection of order. We have achieved continuous bloom, where one flower blossoms before the other dies. And then I look at their garden, if you can call it that. The thickets of shrubs and weeds, intertwined, no longer able to be separated. Everything is enmeshed, a maze. A small third-world kingdom, gone to seed. Then I see something on the ground that catches my eye. Lying in their yard, among the weeds, is a small red heart. It has writing on it, but from where I am standing on the other side of the fence, I can't make out what it says.

Dragging a chair to the fence, I balance myself as I climb. First one leg, then the other. I give a little push from the fence I am straddling and tumble onto the other side where I make a soft landing in the ivy. Little creatures scurry away. I wish I had a machete to chop through the thicket, the lianas and vines that entangle my legs. Thorns scratch and tear at my flesh as I move toward the place where the red heart lies. Reaching down, I pick it up, wishing I'd brought my reading glasses with me. "Scruffy," I make out at last, "I belong to . . ." The rest has been worn away, but it is the tag of a dog long dead. I don't remember them having a dog.

For a moment I feel as if someone is watching me. I glance toward the back windows where the kitchen is. To my surprise, the window is slightly ajar. Making my way through the thick overgrowth until I am standing at the filthy glass, I gaze into a kitchen. I can see a table, a sink, pots, and pans. I jab at the window and it glides open.

The window is low to the ground so I can ease myself in. I land in the kitchen which also serves as a family room. There is a sofa, a TV. It is all in order, fairly neat, though there are dishes in the sink, pots on the stove. I head down a corridor to the living room where I find pictures on a mantel. Budd and Shirlee in a golf cart or standing by a lake—all covered in dust. There is a small painting on the wall of a house in a meadow where wild flowers abound. Behind the house are snow-capped mountains. The painting has no signature so I imagine that Budd or Shirlee must have painted it. Perhaps they went here.

Dust motes flutter past as I double back through the parlor and find myself in the dining room. I am stunned to find the table set, with the remnants of a half-eaten meal still on the plates. The napkins stand on the table like teepees with the tribe long gone. On the plates are small, desiccated piles of what must have been mashed potatoes and peas; the potatoes have fork tracks running through them. Chicken bones have been gnawed. A salad sits, dry and withered like potpourri, in a bowl. When I touch it, it crumbles in my hand.

I pick up the napkin, which is covered with cobwebs and dust, and give it a good shake. A spider who has lived inside scurries away. I pull back the chair and sit at the table. Then I put the napkin in my lap and pull my chair close. I lean forward, resting my arms on the table, as if I'd been invited.

R. K. NARAYAN

Parrots Ltd.

Ramani resolved to become a parrot trader when he saw the following advertisement in a newspaper:

> "Wanted: a parrot trained to repeat the holy names of gods and slokas. Preferably in a musical manner. Prepared to pay Rs.50/- to Rs.1000/- according to the qualification of the parrot. Communications to be addressed to. . . . "

This advertisement caught his eye at a time when he was keenly searching for a congenial occupation. He was the author of *Blood-Bathed Love* and other epic efforts. He was certain that his works would be recognized by coming generations, but, at the moment, all the editors and the publishers in the world stood between him and his public. Hence his search for a 'congenial' occupation. And could there be any profession more suitable to a poet than parrot trade? You lived in the haunts of parrots and spent your time in their lovely company. What an opulent life for a poet! And in this luxury there was money. "Prepared to pay Rs.50/- to Rs.10000/-. . . . " The fifty-rupee variety was not his concern. He was not going to take the trouble to train a fourth-rate parrot. He was going to trade only in the thousand-rupee variety. The Ramani stamp on a parrot was going to stand for the best in parrots and nothing less. One such parrot a month and you made your thousand a month.

He had as yet very vague notions of the parrot business but he believed in luck and intuition. Sometimes he sat down, pen in hand, with next to nothing in his head, and at the end of three hours the sheets of paper before him would be filled with a poetic drama or a wonderful sonnet sequence. How was it done? Through luck and intuition. And the same qualities were now going to see him through the parrot business.

He answered the advertisement. Two days later he received a letter from one Mr. Madusudhan asking to see him at his residence in Saidapet. Ramani had no idea where parrots were available, nor did he know of any parrot that could talk. All the same, he had answered the advertisement in order to study the parrot market.

He inscribed on a blank visiting card "T.M.T. Ramani. Managing Director Parrots Ltd." and started for Saidapet. He took the electric train, found his way to Mr. Madusudhan's bungalow, and sent his card in. He was ushered into a hall where a fat man, sitting cross-legged on thick piles of cushion, welcomed him. "Ah, take that chair, Mr. T.M.T. Ramani," Mr. Madusudhan said. "For years I have been trying to secure a decent parrot. The one I had could recite the Bhagavad Gita at dawn. But the poor creature was mauled by our neighbor's cat, and died in spite of the best medical attention. All sorts of persons promised and disappointed me. I grew desperate and advertised."

"Ah, is that so?" Ramani asked warmly.

"I was able to get parrots that could only say 'How are you?' 'Ranga, Ranga,' 'Who is there?' and such other nonsense, but not one that could utter a prayer. I got another one, a cockatoo this time, beautiful colors, which used to greet visitors with 'Namaste,' and then would recite four stanzas of *Soundarya Lahari,* you know, Shankara's inspired composition. It filled my home with holy sounds morning to night. . . . "

"Don't you like radio programs, which start with devotional songs every morning?"

"No, never. I abominate radio and television and tape-recorder. That is one of the reasons why my wife and children live away from me."

"Where are they?" Ramani asked solicitously.

"Don't ask me. I am happy without them. A parrot is good enough company for me."

"What happened to the cockatoo from Singapore?"

"Some fool of a servant left the cage open one day. It flew off, perched itself on the jack-fruit tree there, and mocked me, fell into bad company, and then I lost sight of it."

"What a pity!" Ramani said sympathetically. "What a pity that we didn't know each other before. We specialize in religious parrots. I am the trainer in our firm, you know." He added as an afterthought, "I have engaged four Brahmin priests in my department to coach the parrots."

"Ah, how cursed am I that I did not know you before. How is it that I don't see your advertisements anywhere?"

"We don't advertise. We have our select clientele and we usually do not take up extra business."

"How is it that I have not had the pleasure of meeting your parrots anywhere in these parts?"

"Our religious parrots sell steadily in Benares and in a few pilgrim centers in the North, but the bulk of our business is in South Africa and Malaya."

Ramani was offered fruits and coffee. "I should like to see your farm sometime," Mr. Madusudhan said.

"With pleasure," Ramani said. "But I am going up north for a few weeks on business. As soon as I return I will take you round our parrot farm." He had a sudden inspiration and added, "I have trained a few parrots in the business line too. They just quote prices and so on and are suitable for business houses. I have some for coffee houses too. These just reel off the menu. All labor-saving devices. In these days of rush and hustle they ought to be very valuable. These business-line parrots save the energy of the shop assistants who have to repeat the same thing over and over again to every customer. All the saved-up energy could be utilized by the principal of the firm for more productive purposes. This is the place of the parrot in modern economy. Would you care to see our business parrots?"

"No," said Mr. Madusudhan. "They aren't useful to me. I have retired from business. My thoughts are with God now. I want a bird that will be filling my house with holy sounds. I want a bird that will utter slokas. I am prepared to pay even one-thousand five-hundred rupees for such a parrot. Please tell me when I can come for my parrot."

"I can't say definitely when I can have one ready for you. I have some advance bookings on hand. In about two months I think I can meet your order."

In fairness to Ramani, it must be said that he had not intended to lie. He had gone there in order to understand the conditions of the parrot market, but in his talk with Mr. Madusudhan his imagination caught fire and he saw Parrots Ltd. gradually revealed to him in all its detail of organization. It was more a loud brown study than a downright falsehood.

Ramani went home and definitely made up his mind to start the parrot business. His first transaction would be with Mr. Madusudhan. He would devote all his waking hours in the next two months to training a parrot for Mr. Madusudhan. The labor would be worth Rs. 1500. In the course of time, with a little practice, he could have a parrot in a month ready for sale. As for customers, he was confident that he could find at least one Madusudhan a month in this wide world. Certain other details of the work bothered him. Once a customer got his parrot, the transaction was done with as long as the parrot lived. What was the normal longevity of a parrot? Probably ten years. So it meant that normally a customer would not return for ten years. For a moment Ramani wondered if it would be wise to earn the confidence of his customers' servants and bribe them to leave the cages open. . . .

The instinct that leads the cow to the grass and the fly to the sugar bowl was responsible for taking Ramani to Moore Market, and there one Kandan became his friend. Kandan had just been loitering around when he noticed Ramani making eager inquiries at the stalls. He introduced himself to him: "Master in need of a parrot?"

"Yes."

"What sort of parrots?"

"A parrot that can be trained to talk. Have you one?"

"Years ago when I was in the army I had a parrot. It could give commands for the troop drill. It was our best companion at Mespot; but my officer took a fancy to it and I gave it to him. I know where parrots are to be had and I can get you one if you want. . . ." In the course of an hour or two, squatting on a patch of grass in front of Moore Market and talking, a great friendship developed between Ramani and Kandan. They came to an agreement. Kandan was to secure a young parrot immediately and train it. He was to deliver the parrot complete in two months and receive twenty rupees in return. In due course he would be employed by Parrots Ltd., on a salary of two hundred rupees a month. Before they parted for the evening, a couple of rupees had changed hands.

Two days later Kandan came to Ramani's house and told him that he had purchased a young parrot from some villager. Thereafter he dropped in frequently to keep Ramani informed of the physical and mental progress of the parrot. Sometimes he demanded an odd rupee or two for buying certain secret drugs essential for the parrot's throat. In a few days he came to announce that the parrot was just able to repeat 'Krishna, Krishna' and also the first two lines of a prayer to God Subramanya. Ramani was quite pleased with Kandan's work and promised to give him a bonus over the agreed amount. Even then the balance would be in his favor. He drafted the balance sheet thus:

EXPENDITURE

		Rs	A	P
Cost of parrot	..	20	0	0
Special throat drugs	..	10	0	0
Trainer's fee	..	50	0	0
Total	..	80	0	0

INCOME

		Rs	A	P
Selling price of trained parrot	..	1500	0	0
Investment	..	80	0	0
Profit	..	1420	0	0

Ramani clamored so much to see the parrot that one dark night Kandan brought a cage with a heavy piece of cloth wrapped round it.

"I say I can't see anything, take away the cover," Ramani said.

"It can't be done," Kandan replied firmly. "The bird is still young. It will die of paralysis if allowed to open its eyes on these new surroundings all of a sudden."

"But how am I to see the bird?" Ramani asked.

"You may peep through this chink if you like."

Ramani lifted the cage and was about to hold it against the light. "Ah, don't do it," Kandan screamed. "Do you want to blind it for life?"

Ramani put down the cage. He applied his eyes to a very small opening in the cloth wrapping and said, "I see some faint shape inside but I can't say whether it is a ball of wool or a chicken or a parrot." At this Kandan looked so hurt that Ramani felt sorry for allowing these frivolous words to cross his lips and apologized. Ramani asked why the bird was not fluttering its wings. There was a danger of its wasting all its energy, Kandan explained. Every ounce had to be conserved for cultivating its voice. Ramani desired to hear the voice of the parrot. Kandan declared that at nights parrots could not be made to talk.

"Well, well. You may deliver it to me in working order on the 13th of next month."

"No sir, thirteen is a bad number. I'll deliver on the 12th or the 14th."

"Very well, don't delay."

"On the 14th definitely. It will be the most garrulous parrot one would ever wish to meet."

"Mere garrulity is not enough," Ramani said. "It must be the most religious-minded parrot."

On the twelfth of the following month Kandan brought a green parrot in a cage. It was a rakish-looking, plump bird. The sight of it sent a thrill through Ramani. He had not thought that an ambition could be so readily realized. A small thread was tied round the beak of the parrot. Kandan explained, "It is better that you keep its beak tied up till you reach your customer's place. Otherwise the rascal will talk all the way and gather a crowd behind you." Ramani insisted on examining the full accomplishments of the parrot now. Kandan requested Ramani to go out of the room for a few minutes and he would untie the thread and coax the bird. Of course it could be made to talk even in Ramani's presence but then it might take time, and he (Kandan) would now have to go and attend his aunt, who was lying in a serious condition in General Hospital. He could coax the bird much quicker if Ramani would oblige him by going out. Ramani went out of the room. Presently he heard the gruff voice of Kandan coaxing the bird. And then the parrot uttered in a melodious voice, "Krishna, Krishna," "Rama, Rama," and the first two lines of a prayer to God Subramanya. "As soon as you take him over to your customer's place, snip off the thread with scissors. If you give him a red, ripe chili he will be very friendly with you in an hour or two, and then you can coax him to utter the holy sounds."

"Right, thanks. Do you want your money now?"

"Hmm, yes," said Kandan. "I have to buy some medicines for my aunt."

Ramani took his savings bank book, went to the Vepery Post Office, bled his account white, and handed fifty rupees to Kandan. The old clerk at the counter looked on Ramani's recent withdrawals with marked disfavor. Ramani said apologetically, "I will come back in the evening and deposit one thousand rupees."

Kandan took leave of Ramani and hurried away to his aunt's bedside.

"Ah! Ah! Come in, Mr. Ramani," said Mr. Madusudhan as soon as Ramani appeared in Saidapet with a parrot in hand. "I am so happy that you have brought the parrot. Really! Really! Or am I dreaming? Ah, you are correct to the hour."

"In business, punctuality is everything," said Ramani. Mr. Madusudhan took him in. He inspected the cage with delight, and asked again and again if the holy names of gods were going to echo through his halls thenceforth. "Does the bird really utter the names of Krishna and Rama?"

"Absolutely," Ramani replied. "It was trained under my personal supervision."

They sat on a sofa with the cage between them. Ramani took a pair of scissors and snipped off the thread tied round the parrot's beak. He took out a ripe chili and gave it to the bird. It ate the chili gratefully.

Ramani said, "Since this is a new place it will take about half an hour for him to open his mouth."

"Let him. Let him take his own time," said Mr. Madusudhan. Ramani thrust another chili into the cage and the parrot attacked it with vigor. They watched it for some time, and then Mr. Madusudhan asked, "Will you have your check immediately or sometime later?"

Ramani was not used to such questions. He grinned awkwardly and said, "Oh, I have not brought the receipt book."

"It does not matter. You can send the receipt later on."

"May we hope for another order from you?"

It was at this stage that the shrieking question was asked in Tamil, "Are you drunk or mad?" It was followed by the command "Get out, you fool!" Ramani looked at the cage in consternation. The parrot had eaten all the chili and was now in a loquacious mood. He chuckled quietly, and winked at Ramani before saying in lucid English, "Hands up or I shoot! You son of a. . . ."

Mr. Madusudhan choked as he asked, "Is this the kind of holy sound that is going to fill my house?" He glared at Ramani.

"There is some mistake," mumbled Ramani. He suddenly rose and fled, leaving the cage behind. He did not stop to turn and look till he reached his house in Vepery.

Two days later a small advertisement in a paper said: "LOST: a green parrot in a cage kept in the frost veranda. Finder will be rewarded. . . ." Ramani wondered for a moment if it would be worth his while to put this person on the track of the parrot. But he realized that he might be hauled up for theft. For some time he lived in terror of being hunted down by Mr. Madusudhan, but fortunately the visiting card he had left behind contained only his name and not his address.

JOYCE CAROL OATES

Mark of Satan

A woman had come to save his soul and he wasn't sure he was ready.

It isn't every afternoon in the dead heat of summer, cicadas screaming out of the trees like lunatics, the sun a soft, slow explosion in the sky, that a husky young woman comes on foot rapping shyly at the screen door of a house not even yours, a house in which you are a begrudged guest, to save your soul. And she'd brought an angel-child with her too.

Thelma McCord, or was it McCrae. And Magdalena who was a wisp of a child, perhaps four years old.

They were Church of the Holy Witness, headquarters Scranton, PA. They were God's own, and proud. Saved souls glowing like neon out of their identical eye sockets.

Thelma was an "ordained missionary" and this was her "first season of itinerary" and she apologized for disturbing his privacy but did he, would he, surrender but a few minutes of his time to the Teachings of the Holy Witness?

He'd been taken totally by surprise. He'd been dreaming a disagreeable churning-sinking dream and suddenly he'd been wakened, summoned, by a faint but persistent knocking at the front door. Tugging on wrinkled khaki shorts and yanking up the zipper in angry haste—he was already wearing a T-shirt frayed and tight in the shoulders—he'd padded barefoot to the screen door, blinking the way a mollusk might blink if it had eyes. In a house unfamiliar to you, it's like waking to somebody else's dream. And there on the front stoop out of a shimmering-hot August afternoon he'd wished to sleep through, this girlish-eager young female missionary. An angel of God sent special delivery to *him*.

Quickly, before he could change his mind, before *no! no!* intervened, he invited Thelma and little Magdalena inside. Out of the wicked hot sun—quick.

"Thank you," the young woman said, beaming with surprise and gratitude. "Isn't he a kind, thoughtful man, Magdalena!"

Mother and daughter were heat-dazed, clearly yearning for some measure of coolness and simple human hospitality. Thelma was carrying a bulky straw purse and a tote bag with a red plastic sheen that appeared to be heavy with books and pamphlets. The child's face was pinkened with sunburn, and her gaze was so downcast she stumbled on the threshold of the door and her mother murmured *Tsk!* and clutched her hand tighter, as if, already, before their visit had begun, Magdalena had brought them both embarrassment.

He led them inside and shut the door. The living room opened directly off the front door. The house was a small three-bedroom tract ranch with simulated redwood siding; it was sparsely furnished, the front room uncarpeted, with a butterscotch-vinyl sofa, twin butterfly chairs in fluorescent lime, and a coffee table that was a slab of weather-stained granite set atop cinder blocks. (The granite slab was in fact a grave marker, so old and worn by time that its name and dates were illegible. His sister Gracie, whose rented house this was, had been given the coffee table slab by a former boyfriend.) A stain the color of tea and the shape of an octopus disfigured a corner of the ceiling but the missionaries, seated with self-conscious murmurs of thanks on the sofa, would not see it.

He needed a name to offer to Thelma McCord, or McCrae, who had so freely offered her name to him. "Flash," he said, inspired, "my name is Flashman."

He was a man no longer young yet by no means old; nor even, to the eye of a compassionate observer, middle-aged. His ravaged looks, his blood-veined eyes, appeared healable. He was a man given, however, to the habit of irony, distasteful to him in execution but virtually impossible to resist. (Like masturbation, to which habit he was, out of irony too, given as well.) When he spoke to Thelma he heard a quaver in his voice that was his quickened, erratic pulse but might sound to another's ear like civility.

He indicated they should take the sofa, and he lowered himself into the nearest butterfly chair on shaky legs. When the damned contraption nearly overturned, the angel-child Magdalena, fluffy pale-blonde hair and delicate features, jammed her thumb into her mouth to keep from giggling. But her eyes were narrowed, alarmed.

"Mr. Flashman, so pleased to make your acquaintance," Thelma said uncertainly. Smiling at him with worried eyes, possibly contemplating whether he was Jewish.

Contemplating the likelihood of a Jew, a descendant of God's chosen people, living in the scraggly foothills of southwestern Pennsylvania, in a derelict ranch house seven miles from Waynesburg with a front yard that looked as if motorcycles had torn it up. Would a Jew be three days' unshaven, jaws like sandpaper, knobbily barefoot and hairy-limbed as a gorilla? Would a Jew so readily welcome a Holy Witness into his house?

Offer them drinks, lemonade, but no, he was thinking, *no.*

This, an opportunity for him to confront goodness, to look innocence direct in the eye, should not be violated.

Thelma promised that her visit would not take many minutes of Mr. Flashman's time. For time, she said, smiling breathlessly, is of the utmost. "That is one of the reasons I am here today."

Reaching deep into the tote bag to remove, he saw with a sinking heart, a hefty black Bible with gilt-edged pages and a stack of pamphlets printed on pulp paper—THE WITNESS. Then easing like a brisk mechanical doll into her recitation.

The man who called himself Flash was making every effort to listen. He knew this was important, there are no accidents. Hadn't he wakened in the night to a pounding heart and a taste of bile with the premonition that something, one of *his things,* was to happen soon? Whether of his volition and calculation, or seemingly by accident (but there are no accidents), he could not know. Leaning forward, gazing at the young woman with an elbow on his bare knee, the pose of Rodin's Thinker, listening hard. Except the woman was a dazzlement of sweaty-fragrant female flesh. Speaking passionately of the love of God and the passion of Jesus Christ and the Book of Revelation of St. John the Divine and the Testament of the Witness. Then eagerly opening her Bible on her knees and dipping her head toward it so that her sand-colored, limp-curly hair fell into her face and she had to brush it away repeatedly—he was fascinated by the contrapuntal gestures, the authority of the Bible and the meek dipping of the head and the way in which, with childlike unconscious persistence, she pushed her hair out of her face. Unconscious too of her grating singsong voice, an absurd voice in which no profound truth could ever reside, and of her heavy, young breasts straining against the filmy material of her lavender-print dress, her fattish-muscular calves and good, broad feet in what appeared to be white wicker ballerina slippers.

The grimy venetian blinds of the room were drawn against the glaring heat. It was above ninety degrees outside and there had been no soaking rains for weeks and in every visible tree hung ghostly bagworm nests. In his sister's bedroom a single-window-unit air conditioner vibrated noisily and it had been in this room, on top of, not in, the bed, that he'd been sleeping when the knocking came at the front door; the room that was his had no air conditioner. Hurrying out, he'd left the door to his sister's bedroom open and now a faint trail of cool-metallic air coiled out into the living room and so he fell to thinking that his visitors would notice the cool air and inquire about it and he would say, Yes, there *is* air conditioning in this house, in one of the bedrooms, shall we go into that room and be more comfortable?

Now the Bible verses were concluded. Thelma's fair, fine skin glowed with excitement. Like a girl who has shared her most intimate secret and expects you now to share yours, Thelma lifted her eyes to Flash's and asked, almost boldly, Was he aware of the fact that God loved him? He squirmed hearing such words. Momentarily unable to respond, he laughed, embarrassed, shook his head, ran his fingers over his sandpaper jaws, and mumbled, No, not really, he guessed that he was not aware of that fact, not really.

Thelma said that was why she was here, to bring the good news to him. That God loved him whether he knew of Him or acknowledged Him. And the Holy Witness was their mediator.

Flashman mumbled, Is that so. A genuine blush darkening his face.

Thelma insisted, Yes, it *is* so. A brimming in her close-set eyes, which were the bluest eyes Flash had ever glimpsed except in glamour photos of models, movie stars, naked centerfolds. He said apologetically that he wasn't one hundred percent sure how his credit stood with God these days. "God and me," he said, with a boyish, tucked-in smile, "have sort of lost contact over the years."

Which was *the* answer the young female missionary was primed to expect. Turning to the little girl, she whispered in her ear, "Tell Mr. Flashman the good, good news, Magdalena!" and like a wind-up doll, the blonde child began to recite in a breathy, high-pitched voice, "We can lose God but God never loses *us*. We can despair of God but God never despairs of *us*. The Holy Witness records, 'He that overcometh shall not be hurt by the second death.'" As abruptly as she'd begun, the child ceased, her mouth going slack on the word *death*.

It was an impressive performance. Yet there was something chilling about it. Flash grinned and winked at the child in his uneasiness and said, "Second death, eh? What about the first?" But Magdalena just gaped at him. Her left eye losing its focus as if coming unmoored.

The more practiced Thelma quickly intervened. She took up both her daughter's hands in hers and in a brisk patty-cake rhythm chanted, "As the Witness records, 'God shall wipe away all tears from their eyes; and there *will be* no more death.'"

Maybe it was so? So simple? *No more death.*

He was bemused by the simplicity of fate. In this house unknown to him as recently as last week, in this rural no-man's-land where his older sister Gracie had wound up a county social worker toiling long grueling hours five days a week and forced to be grateful for the shitty job, he'd heard a rapping like a summons to his secret blood padding barefoot to the dream doorway that's shimmering with light and there she *is.*

"Excuse me, Thelma—would you and Magdalena like some lemonade?"

Thelma immediately demurred out of countrybred politeness as he'd expected, so he asked Magdalena, who appeared to be parched with thirst, poor exploited child, but, annoyingly, she was too shy to even nod her head yes, please. Flash, stimulated by challenge, apologized for not having fresh-squeezed lemonade—calculating that Thelma would have to accept to prove she wasn't offended by his offer —adding that he was about to get some lemonade for himself, icy-cold, and would they please join him, so Thelma, lowering her eyes, said yes. As if he'd reached out to touch her and she hadn't dared draw back.

In the kitchen, out of sight, he moved swiftly—which was why his name was Flash. For a man distracted, a giant, black-feathered eagle tearing out his liver, he moved with surprising alacrity. But that had always been his way.

Opening the fridge, nostrils pinching against the stale stink inside, trying his best to ignore his sister Gracie's depressed housekeeping, he took out the stained Tupperware pitcher of Bird's Eye lemonade— thank God, there was some. Tart chemical taste he'd have to mollify, in his own glass, with an ounce or two of Gordon's gin. For his missionary visitors he ducked into his bedroom and located his stash and returned to the kitchen counter, crumbling swiftly between his palms several chalky-white pills, six milligrams each of barbiturate, enough to fell a healthy horse, reducing them to gritty powder to dissolve in the greenish lemonade he poured into two glasses: the taller for Thelma, the smaller for Magdalena. He wondered what the little girl weighed—

forty pounds? Thirty? Fifty? He had no idea, children were mysteries to him. His own childhood was a mystery to him. But he wouldn't want Magdalena's heart to stop beating.

He'd seen a full-sized man go glassy-eyed and clutch at his heart and topple over stone dead overdosing on—what? Heroin. It was a clean death, so far as deaths go, but it came out of the corner of your eye, you couldn't prepare.

Carefully setting the three glasses of lemonade, two tall and slim for the adults, the other roly-poly for sweet little Magdalena, on a laminated tray. Returning then, humming cheerfully to the airless living room where his visitors were sitting primly on the battered sofa as if, in his absence, they hadn't moved an inch. Shyly yet with trembling hands, both reached for their glasses. "Say 'thankyou, sir,'" Thelma whispered to Magdalena, who whispered, "Thankyou, sir," and lifted her glass to her lips.

Thelma disappointed him by taking only a ladylike sip, then dabbing at her lips with a tissue. "Delicious," she murmured. But setting the glass down as if it were a temptation. Poor Magdalena was holding her glass in both hands taking quick swallows, but at a sidelong glance from her mother, she too set her glass down on the tray.

Flash said, as if hurt, "There's lots more sugar if it isn't sweet enough."

But Thelma insisted, No, it was fine. Taking up, with the look of a woman choosing among several rare gems, one of the pulp-printed pamphlets. Now, Flash guessed, she'd be getting down to business. Enlisting him to join the Church of the Holy Ghost, or whatever it was—Holy Witness?

She named names and cited dates that flew past him—except for the date Easter Sunday, 1899 when, apparently, there'd been a "shower from the heavens" north of Scranton, PA—and he nodded to encourage her though she hardly needed encouraging, taking deep, thirsty sips from his lemonade to encourage her too. Out of politeness Thelma did lift her glass and take a chaste swallow but no more. Maybe there was a cult prescription against frozen foods, chemical drinks? The way the Christian Scientists, unless it was the Seventh Day Adventists, forbade blood transfusions because such was "eating blood," which was outlawed by the Bible.

Minutes passed. The faint trickle of metallic-cool air touched the side of his feverish face. He tried not to show his impatience with Thelma, fixing instead on the amazing fact of her: a woman not known to him an hour before, now sitting less than a yard away addressing him as if, out of all of the universe, *he mattered*. Loving how she sat wide-hipped and settled into the vinyl cushions like a partridge in a nest. Knees and ankles together, chunky farmgirl feet in the discount-mart wicker flats, half-moons of perspiration darkening the underarms of her floral-print dress. It was a Sunday school kind of dress, lavender rayon with a wide, white collar and an awkward flared skirt and cloth-covered buttons the size of half-dollars. Beneath it the woman would be wearing a full slip, no half-slip for her. Damp from her warm, pulsing body. No doubt a white brassiere—D cups—and white cotton panties, the waist and legs of which left red rings in her flesh. Undies damp, too. And the crotch of the panties, damp. Just possibly stained. She was bare-legged, no stockings, a concession to the heat: just raw, female leg, reddish-blond transparent hairs on the calves, for she was not a woman to shave her body hair. Nor did she wear makeup. No such vanity. Her cheeks were flushed as if rouged and her lips were naturally moist and rosy. Her skin would be hot to the touch. She was twenty-eight or -nine years old and probably Magdalena was not her first child, but her youngest. She had the sort of female body mature by early adolescence, beginning to go flaccid by thirty-five. That fair, thin skin that wears out from too much smiling and aiming to please. Suggestion of a double chin. Hips would be spongy and cellulite-puckered. Kneaded like white bread, squeezed, banged, and bruised. Moist heat of a big bush of curly public hair. Secret crevices of pearl drops of moisture he'd lick away with his tongue.

Another woman would have been aware of Flash's calculating eyes on her like ants swarming over sugar, but not this impassioned missionary for the Church of the Holy Witness. Had an adder risen quivering with desire before her, she would have taken no heed. She was reading from one of THE WITNESS pamphlets and her gaze was shining and inward as she evoked in a hushed, little-girl voice a vision of bearded prophets raving in the deserts of Smyrna and covenants made by Jesus Christ to generations of sinners up to this very hour. Jesus Christ was the most spectacular of the prophets, it seemed, for out of his mouth came a sharp, two-edged sword casting terror into all who beheld. Yet he was a poet, his words had undeniable power, for here was Flash the man squirming in his butterfly chair as Thelma recited tremulously, "'And Jesus spake: I am he that liveth, and was death; and, behold, I am alive for evermore; and have the keys of hell and death.'"

There was a pause. A short distance away a neighbor was running a chain saw, and out on the highway cars, trucks, thunderous diesel vehicles passed in an erratic whooshing stream, and on all sides beyond the house's walls the air buzzed, quivered, vibrated, rang with the insects of late summer but otherwise it was quiet, it was silent. Like a vacuum waiting to be filled.

The child Magdalena, unobserved by her mother, had drained her glass of lemonade and licked her lips with a flicking pink tongue and was beginning to be drowsy. She wore a pink rayon dress like a nightie with a machine-stamped lace collar, she had tiny feet in white socks and shiny white plastic shoes. Flash saw, yes, the child's left eye had a cast in it. The right eye perceived you head-on but the left drifted outward like a sly, wayward moon.

A defect in an eye of so beautiful a child would not dampen Flash's ardor. He was certain of that.

Ten minutes, fifteen. By now it was apparent that Thelma did not intend to drink her lemonade though Flash had drained his own glass and wiped his mouth with gusto. Did she suspect? Did she sense something wrong? But she'd taken no notice of Magdalena, who had drifted off into a light doze, her angel-head drooping and a thread of saliva shining on her chin. Surely a suspicious Christian mother would not have allowed her little girl to drink spiked lemonade handed her by a barefoot, bare-legged pervert, possibly a Jew, with eyes like the yanked-up roots of thistles—that was encouraging.

"Your lemonade, Thelma," Flash said, with a host's frown, "it will be getting warm if you don't—"

Thelma seemed not to hear. With a bright smile she was asking, "Have you been baptized, Mr. Flashman?"

For a moment he could not think who Mr. Flashman was. The gin coursing through his veins, which ordinarily buoyed him up like debris riding the crest of a flood and provided him with an acute clarity of mind, had had a dulling, downward sort of effect. He was frightened of the possibility of one of *his things* veering out of his control, for in the past when this had happened the consequences were always very bad. For him as for others.

His face burned. "I'm afraid that's my private business, Thelma. I don't bare my heart to any stranger who walks in off the road."

Thelma blinked, startled. Yet was immediately repentant. "Oh, I know! I have overstepped myself, please forgive me, Mr. Flashman!"

Such passion quickened the air between them. Flash felt a stab of excitement. But ducking his head, boyish-repentant too, he murmured, "No, it's okay, I'm just embarrassed, I guess. I don't truly *know* if I was baptized. I was an orphan discarded at birth, set out with the trash. There's a multitude of us scorned by man and God. What happened to me before the age of twelve is lost to me. Just a whirlwind. A whirlpool of oblivion."

Should have left his sister's bedroom door shut, though. To keep the room cool. If he had to carry or drag this woman any distance—the child wouldn't be much trouble—he'd be miserable by the time he got to where he wanted to go.

Thelma all but exploded with solicitude, leaning forward as if about to gather him up in her arms.

"Oh, that's the saddest thing I have ever heard, Mr. Flashman! I wish one of our elders was here right now to counsel you as I cannot! 'Set out with the trash'—can it be? Can any human mother have been so cruel?"

"If it was a cruel mother, which I don't contest, it was a cruel God guiding her hand, Thelma—wasn't it?"

Thelma blinked rapidly. This was a proposition not entirely new to her, Flash surmised, but one which required a moment's careful and conscious reflection. She said, uncertainly at first and then with gathering momentum, "The wickedness of the world is Satan's hand, and the ways of Satan, as with the ways of God, are not to be comprehended by man."

"What's Satan got to do with this? I thought we were talking about the good guys."

"Our Savior Jesus Christ—"

"*Our* Savior? Who says? On my trash heap I looked up, and He looked down, and He said, 'Fuck you, kid. Life *is* unfair.'"

Thelma's expression was one of absolute astonishment. Like a cow, Flash thought ungallantly, in the instant the sledgehammer comes crashing down on her head.

Flash added, quick to make amends, "I thought this was about me, Thelma, about my soul. I thought the Holy Witness or whoever had something special to say to *me*."

Thelma was sitting stiff, her hands clasping her knees. One of THE WITNESS pamphlets had fallen to the floor and the hefty Bible too would have slipped had she not caught it. Her eyes now were alert and wary and she knew herself to be in the presence of an enemy, yet did not know that more than theology was at stake. "The Holy Witness does have something special to say to you, Mr. Flashman. Which is why I am here. There is a growing pestilence in the land, flooding the Midwest with the waters of the wrathful Mississippi, last year razing the Sodom and Gomorrah of Florida. Everywhere there are droughts and famines and earthquakes and volcanic eruptions and plagues—all signs that the old world is nearing its end. As the Witness proclaimed in the Book of Revelation that is our sacred scripture, 'There will be a new heaven and a new earth, as the first heaven and the first earth pass away. And the Father on His throne declaring, Behold I make all things new—'"

Flash interrupted, "None of this *is* new! It's been around for how many millenia, Thelma, and what good's it done for anybody?"

"—'I am Alpha and Omega, the beginning and the end,'" Thelma continued, unheeding, rising from the sofa like a fleshy angel of wrath in her lavender dress that stuck to her belly and legs, fumbling to gather up her Bible, her pamphlets, her dazed child, "'—I will give unto him that is a thirst of the fountain of life freely but the fearful, and unbeliev-ing, and the abominable, and murderers, and all liars, shall sink into the lake which burneth with fire and brimstone: which is the second death.'" Her voice rose jubilantly on the word *death*.

Flash struggled to disentangle himself from the butterfly chair. The gin had done something weird to his legs—they were numb, and rubbery. Cursing, he fell to the floor, the rock-hard carpetless floor, as Thelma roused Magdalena and lifted her to her feet and half-carried her to the door. Flash tried to raise himself by gripping the granite cof-fee table but this too collapsed, the cinder blocks giving way and the heavy slab crashing down on his right hand. Three fingers were broken at once, but in the excitement he seemed not to notice. "Wait! You can't leave me now! I need you!"

At the door Thelma called back, panting, "Help *is* needed here. There is Satan in this house."

Flash stumbled to his feet and followed the woman to the door, calling after her, "What do you mean, 'Satan in this house'—there is no Satan, there is no Devil, it's all in the heads of people like you. You're religious maniacs! You're mad! Wait—"

He could not believe the woman was escaping so easily. That *his thing* was no thing of *his* at all.

Hauling purse and bulky tote bag, her sleep-dazed daughter on her hip, Thelma was striding in her white wicker ballerina flats swiftly yet without apparent haste or panic out to the gravel driveway. There was a terrible quivering of the sun-struck air. Cicadas screamed like fire sirens. Flash tried to follow after, propelling himself on his rubbery legs which were remote from his head which was too small for his body and at the end of a swaying stalk. He was laughing, crying, "You're a joke, people like you! You're tragic victims of ignorance and superstition! You don't belong in the twentieth century with the rest of us! You're the losers of the world! You can't cope! *You* need salvation!"

He stared amazed at the rapidly departing young woman—at the dignity in her body, the high-held head, and the very arch of the backbone. Her indignation was not fear, an indignation possibly too primitive to concede to fear, like nothing in his experience nor even in his imagination. If this was a movie, he was thinking, panicked, the missionary would be *walking out of the frame,* leaving him behind—just him.

"Help! Wait! Don't leave me here alone!"

He was screaming, terrified. He perceived that his life was of no more substance than a cicada's shriek. He'd stumbled as far as the driveway when a blinding light struck him like a sword piercing his eyes and brain.

He'd fallen to his knees then in the driveway, amid sharp gravel and broken glass, and he was bawling like a child beyond all pride, beyond all human shame. His head was bowed, sun beating down on the balding crown of his head. His very soul wept through his eyes for he knew he would die, and nothing would save him, not even irony. *Don't flatter yourself you matter enough even to be grieved! Asshole!*—no, not even his wickedness would save him. Yet seeing him stricken, the young Christian woman could not walk away. He cried, "Satan *is* here! In me! He speaks through me! It isn't me! Please help me, don't leave me to die!" His limbs shook as if palsied and his teeth chattered despite the heat. Where the young woman stood wavering there was a blurry, shimmering figure of light and he pleaded with it, tore open his chest, belly to expose the putrescent tumor of Satan choking his entrails, he begged for mercy, for help, for Christ's love, until at last the young woman cautiously approached him to a distance of about three feet, knelt too, though not in the gravel driveway but in the grass, and by degrees put aside her distrust. Seeing the sickness in this sinner howling to be saved, she bowed her head and clasped her hands to her breasts and began to pray loudly, triumphantly, "O Heavenly Father, help this tormented sinner to repent of his sins and to be saved by Your Only Begotten Son that he might stand by the throne of Your righteousness, help all sinners to be saved by the Testament of the Holy Witness—"

How many minutes the missionary prayed over the man who had in jest called himself Flashman he would not afterward know. For there seemed to be a fissure in time itself. The two were locked in ecstasy as in the most intimate of embraces in the fierce heat of the sun, and in the impulsive generosity of her spirit the young woman reached out to clasp his trembling hands in hers and to squeeze them tight. Admonishing him, "Pray! Pray to Jesus Christ! Every hour of every day pray to Him in your heart!" She was weeping too and her face was flushed and swollen and shining with tears. He pleaded with her not to leave him, for Satan was still with him, he feared Satan's grip on his soul, but there was a car at the end of the driveway toward which the child Magdalena had made her unsteady way and now a man's voice called, "Thelma! Thel-ma!" and at once the young woman rose to her full height, brushing her damp hair out of her face, and with a final admonition to him to love God and Christ and abhor Satan and all his ways, she was gone, vanished into the light out of which she had come.

Alone, he remained kneeling, too weak to stand. Rocking and swaying in the sun. His parched lips moved, uttering babble. In a frenzy of self-abnegation he ground his bare knees in the gravel and shattered glass, deep and deeper into the pain so that he might bleed more freely, bleeding all impurity from him or at least mutilating his flesh, so that in the arid stretch of years before him that would constitute the remainder of his life he would possess a living memory of this hour, scars he might touch, read like Braille.

When Gracie Shuttle returned home hours later, she found her brother Harvey in the bathroom dabbing at his wounded knees with a blood-soaked towel, picking bits of gravel and glass out of his flesh with a tweezers. And his hand—several fingers of his right hand were as swollen as sausages and grotesquely bruised. Gracie was a tall, lank, sardonic woman of forty-one with deep-socketed eyes that rarely acknowledged surprise; yet, seeing Harvey in this remarkable posture, sitting hunched on the toilet seat, a sink of blood-tinged water beside him, she let out a long, high whistle. "What the hell happened to *you*?" she asked.

Harvey raised his eyes to hers. He did not appear to be drunk or drugged; his eyes were terribly bloodshot, as if he'd had one of his crying jags, but his manner was unnervingly composed. His face was ravaged and sunburnt in uneven splotches as if it had been baked. He said, "I've been on my knees to Gethsemane and back. It's too private to speak of."

From years ago, when by an accident of birth they'd shared a household with two hapless adults who were their parents, Gracie knew that her younger brother in such a state was probably telling the truth, or a kind of truth; she knew also that he would never reveal it to her. She waved in his face a pulp religious pamphlet she'd found on the living room floor beside the collapsed granite marker. "And what the hell is *this*?" she demanded.

But again with that look of maddening calm, Harvey said, "It's my private business, Gracie. Please shut the door on your way out."

Gracie slammed the door in Harvey's face and charged through the house to the rear where wild, straggly bamboo was choking the yard. Since she'd moved in three years before, the damned bamboo had spread everywhere, marching from the marshy part of the property where the cesspool was located too close to the surface of the soil. Just her luck! And her with a master's degree in social work from the University of Pennsylvania! She'd hoped, she'd expected more from her education, as from life. She lit a cigarette and rapidly smoked it, exhaling luxuriant streams of smoke through her nostrils. "Well, fuck you," she said, laughing. She frequently laughed when she was angry, and she laughed a good deal these days.

It *was* funny. Whatever it was, it *was* funny—her parolee kid brother, once an honors student, now a balding, middle-aged man picking tenderly at his knees that looked as if somebody had slashed them with a razor. That blasted-sober look in the poor guy's eyes she hadn't seen in twelve years—since one of his junkie buddies in Philly had dropped over dead mainlining heroin.

Some of the bamboo stalks were brown and desiccated but most of the goddamned stuff was still greenly erect, seven feet tall and healthy. Gracie flicked her cigarette butt out into it. Waiting, bored, to see if it caught fire, if there'd be a little excitement out here on Route 71 tonight, the Waynesburg Volunteer Firemen exercising their shiny red equipment and every yokel for miles around hopping in his pickup to come gape—but it didn't, and there wasn't.

JOSEF ŠKVORECKÝ

A Case for Political Inspectors

We believe in man, in his infinite
capacity for development.
—Dalibor Pechacek,
Of Class Consciousness

There are various reasons why people become "progressive."

Some do it out of hunger and misery.

Others, out of intellectual convictions.

Some do it for the sake of careers.

And some, because they shit in their pants.

The latter was the reason our good Judge Bohadlo progressed in such a progressive fashion, may the Good Lord bless his soul.

Actually, this is one more story about Political Inspectors, individuals entrusted with guarding socialist values and checking people's political correctness. It is a story about watchfulness and vigilance. And though no PIs appear here directly, they hover in the background and are present in spirit.

When I first had the honor of meeting Judge Bohadlo he turned out to be a well-preserved, elderly gentleman. A kindly looking chubby fellow, with delicate, rosy cheeks that bespoke fine meals and choice wines, delicate rosy hands that had never known manual labor, a round little belly and a mouth shining like Klondike gold.

A flat in a modern apartment house, a spouse bedecked with bracelets, an aristocratic little dog—as solid a couple as a Biedermeyer chair or a table at the Hotel Ambassador.

A District Judge or something of the sort, I didn't know his exact title but certainly a few ranks above the ordinary. His schoolmate was the father of my former girlfriend Julie Nedochodil, and it was at the Nedochodils that I had the honor.

In pre-communist days, he used to visit there once in a while, when he had some business to discuss with Papa Nedochodil. After

1945, he formed some sort of connection with cloisters, church organizations, and the Catholic party.

He had already been involved in politics before the war, but in those days he was connected with the Agrarian party.

After discussions in Papa Nedochodil's study, Madam Nedochodil would invite him to the dining room for a bit of refreshment, and there they sat, sipped wine from South-Moravian cloisters, and munched on sandwiches spread with goat cheese from East-Slovakian cloisters, while Judge Bohadlo recounted tales from the good old golden days.

He especially liked to recall the fox hunts on the estates of Prince Schwarzenberg and Baron Simmenthal. But his dearest friend was Count Humprecht Gelenj, who entered the Premonstrates Order in 1945.

The Judge made no secret of his distaste for communism.

And so they lived, grew obese, and enjoyed themselves.

In February 1948, the ground under Judge Bohadlo's feet suddenly gave way, but he grasped the support held out to him and performed a grandiose somersault.

He applied for membership in the Communist party.

And what's more—he was accepted.

And so Judge Bohadlo became a communist.

Naturally, this triggered difficult inner struggles.

Seeking relief for his spiritual torments, he turned to Papa Nedochodil for moral support.

He tried to justify himself:

First of all, he is unused to physical work. Suppose they fired him, what then?

Secondly, he supports a sick wife who needs spa treatments.

And thirdly, somebody's got to stick it out, to save what can be saved.

This third, heroic-sounding argument met with Papa Nedochodil's wholehearted approval.

But the big blow was still to come. The Pope issued an excommunication decree.

And he really let them have it.

Excommunication applied to all members of the Communist party, as well as any person aiding the communist movement directly or indirectly (reading communist books and newspapers, listening to communist broadcasts, etc. etc.).

In other words, it applied to practically everybody.

Above all, of course, to Party members.

For a long time, Judge Bohadlo failed to come to Papa Nedochodil's house. Then one day he appeared. His pink second chin drooped lifelessly, his pince-nez kept dropping off his nose.

Somebody, he said in a shaky voice, has to stick it out, save what can be saved. As long as he remains in inner opposition.

Papa Nedochodil had a rather different opinion and his gaze upon the Judge's pale pink cheeks was somewhat disdainful, yet, because he was basically a kindly soul, he offered his friend such an ingenious construction of *reservatio mentale* as applied to the papal decree that the Judge began to see that ominous document in an entirely new light. He gobbled up the roast pork Madam Nedochodil offered him, washed it down with mead, and left in a virtually buoyant mood.

All the same, an evil deed is an evil deed. One can keep on thinking up excuses and seek relief in dialectical logic, but an evil deed gives rise to a bad conscience, and that works night and day.

With a sledgehammer.

Two days later, we had the Judge back on our neck. Full of torment, near collapse. Somebody, he whispered, has to stick it out. . . .

A new injection of casuistry, combined with almond pastry and mead, put him back on his feet.

He left in much calmer shape.

Two days later, he returned.

Very shaken.

And so it continued, until the mead ran out.

He stopped coming for a long time.

And then one day he suddenly appeared at the door, looking radiant. He announced that he had consulted a confessor.

The confessor had reassured him: somebody indeed has to stick it out and save what can be saved.

I was rather surprised, but then I discussed the matter with Julie in her room, and that clever girl reconstructed the story this way: Imagine, she said, a clergyman who is in every respect a proper priest, except that the poor fellow lacks the courage of the early Christian martyrs. It's hard to condemn him for that, even in this nation of Hussite heroes. And now somebody walks into his confessional, kneels down, and confesses that he sinned by joining the Communist party. What is that poor old fellow to do?

Of course, the matter is clear. According to the papal decree, he is forbidden to absolve him as long as he remains in league with the god-less brood.

Only . . .

Suppose the penitent is an undercover agent? If I refuse him absolution, he may turn me in.

So imagine the situation: the Judge is kneeling in the confessional, trembling, gnawed by his bad conscience.

Behind the grating sits the priest, trembling, the ugly thought of prison oppressing his mind.

This mutual trembling, naturally, could only be ended through compromise.

Thesis approved: somebody's got to stick it out, save what can be saved.

Proviso: the aforementioned somebody must not perform anything evil, and in his heart must continue to oppose those communist ideas that conflict with the teachings of the church.

Please note: "those communist ideas that conflict with the teachings of the church." In other words, not communism as such.

Why not?

Well, because the Reverend Father was suddenly struck by still another terrible possibility: if that penitent is an informer, he could just as well turn him in for giving absolution as for refusing to give it. After all, what would it mean to absolve someone of communism? That would logically imply that the Reverend Father considered communism a sin, and that he was guided by the Pope rather than by the State Bureau for Religious Affairs.

In short, that poor priest spent some very trying moments in connection with Judge Bohadlo's confession.

The compromise lay uneasy on his conscience, and so he at least urged the penitent to practice energetically the virtue of Christian charity: concretely, in terms of the Judge's profession, he should do his utmost to ease the human lot of the prisoners with whom he came in contact.

This was a program to which Judge Bohadlo responded with the greatest of enthusiasm.

He repeatedly reported to us on his acts of charity:

He smuggled chocolate bars to Miss Skladanovska, daughter of the former Senator and friend of my former love Julie Nedochodil, whom he had socked with two years in jail for an attempt at illegal emigration.

He frequently smuggled packages of American vitamins into the cell of Mr. Simms, a former editor whom he had slammed with a fifteen-year sentence.

After meting out a life sentence to a certain wholesale merchant, the Judge patted him on the back and whispered in his ear, Keep up your spirits, friend!

Whereupon that malcontent answered in a loud voice, Shut your trap, you swine!

Ingratitude rules the world. Judge Bohadlo performed his good deeds without thought of reward, like a true Boy Scout.

He would recount these stories to us, always managing to add his denunciation of communist legal and investigative methods, and he let us in on some unbelievably sensational details of political trials.

A bad conscience turned the Judge into an ideal source of juicy information.

The Voice of America would have paid me for them in gold.

But I have always followed the principle: freedom is better than riches.

And it's paid off for me so far.

The Judge kept cursing communism like the prophet Habakkuk, for reasons best known to himself, while furiously munching on hors d'oeuvres and pastry. His eyes burned with indignation. In those moments his conscience grew calmer. But then he'd leave for a street rally or the meeting of some organization where he'd excoriate the imperialists, and his bad conscience stuck out its horns.

At Papa Nedochodil's, of course, he tried as hard as he could to ridicule such proceedings. After indoctrination sessions where they discussed dialectical and historical materialism, he declared (at Papa Nedochodil's), I've forgotten more of this nonsense than they will ever learn. I recognized it for trash when I was still a young puppy like you, he added, turning to me.

He said it in the heat of the moment, so I didn't take offense. I understood him.

But that didn't help.

They promoted him.

His wife won approval for sojourn in a spa, whereas the wife of an impoverished shoemaker in the Judge's basement, who stubbornly insisted on remaining a private entrepreneur, was rejected.

Does that surprise you? You don't seem to understand: Judge Bohadlo was politically sound. A working member of the intelligentsia.

Whereas the shoemaker? Suppose they gave him a bit of leeway. In no time at all, he'd hire apprentices and start exploiting the working class. People of his type are incorrigible. Petty entrepreneurs are the germs of capitalism.

Judge Bohadlo thus became an ever-higher jurist and, in the end, an instructor of political education.

He stuck it out, that's true, and saved what could be saved.

In the single year of 1950, he smuggled in 28 packages of American chocolate, 5 kilos of vitamins, 3 kilos of sugar, 2,000 cigarettes, 18 books for reading, and 22 prayer books.

He kept precise records, including name, date, type of merchandise, and quantity.

In excoriating the Communist party, he reached a McCarthyite level of intensity.

And so it continued.

What's that?

You're asking whether he's still a high judge? Whether they ever unmasked him and got rid of him?

But, my dears, you are so naive!

Of course, obviously, naturally. In the end, our society always gets rid of its internal enemies, even if they managed to lead it by the nose for years. Our society has eliminated—and continues to eliminate—all parasites who believe they can hide behind slogans and phrases, and conceal their foul schemes.

Judge Bohadlo?

Of course our society got rid of him in the end.

How?

He died.

A stroke.

Say what you like, death is still the best Political Inspector.

JANE SMILEY

The Life of the Body

I had been going to call my sister Rhonda when the phone rang, and even then, when I heard her voice, I thought that I could just open my mouth and tell her, but when she heaved a blue, premenstrual sigh and said, "So what are you going to do today," I just said what I always say, oh nothing. I thought, another day. Just another day. Then the time will be more right, somehow.

The fact is that I am in about the worst trouble I have ever heard of anyone being in. After Rhonda hung up, the phone rang four separate times. There is no one I dare to hear from, and so I let it ring. If I had picked it up, I would have said to anyone on the other end that I am pregnant, that Jonathan Ricklefs is the father, not Jake, my husband, and that everything inside me is about to be revealed, layer by layer, to Jake, to Jonathan, to Rhonda and our parents, to my son Ezra and my daughter Nancy, to people who care about me and to people who barely know me. What is it that will shame me most when it is revealed? Maybe it is the crazy force of my desire for Jonathan, the full extent of which I have kept from him and which makes me squirm with discomfort even as a secret. But maybe it is something else, something that has not even been revealed to me yet.

I used to have three children. The third was Dory. Five months ago, when she was almost three, she fell head over heels down the stairs. She went over three times, we think. She broke her neck at the bottom and died that afternoon. Various children around the country have her liver, her kidneys, her corneas. There was no one to receive her heart at that moment. A heart is something that can't be saved for very long. She had a little book in her hand when Jake found her at the bottom. It was a habit we couldn't break her of, "reading" on the stairs. Really, she didn't know how to read yet, but she loved to look at the pictures.

I was getting dressed in our bedroom, Jake was ironing his shirt, Nancy and Ezra were eating breakfast. We all heard the long cry of surprise and fear, the thump of limbs toppling and hitting, the utter silence of the house around those noises. All struck dumb, all thinking, *What's that?* all listening. The rustle of buttonholes, stopped, the swish of the iron, stopped, the interior crunch of cereal and toast, stopped.

I can't say what I would have given to have been standing at the bottom of the stairs, holding out my arms to catch Dory. My inner life isn't very mysterious or symbolic. I often dream that I am there, that she is saved. Some part of me, in the dream, always asserts that even if the last time was a dream, this time it is true. It isn't.

Jake wouldn't let me speak at the funeral. He was afraid I would say something outrageous. I might have. I might have said, What right do I have to grieve, having lost only one? Isn't the society of mothers who have lost some many times bigger than the society of mothers who have kept all theirs? I would have said a lot of contradictory things, since I was very confused. Instead, we thanked God who took her away for giving her to us in the first place. That was Jake's idea. He is a religious person, more so now.

Jonathan is a fatalist rather than a providentialist. Things come and go. Forces arrange themselves so that he will, for example, eat granola instead of a peach. When I think of the way he sees himself, I imagine a kind of pinpoint at the vortex of a whirlpool. Blakean swirls above his head. Streaks of light moving through darkness. He is not a very hopeful person. I used to tease him about it. When I tell him I am pregnant, he will nod slowly, his expectations of the worst confirmed.

Maybe that is what I hate most about this, all the suspicions confirmed, especially the suspicions about me that everyone seems to harbor—that Dory's death has made me crazy, that Jake and I have never gotten along, that I would do anything to tie Jonathan to me, that I wanted to replace Dory at any cost, that women are by nature evil, irresponsible, and deceptive. What does it say in the Bible? *And I find more bitter than death the woman, whose heart is snares and nets, and her hands as bands: whoso pleaseth God shall escape from her; but the sinner shall be taken by her.* All that stuff. Once on the *Today* show, I saw a man who had written a book about the Dionne quintuplets. When they were born, their mother was ashamed. She said, "People will think that we are pigs." So much intercourse revealed to the world. Well, I was never proud of my pregnancies. Just by looking at you, people knew what you were thinking about.

I could have told Jake last night. I could have told Jonathan last night, too, when he brought over some lettuce from his garden. It doesn't make it any easier that this will be the first news Jake has had of my affair with Jonathan. Jonathan talks well to Jake. Not many people do—Jake is antisocial and impatient, and his idea of a serviceable conversational gambit is "What do you want?" Someone else who talks well to Jake is Rhonda. I am tempted to tell her, and let her tell them all. She is a great moaner. "Ooooh, Sarah. Ooh, Sarah." That is how she listens to confidences, moaning those wordless cries that you would like to be moaning yourself. "Ooh, Sarah. Ooooh Sarah." I try it out, out loud, but it isn't the same. I know I should be finishing the sentence, "Oooh Sarah you shithead," which is something Rhonda would never even think of doing.

There is the crunch of wheels in the driveway, Jake returning from work, as he often does. He will find me standing over the sink, as he often does. I get up and position myself there. He comes in and runs up the stairs. There is the slamming of closet doors upstairs, the thump of his heavy feet. He really has forgotten something, he always really has, but he never did before Dory died. The manifestation of his grief is more than forgetfulness, it is perennial searching. Though he gave up smoking years ago, his hands wander his pockets in search of cigarettes. He is always making sure he has his keys, his wallet, his checkbook. I find him in closets looking for sweaters and pairs of slippers and magazine articles we threw out years ago. He turns over the cushions, puts his hands in the cracks, comes up with pennies that he gives to Nancy. He calls his mother and asks if his old yearbooks are at her house, his swimming trunks from high school, his old Bo Diddley records. We are patient with this searching, his mother and I. Even Jake knows what he is searching for, but he can't stop just because he won't find her.

He appears in the kitchen doorway. I have my hands in the water, as if I were doing something, and it might be that, not looking at him, looking out the back window at the peonies blooming in the yard, I will say, "I'm pregnant." I know the words, I've said it before. But of everyone in the whole world, Jake is the only other person who knows that we haven't slept together since the week before Dory died. It is also possible that I will tell no one, just wait for them to notice, and ask. It may be that social nicety will prevent most people from asking. It may be that fear will prevent Jake from asking, and even greater fear will prevent Jonathan from asking, and a year from now I will say, in a cocky voice, "Ever wonder where I got this baby?"

Jake says, "I forgot the reports. I can't believe I actually forgot the reports."

"It's okay."

"Of course it's okay. That isn't what I'm talking about. I just can't believe it. I'm just remarking on that, is all."

"I know."

"What are you going to do today?" He asks suspiciously, because he thinks that my grief is to loiter around the house for hours, then hurry and clean up just before Ezra and Nancy get home. It was. Lately my grief has been to go to bed with Jonathan Ricklefs as much as possible, on every flat surface in his apartment. I say, "I'm going to go to Rhonda's dance class with her again, then I'm going to order meat at the locker, then bake cookies with Nancy for the day camp birthday party. How about cooking out for dinner? It's already getting hot enough."

"Will you make potato salad?" He glides up next to me, kisses me on the neck, as if bribing me. I turn and put my hands on his shoulders. I smile, as if being bribed. "I'll boil the potatoes as soon as you leave."

"The day camp counselor thinks Nancy seems fine. She's playing with everyone, and the shyness has worn off completely. She's making a belt in the crafts class."

"Good."

"Ezra is being more reserved."

"Ezra *is* more reserved."

"How much more?"

"Sweetie, I wish I knew. He likes the horses. Yesterday he told me about the horses for about twenty-five minutes. His favorite is named Herb. He got to go into the stable and give Herb his oats." We smile at Herb. Jake smiles at me. He thinks we are coming out of things when in fact we are just getting started. Another day. I will let him go another day. He pecks me on the cheek and leaves with a number of slams: the kitchen door, the garage door, the car door. He is a noisy man.

*   *   *

Rhonda dances every day. Lately I have been going with her. This is not aerobics, it is serious modern dance. The other students are mostly in their teens and early twenties. The teacher is a black man who dances in a local company. I don't know why he lets me come, except that he is a friend of Rhonda's, and she is my sister. Rhonda, although she is thirty-two and has two children, turns out to have considerable talent for the dance. The first day I came, she warmed up, without shame, by stretching and then doing three slow cartwheels and a couple of handstands. I was amazed. I keep up well with the slower third of the twenty-year-olds, and mostly Henry doesn't pay any attention to us. We pay attention to him, though. Pas de cheval: Henry says, "You know how a puppy licks your arm? So that every pore and hair gets wet? Well, make the sole of your foot lick the floor." Deep second position: "You are in water! Your head is floating upward! Your knees are floating outward! Lift! Lift!" He tells us not to mimic him, but to feel ourselves, our muscles and tendons sliding and rolling, our balls and sockets rotating.

Today we have hamstrings and adductors for half an hour, then chainé turns for half an hour. My days here, as everywhere, are numbered, and so when we lie on our backs and rotate our hips outward and find the place on each side where the tendons split, I am careful to note what it feels like. When we then curl up to standing, I think only of my spine, catlike, and my long, furry tail anchoring me to the floor. When we step and pivot across the floor, I push my toes through the wet mud Henry evokes, and leave long swathes filling with water behind me. After four times across the floor, we lie down and slither through that same mud, chests first, trying not to get our chins wet.

The first to go are Nancy and Ezra, who are active and well taken care of. Then I stop thinking about Rhonda, even though she is just ahead of me in line. Jake vanishes next, with his expectations that are soon to be betrayed. Now Dory, who never knew me as a dancer, who has no associations with this room or these people (they know my first name only, if that). After that, I forget I am pregnant, and at last, sometime in the triple prances ("Sli-i-ide snap! snap!" says Henry), even Jonathan lets go. Henry becomes Henry the dancer rather than Henry the man. We are panting. Henry tells the accompanist to speed up the tempo, and we are running. Henry goes first, down-up-up, arms and chin swooping then lifting. Someone in red and black does it after him, a flute passage on the heels of a bassoon passage, and then it is me, and the only thing I feel is the slick floor under my feet and the rush of my fingers through the air, up-up!

The one in red and black, of course, is Rhonda, who is damp with sweat from ponytail to heel, and when class is over, she says, "God, let's shower and eat at my place. I've got spaghetti left over from last night."

It is words that bring them all back with a suffocating rush. "God." "My place." "Last night." We are fixed in place and time after all. Henry passes us on the way out. "Lovely," he says. He is a big man, happy, Rhonda says, because he gets a lot of oxygen to the brain.

I should tell her in the locker room, naked in the shower, but I make excuses. Now that she is right here, it seems like Jonathan should be the first to know, then Jake, then her. Then our parents, then the children. That's the obvious order, just as Rhonda-Jake-Jonathan was last night, when Jake and Jonathan were standing with their hands in their pockets under the hackberry tree, considering ways to save it from whatever is infesting it.

* * *

There is this space, of course, this carefully made space in the day when I will see Jonathan. After the meatlocker, after lunch, before Nancy and Ezra get home from day camp. I enter the downstairs door quickly, and run up. The door opens at the first brush of my first knock. Jonathan is grinning. "Hi," he says, "Hi, hi, hi." He locks the door behind me. He looks me up and down. I catch sight of a pot of tea steaming behind him on the coffee table and I burst into tears. It isn't the first time, nor does it come from the press of present circumstances. All of this sadness has been there from the beginning. I think, in fact, that this affair was begun as a tribute to sadness, gathered force through sadness, and will result in more sadness for everyone that we can possibly stand.

I feel utterly comfortable weeping here.

Perhaps more importantly, Jonathan feels utterly comfortable with my weeping. I sit on the couch and he pours the tea and then he sits beside me and folds me into his chest, and soon I am weeping and kissing him, and he is wiping my face with a paper napkin and kissing me, and that is how it has gone for months, salty kisses, passion, and grief. I am, as they say, shameless. Often we don't make love, but today we do. Today when he kisses me with his lips, I give him my tongue, only my tongue, and then I feel his, meeting mine, and instantly my nipples, tender with pregnancy, stand up, burning. As much as they hurt, I long to have him lick and suck them, and when I think of that, they tingle suddenly, as if milk were about to come down. They haven't done that since Dory was nursing, and it is the most intense feeling of physical longing, the longing to give suck. I almost tell the news, but I don't.

Jonathan kisses my neck and shoulders, and his erection presses against my leg, presses into my imagination, the thick, smooth shape, the reddish color—I am as familiar with it as I am with my own hand, more familiar, since I have looked at it, tasted it, touched and held it, smelled it. A weighty, living object. Sometimes at night, after Jake goes to sleep and I am lying awake in fear and guilt, I just open my mouth and put my tongue out, wishing, thinking how I would lick the little crease and then run my tongue under the cap, marveling always at the warm shape of it. He sucks my breasts and I push both hands into his pants, unsnapping them, forcing the zipper down. He hops a little on the couch, then pulls my T-shirt up. It tangles in my arms and hair. I am still weeping. I am happy to be trapped inside this shirt with my nipples burning, my cunt throbbing. I open my mouth and put my tongue out.

"Sarah!" he moans. "Oh, Sarah oh oh." And then he strips off my shorts and shoes and sucks my toes and after that he licks my cunt, and licks and licks, parting the lips and putting his fingers in, licking, finding, at last, the spot that burns so that I push him away, his head, his shoulders. He pushes back, licking, his tongue fastened to that spot. My legs turn to water, and my back arches, and for a moment he is gone, and then he eases into me, slow and slick, and his tongue is in my open mouth and his fingers are in my ears and his chest, smooth and firm, in its way, as a penis, is sliding along my chest, and then he does something I always like, which is to lift my legs to my shoulders so that he can get in and in, and he gets in, so far that he relaxes a little, and closes his eyes. I push him off, out. He is shocked, his flesh is shocked at the suddenness of it, but before he realizes, I have it, his penis in my mouth, as I have wanted, and I am licking and stroking. I like to feel this, that he cannot stop himself. He does not. I swallow. He falls back on the couch, pulling me with him, holding me tight, panting. This is the way it has gone for months. I cling to him in desperate fear, but I am no longer weeping.

Sometimes I dream that I am just a torso, and blind, born that way, skin, a mouth, breasts, a cunt more open than any cunt ever, and Jonathan is engulfing me as well as penetrating every orifice. I dream that all I can do in life is fuck and suck and kiss and be embraced, and that I orgasm over and over and never get enough. Sometimes I daydream it.

The tension flows back into his flesh. I feel it along my chest, in his shoulder where my ear and cheek rest. His arm tightens over my back, and his other arm moves. When I lift my head to look at him, I see that he has covered his eyes with his elbow. I lower my head gently and wait, as still as possible. His heart has not relaxed, and is pounding steadily faster. As I open my mouth to speak, he says, "Sarah, talk to me."

I lift my head. "You want me to open the conversation."

"It's hopeless."

"What is hopeless." I can't make it a question, must make it a denial.

"Sarah—"

"Don't say anything, just don't say anything. Do you love me?"

He answers without hesitation but not without pain, "I tell you I do over and over. I do."

"Then don't say anything."

"Do you love me?"

"I think of you without ceasing, day and night."

"Do you love me?"

"You possess me."

"Sarah, do you love me?"

After minutes go by and I don't answer, he sits up and puts me away from him and pours the tea. I reach for my T-shirt and pull it on, but I don't stop shivering. I watch him drink his tea, catching tea leaves on the tip of his tongue and picking them off with his finger. He knows I am looking at him and from time to time turns his gaze to mine. This is another thing that we feel comfortable with, staring and being stared at. He is a big man, broad and muscular, utterly defeated, *as an ox goeth to the slaughter.* When we met, I was attracted to his self-reliance, his detached outlook. Both of those are gone now. I wonder how much he wants them back. He says, "I am terrified."

"Are you terrified that it will go on or are you terrified that it will stop?"

"Both."

"Are you frightened of me or for me?"

"Both."

"Will love find a way? If we stick together, can we make it?"

"Sometimes I think so. Weaker moments. Oh, Sarah." He covers his eyes again. A moment later I see tears on his cheeks. I look away. He goes on. "It's too painful. Sometimes I feel like our clothes are lined with nails and the tighter we embrace, the more blood we draw from each other."

I say, "It was fun at the beginning. That's important. A book I read says that you draw on the strengths of the relationship when you remember the beginning. I used to be known for my sense of humor, actually. Jonathan, suspend choice, all right? No action, no decision, just endurance." But he is slippery. As soon as he admitted fear, I felt it myself, telegraphed from him to me. I felt the size of the betrayal that would be possible just to escape that fear. Which arm, which leg, which sense would I have given just to escape that fear the moment I saw my daughter at the bottom of the stairs?

"A day," I say. "Only another day. Don't make up your mind or even think anything for another day. Go canoeing. Go to the movies. Eat something soothing, with lots of B vitamins. If I leave now, I might beat Nancy home by a minute." I run out the door, down the steps, out the lower door. I know he is watching me from the window. He fell in love with me when Dory died. That is why my chest closes up when I try to say that I love him. I don't want to be loved for my belongings, even if that belonging is only an enlargement that springs from tragedy.

* * *

I make a lot of mistakes. This time it is the potato salad, which I forgot, though Jake asked for it specifically. I forgot about it all the way until he looked in the refrigerator and said, "Didn't you make the potato salad?" and so there was no evasive action possible. I say, "I'll do that thing."

"What thing?"

"That thing where I go to the deli and get some of theirs, then re-dress it. You like that."

"You were going to put the potatoes on as soon as I left."

"I forgot."

"How could you forget? You were standing right here in the kitchen. All you had to do was turn around and take the potatoes out of the cupboard.

"I forgot."

"I'm not mad. I just don't understand you."

"You forgot your reports."

"I was working on them last night. I put them aside."

"I don't want to argue about fine points."

"It means something," he says. "The way people act means something. You know that."

"I forgot."

He shakes his head and goes outside to start the fire. Before he addressed me on the topic of potato salad, I was standing over the dishwater, as always, washing up the cookie things and pondering the recollection of Jonathan sucking my breasts, thinking that I would like him to kiss all of my skin at the same time. Jonathan knows in his heart that what I crave from him are impossibilities. That is why he is afraid of me.

Out the kitchen window, Jake comes into view, carrying the charcoal and the lighter fluid. Most people, including Jonathan, feel lots of sympathy for him. Soon they'll feel more. They think he must grieve a great deal for Dory. I don't know. I wish I had seen the first look on his face when he got to her, but I started from back in the closet in our bedroom upstairs, and by the time I reached them at the bottom of the stairs, he was already practical, had already covered her with the afghan and was calling the ambulance, wouldn't let her be moved. He has never cried in my presence. Nor have I cried in his presence. But we do not pretend that everything is normal. We strive with all our might to make a routine, a little thread that will guide Ezra and Nancy, and maybe ourselves, out of the labyrinth.

That our sex life ended did not surprise me. Jake does not seek comfort in the flesh of others. He has to feel good to reach out. When he does not feel good, he avoids people. All of his brothers are the same way. When their father died three years ago, they gathered in Tallahassee for four days, five men. They built a bathroom out of the downstairs porch of their mother's house, taking maybe four hours out for the funeral and the burial. I asked Jake if they talked about their father in there, while they were grouting and caulking. He said, "Ralph did, a little." He didn't touch me for four months. I didn't mind. I think about Jonathan putting his face between my thighs and licking, sticking his tongue in; Jake comes up behind me and says, "Are you going to get the potato salad now or not?" and I start violently. He turns me around, his hands on my shoulders, and looks into my eyes. His face is very close to mine, and he is serious. He says, "Sarah, can't you pay attention? That's not an accusation. I want to know. Is that the problem, that you can't pay attention?"

"I'm trying. Don't watch me."

"I wish I could help myself."

I pull away. "I'll get the potato salad now, okay? Nancy is over at Allison's house, and Ezra is watching television."

"Don't get distracted. Half an hour, okay? Be back in half an hour."

"I will."

"I mean it."

"I *will*." It is for my own good, so I won't wander, so I'll keep my mind on the business at hand.

That is the beginning. The second incident takes place when I am coming out of Nancy's room after putting her to bed. Jake is in the hallway, looking at the bookshelves. I turn to say one last thing to Nancy, and Jake's arm goes around my waist. Distracted, I stiffen. Then I relax, but the stiffening doesn't go unnoticed. His arm drops. We stand there for an awkward second, then he chooses a book, and I turn and go down the stairs.

In the end, we argue about religion rather than sex. It is dark when I come into our bedroom, and I think Jake is asleep, but he speaks in a firm, clear voice, surprising in the dark. "Can I tell you something?" I push the top drawer of the dresser in, and he takes this for assent. I stand quietly, looking at the parallelogram of moonlight on the top of the dresser. "There was this time, when my mother's younger sister died of complications of childbirth. I guess I was about fourteen. Anyway, we had just moved to that house in Tallahassee, and I came in from doing something outside. Maybe we were helping Dad move that shed. That was one of the first things we had to do. It was almost dark, and Mom was sitting in the dark, snapping beans for dinner, and everyone else was outside, and when I went to turn on the light, she said, 'Jake, leave it dark,' so I left it dark, and she said, 'The Lord helps a man be good, Jake. If you let Him come inside you, He is a tide that carries you to goodness. But you've got to open the door yourself.' That was all she said, and then Richie came in and turned on the light and pretty soon we had dinner. Sarah, I know it's hard to find the door. It took me ten years to find the door, but I found it."

"It's not a door I want to find, Jake. Your mother was a religious woman, and she raised you, and so she was preaching to the converted. Before we got married, she said you'd come back to it, and you did. Big surprise."

"I tried the other way."

"You always thought of it as the other way. I don't believe, Jake. It's not in me. My brain doesn't have that bump. It's not in my horoscope. I went to Sunday school and read the Bible and it didn't take. If you didn't bring it up, I wouldn't think about it."

"But maybe me bringing it up is the Lord's way of trying to get your attention. I can't stop doing it. *I am moved* to do it. Don't you understand what that means?"

By now I have gotten, without realizing it, into the dark corner between the dresser and the wall. I open my mouth, but I know perfectly well how Jake's life looks to him: in retrospect, a series of perfectly timed nudges toward the right path that his mother would have, and often had, called miracles—a moment of despair, and then she looks up to see the minister on the porch, about to ring the bell. That happened more than once. I didn't necessarily discount her interpretation. It does seem to me that the world and the inner life mesh in mysterious ways more often than not.

I run my finger around the edge of the moonlight. More than anything, I want him to stop badgering me. I say, "I understand that you are driving me nuts with this God shit. I got some tracts in the mail again yesterday. Did you send them?"

He is out of bed in an instant, moved to rage by everything unbearable that we have to bear. I find that I am in a tight spot, between the wall and the dresser, and as I am trying to get out, he takes me by the shoulders and bumps my head on the wall. I press against him. His grip tightens, and I can feel the panic roll up from my toes all at once. I know he won't hurt me, but I feel that he will kill me. The walls behind me and to my left are unyielding, cold, terrifying. I bend down. His hands press harder on my shoulders, weights that I cannot evade. I do the only thing that I can possibly do, which is to push hard against the wall with my hip, and hard against the dresser with my hands. It falls over with a crash, and the stained glass box Jake keeps pennies in flies toward the window. I see this out of the corner of my eye. Jake does it again, bumps my head against the wall, this time hard, and simultaneously with the sound of breaking glass. Then I get out from under him, clamber over the dresser, and flee the room. For the rest of the night, which I spend on the sofa, every time I fall into a doze, I seem to feel my head being slammed into glass, and I wake up expecting to reach up and find blood pouring down my face.

When I loved Jake, when our relationship wasn't too complicated to have a label like that, it was this absolute quality that I loved, this straightness, this desire for goodness, and mostly the struggle he put up with himself, the manly difficulty of that. I didn't know anyone like him. I don't know that this appreciation is reciprocated—when he talks about me to his pastor and other men he likes who are religious, they will have a long tradition of misogyny to consult. He will not be guided to see things from my point of view. Well, deep in the night, curled up on the couch with the pillow over my head, somewhere in the realm of sleep, I do feel what he felt and see what he saw and hear what he heard: the flippant and dismissive tone of my voice, the indifference of my face in the half light, the inviting and unusual way I was wedged into that space, easy prey, and deserving of punishment too. I feel again the corner enclosing my flesh, the panic surging out of me in a flood, and I wake up with a start. Containing both points of view at once makes me short of breath. I sit up and gaze around the living room. For the first time in weeks, I don't want Jonathan. I try to make myself think of him, but my mind won't fix.

Jonathan used to run a millworks, producing hardwood moldings for lumberyards. He made some money and sold the business, and now he goes to school in horticulture and landscape architecture. He taught an extension course in tree fruits, which is where I met him, and which is why he has his days free and why he can talk to Jake, whose only ambition in life is to run a market garden with his brother Richie. Richie would grow only corn, Jake would do the other vegetables and press cider in the fall. I would do fresh-cut flowers in season and apples in the fall. Right now Jake and Richie have other jobs: Richie manages a big A & P in the next town and Jake works for the county government as an accountant. Jake and Richie and I own 57 acres, free and clear. Next summer, the five brothers are going to begin building a house on the land. Every weekend, all spring, Jake and Richie have gone out to the property and walked its every inch, looking for the best site for the house and the garden and the garden buildings. That gave Jonathan and me four or five extra hours every week that we wouldn't have had, and it was on one of those weekends, when I forgot my diaphragm, that I got pregnant. In the ten years of marriage, I have forgotten it off and on, without consequences, and each of the other pregnancies took a number of months, and so I was careless. Careless and lazy: I realized I had forgotten it before I was to the end of our street, but I couldn't bear to turn back and thought I would trust to luck, as I had in the past. Careless and lazy and possessed. There have been times in the last seven months when putting off seeing Jonathan for even ten minutes was the cruelest torture.

We bought the property two years ago, with savings and with Jake's and Richie's portions of their father's estate. I like Richie. All that summer he would come over about dinnertime and sit on the porch swing, talking to Jake about what sort of house they would build and watching Dory. Dory was sixteen months when we bought the land. When Richie was here, we would prop open all the doors and she would charge through all the rooms and in and out of the house. He would help her down the front steps, and she would tear around the yard, which was fenced. She was utterly safe and utterly free, and maybe for that reason, much happier than Nancy and Ezra were at that age. Rhonda and Walker came over a lot too. We have all known each other for a long time. Lots of times, Rhonda would go into the kitchen and open the cabinets and start making dinner, and though I had disagreements with Jake that everyone knew about, there was a largeness and comfort to family life that soothed me. It spread in every direction, over the landscape, from the past into the future. It was enough to buy land and plan, to care for the children, to dig and plant. Richie and Walker distracted Jake, engaged him in conversation, made him feel at ease. Whatever was missing between us got to seem like just a certain coloring, a certain way the landscape might be lit but wasn't, nothing particular, considering everything else that was there. Richie, after all, wasn't even married, had never, as far as we knew, had a steady girlfriend.

Usually, these days, it seems like nothing, what we had at all those dinnertimes, but just now, when I am cold and tired and frightened of sleep, it seems like a thing of substance and weight, safe as a vault, with the child rolling through it like a golden ball.

I don't know anyone who has had an abortion, but it can be done. Rhonda would know all about it. And if this were the moment when it was to be done, I would do it, because no one else is here, not Jonathan or Nancy or Ezra or Jake or Richie or Rhonda or my mother. Only I am here, and for the moment Jake has pounded sentiment out of me. Nothing in this room, which we bought and filled with our purchases, means a thing to me, not even the pictures. Nothing I have ever felt or thought or given voice to remotely interests me just now, no principle or affection or intention. I sit against the arm of the couch, waiting to make up my mind to have an abortion.

Instead it must be that I fall asleep, because Ezra wakes me, and it is daylight, though just barely. Ezra always comes down early and expects to have the house to himself for an hour. He says, "Mommy, can I turn on the TV?" and the day is begun. I look at him for a long moment, until he smiles in self-defense, and then I say, "Do you have riding again today?" and he grins. He says, "Alan, you know, the head of riding, he said I could ride Herbie every time, if I asked." He goes and turns on the TV, then glances back at me. "He's a real good horse, Mom. And he's a horse, not a pony."

"Hmm."

"Do you know the difference?"

"I do, actually."

"Well, he's a horse."

"Good, sweetie." I pull myself up the stairs and into the bathroom.

At breakfast I act as if nothing has happened, and Jake can think he is getting away with something if he wants. I put his eggs in front of him and meet his gaze, and I am nearly as tender with him as I am with the children, brushing their shoulders or hair with my hand. And then they are gone, and I pick up the phone and I call Jonathan and make a date with him for lunch. His voice is distant, distracted. After that I make sure that Rhonda is going to her dance class and that I can come along. Then I do the dishes and sweep the kitchen. In fact, I get down on my hands and knees with the butler's brush and sweep like I've never swept before, getting the dust and sand of seven years out of the corners, off the top edge of the moldings, out from under the stove and refrigerator. When I am finished, I am dusty and sweaty. I go around and open the windows, catching what breeze there is. After that I take another shower.

The fact is that this is the last hour of the old life. Things that are soft are about to harden and take the simple shapes that may last them the rest of my life. For example, I don't hate Jake and I don't love Jonathan. Whatever I feel for each of them is like one of those dye baths that you dip the endpapers of books in—a riot of colors swirled together, compounded of everything each has confided in me and everything I have confided in each of them. At this moment, I have the feeling that each time I have looked at each one of them is distinct and significant, that I know some discrete grain of truth about each of them as a result of every glance. The large thing that I know about them is that they are not each other, but that large thing is compounded of the numberless small ways in which they are not each other. I don't blame them for not being each other, but as soon as I speak, they will move into position. Jake, betrayed, will become my enemy. Jonathan, responsible, will become my partner. I would be deluding myself if I didn't know that he will consider my pregnancy a moral outrage in addition to an injury to himself. If he doesn't tell his brothers, and probably my children, that I am a whore, then he won't be the Jake I have known for ten years. And so the children will move into position too: confused at first, judgmental later, damaged forever. And Jonathan. Well, Jonathan. Just because I know that he will do the right thing, does that mean I planned for him to? At lunch I'll tell him I'm pregnant before he tells me we have to end our affair, and for a lot of reasons, he will swallow his doubts, and I will swallow mine, and sometime soon I will tell him that I love him, because I will love him. I will move into position too. Maybe.

A week after the funeral, when the children were back in school, I walked to the library and then to Jonathan's house. It was the day before Valentine's Day, warm and sunny, with snow melt trickling down every gutter. I had thrown away the valentine I intended to give him— it was one of those cynical and sexy ones, and when I found it in my purse the day after the funeral, it seemed to be cursed, so I tore it up, tore it up again, took it down the street, and threw it into some dry cleaner's dumpster. I was chastened. Everything having to do with Jonathan Ricklefs frightened me. We hadn't slept together very often— our friendship was more teasing and drinking tea than anything else. He seemed invulnerable, possibly dating someone else, though I wasn't sure. Jake was at work, my mother had left, the children were back in school, and I was walking down the street, glad to be put back together a little bit, glad that the previous night was over and the night to come wasn't yet upon me. I climbed the step and rang the bell, and I remember turning and looking down the street, idly, thinking of nothing for a moment. And then the door opened, and Jonathan was there, and his hand closed around my elbow, and he pulled me into the hallway where he hugged me and looked at me and put his hand on my face and then hugged me again, and just at that moment when he looked at me, I knew two things at once, that Dory was dead and that Jonathan loved me as he had not loved me ten days before. I don't know that any relationship can survive that sort of birth for long. Or maybe the root is this, that when I was standing in the closet that morning, buttoning my shirt, it was Jonathan I was thinking of, Jonathan who had delayed me in the closet, taking off one shirt and putting on another. I was thinking about him sucking my breasts; I could feel my nipples rise against the cotton of the shirt as I thought, *What's that noise?*

In the first hour of the new life, I will speak and act and justify and choose. I will summarize and simplify, in order to make the new life. I will start forgetting what I know in the last hour of the old life. I don't think this is the least of the things that will be destroyed.

I am pulling up my tights in the locker room when Rhonda comes in. She is lovely, my sister. She has two dimples, still, one just under her left eye, the other just to the right of her smile. In the humidity, her hair springs out of her bun with curly abandon. "Sary!" she roars. Her voice is always gravelly and ironic, because in spite of everything she still smokes cigarettes. "Am I late? I had to buy these new tights! Look at this! Is that shine? Don't you love it?" She goes over and stubs out her cigarette in the sink, then wets the end and throws it in the trashcan. "Shit. We've got to hurry. Henry always notices if you're late. Last week he wouldn't let one of them dance, that one who always wears the silver leotard."

I run after her. She snaps the front of her leotard as we trot down the hall. At the door, I put my hand on hers, holding it closed. She looks at me. I say, "Rhonda. Wait a minute." And I tell her. Then I open the door and walk in. Henry has started pliés. I take my place in line. Two minutes later, I feel Rhonda behind me, everything about her, her sadness and her fear as well as her presence. She gives out a little moan. Henry casts her a glance.

He says, "There is a thread attached to that spot on the back of your head where the hair swirls around. You know that spot? Just a thread. If you let your spine stretch upward as your buttocks drop down, you won't break that thread." My chin drops, the vertebrae seem to release one another and float. This is it, isn't it, what Jake calls God and Jonathan calls passion. I lift my arms and drop and spread my shoulders, then turn. Rhonda is there, and her face is white and her expression dismayed. She would like a cigarette. This is it, isn't it, this movement, movement, only movement, only the feeling of life running through the tissues. After all, it makes me smile. A second later, my sister smiles back.

WILLIAM TREVOR

The Potato Dealer

Mulreavy would marry her if they paid him, Ellie's uncle said: she couldn't bring a fatherless child into the world; he didn't care what was done nowadays; he didn't care what the fashion was; he wouldn't tolerate the talk there'd be. "Mulreavy," her uncle repeated. "D'you know who I mean by Mulreavy?"

She hardly did. An image came into her mind of a big face that had a squareness about it, and black hair, and a cigarette butt adhering to the lower lip while a slow voice agreed or disagreed, and eyes that were small, and sharp as splinters. Mulreavy was a potato dealer. Once a year he came to the farm, his old lorry rattling into the yard, then backed up to where the sacks stood ready for him. Sometimes he shook his head when he examined the potatoes, saying they were too small. He tried that on, Ellie's uncle maintained. Cagey, her uncle said.

"I'll tell you one thing, girl," her uncle said when she found the strength to protest at what was being proposed. "I'll tell you this: you can't stay here without there's something along lines like I'm saying. Nowadays is nothing, girl. There's still the talk."

He was known locally as Mr. Larrissey, rarely by his Christian name, which was Joseph. Ellie didn't call him "Uncle Joseph," never had; "Uncle" sometimes, though not often, for even in that there seemed to be an intimacy that did not belong in their relationship. She thought of him as Mr. Larrissey.

"It's one thing or the other, girl."

Her mother—her uncle's sister—didn't say anything. Her mother hadn't opened her mouth on the subject of Mulreavy, but Ellie knew that she shared the sentiments that were being expressed, and would accept, in time, the solution that had been offered. She had let her mother down; she had embittered her; why should her mother care what happened now? All of it was a mess: in the kitchen of the farmhouse her mother and her uncle were thinking the same thing.

Her uncle—a worn, tired man, not used to trouble like this—didn't forgive her and never would. So he had said, and Ellie knew it was true.

Since the death of her father she and her mother had lived with him on the farm on sufferance: that was always in his eyes, even though her mother did all the cooking and the cleaning of the house, even though Ellie, since she was eleven, had helped in summer in the fields, had collected and washed the eggs and nourished the pigs. Her uncle had never married; if she and her mother hadn't moved on to the farm in 1978, when Ellie was five, he'd still be on his own, managing as best he could.

"You have the choice, girl," he said now, the repetition heavy in the farmhouse kitchen. He was set in his ways, Ellie's mother often said; lifelong bachelors sometimes were.

He'd said at first—a fortnight ago—that his niece should get herself seen to, even though it was against religion. Her mother said no, but later wondered if it wasn't the only way out, the trip across the water that other girls had gone on. What else was there? They could go away and have it quietly done, they could be visiting the Galway cousins, no one would be the wiser. But Ellie, with what spirit was left in her, though she was in disgrace and crying, would not agree. In the fortnight that passed, she many times, tearfully, repeated her resolve to let the child be born.

Loving the father, Ellie already loved the child. If they turned her out, if she had to walk the roads, or find work in Moyleglass or some other town, she would. But Ellie didn't want to do that; she didn't want to find herself penniless because it would endanger the birth. She would never do that was the decision she had privately reached the moment she was certain she was to have a child.

"Mulreavy," her uncle said again.

"I know who he is."

Her mother sat staring down at the lines of grain that years of scrubbing had raised on the surface of the kitchen table. Her mother had said everything she intended to say: disgrace, shame, a dirtiness occurring when people's backs were turned, all the thanks you get for what you give, for sacrifices made. "Who'd want you now?" her mother had asked her, more than once.

"Mind you, I'm not saying Mulreavy'll bite," Ellie's uncle said. "I'm not saying he'd take the thing on."

Ellie didn't say anything. She left the kitchen and walked out into the yard, where the turkeys screeched and ran toward her, imagining she carried meal to scatter, as often she did. She passed them by and let herself through the black iron gate that led to the sloping three-cornered field beyond the outbuildings, the worst two acres of her uncle's property. Ragweed and gorse grew in profusion, speckled rock-surfaces erupted. It was her favorite field, perhaps because she had always heard it cursed and as a child had felt sorry for it. "Oh, now, that's nice!" the father of her unborn child had said when she told him she felt sorry for the three-cornered field. It was then that he'd said he wished he'd known her as a child, and made her describe herself as she had been.

*   *   *

When it was put to Mulreavy he pretended offense. He didn't expostulate, for that was not his way. But as if in melancholy consideration of a personal affront he let the two ends of his mouth droop, as he sometimes did when he held a potato in his palm, shaking his head over its unsatisfactory size or shape. Ash from his cigarette dribbled down his shirt-front, the buttons of a fawn cardigan open because the day was warm, his shirtcollar open also and revealing a line of grime where it had been most closely in contact with the skin of his neck.

"Well, that's a quare one," Mulreavy said, his simulated distaste slipping easily from him, replaced by an attempt at outraged humor.

"There's a fairish sum," Mr. Larrissey said, but didn't say what he had in mind and Mulreavy didn't ask. Nor did he ask who the father was. He said in a by-the-way voice that he was going out with a woman from Ballina who'd come to live in Moyleglass, a dressmaker's assistant; but the information was ignored.

"I only thought it was something would interest you," Mr. Larrissey said.

Their two vehicles were drawn up on the road, a rusting Ford Cortina and Mulreavy's lorry, the driving-side windows of both wound down. Mulreavy offered a cigarette. Mr. Larrissey took it. As if about to drive away, he had put his hand on the gear when he said he'd only thought the proposition might be of interest.

"What's the sum?" Mulreavy asked when the cigarettes were lit, and a horn hooted because the vehicles were blocking the road. Neither man took any notice: they were of the neighborhood, local people; the road was more theirs than strangers'.

When the extent of the money offered was revealed Mulreavy

knew better than to react, favorably or otherwise. It would be necessary to give the matter thought, he said, and further considerations were put to him, so that at leisure he could dwell on those also.

* * *

Ellie's mother knew how it was, and how it would be: her brother would profit from the episode. The payment would be made by her: the accumulated pension, the compensation from the time of the accident in 1978. Her brother saw something for himself in the arrangement he hoped for with the potato dealer; the moment he had mentioned Mulreavy's name he'd been aware of a profit to be made. Recognizing at first, as she had herself, only shame and folly in the fact that his niece was pregnant, he had nonetheless explored the situation meticulously: that was his way. She had long been aware of her brother's hope that one day Ellie would marry some suitable young fellow who would join them in the farmhouse and could be put to work, easing the burden in the fields. That was how the debt of taking in a sister and a niece might at last be paid. But with a disaster such as there had been, there would be no young fellow now. Instead there was the prospect of Mulreavy, and what her brother had established in his mind was that Mulreavy could ease the burden too. A middle-aged potato dealer wasn't ideal for the purpose, but he was better than nothing.

Ellie's mother, resembling her brother in appearance, lean-faced and with his tired look, often recalled the childhood he and she had shared in this same house. More so than their neighbors, they were known to be a religious family, never missing Mass, going all together in the trap on Sundays and later by car, complimented for the faith they kept by Father Hanlon and his successor. The Larrisseys were respected people, known for the family virtues of hard work and disdain for ostentation, never seeming to be above themselves. She and her brother had all their lives been part of that, had never rebelled against these laid-down *mores* during the years of their upbringing.

Now, out of the cruel blue, there was this; and as far as brother and sister could remember, in the farmhouse there had never been anything as dispiriting. The struggle in bad seasons to keep two ends together, to make something of the rock-studded land even in the best of times, had never been lowering. Adversity of that kind was expected, the lot of the family they had been born into.

It had been expected also, when the accident occurred to the man she'd married, that Ellie's mother should return to the house that was by then her brother's. She was forty-one then; her brother forty-four, left alone two years before when their parents had died within the same six months. He hadn't invited her to return, and though it seemed, in the circumstances, a natural consequence to both of them, she knew her brother had always since considered her beholden. As a child, he'd been like that about the few toys they shared, insisting that some were more his than hers.

"I saw Mulreavy," he said on the day of the meeting on the road, his unsmiling, serious features already claiming a successful outcome.

* * *

Mulreavy's lorry had reached the end of its days and still was not fully paid for: within six months or so he would find himself unable to continue trading. This was the consideration that had crept into his mind when the proposition was put to him, and it remained there afterwards. There was a lorry he'd seen in McHugh Bros. with thirty-one thousand on the clock and at an asking price that would be reduced, the times being what they were. Mulreavy hadn't entirely invented the dressmaker from Ballina in whom he had claimed an interest: she was a wall-eyed woman he had recently seen about the place, who had arrived in Moyleglass to assist Mrs. Toomey in her cutting and stitching. Mulreavy had wondered if she had money, if she'd bought her way into Mrs. Toomey's business, as he'd heard it said. He'd never spoken to her or addressed her in any way, but after his conversation with Mr. Larrissey he made further inquiries, only to discover that rumor now suggested the woman was employed by Mrs. Toomey at a small wage. So Mulreavy examined in finer detail the pros and cons of marrying into the Larrisseys.

"There'd be space for you in the house," was how it had been put to him. "Maybe better than if you took her out of it. And storage enough for the potatoes in the big barn."

A considerable saving on day-to-day expenses would result, Mulreavy had reflected, closing his eyes against the smoke from his cigarette when those words were spoken. He made no comment, waiting for further enticements, which came in time. Mr. Larrissey said, "Another thing is, the day will come when the land'll be too much for me. Then again, the day will come when there'll be an end to me altogether."

Mr. Larrissey crossed himself. He said no more, allowing the references to land and his own demise to dangle in the silence. Soon after that he jerked his head in a farewell gesture and drove away.

He'd marry the girl, Mulreavy's thoughts were later, after he'd heard the news about the dressmaker; he'd vacate his property, holding on to it until the price looked right and then disposing of it, no hurry whatsoever since he'd already be in the Larrisseys' farmhouse, with storage facilities and a good lorry. If he attended a bit to the land, the understanding was that he'd inherit it when the day came. It could be done in writing; it could be drawn up by Blaney in Moyleglass.

Eight days after their conversation on the road the two men shook hands, as they did when potatoes were bought and sold. Three weeks went by and then there was the wedding.

* * *

The private view of Ellie's mother—shared with neither her daughter nor her brother—was that the presence of Mulreavy in the farmhouse was a punishment for the brazen sin that had occurred. When the accident that made a widow of her had happened, when she'd looked down at the broken body lying there, knowing it was lifeless, she had not felt that there was punishment in that, directed either at her or at the man she'd married. He had done little wrong in his life; indeed, he had often sought to do good. Neither had she transgressed, herself, except in little ways. But what had led to the marriage of her daughter and the potato dealer was deserving of this harsh reprimand, which was something that must now be lived with.

* * *

Mulreavy was given a bedroom that was furnished with a bed and a cupboard. He was not offered, and did not demand, his conjugal rights. He didn't mind; that side of things didn't interest him. Instead, daily, he surveyed the land that was to be his inheritance. He walked it, lovingly, at first when no one was looking, and later to identify the weed that had to be sprayed and to trace the drains. He visualized a time when he no longer traveled about as a middleman, buying potatoes cheaply and selling at a profit, when the lorry he had acquired with the

dowry would no longer be necessary. On these same poor acres, sufficient potatoes could be grown to allow him to trade as he'd traded before. Mulreavy wasn't afraid of work when there was money to be
made.

*　*　*

The midwife called down the farmhouse stairs a few moments after
Mulreavy heard the first cry. Mr. Larrissey poured out a little of the
whiskey that was kept in the wall-cupboard in case there was toothache
in the house. His sister was at the upstairs bedside. The midwife said a
girl had been born.

A year ago, it was Mr. Larrissey, not his sister, who had first
known about the summer priest who was the father of this child. On his
way back from burning stubble he had seen his niece in the company of
the man and had known from the way they walked that there was
some kind of intimacy between them. When his niece's condition was
revealed he had not, beneath the anger he displayed, been much
surprised.

Mulreavy, clenching his whiskey glass, his lips touched with a
smile, had not known he would experience a moment of happiness
when the birth occurred; nor had he guessed that the dourness of Mr.
Larrissey would be affected, that whiskey would be offered. The thing
would happen, he had thought, maybe when he was out in the fields.
He would walk into the kitchen and they would tell him. Yet in the
kitchen, now, there was almost an air of celebration, a satisfaction that
the arrangement lived up to its promise.

Above where the two men sat, Ellie's mother did as the midwife directed in the matter of the afterbirth's disposal. She watched the baby
being taken from its mother's arms and placed, sleeping now, in the
cradle by the bedside. She watched her daughter struggling for a moment against the exhaustion that possessed her, before her eyes closed
too.

*　*　*

The child was christened Mary Josephine—these family names chosen
by Ellie's mother, and Ellie had not demurred. Mulreavy played his
part, cradling the infant in his big arms for a moment at the font, a suit

bought specially for the occasion. It wasn't doubted that he was the father, although the assumption also was that the conception had come first, the marriage later, as sometimes happened. There'd been some surprise at the marriage, not much.

Ellie accepted with equanimity what there was. She lived a little in the past, in the summer of her love affair, expecting of the future only what she knew of the present. The summer curate who had loved her, and whom she loved still, would not miraculously return. He did not even know that she had given life to his child. "It can't be," he'd said when they lay in the meadow that was now a potato field. "It can't ever be, Ellie." She knew it couldn't be: a priest was a priest. There would never, he promised, as if in compensation, be another love like this in all his life. "Nor for me," she swore as eagerly, although he did not ask for that, in fact said no, that she must live her normal life. "No, not for me," she repeated. "I feel it too." It was like a gift when she knew her child was to be born, a fulfillment, a forgiveness almost for their summer sin.

As months and then years went by, the child walked and spoke and suffered childhood ills, developed preferences, acquired characteristics that slipped away again or stubbornly remained. Ellie watched her mother and her uncle aging, while they in turn were reminded by the child's presence of their own uneasy companionship in the farmhouse when they were as young as the child was now. Mulreavy, who did not go in for nostalgia or observing changes in other people, increased his potato yield. Like Mr. Larrissey, he would have preferred the child who had been born to be a boy, since a boy, later on, would be more useful, but he did not ever complain on this count. Mr. Larrissey himself worked less, in winter often spending days sitting in the kitchen, warm by the Esse stove. For Ellie's mother, passing time did not alter her belief that the bought husband was her daughter's reprimand on earth.

All that was how things were on the farm and in the farmhouse. A net of compromise and acceptance and making the best of things held the household together. Only the child was aware of nothing, neither that a man had been bought to be her father, nor that her great-uncle had benefited by the circumstances, nor that her grandmother had come to terms with a punishment, nor that her mother still kept faith with an improper summer love. The child's world when she was ten had more to do with reading whole pages more swiftly than she had a year ago, and knowing where Heligoland was, and reciting by heart *The Wreck of the Hesperus*.

But, without warning, the household was disturbed. Ellie was aware only of some inner restlessness, its source not identified, which she assumed would pass. But it did not pass, and instead acquired the intensity of unease: what had been satisfactory for the first ten years of her child's life was strangely not so now. In search of illumination, she pondered all that had occurred. She had been right not to wish to walk the roads with her fatherless infant, she had been right to agree to the proposal put to her; looking back, she could not see that she should, in any way whatsoever, have done otherwise. A secret had been kept; there were no regrets. It was an emotion quite unlike regret that assailed her. Her child smiled back at her from a child's innocence, and she remembered those same features, less sure and less defined, when they were newly in the farmhouse, and wondered how they would be when another ten years had passed. Not knowing now, her child would never know. She would never know that her birth had been accompanied by money changing hands. She would never know that, somewhere else, her father forgave the sins of other people, and offered Our Savior's blood and flesh in solemn expiation.

"Can you manage them?" Ellie's husband asked when she was loading sacks onto the weighing scales, for she had paused in the work as if to rest.

"I'm all right."

"Take care you don't strain yourself."

He was often kind in practical ways. She was strong, but the work was not a woman's work and although it was never said, he was aware of this. In the years of their marriage they had never quarreled or even disagreed, not being close enough for that, and in this way their relationship reflected that of the brother and sister they shared the house with.

"They're a good size, the Kerrs," he said, referring to the produce they worked with. "We hit it right this year."

"They're nice, all right."

She had loved her child's father for every day of their child's life and before it. She had falsified her confessions and a holy baptism. Black, ugly lies were there when their child smiled from her innocence, nails in another cross. It hadn't mattered at first, when their child wouldn't have understood.

"I'll stop now," Ellie said, recording in the scales book the number of sacks that were ready to be sealed. "I have the tea to get."

Her mother was unwell, confined to her bedroom. It was usually her mother who attended to the meals.

"Go on so, Ellie," he said. He still smoked forty cigarettes a day, his life's indulgence, a way to spend a fraction of the money he accumulated. He had bought no clothes since his purchase of the christening suit except for a couple of shirts, and he questioned the necessity of the clothes Ellie acquired for herself or for her child. Meanness was a quality he was known for; commercially, it had assisted him.

"Oh, I got up," Ellie's mother said in the kitchen, the table laid and the meal in the process of preparation. "I couldn't lie there."

"You're better?"

"I'd say I was getting that way."

Mr. Larrissey was washing traces of fertilizer from his hands at the sink, roughly rubbing in soap. From the yard came the cries of the child, addressing the man she took to be her father as she returned from her evening task of ensuring that the bullocks still had grass to eat.

*　　*　　*

All the love there had been, all the love there still was—love that might have nourished Ellie's child, that might have warmed her—was the deprivation the child suffered. Ellie remembered the gentle, pale hands of the lover who had given her the gift of her child, and heard again the whisper of his voice, and his lips lingered softly on hers. She saw him as she always now imagined him, in his cassock and his surplice, the embroidered cross that marked his calling repeated again in the gestures of his blessing. His eyes were still a shade of slate, his features retained their delicacy. Why should a child not have some vision of him too? Why should there be falsity?

"You've spoken to them, have you?" her husband asked when she said what she intended.

"No, only you."

"I wouldn't want the girl told."

He turned away in the potato shed to heft a sack onto the lorry. She felt uneasy in herself, she said, the way things were, and felt that more and more. That feeling wasn't there without a reason. It was a feeling she was aware of most at Mass and when she prayed at night.

Mulreavy didn't reply. He had never known the identity of the father. Some runaway fellow, he had been told at the time by Mr. Larrissey, who had always considered the shame greater because a priest was involved. "No need Mulreavy should know that," Ellie had been instructed by her mother, and had abided by this wish.

"It was never agreed," Mulreavy maintained, not pausing in his loading. "It wasn't agreed the girl would know."

Ellie spoke of a priest then; her husband said nothing. He finished with the potato sacks and lit a cigarette. That was a shocking thing, he eventually remarked, and lumbered out of the barn.

"Are you mad, girl?" Her mother rounded on her in the kitchen, turning from the draining board, where she was shredding cabbage. Mr. Larrissey, who was present also, told her not to be a fool: what good in the world would it do to tell a child the like of that?

"Have sense, for God's sake," he crossly urged, his voice thick with the bluster that obscured his confusion.

"You've done enough damage, Ellie," her mother said, all the color gone from her thin face. "You've brought enough on us."

When Mulreavy came into the kitchen an hour later, he guessed at what had been said, but he did not add anything himself. He sat down to wait for his food to be placed in front of him. It was the first time since the arrangement had been agreed upon that any reference to it had been made in the household.

"That's the end of it," Ellie's mother laid down, the statement made as much for Mulreavy's benefit as for Ellie's. "We'll hear no more of this."

Ellie did not reply. That evening she told her child.

* * *

People knew, and talked about it now. What had occurred ten years ago suddenly had an excitement about it that did not fail to please. Minds were cast back, memories ransacked in a search for the name and appearance of the summer priest who had been and gone. Father Mooney, who had succeeded old Father Hanlon, spoke privately to Ellie, deploring the exposure she had "so lightly" been responsible for.

With God's grace, he pointed out, a rough and ready solution had been found and disgrace averted ten years ago. There should have been gratitude for that, not what had happened now. Ellie explained that every time she looked at her child she felt a stab of guilt because a deception of such magnitude had been perpetrated. "Her life was no more than a lie," Ellie said, but Father Mooney snappishly replied that that was not for her to say.

"You flew in the face of things once," he fulminated, "and now you've done it again." When he glared at her, it showed in his expression that he considered her an unfit person to be in his parish. He ordered Hail Marys to be repeated, and penitence practiced, with humility and further prayer.

But Ellie felt that a weight had been lifted from her, and she explained to her child that even if nothing was easy now, a time would come when the difficulties of the moment would all be gone.

* * *

Mulreavy suffered. His small possession of pride was bruised; he hardly had to think to know what people said. He went about his work in the fields, planting and harvesting, spreading muck and fertilizer, folding away checks until he had a stack ready for lodgment in Moyleglass. The sour atmosphere in the farmhouse affected him, and he wondered if people knew, on top of everything else, that he occupied a bedroom on his own and always had, that he had never so much as embraced his wayward young bride. Grown heavier over the years, he became even heavier after her divulgence, eating more in his despondency.

He liked the child; he always had. The knowledge that a summer priest had fathered her caused him to like her no less, for the affection was rooted in him. And the child did not change in her attitude to him, but still ran to him at once when she returned from school, with tales of how the nuns had been that day, which one bad-tempered, which one sweet. He listened as he always had, always pausing in his work to throw in a word or two. He continued to tell brief stories of his past experiences on the road; he had traded in potatoes since he was hardly more than a child himself, fifteen when he first assisted his father.

But in the farmhouse Mulreavy became silent. In his morose mood he blamed not just the wife he'd married but her elders too. They had deceived him. And knowing more than he did about these things, they should have foreseen more than they had. The child bore his name. "Mrs. Mulreavy" they called his wife. He was a laughingstock.

* * *

"I don't remember that man," he said when almost a year had passed, on a September morning. He had crossed the furrows to where she was picking potatoes from the clay he'd turned, the plough drawn by the tractor. "I don't know did I ever see him."

Ellie looked up at the dark, jowled features above the rough, thick neck. She knew which man he meant. She knew, as well, that it had required an effort to step down from his tractor and cross to where she was, to stand unloved in front of her. She said at once, "He was here only a summer."

"That would be it, so. I was always traveling then."

She gave the curate's name and he nodded slowly over it, then shook his head. He'd never heard that name, he said.

The sun was hot on her shoulders and her arms. She might have pointed across the ploughed clay to the field that was next to the one they were in. It was there, below the slope, that the conception had taken place. She wanted to say so, but she didn't. She said, "I had to tell her."

He turned to go away, then changed his mind, and again looked down at her.

"Yes," he said.

She watched him slowly returning to where he'd left the tractor. His movements were always slow, his gait suggesting an economy of energy, his arms loose at his sides. She mended his clothes, she kept them clean. She assisted him in the fields, she made his bed. In all the time she'd known him she had never wondered about him.

The tractor started. He looked behind to see that the plough was as he wanted it. He lit another cigarette before he set off on his next brief journey.

TOBIAS WOLFF

Two Boys and a Girl

Gilbert saw her first. This was in late June, at a party. She was sitting alone in the back yard, stretched out on a lawn chair, when he came out to get a beer from the cooler. He tried to think of something to say to her but she seemed complete in her solitude and he was afraid of sounding intrusive and obvious. Later he saw her again, inside—a pale, dark-haired girl with dark eyes and bright red lipstick, some of which had gotten smeared on her teeth. She was dancing with Gilbert's best friend, Rafe. The night after that she was with Rafe when he picked Gilbert up to go to another party, and again the night after that. Her name was Mary Ann.

Mary Ann, Rafe, and Gilbert. They went everywhere together that summer, to parties and movies and the lake, to the pools of friends, and on long, aimless drives after Gilbert got off work at his father's bookstore. Gilbert didn't have a car, so Rafe did the driving; his grandfather had given him his immaculate old Buick convertible as a reward for getting into Yale. Mary Ann leaned against him with her bare white feet up on the dash while Gilbert sprawled like a pasha in the back and handed out the beers and made ironic comment on whatever attracted his notice.

Gilbert was very ironic. At the high school where he and Rafe had been classmates, the yearbook editors voted him "Most cynical." That pleased him. Gilbert believed disillusionment to be the natural consequence, even the duty, of a mind that could cut through the authorized version to the true nature of things. He made it his business to take nothing on trust, to respect no authority but that of his own judgment, and to be elegantly unsurprised at the grossest crimes and follies, especially those of the world's anointed.

Mary Ann listened to what he said even when she seemed to be occupied with Rafe. Gilbert knew this, and he knew when he'd managed to shock her. She clenched her hands, blinked rapidly, and a red splotch, vivid as a birthmark, appeared on the milky skin of her neck. It wasn't hard to shock Mary Ann. Her father, a captain in the Coast

Guard, was the squarest human being Gilbert had ever met. One night when he and Rafe were waiting for Mary Ann, Captain McCoy stared at Gilbert's sandals and asked what he thought about the beatniks. Mrs. McCoy had doilies all over the house, and pictures of kittens and the Holy Land and dogs playing poker, and in the toilets these chemical gizmos that turned the water blue. Whenever Gilbert took a leak at Mary Ann's house he felt sorry for her.

In August Rafe went fishing in Canada for two weeks with his father. He left Gilbert the keys to the Buick and told him to take care of Mary Ann. Gilbert recognized these words as what the hero of a war movie says to his drab sidekick before he leaves on the big mission.

Rafe delivered this line while he was in his room packing for the trip. Gilbert lounged on the bed watching him. He wanted to talk but Rafe was playing his six-record set of *Il Pagliacci*, which Gilbert didn't believe he really liked, though Rafe made occasional singing noises as if he knew the whole score by heart. Gilbert thought he was taking up opera the same way he'd taken up squash that winter, as an accessory. He lay back and was silent. Rafe went about his business. He was graceful and precise and he assembled his gear without waste of motion or any hesitation as to where things were. At one point he walked over to the mirror and studied himself as if he were alone, and Gilbert was surprised by the anger he felt. Then Rafe turned to him and tossed the keys on the bed and spoke his line about taking care of Mary Ann.

The next day Gilbert drove the Buick around town all by himself. He double-parked in front of Nordstrom's with the top down and smoked cigarettes and watched the women come out as if he were waiting for one of them. Now and then he examined his watch and frowned. He drove onto a pier at the wharf and waved at one of the passengers on the boat to Victoria. She was staring down at the water and didn't see him until she raised her eyes as the boat was backing out of the slip and caught him blowing a kiss at her. She stepped away from the rail and vanished from sight. Later he went to La Luna, a bar near the university where he knew he wouldn't get carded, and took a seat from which he could see the Buick. When the bar filled up he walked outside and raised the hood and checked the oil, right outside La Luna's big picture window. To a man walking past he said, "This damn thing drinks oil like it's going out of style." Then he drove off with a grave expression, as if he had some important and not entirely pleasant business to perform. He stopped and bought cigarettes in two different drugstores. He called home from the second drugstore and told his mother he wouldn't be in for dinner and asked if he'd gotten any mail. No, his mother said, nothing. Gilbert ate at a drive-in and cruised for a while and then went up to the lookout above Alki Point and sat on the hood of the Buick and smoked in a moody, philosophical way, deliberately ignoring the girls with their dates in the cars around him. A heavy mist stole in from the sound. Across the water the lights of the city blurred, and a foghorn began to call. Gilbert flipped his cigarette into the shadows and rubbed his bare arms. When he got home he called Mary Ann, and it was agreed that they would go to a movie the following night.

After the movie Gilbert drove Mary Ann back to her house, but instead of getting out of the car she sat where she was and they went on talking. It was easy, easier than he had thought it would be. When Rafe was with them Gilbert could speak through him to Mary Ann and be witty or deep or outrageous. But in the moments they'd been alone, waiting for Rafe to rejoin them, he had always found himself tongue-tied. It was a kind of panic. He'd cudgel his brains for something to say, and whatever he did come up with sounded tense and sharp. But that didn't happen, that night.

It was raining hard. When Gilbert saw that Mary Ann wasn't in any hurry to get out he cut the engine and they sat there in the faint marine light of the radio tuning band with liquid shadows playing over their faces from the rain streaming down the windshield and the sides of the car. The rain drummed in gusts on the canvas roof, but inside it was warm and close, like a tent during a storm. Mary Ann was talking about nursing school, about her fear that she wouldn't be able to make it in the tough courses, especially Anatomy and Physiology. Gilbert thought she was being ritually humble and said, Oh, come on, you'll do fine.

I don't know, she said. I just don't know. And then she told him how badly she'd done in biology and chemistry and math, and how two of her teachers had personally gone down to the nursing school admissions office to help her get in. Gilbert saw that she really was afraid of failing, and that she had reason to be afraid. Now that she'd said so herself, it made sense to him that she struggled in school. She wasn't quick that way; wasn't clever. There was a simplicity about her.

She leaned back into the corner, watching the rain. She looked sad. Gilbert thought of touching her cheek with the back of his hand to reassure her. He waited a moment and then told her it wasn't exactly true that he was trying to make up his mind whether to go to the University of Washington or Amherst. He should have corrected this misunderstanding before. The actual truth was that he hadn't gotten into Amherst. He'd made it onto a waiting list, but with only three weeks left until school began he figured his odds were just about nil.

She turned and regarded him. He couldn't see her eyes. They were pools of shadow with only a glint of light at the bottom. She asked him why he hadn't gotten in.

To this question Gilbert had no end of answers. He thought of new ones every day, and he was sick of them all. I stopped working, he said. I just completely slacked off.

But you should have gotten in wherever you wanted. You're smart enough.

I talk a pretty good game, I guess. He took out a cigarette and tapped it on the steering wheel. I don't know why I smoke these damn things, he said.

You like the way they make you look. Intellectual.

I guess. He lit it.

She watched him closely as he took the first drag. Let me, she said. Just a puff.

Their fingers touched when he handed her the cigarette.

You're going to be a great nurse, he said.

She took another puff of the cigarette and blew it out slowly.

Neither of them spoke for a while.

I'd better go in, she said.

Gilbert watched her go up the walkway to her house. She didn't hunch and run but moved sedately through the lashing rain as if it were a night like any other. He waited until he saw her go inside and then turned the radio back up and drove away. He kept tasting her lipstick on the cigarette.

When he called from work the next day her mother answered and asked him to wait. Mary Ann was out of breath when she came to the phone. She said she'd been outside on a ladder, helping her dad paint the house. What are you up to? she asked.

I was just wondering what you were doing, he said.

He took her to La Luna that night, and the next. Both times they got the same booth, right near the jukebox. "Don't Think Twice, It's Alright" had just come out and Mary Ann played it again and again while they talked. On the third night some guys in baseball uniforms were sitting there when they came in. Gilbert was annoyed and saw that she was too. They sat at the bar for a time but kept getting jostled by the drinkers behind them. They decided to go someplace else. Gilbert was paying his tab when the baseball players stood up to leave and Mary Ann slipped into the booth just ahead of an older couple who'd been waiting nearby.

We were here first, the woman said to Mary Ann as Gilbert sat down across from her.

This is our booth, Mary Ann said, in a friendly, informative way.

How do you figure that?

Mary Ann looked at the woman as if she had asked a truly eccentric question. Well, I don't know, she said. It just is.

Afterwards it kept coming back to Gilbert, the way Mary Ann had said "our booth." He collected such observations and pondered them when he was away from her: her breathlessness when she came to the phone, the habit she'd formed of taking puffs from his cigarettes and helping herself to his change to play the jukebox, the way she listened to him, with such open credulity that he found it impossible to brag or make excuses or say things merely for effect. He couldn't be facetious with Mary Ann, she always thought he meant exactly what he said, and then he had to stop and try to explain that he'd actually meant something else. He had begun to dislike the sound of his voice when he was employing irony. It sounded weak and somehow envious. It sounded thin and unmanly.

Mary Ann gave him no occasion for it. She took him seriously. She wrote down the names of the books he spoke of, *On the Road, The Stranger, The Fountainhead,* and some others that he hadn't actually read but knew about and intended to read as soon as he found the time. She listened when he explained what was wrong with Barry Goldwater and *Reader's Digest* and the television shows she liked, and she agreed that he was probably right. In the solemnity of her attention he heard himself saying things he had said to no one else, confessing hopes so implausible he had barely confessed them to himself. He was often surprised by his own honesty. But he stopped short of telling Mary Ann what he believed she already knew, because of the chance that she didn't know, or wasn't ready to admit to what she knew. If he said it, everything would change, for all of them. By saying a few words he would change everything and he was afraid to do this.

They went out every night but two, once when Gilbert had to work overtime and once when Captain McCoy took Mary Ann and her mother to dinner. They saw a couple more movies and went to a party and to La Luna and drove around the city. The nights were warm and clear and Gilbert put the top down and poked along in the right lane. He used to wonder, with some impatience, why Rafe drove so slowly. Now he knew. To command the wheel of an open car with a girl on the seat beside you was to be established in a condition that only a fool would hasten to end. He drove slowly around the lake and downtown and up to the lookouts and then back to Mary Ann's house. The first few nights they sat in the car. After that, Mary Ann invited Gilbert inside.

He talked, she talked. She talked about her little sister Kathleen who had died of cystic fibrosis two years before, and whose long, hard dying had brought her family close and given her the idea of becoming a nurse. She talked about friends from school and the nuns who had taught her. She talked about her parents and grandparents and Rafe. All her talk was of her affections. Unconditional enthusiasm generally had a wearying effect on Gilbert, but not on these nights with Mary Ann. She gave praise, it seemed to him, not to shine it back on herself or to dissemble some secret bitterness but because that was her nature. That was how she was, and he liked her for it, as he liked it that she didn't question everything but took the appearance of good for good itself, like a child.

She had been teaching herself the guitar and sometimes she would consent to play and sing for him, old ballads about mine disasters and nice lads getting hung for poaching and noblewomen drowning their babies. He could see how the words moved her: so much that her voice would give out for moments at a time, during which she would bite her lower lip and gaze down at the floor. She put folk songs on the record player and listened to them with her eyes closed. She also liked Roy Orbison and the Fleetwoods and Ray Charles. One night she was bringing some fudge from the kitchen just as "Born to Lose" came on. Gilbert stood and offered his hand with a dandified flourish that she could have laughed off if she'd chosen to. She put the plate down and took his hand and they began to dance, stiffly at first, from a distance, then easily and close. They fit perfectly. Perfectly. He felt the rub of her hips and thighs, the heat of her skin. Her warm hand tightened in his. He breathed in the scent of lavender water with the sunny smell of her hair and the faint salt smell of her body. He breathed it in again and again. And then he felt himself grow hard and rise against her, so that she had to know, she just had to know, and he waited for her to move away. But she did not move away. She pressed close to him until the song ended, and for a moment or two after. Then she stepped back and let go of Gilbert's hand and in a hoarse voice asked him if he wanted some fudge. She was facing him but managing not to look at him.

Maybe later, he said, and held out his hand again. May I have the honor?

She walked over to the couch and sat down. I'm so clumsy.

No you're not. You're a great dancer.

She shook her head.

He sat down in the chair across from her. She still wouldn't look at him. She put her hands together and clamped them between her knees and stared at them.

Then she said, How come Rafe's dad picks on him all the time?

I don't know. There isn't any particular reason. Bad chemistry, I guess.

It's like he can't do anything right. His dad won't let him alone, even when I'm there. I bet he's having a miserable time.

It was true, neither Rafe's father nor his mother could take any pleasure in their son. Gilbert had no idea why this should be so. But it was a strange subject to have boiled up out of nowhere like this, and for her to be suddenly close to tears about it. Don't worry about Rafe, he said. Rafe can take care of himself.

The grandfather clock chimed the Westminster Bells, then struck twelve times. The clock had been made to go with the living room ensemble and its tone was tinny and untrue. It set Gilbert on edge. The whole house set him on edge: the pictures, the matching Colonial furniture, the single bookshelf full of condensed books. It was like a house Russian spies would practice being Americans in.

It's just so unfair, Mary Ann said. Rafe is so sweet.

He's a good egg, Rafe, Gilbert said. Most definitely. One of the best.

He is the best.

Gilbert got up to leave and then Mary Ann did look at him, with something like alarm. She stood and followed him outside, onto the porch. When he looked back from the end of the walkway she was watching him with her arms crossed over her chest. Call me tomorrow, she said. Okay?

I was thinking of doing some reading, he said. Then he said, I'll see. I'll see how things go.

The next night they went bowling. This was Mary Ann's idea. She was a good bowler and frankly out to win. Whenever she got a strike she threw her head back and gave a great bark—*hah!* She questioned Gilbert's score-keeping until he got rattled and told her to take over, which she did without even a show of protest. When she guttered her ball she claimed she'd slipped on a wet spot and insisted on bowling that frame again. He didn't let her, he understood that she would despise him if he did, but her shamelessness somehow made him happier than he'd been all day.

When he pulled up to her house Mary Ann said, Next time I'll give you some pointers. You could be half decent if you knew what you were doing.

He heard that "next time." He killed the engine and turned and looked at her.

Mary Ann, he said.

He had never said so much before.

She looked straight ahead and didn't answer. Then she said, I'm thirsty. You want a glass of juice or something? Before Gilbert could say anything, she added, We'll have to sit outside, okay? I think we woke up my dad last night.

Gilbert waited on the steps while Mary Ann went into the house. The air was pungent with the smells of paint and turpentine. Cans and brushes were lined up along the porch railing. Captain McCoy scraped and painted one side of the house every year. This year he was doing the front. That was just like him, to eke it out one side at a time. Gilbert had once helped the Captain make crushed ice for drinks. The way the Captain did it, he held a single cube in his hand and clobbered it with a hammer until it was pulverized. Then another cube. Then another. Etcetera. When Gilbert wrapped a whole tray's worth in a towel and started to bang it on the counter the Captain grabbed the towel away from him. That's not how you do it! he said. He found Gilbert another hammer and the two of them stood there hitting ice cubes.

Mary Ann came out with a couple of glasses. She sat beside Gilbert, and they drank and looked out at the Buick gleaming under the streetlight.

I'm off tomorrow, Gilbert said. You want to go for a drive?

Gee, I wish I could. I promised my dad I'd paint the fence.

We'll paint, then.

That's all right. It's your day off. You should do something.

Painting's something.

Something you like, dummy.

I like to paint. I love to paint.

Gilbert.

No kidding, I love to paint. Ask my folks. Every free minute, I'm out there with a brush.

Like fun.

So what time do we start? Look, it's only been three hours since I did my last fence and already my hand's starting to shake.

Stop it! I don't know. Whenever. After breakfast.

He finished his orange juice and rolled the glass between his hands. Mary Ann.

He felt her hesitate. What, she said.

He kept rolling the glass. What do your folks think about us going out so much?

They don't mind. I think they're glad, actually.

I'm not exactly their type.

Ha. You can say that again.

What're they so glad about, then?

You're not Rafe.

What, they don't like Rafe?

Oh, they like him, a lot. A whole lot. They're always saying how if they had a son, and so on. But my dad thinks we're getting too serious.

Ah. Too serious. So I'm comic relief.

She shook her head.

I'm not comic relief?

No.

Gilbert put his elbows on the step behind him. He looked up at the sky and said, carefully, He'll be back in a couple of days.

I know.

Then what?

She leaned forward and stared into the yard as if she'd heard a sound.

He waited for a time, aware of every breath he took. Then what? he said again.

I don't know. Maybe . . . I don't know. I'm really kind of tired. You're coming tomorrow, right?

If that's what you want.

You said you were coming tomorrow.

Only if you want me to.
I want you to.
Okay. Sure. Tomorrow, then.

Gilbert stopped at a diner on the way home. He ate a piece of apple pie, then drank coffee and watched the cars go past. To an ordinary person driving by he supposed he must look pretty tragic, sitting here alone over a coffee cup, cigarette smoke curling past his face. And the strange thing was, that person would be right. He was about to betray his best friend. He was about to cut Rafe off from the two people he trusted most, possibly, he understood, from trust itself. Himself, too, he would betray—the idea he had of himself, held deep under the stream of his flippancy, as one who would die before he'd betray a friend. And he knew what he was doing. That was why this whole thing was tragic, because he knew what he was doing and could not do otherwise.

He had thought it all out. He could give himself reasons. Rafe and Mary Ann would have broken up anyway, sooner or later. Rafe was moving on. He didn't know it, but he was leaving them behind. He'd have roommates, guys from rich families who'd invite him home for vacation, take him skiing, sailing. He'd wear a tuxedo to debutante parties where he'd meet girls from Smith and Mt. Holyoke, philosophy majors, English majors, girls with ideas who were reading the same books he was reading and other books too, who could say things he wouldn't have expected them to say. He'd get interested in one of these girls and go on road trips with his friends to her college. She'd come to New Haven. They'd rendezvous in Boston, New York. He'd meet her parents. And on the first day of his next trip home, honorable Rafe would enter Mary Ann's house and leave half an hour later with a sorrowful face and a heart leaping with joy. There wouldn't be many more trips home, not after that. What was here to bring him all that way? Not his parents, those crocodiles. Not Mary Ann. Himself? Good old Gilbert? Please.

And Mary Ann, what about Mary Ann? When Rafe double-timed her and then dropped her cold what would happen to that simple goodheartedness of hers? Would she begin to suspect it, stand guard over it? He was right to do anything to keep that from happening.

These were the reasons, and they were good reasons, but Gilbert could not make use of them. He knew that he would do what he was going to do even if Rafe stayed at home and went to college with him, or if

Mary Ann was somewhat more calculating. Reasons always came with a purpose, to give the appearance of struggle between principle and desire. But there'd been no struggle. Principle had power only until you found what you had to have.

Captain McCoy was helping Mrs. McCoy into the car when Gilbert pulled up behind him. Captain McCoy waited as she gathered her dress inside, then closed the door and walked back toward the Buick. Gilbert came around to meet him.

Mary Ann tells me you're going to help with the fence.

Yes, sir.

There's not that much of it—shouldn't take too long.

They both looked at the fence, about forty feet of white pickets that ran along the sidewalk and joined up with the two privet hedges that formed the side boundaries of the yard. Mary Ann came out on the porch and mimed the word Hi.

Captain McCoy said, Would you mind picking up the paint? It's that Glidden store down on California. Just give 'em my name. He opened his car door, then looked at the fence again. Scrape her good. That's the secret. Give her a good scraping and the rest'll go easy. And try not to get any paint on the grass.

Mary Ann came through the gate and waved as her parents drove off. She said that they were going over to Bremerton to see her grandmother. Well, she said. You want some coffee or something?

I'm fine.

He followed her up the walk. She had on cutoffs. Her legs were very white and they flexed in a certain way as she climbed the porch steps. Captain McCoy had set out two scrapers and two brushes on the railing, all four of them exactly parallel. Mary Ann handed Gilbert a scraper and they went back to the fence. What a day! she said. Isn't it the most beautiful day? She knelt to the right of the gate and began to scrape. Then she looked back at Gilbert watching her and said, Why don't you do that side over there? We'll see who gets done first.

There wasn't much to scrape: some blisters, a few peeling places here and there. This fence is in fine shape, Gilbert said. How come you're painting it?

It goes with the front. When we paint the front, we always paint the fence.

It doesn't need it. All it needs is some retouching.

I guess. Dad wanted us to paint it, though. He always paints it when he paints the front.

Gilbert stopped, looked behind him at the gleaming white house, the bright, weedless lawn trimmed to the nap of a crew cut.

Guess who called this morning, Mary Ann said.

Who.

Rafe! There was a big storm coming in, so they left early. He'll be back tonight. He sounded really great. He said to say hi.

Gilbert resumed running the scraper up and down the pickets.

It was so good to hear his voice, Mary Ann said. I wish you could have been here to talk to him.

A kid went by on a bicycle, balloons thrumming against the spokes.

We should do something, Mary Ann said. Surprise him. Maybe we could take the car over to the house, be waiting out front when he gets back. Wouldn't that be great?

I wouldn't have any way to get home.

Rafe can give you a ride.

Gilbert sat back and watched Mary Ann. She was halfway down her section of the fence. He waited for her to turn and face him. Instead she knelt to work at a spot near the ground. Her hair fell forward, exposing the nape of her neck. Maybe you could invite someone along, Mary Ann said.

Invite someone. What do you mean, a girl?

Sure. It would be nice if you had a girl. It would be perfect.

Gilbert threw the scraper against the fence. He saw Mary Ann freeze. It would *not* be perfect, he said. When she still didn't turn around he stood and went up the walk and through the house to the kitchen. He paced back and forth. He went to the sink, drank a glass of water, and stood with his hands on the counter. He saw what Mary Ann was thinking of, the two of them sitting in the open car, herself jumping out as Rafe pulled up, the wild embrace. Rafe unshaven, reeking of smoke and nature, a little abashed at all this emotion in front of his father but pleased too, and amused. And all the while Gilbert looking coolly on, hands in his pockets, ready to say the sly, mocking words that would tell Rafe that all was as before, Mary Ann unchanged, himself unchanged. That was how she saw it going. As if nothing had happened.

Mary Ann had just about finished her section when Gilbert came back outside. I'll go get the paint, he told her. I don't think there's much left to scrape on my side, but you can take a look.

She stood and tried to smile. Thank you, she said.

He saw that she had been in tears, and this did not soften him but confirmed him in his purpose.

Mary Ann had already spread out the tarp, pulling one edge under the fence so the drips wouldn't get on the grass. When Gilbert opened the can she laughed and said, Look! They gave you the wrong color.

No, that's exactly the right color.

But it's *red*. We always do white. Like it is now.

You don't want to use white, Mary Ann. Believe me.

She frowned.

Red is the perfect color here. No offense, but white is the worst choice you could make.

But the house is white.

Exactly, Gilbert said. So are the houses next door. You put a white fence here, what you end up with is complete boredom. It's like being in a hospital, you know what I mean?

I don't know. I guess it is a lot of white.

What the red will do, the red will give some contrast and pick up the bricks in the walk. It's just what you want here.

Well, maybe. The thing is, I don't think I should. Not this time. Next time, maybe, if my dad wants to.

Look. Mary Ann. What your dad wants is for you to use your own head.

Mary Ann squinted at the fence.

He said, You have to trust me on this, okay?

She sucked in her lower lip, then nodded. Okay. If you're sure.

Gilbert dipped his brush. The world's bland enough already, right? Everyone's always talking about the banality of evil—what about the evil of banality?

They painted through the morning and afternoon. Every now and then Mary Ann would back off a few steps and take in what they'd done. At first she kept her thoughts to herself. The more they painted, the more she had to say. Toward the end she went out into the street and stood there with her hands on her hips. It's interesting, isn't it? Really different. I see what you mean about picking up the bricks. It's pretty red, though.

It's perfect.
Think my dad'll like it?
No question. He'll be crazy about it.
Think so? Gilbert? Really?
Wait till you see his face.

JOHN ASHBERY

Dangerous Moonlight

Of course you will. It happens even after you're dead.
Or, in some cases, the results are positive, but the verdict
negative. "In such a muddle," you said, and "all muddled up."
I wish I could help, but I've a million things to do
and restoring your peace of mind isn't one of them. There goes my
     phone. . . .

The professor's opinion on all this was: "Well, he leaps around,
doesn't he, your little surgeon poet. Seems to lead an agitated life
on the surface, but if you really listen to him, you find he's got
everything down pat. Knows where his bread is buttered, and his ass.
I could open a drawer of rhetorical footnotes, translated from
the Japanese or Old Church Slavonic, if I felt like it, and in there'd
be something that rhymes with him and his coziness, his following the
     trail
all the way back to its point of origin. Plus his lively friendliness, which
co-exists, numinously I grant, with a desire to inflict harm.

"There is a kind of poetry in mere existence.
the kind shopkeepers and people walking along the street lead,
you know, and evenness, that fills them up to whatever brim
is there, and stays, transient, all the days of their lives.
Such enharmonics are not for your poet-person. He sees, and breeds:
otherwise the game isn't worth the candle to him. He'd as soon rhyme
     breeze
with breathes as walk over to that fire hydrant in the grass
to examine it, see what it's made of, make sure it's not an idea in some
philosopher's mind that will bruise and cloud over once that mind's
removed, leaving but a dubious trace of itself, like a ring of puffball
     dust. . . ."

Suppose we grant its power of conserving to listening,
so it's really a full-fledged element in the creative process.
Well, others have done just that from time immemorial,
when women wore tall cones on their heads with sails attached to them.
But, as mattering ages, it hardens into something smooth like good
    luck,
no longer kinetic. Then you can listen all you want
at palace doors, creaky vents. . . .

This imploring precess is twofold. First, let's not forget its root
in implosive. That's something it's got up its sleeve.
Did you ever seen an anarchist without his round bomb?
And then the someone that's got to be implored,
how does he fit in? I'll tell you: like a wedge that was subtracted
from a wheel of cheese and is replaced, so that it fits perfectly;
no one can see where the cut was. Well, that's
poetic argument for you. It stands on its own ("The cheese stands
    alone")
but can at the drop of a speculation be seen again as a part,
a vital one, of the mucus cloud that is generalized human thought
    aimed at
a quarrel or a rebus in the lining. And that's the way
we get old with poetry. Comes a time when no one has a notion
of anything else, and the odor of fried brains contends
with the damp of vacant ancestral halls, to their mutual
betterment, actually. Here, had me that cod. . . .

FRANK BIDART

A Coin for Joe, with the Image of a Horse;
c.350–325 BC

COIN

        chip of the closed,—L O S T world, toward whose unseen grasses

this long-necked emissary horse

               eagerly still
               stretches, to graze

       *

                                World; Grass;

stretching Horse;—ripe with hunger, bright circle
summoned back to us now to famish us, exiled, scarred
                            underground . . . for

you   chip of the incommensurate
closed world   *A n g e l*

LUCIE BROCK-BROIDO

Evangelical

The Hood is far under way & I think it a Beauty.
You resemble the one who wears

The cloth mask & is paid for putting
Down a man—the gentility of strangers is stranger

Than the sweetness of the more corporeal, a friend.
These behaviors of the year bewilder

Me, the branches do not know
To flourish or to char & bend, like the evangelicals.

I wanted so much to mingle with them
In their pageantry, herding like pachyderms

In their dry domain, standing still, grazing
On nothing, like flocks of firemen asbestos-

Robed, collecting on a parking lot, witnessing
A velvet building as it burns to ground.

Ninety-seven percent of my world is wizardry,
Three percent is organ, bone.

I was a passenger or a witness
In the crowd, anonymous & angelical.

Does not my heart astound you?
An executioner's career is all applause.

JOSEPH BRODSKY

Anti-Shenandoah: Two Skits and a Chorus of Going East

I. Departure

"Why don't we board a train and go off to Persia?
Persia doesn't exist, obviously, but inertia
does. It's a better vehicle than any old engine, Johnny,
and we may have a comfortable, an eventful journey."

"Why do you call me 'Johnny' when you know I am Billy, Mary?
Perhaps because of inertia? It's Johnny you want to marry,
not me. But he is not in Persia, he went off to Warsaw,
although after 1945 it's a different city also."

"Of course, you are Billy, Billy; and I'm not Mary, either.
Actually, I am Suzy: you are welcome to check my visa.
But let's be Mary and Johnny, like in the Ark of Noah,
or nameless, the way we were when we were spermatozoa."

"Because there are but two sexes, there is a lot of nuance,
and history's where our exes join kings and ruins.
When someone's whereabouts become a mystery,
you should take the train of thought that goes to history."

"Ah, there is so much action! In history, willy-nilly,
Mary becomes just Suzy, and Johnny Billy,
B.C. becomes A.D., and Persia Warsaw.
For history breeds inertia, and vice versa."

"Ah, mixing inertia with history bespeaks individuality!
  Mary, let's take a chance, this father of causality:
  let's take the Express to where folks live in utter penury
  and where the reality quickly becomes a memory."

"Oh, he is my dear boy, my slowly peeled banana!"
"And she is my sweetheart filled with Tampax Americana!"
"The future arrives on time whistling Domine Gloria.
  and we must take it Eastward, where it's always earlier."

II. Arrival

"What is this place? It looks kind of raw.
  The trees stand as if they are about to draw,
  their rustle is so menacing. They, no doubt,
  have seen too many movies—but were they dubbed?"

"I don't mind the place, but who are these guys?
  Is this their true appearance, or disguise?
  They all sell shoelaces but wear no shoes.
  Can we explain to them that we are not Jews?"

"I never knew that history is so much
  inhabited and curious, and prone to touch.
  Oh, do they have a leader? A shah? A khan?
  Frankly, I regret I don't have my gun."

"But I've read many people can't wish the same
  wish. Unless, of course, they are insane.
  I think we are quite safe; they don't want to kill,
  though frankly I regret I am off the pill."

"Ah, this is the past, and it's rather vast,
  and in the land of the cause its effects go bust
  or else get outnumbered in more ways than one:
  we've brought them all the future, and we are left with none."

"One shouldn't speak for others when things get tight.
　You might not have the future, but I just might.
　The future is derivative; they may crack skulls,
　but because they've been so primitive, we've had Pascals."

"So it's goodbye, dear Mary. Hope all goes well.
　We'll meet not in the future but, say, in Hell."
"Oh, that would be nice, dear Johnny, that would be great.
　But the afterlife in history occurs quite late."

III. Chorus

　Here they are, for all to see,
　　the fruits of complacency.
　Beware of love, of A.D., B.C.,
　　and the travel agency.

　A train may move fast, but time is slow.
　　History's closer
　to the Big Bang than to Roman Law,
　　and you are the loser.

CHARLES BUKOWSKI

Between the Earthquake, the Volcano and the Leopard

Fante

every now and then it comes back to
me,
him in bed there, blind,
being slowly chopped away,
the little bulldog.
the nurses passing through, pulling
at curtains, blinds, sheets.
seeing if he was still alive.
the Colorado Kid.
the scourge of the *American
Mercury.*
Mencken's Catholic bad boy.
gone Hollywood.
and tossed up on shore.
being chopped away.
chop, chop, chop.
until he was gone.

he never knew he would be
famous.
I wonder if he would have given
a damn.
I think he would have.

John, you're big time now.
you've entered the Books of
Forever
right there with Dostoevsky,

Tolstoy, and your boy
Sherwood Anderson.

I told you.
and you said, "you wouldn't
shit an old blind man,
would you?"

ah, no need for that,
bulldog.

the observer

every time I drove past the hospital
I looked at it and thought, some day
I'll be in there.
and eventually I was in there,
sometimes sitting at this long
narrow window
and watching the cars pass on the
street below, as I once had
done.

it was a stupid window.
I had to sit on two folded blankets so that
I could see out.
they had built the window so that part of
the wooden frame
was eye-height
so you either had to look over or
under it.
so I sat on the blankets and looked
over.
well, the window wasn't stupid,
the designers
were.

so I sat there and watched the cars
pass on the street and I thought,
those lucky sons of bitches don't

know how lucky they
are
just to be dumb and driving through
the air
while I sit here on top of my
years
trapped,
nothing but a face in the window
that nobody ever
saw.

August, 1993

easy, go easy, you can't outlast the mountain,
you've just come back from another
war,
go easy.
they are clamoring for you to do it for them once
again,
let them wait.
sit in the shade, wait for your strength to
return.
you'll know when the time is here.
then you'll arrive
for yourself and for them.
a bright sun.
a new fire.
a new gamble.
but
for now
go easy.
let them wait.
let them watch the new boys, the old
boys
meanwhile, you'll need a day or two
to sharpen the
soul,
musing through these D. H. Lawrence
afternoons,
these horseless days,

these nights of music trickling from the
walls,
this waiting for the fullness and the
charge.

this night

I sit in a chair on the balcony
and drink natural spring
water.
the large palms run down the
hill with their dark
heads.
I can see the lights of this
city, of several
cities.

I sit in this balcony chair
where a high voltage wire runs
down and connects underneath
here
where I can reach out and
touch it.
(we can go very fast around
here.)
I hold a bottle of natural
spring water.
a plane flies high in the
overcast, I can't see him,
he can't see
me.
he is very fast.
I can't catch him but I can
pass him by
stretching out
my hand.

it's a cool summer night.
hell trembles near by,
stretches.

I sit in this chair.
my 9 cats are
close by.

I lift the bottle of water,
take a large
swallow.

things will be far worse than
they are
now.
and far
better.

I wait.

betting on now

I am old enough to have died several
times and I almost have,
now I drive my car through the sun
and over the freeway and past
Watts and to the racetrack
where the parking lot attendants
and the betting clerks
throw garlands of flowers at
me.
I've reached the pause before the full
stop and they are celebrating
because it just seems proper.
what the hell.
the hair I've lost to chemo-
therapy is slowly growing
back but my feet are numb
and I must concentrate on my
balance.
old and battered, olden
matter,
I am still lucky with the
horses.

the consensus is that I
have a few seasons
left.
you would never believe
that I was once young
with a narrow razor face
and crazy eyes of
gloom.
no matter, I sit at my
table
joking with the waiters.
we know it's a fixed
game.
it's funny, Christ, look
at us:
sitting ducks.
"what are you having?"
asks my waiter.
"oh," I say and
read him something
from the menu.
"okay," he says
and walks away
between the earthquake,
the volcano and the
leopard.

C. P. CAVAFY

TRANSLATED BY EDMUND KEELEY AND DIMITRI GONDICAS

The Ships

From Imagination to the Blank Page. A difficult crossing, the waters dangerous. At first sight the distance seems small, yet what a long voyage it is, and how injurious sometimes for the ships that undertake it.

The first injury derives from the highly fragile nature of the merchandise that the ships transport. In the marketplaces of Imagination most of the best things are made of fine glass and diaphanous tiles, and despite all the care in the world, many break on the way, and many break when unloaded on the shore. Moreover, any such injury is irreversible, because it is out of the question for the ship to turn back and take delivery of things equal in quality. There is no chance of finding the same shop that sold them. In the marketplaces of Imagination, the shops are large and luxurious but not long-lasting. Their transactions are short-lived, they dispose of their merchandise quickly and immediately liquidate. It is very rare for a returning ship to find the same exporters with the same goods.

Another injury derives from the capacity of the ships. They leave the harbors of the opulent continents fully loaded, and then, when they reach the open sea, they are forced to throw out a part of the load in order to save the whole. Thus, almost no ship manages to carry intact as many treasures as it took on. The discarded goods are of course those of the least value, but it happens sometimes that the sailors, in their great haste, make mistakes and throw precious things overboard.

And upon reaching the white paper port, additional sacrifices are necessary. The customs officials arrive and inspect a product and consider whether they should allow it to be unloaded; some other product is not permitted ashore; and some goods they admit only in small quantities. A country has its laws. Not all merchandise has free entry, and contraband is strictly forbidden. The importation of wine is restricted, because the continents from which the ships come produce wines and spirits from grapes that grow and mature in more generous temperatures. The customs officials do not want these alcoholic products in the least. They are highly intoxicating. They are not appropriate for all palates. Besides, there is a local company that has the monopoly in wine. It produces a beverage that has the color of wine and the taste of water, and this you can drink the day long without being affected at all. It is an old company. It is held in great esteem, and its stock is always overpriced.

Still, let us be pleased when the ships enter the harbor, even with all these sacrifices. Because, after all, with vigilance and great care, the number of broken or discarded goods can be reduced during the course of the voyage. Also, the laws of the country and the customs regulations, though oppressive in large measure, are not entirely prohibitive, and a good part of the cargo gets unloaded. Furthermore, the customs officials are not infallible: some of the merchandise gets through in mislabeled boxes that say one thing on the outside and contain something else; and, after all, some choice wines are imported for select symposia.

Something else is sad, very sad. That is when certain huge ships go by with coral decorations and ebony masts, with great white and red flags unfurled, full of treasures, ships that do not even approach the harbor either because all of their cargo is forbidden or because the harbor is not deep enough to receive them. So they continue on their way. A favorable wind fills their silk sails, the sun burnishes the glory of their golden prows, and they sail out of sight calmly, majestically, distancing themselves forever from us and our cramped harbor.

Fortunately, these ships are very scarce. During our lifetime we see two or three of them at most. And we forget them quickly. Equal to the radiance of the vision is the swiftness of its passing. And after a few years have gone by, if—as we sit passively gazing at the light or listening to the silence—if someday certain inspiring verses return by chance to our mind's hearing, we do not recognize them at first and we torment our memory trying to recollect where we heard them before. With great effort the old remembrance is awakened, and we recall that those verses are from the song chanted by the sailors, handsome as the heroes of the *Iliad,* when the great, the exquisite ships would go by on their way—who knows where.

Translators' note: This early prose poem, among the very few Cavafy wrote, is here translated into English for the first time. It was among the unpublished works found in the Cavafy archive and was first published in Athens in 1986 by George Savidis, who estimates the date of composition to be between 1895 and 1896. Only a few poems in the

Cavafy canon have been assigned an earlier date of composition, though the most famous poem in the canon, "Waiting for the Barbarians," was written just two years later. The language of "The Ships" ("Ta Ploia") is fairly strict *katharevousa*, or purist Greek, more formal and stilted than the mixed purist and demotic language of Cavafy's maturest work.

DEBORAH DIGGES

Rune for the Parable of Despair

Little left of me that year—I had a vision
I was strata, atmosphere.
Or it was that the host entire coded in my blood
found voice and shrieked, for instance,
at what we now call *roads*
and I must maneuver freeways, bridges with these inside me
falling to their knees beating the ground howling.
One might well ask why they'd come forward—
fugitive flushed from a burning house,
converts fed down the aisles,
bumping and blubbering their way into revival light,
light so eroding, the human face is aberration,
the upright stance a freak
with no means otherwise.

Some things won't translate backwards.
Some things can't be undone,
though it takes years to learn this, years.
Such were the serial exhaustions of my beliefs,
whatever drug worn off that must belong to youth,
or to the feminine, or simply to the genes begun a wintering.
Then I knew the purest bitterness,
as if my heart were a wrecking ball,
my love for the man an iron bell used of the wind,
calling to task a population,
calling them in, as from these fields,
before the stone wheel became speech,
before fire dropped from the sky to be caged and carried into the caves.
And so they came to be with me,

whom I suspect was nothing more to them than shelter,
a ransomed hall, a shipwreck among dead trees,
the fallen branches lichen-studded,
which they dragged into my rooms.
And when the lights burned out they wept,
and when the heat was gone they gathered my rugs around them.
I'd never known how quickly a house
can be taken back, taken down,
nor will I grant myself the balm—
though it's been centuries—
that I was blessed to see it turned inside out,
the furniture thrown through the windows, and the books
to lie face up, riffling, swelling, until the pages
emptied into a thousand seasons,

books that once possessed the magnet pull of stars!
In the end I let them keep the house
the way they wanted, wash from the toilet,
hang yew boughs from the eaves,
my sturdy doors fallen from the hinges,
even my hair commingling with theirs—
huge animal clumps aswirl in the eddies
of spiders' eggs and broken teeth and cemetery moss and pine needles—
until not one ornament was left that said I lived,
not even a drinking glass
I might have toasted with just as the clouds
shifted, my shadow disappeared.
O, drink from once before my leaving, leaving.
With any luck, I sang, I'll be in hell by Christmas.

ANNIE DILLARD

Pastoral

—Max Picard, The World of Silence, *1948. Trans.*
Stanley Godman, 1952.

Sometimes when a peasant moves with the plough and the oxen
Over the broad surface of the field,
It is as if the vault of the sky might take

Up into itself the peasant, the plough, and the oxen.
It is as though time had been sown into silence.
The cattle: the broad surface of their backs . . .

Animals lead silence through the world of man.
It is as if they were carrying silence.
A bird flies slowly into the sky. Its movements

Are trails that keep the silence enclosed. Grain
And stars both shine through the mist and haze.
Two cows in a field moving with a man beside them:

It is as if the man were pouring down silence
From the backs of the animals on to the fields.
The eye of the gods falls on the figures, and they increase.

STEPHEN DOBYNS

Painful Fingers

for Joel Brouwer

In the Museum of the Ethical Neutrality of Tools,
Billy the Kid's sixgun rests on a red cushion
like a virgin anticipating the caresses
of her first lover. The razor of Jack the Ripper

wonders what the fuss is about. The dagger
of Lady Macbeth drowsily dreams of fog-smeared
hills and the Hey-what-the-heck attitude of sheep.
Racks of bombs, boxes of grenades, glass cases

of tommy guns, brass knuckles, executioners' axes
variously contemplate trips to the beach, nights
staring up at the stars, the innocent delight
of hearing an old lady's giddy and abandoned laugh.

And there in the corner, in a place of honor,
the sword of Achilles neither broods nor weeps.
Taffeta tints drift through its childish sensibilities.
For us the past was murder; it felt it was dancing.

Don't go near it! Do you see the guard at the exit
with the bandaged hand? Mistakenly, believing
himself secure, he unlocked the padlocked door.
Who could have told him the blade still burned?

STEPHEN DUNN

The Living

Our trees limb-heavy and silver—
the beautiful never more on the edge
of breaking—and the indiscriminate
freezing rain slicking
the side streets and back alleys,
the long driveways of the rich.

Nothing moving except kids, the stopped world
just slippery to them, permissive, good.

Our cupboards are near empty.
The liquor cabinet too.
Under the eaves some unfrozen logs
in case the electricity goes.
Bosnians, Sudanese flicker into our lives,
flicker out. To think of them is to lose
any right to complain.

Will the mail get through? What is uppermost
and most deep down?
I'd like to feel, once again, what I know.

Now a lone car braving it, going slow,
kids on its fender.
Icicles exclamatory from the shed's roof.
Everywhere a whiteness, a dare.
What's underneath is sure
to have something underneath it.
All the way in: that's where crazy is.
The cable's out, or down.
The TV screen is snow.

A branch snaps,
and the comparisons that come
are whipcrack, gunshot—the almost dead.
What to do with the barely living
before they die? Exhaust them, I say,
shellac them with our tongues.
Isn't overuse a form of love?
Like a gunshot; like a whipcrack; both,
one last time.

The forecast is more of the same.
And then a few things worse.

I feel like making a little path
from house to car,
then I'm going to scrape.
Wait until it all stops, my wife says.
Is she a realist or an optimist?
I've got my coat on.
I've got the hard-edged shovel in my hand.

ALLEN GINSBERG

Apocalypse of Les Halles

Vast barn over the streets
Puddles of mud and blood in the gutter
Red truck heads growl and push asleep
Carts full of lungs carts full of liver carts full of hearts
Carts full of heads
The lungs shaking and quivering
A huge cow's head ogled and nodded at the curb
A cart full of flowers, cortege piled on wooden rollers from the basement
A cart full of jaws entering the elevator
Enamel trays tin buckets and stomachs emerging
Hollow bong, an empty cart bellowing against the wall
An old woman stained with blood
Six men stand on the street corner shaking hands, blood running down
      white smocks
A man with the head of a skinned pig walks the cobble street
A man with head full of wires appears Plug him in
Slowly judiciously methodically a red corpse on his shoulders he
      marches the slippery aisle
A cart full of hooves
Red tails hang the streaky thighs rap the laborer's back
A grey shirt under his smock sways over dungareed buttocks he pushes
      his meat into the door
Snuffle and grunt of dopey trucks
Rumble of iron wheels against splintered wood, Mud-track of truck
      wheels huge sneakers of Martian athletes laid across the road
Corpses identical hanging in hundred perspective under the staring
      light bulb
Candelabra of the racks
Legs laid out on the ground like silverware
Heads of sudden menace the herds of trucks the bloody smeared apron
      of a fool

Fat butchers clutching their corpse breasts split down the middle with
    an ax
Ribs and backbones in rows Six carts coming at once in different
    directions.
Pushers in hip boots
Elevators full of blood descending
Six wheeled carts rumbling empty over Rimbaud's grave
Sweet lady in an apron what're you doing here
Ten fat men struggling with the ass end of a cow
A ballet dancer pushes an empty cart to midstreet and leaves it there
    with a despairing gesture
Comes back pulling a cart full of cows heads
Here come secret prisoners wrapped in brown burlap
Here come mummies of Egypt for breakfast
Layers of lard trains full of pigeons
Great bellies limping in the void
Peter demanding "pigs feet sticking out of boxes like strawberries" be
    noticed
A 5 foot huge brown basket full of brains
I thought it was a prehistoric six-feet hairy skull
Horns sticking out of naked goats heads
Who little boys holding hands peering at the flowers
O the rumble! two shiny pigs heads snouts to Heaven
O the roar! wide eyed head of truck charging at my pen
High halls
A man in beret feels up the assholes of hanging pigs he's an official
O the Fish smell! O the Liver stink! O itchy nosed butchers of Paris!
Bicyclists balancing boxes of chest muscles
Ox breasts jiggling up and down like great rubbery jokes at dawn
Burlap spread over the scene Heavenly burlap for curtain
Cows rise up dancing
A whiff of mammal smell in the atmosphere a peep of blue gowns of
    angels' bloody aprons.
Fellow conspirators, Eat!

September 1958

LOUISE GLÜCK

Symposium

You don't love the world.
If you loved the world you'd have
images in your poems.

John loves the world. He has
a motto: judge not
lest ye be judged. Don't

argue this point
on the theory it isn't possible
to love what one refuses
to know: to refuse

speech is not
to suppress perception.

Look at John, out in the world,
running even on a miserable day
like today. Your
staying dry is like the cat's pathetic
preference for hunting dead birds—completely

consistent with your risk-free spiritual themes:
autumn, loss, darkness, etc.

We can all write about suffering
with our eyes closed. You should show people
more of yourself; show them your clandestine
passion for red meat.

JORIE GRAHAM

Flood

So in the cave of the winds he prisoned the north wind.

(no, it's too heavy, besides, how shall I put it)

And the north wind and the west wind and such others as

(sometimes the mood of a moment, sometimes an almond tree)

as cause the clouds of the sky to flee, and he turned loose

(oh empty cupboards, waiting for sleep, sleep)

turned the southerly loose and the southerly came

(we are far into the cave of seem, uneven rain, how

shall I put it) came out streaming, with drenched wings

dripping, and pitch black (how the Prince would laugh)

darkness veiling his terrible

(in those days and how his stories)

countenance, his beard

(but look out this window)(how solemn you are!)

heavy with rain, his locks a torrent, mists his chaplet,

and his wings (and you slept) and his linens and his other garments

running with rain. . . .

2

Now his wide hands squeeze together the wide low-hanging

clouds. Crash and rumble. Cloudbursts. Rainbow.

We are so happy in our way of life.

Thunder fills the apartment like news then is re-
                              placed—
(because it's true?)

and then the doorbell rang—

and then the rainbow's there, light drawing water from
                              the teeming mud
and sucking it up into the cloud again. Nothing

remains. (To say how pleased). Although a rumbling's

drawn across the sky. And tiny insuck where the cigarette
                              is lit.
And hums. And clicks. And lower tones. . . . Well that will do. So in the end
                              something
remains? But what? The crops aren't spared. The farmer

prays. See him now in his dark kitchen at the
                              seeping
end of day—back bent at prayer—right there at the heart

of events—the hollow inside him

swinging, dusty, Yahweh's gamble, Jove's quick

rage, and a sudden breeze at the very end now of
                              this day

lifting the curtains, lifting the tiny beaded seam of sun
                                        in them—
something that won't rub off if you should wish

to take it in your hands. (Oh take it in your hands). Then it is night.

3

Next day, blue skies. Below, blue mud with sky in it.

Above, blue sky with its mud hidden—

mud opening its seams, mud slackening the hard em-
                                        bankments—
thinning them—silt—chalk—as if the whole thing should be
                                sky—fieldwalls

dissolving—hedgerows stringy streams—roots splayed—

roots rotted off—white slush—and cellwalls, slush—

and the honeycombing masonry that separates and breeds, slush—

whole hillsides of thread-thin ash-white roots exposed,

all running downhill, gleaming, watery,

slipping their threaded, knotted

source, and the stems
    are set free
and the leafy ex-
    tensions of rootline, the sun's
outermost meta-
    morphoses, light's outstretched
nailtip, light's beckonings, light's green
    in-chatters with sun

now glazed-down
    darkly, drawn down over the newly exposed scree—
wilty, syrupy—

—(as if the whole world must dissolve again)—

scummy, sleek—all the stubby quickenings of difference now

crushed back into one inky mottling, dank—the world
                              a sudden ripening
over rock and then, in the rush, the world just shiny
                                rock again—

4

Oh let the river horses run wild as ever they would.

Their hooves: the rocks amid the deep roots loosening.

Their heavy breathing: the acceleration; rivulets
                          venting in sudden
loose spots—whitewaters, incurlings—

foam and tossing of manes over bedrock, tossing
                where the muscle of taproot snaps—
gleaming withers where rock-lichens are stripped off, where
                         difference is sanded

off. . . .
    And they obeyed, running.

And the earth opened for them.

And orchards are swept away, grain stores and cattle.

And men and houses, bridges, (temples) (shrines with

holy fires)—

5

An anchor drags the still-green meadow. A dog

barks, or is it a piece of cornice floating by. A feature. A
                             distinction . . . Do you wish
                        to pick it up?
A living cow floats among the floating carcasses.

Dogs come swimming with curious wonders.

(It is an honor)(this carrying what is being said)

Sun fingers down, weakening, to the city-park
                                  below;
row-houses; fencing. Schools turn abruptly, catching
                                  the light,
the private life, what is the private life, what is it
                        that is *nobody's*
                        business
through this glassless display case,

through this length of hallway holding corridors of water?

Bass dive through the woods.

A wolf swims frantic by the floating lamb.

A living deer and then a doll—dress wide with floating—

are borne along—

the wild pig finds all his strength useless—

is there impatience now? there is no impatience—

the deer cannot outspeed the current—

the wind tries to billow the surface of water
but finds itself slowed to a thick ripple—

birds fly low looking for someplace to land—
one tumbles, exhausted, into the current—

the wings are turned again and again by waters—
frothings, suctions: they change shape
                              slightly
but do not vary . . .

Those are not hills, nor are they caves—
(the deep has buried the hills)—

Those are not depths nor are they walls—
(the deep has taken the downtown in)—

Those are not pearls nor are they eyes—
(like a bored salesgirl, current gnaws the banks)—
and all whom the water has spared will now
                              begin
to starve.

JIM HARRISON

Sonoran Radio
(FREELY TRANSLATED)

Looking at a big moon too long
rusts the eyes.

*

The raped girl stood all day naked
in the cold rain holding a plaster virgin.
Their colors ran into the ground.

*

Tonight the Big Dipper poured down
its dark blood into the Sea of Cortez,
El Oso Grande, the hemorrhaged bear.

*

In the supermarket beef feet, chicken feet,
one lone octopus losing its charm.
An old woman named Octavia
who stared at my blind eye
carried out the 100-lb. gunnysack of pintos,
a bag of groceries in the other hand.

*

Just over the mountains
this other country, despised
and forsaken, makes more sense.
It admits people are complicated,

it tries to ignore its sufferings,
it cheats and loves itself,
it admits God might be made
of stone.

*

The red bird sits
on the dead brown snake.

*

The lobo admits its mistake
right after eating
the poisoned calf.

*

In the forms of death
we are all the same;
destinies are traded
at the very highest levels
in very high buildings
in clear view of the dump-pickers.

*

My heart and your heart!

*

The horses are running from flies.
Twenty-three horses run
around and around from the flies
in the big mesquite *retaque* corral
while five boys watch,
each one smaller
than the next biggest.

*

In the valley of the Toltecs
the American hunter from Palm Beach
shot one thousand white-wing doves
in a single day, all by himself.

*

The shark was nearly on shore
when it ate the child in three bites
and the mother kicked the shark in the eye.

*

The dopers killed the old doctor
in the mountain village,
but then the doctor's patients
stoned the dopers to death,
towing their bodies through town
behind Harley Davidsons.

*

It is the unpardonable music
stretching the soul
thinner than the skin.
Everyone knows they are not alone
as they suffer the music together
that gives them greater range
for greater suffering.

*

In the vision
the virgin who sat in the sycamore
speaks in the voice
of the elegant Trogan,
a bird so rare it goes
mateless for centuries.

*

The lagoon near the oil refinery
outside Tampico caught fire one night.
Everywhere tarpon were jumping
higher than a basketball hoop,
covered with oily flames,
the gill plates rattling,
throwing off burning oil.

*

The black dove and white dove
intermarried, producing not brown doves
but some white doves and black doves.
Down the line, however,
born in our garden a deep yellow dove
more brilliant than gold
and blind as a bat.
She sits on my shoulder
cooing night songs in the day,
sleeping a few minutes at noon,
and always at midnight, wakes
as if from a nightmare
screaming *Guadalupe.*

*

She said that outside Magdalena
on a mountainside
she counted thirteen guitarists
perched just below a cave
from which they tried to evoke
the usual flow
of blood and flowers.

*

Up in the borderland mountains
the moon fell slowly on Animas Peak

until it hit it directly
and broke like an egg,
spilling milk on the talus
and scree, sliding in a flood
through a dozen canyons.
The wind rose to fifty knots,
burning the moon
deep into the skin.

*

In a seaside restaurant
in Puerto Vallarta
a Bosnian woman killed a Serbian man
with a dinner fork,
her big arm pumping the tines
like a jackhammer
before the frightened diners,
who decided not to believe it.
She escaped the police net,
fleeing into the green mountains,
fork in hand.

*

The preying mantis crawled
up the left nostril of our burro
and killed it.

*

Nightjars and goat suckers,
birds from the far edge of twilight
carrying ghosts from place to place.
"Just hitching a ride," the ghosts
say to the birds, slapping
on the harness of black thread.
Even in *el norte* the whippoorwill's
nest is lined with the gossamer thread
of this ghost harness.

*

The cowdogs
tore apart
and ate
the pregnant housecat.

*

The grey hawk
(Only twenty pairs left in the U.S.)
flew close over
the vermilion flycatcher
perched on the tip
of the green juniper tree.

*

The waitress in the diner
where I ate my menudo
told me that Christ actually
bled to death. Back in those days
nails were the same as railroad spikes,
and the sun was hot as hell.
She sees the Resurrection
without irony or backspin.
"We are so lucky," she said.
"I couldn't live with all the things
I've done wrong in my life.
I feel better when I'm forgiven."

*

His dog sneezed
and crawled under a pickup
to get away from the sun.
The guitar and concertina music
swept down the mountainside
from the old cowboy's funeral,

hat and bridle
hanging from a white cross
in a cluster of admirable
plastic flowers.

                    *

The ravens are waiting
in the oak at twilight
for the coyotes to come
and open up the dead steer.
The ravens can't break through
cowhide with their beaks
and have been there since dawn
eager for the coyotes to get things started.
There's plenty for everyone.

                    *

These black beetles
big as a thumb
are locked in dead embrace,
either in love or rage.

                    *

The bull does not want
to be caught. For five
hours and as many miles
on a hot morning
three cowboys and a half-dozen
cowdogs have worked
the bull toward the pen.
The truck is ready to take
him to the sale. He's known
as a *baloney bull*, inferring
his destiny: old, used up,
too lazy and tired to mount cows.
Meanwhile he's bawling, blowing
snot, charging, hooking a horn

at the horses, dogs, a stray tree.
Finally loaded, I say goodbye
to his blood-red eyes.
He rumbles, raises his huge neck,
and bawls at the sun.

*

The cowdog licks her cancerous
and bloated teats.
Otherwise, she's the happiest
dog I know, always smiling,
always trying to help out.

*

I gave the woman seven roses
and she smiled, holding
the bouquet a couple of hours
at dusk before saying goodbye.
The next day I gave her
a brown calf and three chickens
and she took me to bed.
Over her shoulder a rose
petal fell for an hour.

*

From a thicket full
of red cardinals
burst seven black javelinas
including three infants
the size of housecats.

*

There were so many birds
at the mountain spring
they drove one insane
at dawn and twilight;

bushes clotted with birds
like vulgar Christmas trees.
I counted thirteen hundred
of a hundred different kinds,
all frozen in place
when the grey hawk flew by,
its keening voice
the precise weight of death.

*

Magdalena kept taking off her clothes
for hours until there was nothing left,
not even a trace of moisture on the leather chair.
Perhaps it was because
she was a government employee
and had lost a child.
It was the sleight of her hand.
I never saw her again.

*

O lachrymae sonorense,
from the ground
paced with stars through the ribs
of ocotillo, thin and black
each o'clock till dawn,
rosy but no fingers except
these black thin stalks
directing a billion bright stars,
captured time swelling outward
for us if we are blessed
to be here on the ground,
night sky shot with measured stars,
night sky without end
amen.

ROBERT HASS

Dragonflies Mating

I

The people who lived here before us
also loved these high mountain meadows on summer mornings.
They made their way up here in easy stages
when heat began to dry the valleys out,
following the berry harvest probably and the pine buds:
climbing and making camp and gathering,
then breaking camp and climbing and making camp and gathering.
A few miles a day. They sent out the children
to dig up the bulbs of the mariposa lilies that they liked to roast
at night by the fire where they sat talking about how this year
was different from last year. Told stories,
knew where they were on earth from the names,
owl moon, bear moon, gooseberry moon.

2

Jaime de Angulo (1934) was talking to a Channel Island Indian
in a Santa Barbara bar. You tell me how your people said
the world was made. Well, the guy said, Coyote was on the mountain,
and he had to pee. Wait a minute, Jaime said,
I was talking to a Pomo the other day and he said
Red Fox made the world. They say Red Fox, the guy shrugged,
we say Coyote. So, he had to pee,
and he didn't want to drown anybody, so he turned toward the place
where the ocean would be. Wait a minute, Jaime said,
if there were no people yet, how could he drown anybody?
The Channelleno got a funny look on his face. You know,
he said, when I was a kid, I wondered about that,
and I asked my father. We were living up toward Santa Ynez.

He was sitting on a bench in the yard shaving down fence posts
with an ax, and I said, How come Coyote was worried about people
when he had to pee and there were no people? The guy laughed.
And my old man looked up at me with this funny smile
and said, You know, when I was a kid, I wondered about that.

3

Thinking about that story just now, early morning heat,
first day in the mountains, I remember stories about sick Indians
and—in the same thought—standing on the free-throw line.

St. Raphael's parish, where the northernmost of the missions
had been, was founded as a hospital, was named for the angel
in the scriptures who healed the blind man with a fish

he laid across his eyes. I wouldn't mind being that age again,
hearing those stories, eyes turned upward toward the young nun
in her white, fresh-smelling, immaculately laundered robes.

The Franciscan priests who brought their faith in God
across the Atlantic, brought with the baroque statues and metal-work
        crosses
and elaborately embroidered cloaks, influenza and syphilis and the
        coughing disease.

Which is why we settled an almost empty California.
There were drawings in the mission museum of the long, dark wards
full of small, brown people, wasted, coughing into blankets,

the saintly Franciscan fathers moving patiently among them.
It would, Sister Marietta said, have broken your hearts to see it.
They meant so well, she said, and such a terrible thing

came here with their love. And I remembered how I hated it
after school—because I loved basketball practice more than anything
on earth—that I never knew if my mother was going to show up

well into one of those weeks of drinking she disappeared into
and humiliate me in front of my classmates with her bright, confident
       eyes
and slurred, though carefully pronounced words and the appalling

impromptu sets of mismatched clothes she was given to
when she had the dim idea of making a good impression in that state.
Sometimes from the gym floor with its sweet, heady smell of varnish

I'd see her in the entryway looking for me, and I'd bounce
the ball two or three times, study the orange rim as if it were,
which it was, the true level of the world, the one sure thing

the power in my hands could summon. I'd bounce the ball
once more, feel the grain of the leather in my fingertips, and shoot.
It was a perfect thing; it was almost like killing her.

                              4

This is the owl moon.
Fear is a teacher.
Sometimes you thought that
nothing could reach her,
nothing can reach you.
Wouldn't you rather
sit by the river, sit
on the dead bank,
deader than winter,
where all the roots gape?

                              5

This morning in the early sun, steam
rising from the pond the color of smoky topaz,
a pair of delicate, copper-red, needle-fine insects
are mating in the unopened crown of a Shasta daisy
just outside my door. The green flowerheads look like wombs
or the upright, supplicant bulbs of a vegetal pre-erection.
The insect lovers seem to be transferring the cosmos into each other
by attaching at the tail, holding utterly still, and quivering intently.

I think (on what evidence?) that they are different from us.
That they mate and are done with mating.
They don't carry all this half-mated longing up out of childhood
and then go looking for it everywhere. And so,
I think, they can't wound each other the way we do.
They don't go through life dizzy or groggy with their hunger,
kill with it, smear it on everything, though it is perhaps also true
that nothing happens to them quite like what happens to us
when the blue-backed swallow dips swiftly toward the green pond,
and the pond's green and blue reflected swallow marries it a moment
in the reflected sky, and the heart goes out to the end of the rope
it has been throwing into abyss after abyss, and a singing shimmers
from every color the morning has risen into.

My insect instructors have stilled, they are probably stuck together
in some bliss and minute pulse of after-longing
evolution worked out to suck the last juice of the world
into the receiver body. They can't separate, probably,
until it is done.

SEAMUS HEANEY

Damson

i

Gules and cement dust. A matte, tacky blood
On the bricklayer's knuckles, like the damson stain
That seeped through his packed lunch.

        A full hod stood
Against the mortared wall; his big, bright trowel
In his left hand for once was pointing down
As he marvelled at his right, held high and raw:
The profiled one, the scaffold-stepper, shown
Bleeding to the world.

       Wound that I saw
In glutinous color fifty years ago—
Damson as omen, weird, a dream to read—
Streams with the desperate, held-at-arm's-length dead
From everywhere and nowhere, here and now.

ii

Over and over, the slur, the scrape and mix
As he trowelled and retrowelled and laid down
Courses of glum mortar. Then the bricks,
Jiggled and settled, tocked and tapped in line.
I loved especially the trowel's shine,
Its edge and apex always coming clean
And brightening itself by mucking in.
It looked light but felt heavy as a weapon,
Yet when he lifted it there was no strain.
It was all dint and trim and float and glisten
Until he washed and lapped it tight in sacking
Like a cult blade that had to be rehidden.

iii

Ghosts with their tongues out for a lick of blood
Are crowding up the ladder, all unhealed,
And some of them rigged out in killing gear.
Drive them back to the doorstep or the road
Where they lay in their own blood once, in the hot
Nausea and last gasp of dear life.
Trowel-wielder, woundie, drive them off
Like Odysseus in Hades lashing out
With his sword that dug the trench and cut the throat
Of the sacrificial lamb.
                          But not like him—
Builder, not sacker, your shield the mortarboard—
Drive them back to the wine-dark taste of home,
The smell of damsons simmering in a pot,
Jam ladled thick and steaming down the sunlight.

BRENDA HILLMAN

The Unbeginning

—or maybe you could just
give up on beginnings. After all,

this notion that things "start"
and "end" somewhere
has caused you so much trouble!

Look at the wild radish in the fields out there.
Isn't it always row
and row of pastel pink-
yellow-blue like some bargain
print of itself, in new pillowcases, on sale;

and you stumble
through it thinking art must come
from the book of splendor
or the book of longing
until the rhythms curve

and the previous music
hasn't ended yet:

the whir the blackbirds make,
as they land, sounds like Velcro,
like a child undoing
Velcro from the winter jacket

(from the *hood*
of a winter jacket)—

EDWARD HIRSCH

Days of 1968

She walked through Grant Park during the red days of summer.
One morning she woke up and smelled tear gas in her hair.

She liked Big Brother and the Holding Company, Bob Dylan,
Sly & the Family Stone, The Mothers of Invention.

When Jimi Hendrix played *Purple Haze* in a jam session
she had a vision of the Trail of Tears and the Cherokee Nation.

She dropped acid assiduously for more than a year.
She sang, "I want to take you higher and higher,"

and dreamt of cleansing the doors of perception.
After she joined the Sky Church I never saw her again...

Days of 1968, sometimes your shutters open
and I glimpse a star gleaming in the constellations.

I can almost reach up and snag her by the hand.
I can go to her if I don't look back at the ground.

MICHAEL HOFMANN

Intimations of Immortality

for F. C. Delius

Have a nice day and get one free—
this is retirement country,
where little old ladies

squinny over their dashboards
and bimble into the millennium,
with cryogenics to follow;

the shuttle astronauts
hope to fluff re-entry and steal
one last record-breaking orbit;

where they give a man
five death sentences
to run more or less concurrently.

I take turns in my three chairs,
and try to remember two switches for lights,
the third for waste.

My eyes sting from salt and sunoil,
and I drink orange juice
till it fizzes and after.

The sight of a cardinal
or the English Sundays on Thursday
make it a red-letter day.

Lizards flirt in the swordgrass,
grasshoppers advertise their thighs
on the stroke of six, and quite suddenly,

after seventy-five years,
the laurel oak crashes out.
See you later, if not before.

RICHARD HOWARD

Homage to Antonio Canaletto

Venice spent what Venice earned

    The operas for which he made designs
in his father's shop
had consequences;
      he never got over the Bibienas'

                    groundless perspectives,
                    and until he died
    such vistas would haunt him: however close
to veritable
palaces he came,
      their porticoes and balustrades composed

                    a proscenium
                    of hysteria.
    But who could count on theaters for pay?
Workmen were always
threatening to quit,
      impresarios "embarrassed," castrati

                    and sopranos in
                    reciprocal fits—
    what could a talent do but "solemnly
excommunicate
the stage" (his own words)
      and set up shop in Rome? A year later

                    he was home again,
                    Roman lessons learned:
    certifiable views of City Life
mattered a good deal
more than the *Scena*
    all'angolo. Unvarying Venice

                    mattered most of all,
                    the abiding dream:

little canals (what else?) colonized by
perfunctory dolls.
First a sketch was made
        (recorded by the *maestro* on the spot),
                        then redrawn by him
                        more decorously
        indoors, where the *product* could be prepared:
the sky painted in,
sometimes even clouds,
        across the canvas acres, inch by inch,
                        and then the contours
                        of buildings incised
        into that sky-skin to provide guidance
for eventual
roofs and cornices,
        hemicircles marking an arch, a dome
                        (all this done of course
                        by apprentices).
At times he was obsessively precise
and in exquisite
detail would devise
        the reigning Doge's coat of arms to fill
                        a space smaller than
                        a baby's thumbnail
        on the ducal barge; but more likely
San Marco would glow
or gloom as it had
        generations ago. Venice might change,
                        storeys be added,
                        campaniles fall,
        but master-drawings in the studio
perdured his pattern
Serenissima
        years on end, a topographical hoax,
                        though one sure to work
                        as long as *he* worked:
        Grand Tourists continued to pay dear for
proof that they had been
duly discerning
        guests of the carnival Republic by

　　　　　　　　　　acquiring views from
　　　　　　　　　　Canaletto's hand.
　　"His merit lyes in painting things which fall
immediately
under his ogle,"
　　　　McSwiny wrote to England. Why not go
　　　　　　　　　　to England as well
　　　　　　　　　　as to Rome? Respite
　　　from the routine of Venetian *vedute*
lured him a moment
that endured ten years:
　　　armed with letters to the Noble Lords, he
　　　　　　　　　　proved (what could he prove?)
　　　　　　　　　　a disappointment
　　　to potential patrons who claimed they saw
deterioration
in his dirty Thames,
　　　and rumors even started he was not
　　　　　　　　　　"the veritable
　　　　　　　　　　virtuoso, no
　　Canalet at all, but an impostor!"
—easily foiled by
his cool reportage:
　　a *View of Whitehall* scrupulous enough
　　　　　　　　　　to rout all skeptics.
　　　　　　　　　　He stayed on, well-paid
　　　but never (as aristocrats assumed)
to paint their houses,
their horses, their dogs. . . .
　　　Nature he loathed, and next to nature, sport.
　　　　　　　　　　Having provided
　　　　　　　　　　plausible prospects
　　of Warwick Castle, Cambridge, Eton, Bath!
he was heard to sigh,
as longed-for Venice
　　　loomed upon his homing horizon, how
　　　　　　　　　　glad he was, never
　　　　　　　　　　to have to portray
　　　another tree. Another thirteen years'
practice made perfect

sense; he persisted.

     Hester Thrale (become Piozzi) bought,
                        long after his death,
                        "seven Canalets,
   to which his myriad imitators seem
hardly more than a
camera obscura
   in the window of a London parlour." . . .
                        Remembered, required!
                        in attestation:
   "Your own Canalettos will have given
a better idea
of the gondola
   than I can convey," a friend of Byron
                    wrote to Hallam,
                    and a few years on,
   for Théophile Gautier (and not for us?)
Venice had become
"avec ses palais,
   ses gondoles, la ville de Canaletto!"
                    On a last drawing
                    (made inside St. Mark's)
   this busy little man, so early prized
for reproducing
whatever might fall
   under his eye, proudly informs us: "Done
                    without spectacles.
                    A. Canaletto."

TED HUGHES

The Locket

Sleeping and waking in the Song of Songs
You were half-blissful. But on occasion,
Casually as a yawn, you'd open
Your death and contemplate it.

Your death
Was so utterly within your power,
It was as if you had trapped it. Maybe by somehow
Giving it some part of you, for its food.
Now it was your curio pet,
Your familiar. But who else would have nursed it
In a locket between her breasts!

Smiling, you'd hold it up.
You'd swing it on its chain, to tease life.
It lent you uncanny power. A secret, blueish,
Demonic flash
When you smiled and gently bit the locket.

I have heard how a fiery cross
Can grow and brighten in the dreams of a spinster.
But a crooked key turned in your locket.
It had sealed your door in Berlin
With the brand of the burnt. You knew exactly
How your death looked. It was a long-cold oven
Locked with a swastika.

The locket kept splitting open.
I would close it. You would smile.
Its lips kept coming apart—just a slit.
The clasp seemed to be faulty.
Who could have guessed what it was trying to say?

Your beauty, a folktale wager,
Was a quarter century posthumous.

While I juggled our futures, it kept up its whisper
To my deafened ear: *fait accompli.*

GALWAY KINNELL

"The Music of Poetry"

And now—after putting forward a "unified theory":
that the music resulting from any of the methods
of organizing English into rhythmic surges
can sound like the music resulting from any other,
being the music not of a method but of the language;
and after proposing that free verse is a variant
of formal verse, using unpredictably the acoustic
repetitions that formal verse uses systematically;
and after playing recordings of the gopher frog's
long-lined chant, sounding like musical rumblings
in an empty stomach, and the notes the hermit thrush
pipes one after another, then twangles together,
and the humpback whale's gasp-cries as it passes
out of the range of human perception of ecstasy,
and the wolf's howls, one, and then several,
and then all the pack joining in a polyphony
to whatever in the sunlit midnight sky
remains keeper of the axle the earth and
her clasped lovers turn upon and cry to;
and after playing recordings of an angakoq singing
in Inuktitut of his trance-life as a nanuk,
a songman of Arnhem Land, Rahmani of Iran,
Neruda of Chile, Yeats, Thomas, Rukeyser,
to let the audience hear that our poems
are of the same order as those of the other animals,
and are composed, like theirs, when we find ourselves
synchronized with the rhythms of the earth,
no matter where, in the city of Brno, which cried
its vowel too deep into the night to get it back,
or at Ma'alaea on Maui in Hawaii, still plumping
itself on the actual matter of pleasure there,
or here in St. Paul, Minnesota, where I lean

at a podium trying to draw my talk to a close,
or a time zone away on Bleecker Street in New York,
where only minutes ago my beloved may have
put down her book and drawn up her eiderdown
around herself and turned out the light—now,
causing me to garble a few words and tangle
my syntax, I imagine I hear
her say my name into the slow waves
of the night and, faintly, being alone, sings.

CAROLYN KIZER

Reunion

For more than thirty years we hadn't met.
I remembered the bright query of your face,
That single-minded look, intense and stern,
Yet most important—how could I forget?—
Was what you taught me inadvertently
(tutored by books and parents, even more
By my own awe at what was yet to learn):
The finest intellect can be a bore.

At this, perhaps our final interview,
Still luminous with your passion to instruct,
You speak to that recalcitrant pupil who
Inhaled the chalk-dust of your rhetoric.
I nod, I sip my wine, I praise your view,
Grateful, my dear, that I escaped from you.

CYNTHIA MacDONALD

Children Who Fall Off the Edge of the World Because of Secrets

I

Cloves. Like the nipples of a child emerging from the falls' cold water
in the Molucca Islands. Spice: embedded in the Indonesian
Archipelago. Cloves stuck in Easter ham, remnant of that time
when cloves preserved the meat from iridescent spoils.

Spice routes. Sought and fought for. Through the dark continent—
its pungent wetnesses, its dry and curving inland seas—Spain,
Portugal, the Netherlands, and France searched for routes;
they probed the oceans past yellow-streaked Canary Isles,
past silk cloak green Cape Verde Islands, and round
the Atlantic curve of land which would become the Ivory Coast.

Searching for the passage, bumping once and twice and then
times beyond count into the coast (like children's sailboats, rudder set,
bumping against the stone rim of the park's calm sailing pond),
hoping to find a shining water pathway to the studded isles.
In 1499, da Gama did. It took two years, three months
from Lisbon round Good Hope to Calicut and the Spice Islands.

II

The Portuguese, who'd banked on being first and were,
knew that the secret must be kept. The sailors pledged to secrecy
on pain of death—and it was painful, long and full of suffering
to make example of the fate of slippery tongues—did learn to
hold them. But still, there was the question of the maps and charts.
How to create and store them, keep them safe from foreign bribes?

The answer: children who'd just been taught to read and write.
Not old enough to understand the import of the whole.
Yet even so, each child was given only a small part to copy
From a slivered portion of a map. And then moved to the next.
A fifteenth-century assembly line. No way
that she or he could possibly make sense out of the whole.
As children never can. We try to put the map together,
placing pink with pink, assessing a small sweep of curve
to find a match, puzzling over *Mada* to see if
land or *nesia* or *gascar* will fit and tell us what we
need to know to let us know the edge of love is close.

III

A mother writes from Lisbon to her older sister in 1499:
"Our dear Luiz, just six, came home this day. We did not know he'd
smuggled out the quill with which he wrote upon the maps.
Into the olive grove, he went with it; I know not why.
We found him there already stiffening.
He'd got the point part of the pen cross-throat. I catched him in
my arms and put my fingers down. Of course, it was too late.

And this after tansy, sotherwood and cloves mixed in with Port
had kept him from the plague. We do not know what means to take. . . .
His delicate favour and bright amber eye was so deep
imprinted in our hearts, far to surpass our grief for the decease
of his three elder brothers who, dying soon as they were
born, were not so sweet endeared to us as this one was.
God grant that he may find safe harbour and a trusty map of heaven
to bring him to the laps of angels. God grant us sorrow's peace."

WILLIAM MATTHEWS

Cancer Talk

Of course it's not on the X-rays: tumors
have no bones. But thanks to the MRI
we see its vile flag luffing from your spine.
To own a fact you buy many rumors:

is the blob benign, or metastatic
to the bone and fatal, or curable?
There will be tests. How good were you in school?
Cells are at work on your arithmetic.

You don't have to be a good soldier.
Lymphoma is exquisitely sensitive
to radiation, but it's not what you have.
How easy it once seemed to grow older.

Don't you hate the phrase "growth experience"?
Big as a grapefruit? Big as a golf ball?
You'll learn new idioms (how good in school
were you?) like "protocol" and "exit burns."

"You'll be a cure," a jaunty resident
predicts. What if you could be you, but rid
of the malignant garrison? How would
it feel to hear in your own dialect—

not Cancer Babble, but clear Broken Heart.
Bald, queasy, chemotherapeutic beauty, welcome home from Port-a-Cat and eu-
phemism. Let the healing candor start.

ROBERT MAZZOCCO

Elegy for Three

There was a sprig of heather at a cemetery
And the grave of a mother and a father
There was a cradle and I was in it
And my parents kept rocking me between them

There was a life and I did not live it
And a smile as pale as milk
Or a scowl on the face of a lost harlequin . . .
There was a *cri de coeur* or a teething ring
Whirling about us in my dream

And a cradle and I was in it
By then an old man
As my parents kept rocking me between them
A young couple whom I had once known and never knew
In life as in death . . .

Till suddenly a curtain was slit open
And an horizon became a cage
Apples hung in the sky like stars
A train swept by like an assassin
A wreath lay crumpled on the floor of a rogue's gallery

And geese sailed on to the tip of an icy mountain . . .
Yet whatever the darkness there may be in grief
There is also a flower a white rose
And in the desert the water jet of the heart

CAMPBELL McGRATH

The First Trimester

This morning we find dead earthworms in the dining room again.

Yesterday there were three; the day before one,

solitary traveller, lone pilgrim or pioneer shrivelled up hard and black
as the twist-tie I first mistook it for, shrunken and bloodless, brittle as
wire.

Today it's two, a couple, bodies entwined in a death-embrace

become a cryptic glyph or sign, some Masonic rune or Buddhist
talisman glimpsed in a
Chinatown junk shop—

the ideogram of this mysterious manifestation.

So shall they come amongst us, singly and by pairs.

But where have they come from? The ficus? The yucca? A paltry,
crumbled trail of soil
implicates the rubber tree, solemn in its dusty corner, in its green
wicker basket among the
bookshelves. Is it possible? After all these years, how could it contain so
much primordial,
undomesticated life, so many wandering waves of worms? And what
would induce them to
leave it now, that safe haven of roots and humus, to migrate out into the
great wide world,
to wither and die in the vast dilapidated Sahara of our dining room
floor?

Inseparable love? Biological compulsion? The change

of seasons? Autumn. Former students call

to speak of their suicides; the last yellowjackets

dive like enraged kamikazes to die enmeshed in our window screens,
rusted auto-bodies awaiting the wrecker;

higher up, two geese,

vectored west against the contrails from O'Hare.

Last week two squirrels burst into my sister-in-law Becky's apartment
and ran amok in a
leaf-storm of old mail and newspapers, chewing through a blueberry
muffin and a box of
after-dinner mints, whirling like the waters of the southern hemisphere
counterclockwise
around the living room until she chased them with a broom back out
the open window.

From my window I watch the local squirrels settling in for the season,
hoarding burrs and
acorns and catkins, feathering their nest in the hollow limb of the big
elm tree with pink
fiberglass insulation stolen by the mouthful from our attic.

At the church next door kids released early from evening service toss
Ping-Pong balls into
colored buckets;

chimney swallows emerge from the unused smokestack that marks its
former existence as a
carriage factory to scour the dusk for insects, scattering and coalescing
in fugitive rings,

coming together, breaking apart, coming together, breaking apart,

circling and circling in an undulant wreath, ecstatic ash from the soul's
bright burning.

Dusk: bicyclists; cricket chimes; the blue moon;

a single green planetary orb to grace the withered stalks of the tomato
plants

in the garden. In the kitchen,

after removing the oatmeal-raisin cookies to cool, Elizabeth has fallen
asleep in the flour-dusted afterglow of baking,

in the sluice of pooled heat spilled like sugared lava from the oven,

in her clothes, on the floor,

sitting up.

JAMES MERRILL

Scrapping the Computer

Like countless others in the digital age, I seem
To have written a memoir on my new computer.
It had no memories, of course. So anyone's
Would have done, and mine were as good as anyone's.
This playmate was programmed for my "personal" needs
(A bit too intricately, it would transpire),
But all was advancing at the smooth pace of dream

Until that morning when a faint mechanical shriek
Took me aback. As I watched, the paragraph
Then under way deconstructed itself into
Mathematical symbols, musical notation—
Ophelia's mad scene in a Czech production
Fifty years hence. The patient left on a gurney,
Returned with a new chip the following week.

Another year or two, the memoir done
And in the publishers' hands, the pressure's off.
But when I next switch it on, whatever Descartes meant
By the ghost in the machine—oh no!—gives itself up:
Experts declare BRAIN DEATH. (The contriver of my program
Having lately developed a multiple personality,
My calls for help keep reaching the wrong one.)

Had it caught some "computer virus"? For months now a post-
Partum depression holds me prisoner:
Days spent prone, staring at the ceiling,
Or with an arm flung over my eyes. Then sleepless nights
In which surely not *my* fingertips upon the mattress
Count out Bach, Sousa, Gershwin, trying to fit
Into groups of five or ten their metronomanic host.

Or was the poor thing taking upon itself a doom
Headed my way? Having by now a self of sorts,
Was it capable of a selfless act
As I might just still be, for someone I loved?
Not that a machine is capable of anything *but*
A selfless act. . . . We faced each other wordlessly,
Two blank minds, two screens aglow with gloom.

Or perhaps this alter ego'd been under "contract"—*Yep,*
You know too much, wise guy. . . . Feet in cement,
A sendoff choreographed by the Mob.
But who the Mob is, will I ever know?
Short of the trillionfold synaptic flow
Surrounding, making every circumstance
Sparkle like mica with my every step

Into—can that be sunlight? Ah, it shines
On women in furs, or dreadlock heads on knees
(Hand-lettered placards: BROKE. ILL. HELP ME PLEASE),
This prisoner set down in the Free World,
His dossier shredded. Now for new memories,
New needs. And while we're at it a virgin laptop
On which already he's composed these lines.

W. S. MERWIN

Possessions

Such vast estates such riches beyond estimation
    of course they all came out of the ground at some time
out of dark places before the records were awake
    they were held by hands that went out like a succession of flames
as the land itself was held until it named its
    possessors who described and enumerated it
in front of magistrates dividing the huge topography
    multiplying the name extending the chateau
house gardens fields woods pastures those facing
    the hill of Argentat with also the road leading
through them and the land called Murat and the fields and woods
    of the hill of Courtis and other designated
dependencies chapel stables dovecote additional
    lands south of the lane to which others were added by
marriage by death by purchase by reparation
    complicating the names of the legitimate offspring
lengthening the testaments meant to leave nothing out
    furnishings plates linens each mirror and its frame
the barrels and oxen and horses and sows and sheep
    the curtained beds the contents of the several kitchens
besides all such personal belongings as money
    and jewels listed apart which were considerable
by the time Mme. la Vicomtesse who was heir to it all
    found it poor in variety and after her marriage
was often away visiting family and so on
    leaving the chateau in the keeping of her
father-in-law who was almost totally deaf
    so it happened that one night during a violent
thunderstorm the son of a laborer managed
    to climb through an upper window and into Madame's
bedroom where with the point of a plowshare he opened
    her jewel case and removed everything in it

and two nights later the gold crown studded with precious
     stones a gift of His Holiness Pius the Ninth
also was missing it was these absences
     that were commemorated at the next family wedding
at which the Vicomtesse wore at her neck and wrists
     pink ribbons in place of the jewels that had been hers
it was for the ribbons that she was remembered

CZESLAW MILOSZ

TRANSLATED BY THE AUTHOR AND ROBERT HASS

This World

It appears that it was all a misunderstanding.
What was only a trial run was taken seriously.
The rivers will return to their beginnings.
The wind will cease in its turning about.
Trees instead of budding will tend to their roots.
Old men will chase a ball, a glance in the mirror—
They are children again.
The dead will wake up, not comprehending.
Till everything that happened will unhappen.
What a relief! Breathe freely, you who suffered much.

SUSAN MITCHELL

Music

sucked into the nasal cavities.

, which doesn't mean I am smelling this music
like an iris haunting my head, taking
over a room with one explosion after another.
To live among flowers is bewildering
after a while, and challenging.

To keep opening. To have that as one's
life work, all those crinkles
of the rose, those petals, and how exciting
for the thumb ever so gently to
and then extract itself

slowly, the rose smacking its lips, it
can almost taste itself tasted,
or is it the thumb?
What the thumb has entered
is time, is tomorrow and tomorrow, but not
yet unfurled, the flags and umbrellas
still wrapped tight, and that,

I'm told, is how a theme came to Beethoven,
not melody, but a single note
he went at with his beak
cracking it like a seed, then the two
halves, then those halves, the music getting
smaller as it grew bigger, as

if to get the entire score he had
to hack back to core and from core extract
ore, and what I love
is the way it's possible to carry
all that in something as small as a nut,
and just thinking about this
I feel it enter me like buckshot, each note
a fig, the many seeds
lodged in my ear.

when I was nineteen, something happened, I

a froth where the music was starting
to leave itself for air
or darkness, as a violin's bow over the string,
glissando or with gasp and fret,

wax to make slippery, so as not to stick
as the hummingbird, obsessive,
sticks to the air
                              attacking
the air where it
the nest more scratch than notes.

Listening, I could hear how little
of my life I filled, the long shadows the possible
cast as it flew off like birds into
another language   by dropping

stones down a shaft, someone could hear
the distances, the music not yet
scrolled, the time not
decided with imbecile signatures.

;   or houses open
on one side to receive the ocean thundering
hundreds of feet below, to be lowered
into the dangers

I want to sleep close to that and hear it
mumbling, a girl with one long dark
strand of hair in her mouth,
so I can't understand what she is saying, all
her underwater reverberations
through the caves of the cavernous and obscure,

especially the disruptions, the long pauses
when nothing is said, only the
bulging of a wave starting to fill up

I could call it Sonata of the Future
this silence, and all the
pieces of broken churned up and polished

about *oscuro*   clouds are a part of it and passages
are, vast fields of air
for which the word is entry

as to a smoke-filled bar or a steamy
that's pitch and polluted
the dark murky, the turnpikes and malls of, say, New Jersey

or a passage that's enigmatic

what I feel when I look at the faces
of ancient Greek sculptures, the
way the eyes seem to be looking at still what
they broke off from. Is that why
they are calm?

I'm only guessing, immersed in blur and bludgeon,
Give me visions that whir
the optic nerve, a wind turned inside
out like a glove.

Lately, I've been thinking about the problem
of what is singable. Is everything
singable? And what does it

mean to sing when the intervals are like arches
spanning a river and the river
is transported bodily, its bubbles
breaking, the glass from which
one drinks these waters
breaking?

universe in which the measured violets and blues

and all those things for which I haven't
a name existing like a hum
a field of crescendos

the rib cage opening and closing
on them, as if testing
wings of something just broken through
a chrysalis, the sound, that hum, opening
and closing its leaves, its buds about

protracted, if necessary,

as if the diaphragm were a chrysalis

its buds all along the about to

What does it mean to draw? To draw
the voice out of the long, each column of air
ictus and glide   It has the string on which to
string itself along, on which to lose
and find itself back to

one has to be ready to record
what one doesn't understand and even what
one doesn't hear, like Webern

in his bagatelles, to include the silences, to start
with them because someone else
might hear the inaudible for him, below
the level of hearing, though
going on, a crackle or persistence, a gate

through or something metal knocking
against something metal
or plastic, noise
of birds, many   what he

broke it off from, a jaggedness
where he struck and kept striking, some of it

its stopping only another way of continuing

and if one language no longer, then rushing
at once to where another, like a spring
starting up   and will

feel their way along

a rope ladder, swaying above and slippery
and those places where the nails
hammered down have fallen out, the orange swirls
still visible in the waves below

or consumed as smell, the vapors, the fumes
rising up out of, to breath that
if there are no

steps for the voice to follow and one has to
swing out again and again
like a spider throwing its lassoes of spit

like a bird glancing the et cetera of light

SHARON OLDS

Sunday Night

When the family would go to a restaurant, my
father would put his hand up a waitress's
skirt if he could—hand, wrist,
forearm. Suddenly, one couldn't see
his elbow, just the upper arm.
His teeth were wet, the whites of his eyes
wet, a man with a stump of an arm,
as if he had reached behind the night.
It was always the right arm, he wasn't
fooling. Places we had been before
no one would serve us, unless there was a young
unwarned woman, and I never warned her.
Woop! he would go, as if we were having
fun together. Sometimes, now,
I remember it as if he had had his
arm in up to his shoulder, his arm
to its pit in the mother. He laughed with teary
eyes, as if he was weeping with relief.
His other arm would be lying on the table—
he liked to keep it motionless, it
improved the joke, ventriloquist
with his arm up the dummy, his own shriek
coming out of her mouth. I wish I had stuck
a fork in that arm, driven the tines
deep, heard the squeak of muscle,
felt the skid on bone. I may have
met, since then, someone related
to one of the women at the True Blue
or at the Hick'ry Pit. Sometimes
I imagine my way back into the skirts
of the women my father hurt, those bells of
twilight, those sacred tented woods.

I want to sweep, tidy, stack—
whatever I can do, clean the stable
of my father's mind. Maybe undirty
my own, come to see the whole body
as holy and lovely. I want to work off
my father's and my sins, stand
beneath the night sky with the moon
glowing, knowing I am under the dome
of a woman who forgives me.

MICHAEL ONDAATJE

Night Fever

overlooking a lake
that has buried a city

bent over a table
shaking from fever
listening for the drowned
name of a town

Teldeniya   Teldeniya

there's water in my bones
a ghost of a chance
methods of death

rock paintings eaten
by amoebic bacteria
streets and temples
that shake within
cliffs of night water
someone with fever
buried
in the darkness of a room

ROBERT PINSKY

Poem with Refrains

The opening scene. The yellow, coal-fed fog
Uncurling over the tainted city river,
A young girl rowing and her anxious father
Scavenging for corpses. Funeral meats. The clever
Abandoned orphan. The great athletic killer
Sulking in his tent. As though all stories began
With someone dying.

                 When her mother died,
My mother refused to attend the funeral—
In fact, she sulked in her tent all through the year
Of the old lady's dying, I don't know why:
She said, because she loved her mother so much
She couldn't bear to see the way the doctors
Or her father or—someone—was letting her mother die.
"Follow your saint, follow with accents sweet;
Haste you, sad notes, fall at her flying feet."

She fogs things up, she scavenges the taint.
Possibly that's the reason I write these poems.

But they did speak: on the phone. Wept and argued,
So fiercely one or the other often cut off
A sentence by hanging up in rage—like lovers,
But all that year she never saw her face.

They lived on the same block, four doors apart.
"Absence my presence is; strangeness my grace;
With them that walk against me is my sun."

"Synagogue" is a word I never heard,
We called it *shul*, the Yiddish word for school.

Elms, terra cotta, the ocean a few blocks east.
"Lay institution": she taught me we didn't think
God lived in it. The rabbi just a teacher.

But what about the hereditary priests,
Descendants of the Cohanes of the Temple,
Like Walter Holtz—I called him Uncle Walter
When I was small. A big man with a face
Just like a boxer dog or a cartoon sergeant.
She told me whenever he helped a pretty woman
Try on a shoe in his store, he'd touch her calf
And ask her, "How does that feel?" I was too little
To get the point but pretended to understand.
"Desire, be steady; hope is your delight,
An orb wherein no creature can be sorry."

She didn't go to my bar mitzvah, either.
I can't say why: she was there, and then she wasn't.
I looked around before I mounted the steps
To chant that babble and the speech the rabbi wrote
And there she wasn't, and there was Uncle Walter
The Cohane frowning with his doggy face:
"She's missing her own son's *musaf.*" Maybe she just
Doesn't like rituals. Afterwards, she had a reason
I don't remember. I wasn't upset: the truth
Is, I had decided to be the clever orphan
Some time before. By now, it's all a myth.
What is a myth but something that seems to happen
Always for the first time over and over again?
And ten years later, she missed my brother's too.
I'm sorry: I think it was something about a hat.
"Hot sun, cool fire, tempered with sweet air,
Black shade, fair nurse, shadow my white hair;
Shine, sun; burn, fire; breathe, air, and ease me."

She sees the minister of the Nation of Islam
On television, though she's half-blind in one eye.
His bow tie is lime, his jacket crocodile green.
Vigorously he denounces the Jews who traded in slaves,
The Jews who run the newspapers and the banks.

"I see what this guy is mad about now," she says,
"It must have been some Jew that sold him the suit."
"And the same wind sang and the same wave whitened,
And or ever the garden's last petals were shed,
In the lips that had whispered, the eyes that had lightened."

But when they unveiled her mother's memorial stone,
Gathered at the graveside one year after the death,
According to custom, while we were standing around
About to begin the prayers, her car appeared.
It was a black car; the ground was deep in snow.
My mother got out and walked toward us, across
The field of gravestones capped with snow, her coat
Black as the car, and they waited to start the prayers
Until she arrived. I think she enjoyed the drama.
I can't remember if she prayed or not,
But that may be the way I'll remember her best:
Dark figure, awaited, attended, aware, apart.
"The present time upon time passëd striketh;
With Phoebus's wandering course the earth is graced.

The air still moves, and by its moving, cleareth;
The fire up ascends, and planets feedeth;
The water passeth on, and all lets weareth;
The earth stands still, yet change of changes breedeth."

STANLEY PLUMLY

Panegyric for Gee

The anachronistic face of the bulldog,
the anachronistic, Churchillian face of the bulldog,
the anachronistic, Churchillian, gargoylean
face of the bulldog, the anachronistic, Churchillian,
gargoylean, Quasimodian face of the bulldog,
whose ears are silk purses,
whose eyes, like a bullfrog's, enlarge,
whose flat black wet gorilla's nose sucks the air
out of the dust, whose mouth is as wide
as a channel cat's feeding for years in solitude
on the bottom, whose two lower utter canines
show one at a time, bite that is worse than its bark,
whose slobber is the drool of herbivores,
whose brooding pose is the seal's,
who climbs and descends, who stands, who climbs again,
who at the top of the stairs in the morning dark
is beef-faced drowsy as the mastiff god—
the andiron-large front legs welded like doorstops to the paws—
who peers down from prehistory over the edge.
O gnomic skin and bone too big for a soul
squeezed from a root-slip in the earth,
O antediluvian noises in the throat,
O silences of staring straight ahead,
O dogtrot, O dreams of the chase ten yards and then a rest—.
To sleep by a bulldog is to return to the primal nasal
sleep of the drunk, the drunk whose carnal snore self-purifies
the breath with the sanctity of opera,
the rich deep long great breath of the animal beached but flying.
When my father slept he slept the sleep of a drunk

who'd have loved this bulldog, so stubborn at the forehead,
so set on plowing through to the conclusion of a door
too thick to pass, except in spirit,
whose singing sober voice alone breaks hearts.

DAVID ST. JOHN

The Figure You

The figure *you*
Remains the speculative whip of my aesthetic

As in the latest chapter I've been writing
Called "The Erotics of the Disembodied Self"

Although I suppose the figure
You still suppose yourself to be is nevertheless

& upon reflection nothing more than the presence
Of someone else's moon-stunned body

Held quietly against your own just like the air
Or any other absence by which we learn to mark

The passing of yet another impossibly forgiven
& long-punishable night

GRACE SCHULMAN

Expulsion

Half-rotten, half-sweet,
it lay on the ground for days
before I tried it

and offered another
to my love, who said,
"I've never liked apples."

When I walked on,
he ate it, core and all.
And that's when it began.

We bought enough Rome Beauties
to make apple marmalade
and apple chutney—

then curries, soufflés,
pirozhki.
We grew restless,

even before the storm
cut off our water supply,
and winds lopped the elm

that cracked over telephone wire.
I remember
how in mild air

the sun lit the sheep laurel
and fell, along with quiet.
He called the perennials

by names once unfamiliar to us,
each with a resonance:
monkshood, purple iris,

foxglove, nightshade;
some we tended,
others grew wild,

recurring gifts.
But all was not right.
There were shrill insects,

scorpions, snaky vines
that twisted up cedars
and strangled white pines.

Here in the city,
things are less clear;
a rickety

ambulance snorts,
carrying the half-dead—
a pedestrian shot

during a robbery—
while toddlers embrace
twenty blocks away.

That square of street
not covered with grime
glitters in moonlight.

My love does not
give names to anything.
Instead, he falls silent

before a grove
of trees among buildings.
We cherish what little we have:

one side is bright,
the other dark.
We praise it.

CHARLES SIMIC

Relaxing in a Madhouse

They had already attached the evening's tears to the windowpanes.

The general was busy with the ant farm in his head.

The holy saints in their tombs were burning. One of the them, flames and all, was the prisoner of several female movie stars.

Moses wore a false beard and so did Lincoln.

X reproduced the Socratic method of interrogation by demonstrating the ceiling's ignorance.

"They stole the secret of the musical matchbook from me," confided Adam.

"The world's biggest rooster was going to make me famous," said Eve.

O to run naked over the darkening meadow after the cold shower!

In the white pavilion the nurse was already turning water into wine.

Hurry home, dark cloud.

GARY SNYDER

Daconstruction

They're slogging through the worksite,
rubber boots, pumps running, foot-wide hose
gushing steely water in a frothy pond

the link-belt crane turns like a Nō stage dancer
dangles a trembling sixty-foot pipe,
young guys in hardhats and T-shirts
hand-signal as it swings

to lower it tenderly
into a three-foot-wide casing
—a whomping cement truck backs in and
dumps down the pipe.

Eight at night—job lights glaring—
shrieks and whistles—
soupy mudponds—rebar and wire snipper trash
a high-rise building start
chain-linked off from the gridlocked streets,

another "economic miracle" of Asia,
smoking cigarettes and shouting—
laying new horizons on old swampy soils,
long-lost wetlands,
rainy noisy sticky city night,

Taipei.

JAMES TATE

A Missed Opportunity

A word sits on the kitchen counter
next to the pitcher of cream
with its blue cornflowers bent.
Perhaps a guest left it in a hurry
or as a tip for good service
or as a fist against some imagined
insult. Or it fell with some old
plaster from the ceiling, a word
some antediluvian helpmate
hushed up. It picked itself up
from the floor, brushed itself off
and, somehow, scratched its way
up the cupboards. It appears to be
a word of considerable strength
and even significance, but I can't
bring myself to look into its gaze.
The cornflowers are pointing toward
the cookies not far away. An expert
could be called to defuse the word,
but it is Sunday, and they are still
sleeping or singing, and, besides that,
the word seems to have moved again
on its own, and now it appears warm
and welcoming, it throbs with life
and a sincere desire to understand me.
It looks slightly puzzled and hurt,
as though I.... I take a step toward it,
I hold out my hand. "Friend," I say,
but it is shrinking, it is going away
to its old home in the familiar
cold dark of the human parking lot.

CHASE TWICHELL

Recorded Birds

I was watching the suffering on TV,

one of the wars—
smoke and broken houses and bafflement,

a row of children lying under a tarp,
the sound of weeping.

The ruins from the last war
had not yet healed. Vines were undoing

what was left of the walls.

Small birds with split tails
twittered on the soundtrack,
swaying in the leaves

behind the reporter and his microphone,

their voices netted
from the wilderness of sound in space,

centuries of animal and human voices

preserved in the airwaves,
immortal, without destination,
perpetually travelling

through what looks from here
like an ocean. If only we knew how,

we might call back to us the sounds

of those that have departed earth,
if only we could find a way

to trap the shards, the long
ribbony trails. Keats, Jesus—

the voices I would love to hear.
Walt Whitman. Dickinson.

My ancestors, all the way back.
The first birds, before they were named.

The silence of the first fox stalking them.

BRUCE WEIGL

From the House on Nguyen Du

One pile of squid
stretched on small bamboo kites
drying in the sun

One driver asleep near his cyclo
in the shade of banyans
by the Lake of the Sword

One wild dog
chasing rats into the sewer
his head like a fox

His tail like the rat's
he does not speak my tongue
my smell is foreign to him

One pile of gladiolus
pink and white
in the cyclo's empty seat

Waiting to be taken
to the lover who tends her misery
in the city's ancient heart

One street of paper shoes
and votive paper
clothes for the dead

One ball of fire
hurling itself into my face
in the first dream in country

One long fever that took me
so far up heaven's ladder
I was surrounded by two men

And a boy
lovely as the Buddha
in failing light

One set of needles
twisted and tapped
into the meridian

Of nerves in my back and arms
one set of joss sticks
white-hot as charcoal

Held by the men and the boy
to the bridges of my blood
until my heart is warmed

One scream
when the nerve of sickness
is finally tapped

One hour of sweat and delusion
until the small reed boat
piled with lotus blossoms

Sails a wide circle
out and away
that signifies the world

C. K. WILLIAMS

Secrets

I didn't know the burly old man who lived in a small house like ours
     down the block in Newark
was a high-up in the mob on the docks until I was grown and my father
     told me about him.

I didn't know until much too much later that my superior that year in
     the stockroom at Nisner's,
a dazzlingly bright black man, would never in those days climb out of
     his airless, monotonous cellar.

Neither did I know that the club where I danced every night in Philly in
     the early seventies—
it was almost my home—was controlled by loansharks and infested by
     addicts and coke-heads.

The councilman on the take, the grocer gambler, the blonde girl
     upstairs giving free oral sex—
it was all news to me: do people hide things from me to protect me? Do
     they mistrust me?

Even when Sid Mizraki was found beaten to death in an alley, I didn't
     hear till years later.
Sid murdered! Oh, god, my god, was all I could say: poor, sad Sid, poor
     hard-luck Sidney!

I didn't know Sidney that well, but I liked him: plump, awkward, he
     was gentle, eager to please,
the way unprepossessing people will be; we played ball, went to
     Chinatown with the guys.

He'd had a bleak life: lonely childhood in the streets, bad education,
    no women, irrelevant jobs;
when I knew him he worked for the city, then stopped; I had no idea
    of his true tribulations.

As the tale finally found me, Sid had a boss who hated him, rode him,
    drove him insane,
and Sid one drunk night in a bar bribed some burglars he knew to kill
    the creep for him.

I can't conceive how you'd dream up something like that, or how you'd
    know people like that,
but apparently Sid had access to tax rolls, and rich people's addresses
    he was willing to trade.

Then suddenly he was transferred, got a friendlier boss, forgot the
    whole witless affair,
but a few years later the thieves were caught and as part of their plea
    bargain sold Sid.

Sid got off with probation, but was fired, of course, and who'd hire him
    with that record?
He worked as a bartender, went on relief, drifted, got into drugs and
    some small-time dealing.

Then he got married—"to the plainest woman on earth," someone told
    me—but soon was divorced;
more drugs, more dealing, run-ins with cops, then his unthinkable
    calvary in that alley.

It was never established who did it, or why; no one but me was
    surprised it had happened.
A bum found him, bleeding, broken, inert; a friend from before said,
    "His torments are over."

So, Sidney, what now? Shall I sing for you, celebrate you with some
    truth? Here's truth:
add up what you didn't know, poor friend, and I don't, and you might
    have one conscious person.

No, this has nothing to do with your omissions or sins or
    failed rectifications,
to come so close to a life and not comprehend it, acknowledge it, truly
    know it is life.

How can I feel so clearly the shudder of blows, the blessed oblivion
    breaking on you,
and not really grasp what you were in yourself to yourself, what secrets
    sustained you.

So maybe if anyone's soul should be singing, it's yours: I think I know
    what you'd tell me:
*poor sensitive, sheltered creature; poor poet: if you can't open your eyes, stay at least
    still.*

CHARLES WRIGHT

Omaggio a Montale

It's come to meet you at last,
That endless high humming,
                    like sounds in a summer's night,
And rasp of rocks in the tide's suck
As you walk on the dune-hummocked shore
Alone, the way you used to,
                    the sea as black as a cassock
Around you, no wind, no lights,
And rain, the dry, steady drops of forever
Filling your shoes,
                tracing the contours of all your face
Like ants with their cleansing tongues. . . .

Maestro, the 11th Commandment is now in effect,
And no one will bother you ever gain.

Is everything still familiar there,
Umbrellas spread open against the sky, the cliff-rise
And colorless surf
              fixed in the mind of God
As they were from the first time?
And do the prayer flags still turn when the tides turn?
I like to imagine the one syllable
                    rising out of your mouth
Like a sun as you stand at the edge
Of the sea's reach and look into everywhere
And there's no one, no one at all.
                And the syllable comes, and it's *Yes*.

(1981)

ROY BLOUNT JR.

There Once Was a Lady Who Did, and Other 'Do-Me Feminist' (I Believe the Expression Is) Limericks

Note: The above title is one man's attempt to justify, in terms of contemporary gender politics, a number of limericks—and limerick *sequences*—that spring from the same man's sincere desire to rectify the dearth in our tradition of limericks that are indecent and also female-positive. *(Risquée?)* After I came up with the title, however, I found myself writing inferior, topical limericks that predictably rhymed *politicize* with *titty size, agenda* with *pudenda*. Those I junked. Herewith the limericks of sincere desire.

There once was a lady who did
Whatever her well-rounded id
    Required of her ego.
    And I say, "Whoo-wee, go
To it, you wonderful kid."

Her skirt and her halter were mini,
Her bellybutton an inny.
    She read Derida,
    So *n'yah, n'yah, n'yah,*
If you presumed her a ninny.

There once was a lady with hips so
Perfectly beveled that *ipso*
    Facto whatever adj-

Ustments of leverage
They made were a form of calypso.

There once was a lady who'd start out
With "You can eat your heart out."
       By the time you had gnawed
       To the cockles, she'd thawed
And moved on to "Let's get your part out."

There once was a lady who quite
Properly wouldn't, at night,
       Let anyone touch her,
       Thanks very much. Her
Taste ran to broad morning light.

Her name, as it happened, was Dawn.
In summer her skin was all fawn
       From gamboling nude.
       I reckon that you'd
Not, upon meeting her, yawn.

An icy-eyed lady named Maude
Does not like to be pawed.
       Or not very much.
       But if you'll just touch . . .
After a pause, she'll have thawed.

With Melanie Green one would oft
Turn and find she had doffed
       Every stitch.
       The reason for which:
Clothes made her nipples get soft.

I know a lady whose pet
Calico cat she will set
       On her lap, fur to fur,
       And stroke it and purr,
"Bulldog, take all you can get."

There once was a lady whose lashes
Fluttered a fireman's mustaches.
  He said, "Hotcha, Sweetie!"
 "My *name*'s Nefertiti,"
She said, and reduced him to ashes.

There once was a lady who romped
In Cannes with a hot-blooded *compte*
  Who cried, *"Sacre bleu,*
  J'arrive!" She said, "You
Needn't have been quite so . . . prompt."

To too-sharply-focussed Pierre,
A lady protested, "I *swear.*
  Don't be so literal.
  When I speak of clitoral
I mean all around down in there."

"Okay," responded Pierre,
"But *I* thought, if I'm going to err
  In any direction
  In the area of sex. . . . Y'kn-
Ow you make me wanna *SHOUT.* . . . Sorry, where

Was I?" "Forget it, galoot,
Go ahead, rooty-toot-toot.
  However you do it,
  Deep down, I intuit
An honest intention." "Oh shoot,"

Sighed Pierre, "I have spent
Sooner than I had meant."
  "Now don't get too low,"
  She said, "let's just go
For seconds." For *hours* they went.

There once was a lady, Elaine,
Who had an affair on a plane.
    Perhaps it was wrong,
    But it didn't last long,
Which is why she returned on the train.

A traveling lady who whirled
Through airports all over the world
    In clothes that were see-through
    Once met me in Heathr—*ooo,*
Was my welcome banner unfurled!

There once was a lady named Harriet
Who rode around in a chariot
    Drawn gladly by men
    Proud to have been
Roped by her smile like a lariat.

There once was a priestess who would
Do whatever she could—
    Ride in on a mastiff
    Entirely bare-assed if
She thought it would do any good.

A spirited medium, Miriam,
Frequently entered delirium.
    But graciously when
    She brought along men,
She kept an eye out, not to weary 'em.

There once was a lady whose hair
Was so abundantly *there*
    You'd run barefoot through it,
    And you know she knew it.
And then, when *her* feet were bare,

Her little toes there for the countin'
Counterpointed that fountain
    Of auburn bravura. . . .
    I blurted out, "You're a
Tippy-based volcanic mountain!"

"A *what*?" she said. "Oh—I don't *know*," I
Said, "it's just that I'm *so* high
    On you, top to toes,
    Words fail, I suppose—"
"Thanks, Ray." "Uh, excuse me, that's *O*-Y."

There once was a lady named Sims
Whose smoothly continuous limbs
    Made numerous men's
    Previous yens
Come to seem no more than whims.

There once was a lady whose dimple
Was not automatic or simple.
    It faded and deepened
    In passion and sleep, and
Jumped sometimes like a chimp'll.

A lady there was with a bottom
Whose halves were so full when you got 'em
    In hand, your heart
    Cried, "Ease them apart!
What *was* all that fuss about Sodom?"

There once was a lady, Sue Ewing,
Who got into rare ways of screwing—
    Some so *outré*,
    Her lover would say,
"Now what is it, dear, that we're doing?"

Her sister, *nee* Marylou Ewing,
In lieu of cohabitant screwing,
    Sits home on Sundays
    In elegant undies
And calls up her spouse, whom she's suing.

A lady of lower Manhattan
For some reason got off on *Patton.*
    She dreamed a lot
    Of George C. Scott
In ripped fatigues of black satin.

A lady who went to Oahu
Said, "Was it Gauguin or Seurat who
    Went all Polynesian?
    Though I'm no Parisian,
If Samoans will pose for me—Yahoo!"

When her mural's still wet, I give Coral—
Backed up against it—some oral,
    Producing broad tushstrokes.
    And then she adds bushstrokes
By means I've a hunch are immoral.

A lady, Felicity Monk,
When touched near the ribcage was sunk.
    Though not at all sickly, she
    Was rather ticklish? E-
normously: *WOOO-HA,* kerplunk.

Then someone touched near her heart.
She found, with a nice easy start,
    She savored the *WOOO*
    And the *HA* and could do
Entirely without the last part.

There once was a lady whose sighs   *huhhhh*
You just couldn't quite analyze   *huhhhh*
    (Not sorrow, not guilt),
    Except when they built
Into *huh'h'h'YES!* Otherwise . . .   *huhhhh*

An active lady named Jean
Found being on bottom obscene.
    So firm was her tone,
    Men served as her throne,
Her Harley, her rowing machine.

And as for Evangeline Keith, her
View was, a man was beneath her.
    By that she meant he
    Laid a bass line while she
Rocked somewhere off lost in the ether.

There once was a tough lady cop
Who liked to do it on top—
    Oh hell, everwhichways,
    Spoons, sideways, bitchways
And up 'gainst the wall for lagniappe.

There once was a lady who voiced
the level opinion you'd foist
    Nothing on her,
    Although her lips were,
While saying this, parted and moist.

There once was a lady named Joyce
Who had a catch in her voice
    That made men decide
    They'd not be denied—
As if they had any choice.

A lady was feeling frustration
In bed with her man's conversation.
    Asked "What do you *feel*?"
    All he'd reveal
Was "You. And you're a sensation."

"No, your emotions I mean—
Open up, mister, come clean.
    And that's not a straight line.
    You know that I hate lyin'
Beside you with nothing between

Us but jokes and physical movement."
"But dear, to tell you what you've meant
    To me would take bins
    Of gems, violins—"
"Well, that would be an improvement."

There once was a lady named Faye
Who took due pride in the way
    The line of the small
    Of her back met the—all
Together now, hip, hip, hooray!

Our geometry lecturer's knees
Pose a Euclidean tease—
    As the points of them flirt
    With the hem of her skirt
We guess at the apex of these.

A lady whose skin was like honey
When licked responded quite une-
    quivocally:
    All over she'd be
Mellifluously runny.

There once was a babe in whose arms
I felt secure from all harms.
　　Wasn't quite so;
　　However, I know
We had both the hots and the warms.

Of a full-breasted lady named Susie,
I asked, as we shared her Jacuzzi,
　　"Mind if I note
　　How nicely they float?"
"*Feel* 'em," she said. I felt woozy.

There once was a lady whose smile
Said, "You'll be delighted, and I'll
　　Be all that I wanna.
　　And then, in the sauna,
We'll mull it all over awhile."

ITALO CALVINO

TRANSLATED FROM THE ITALIAN BY PATRICK CREAGH

The Birds of Paolo Uccello

We see no birds in the paintings of Paolo Uccello. In all his teeming world the skies are empty. One looks up in hope, and sees no feathered creatures in flight or perched on the branches of trees. Lowering one's eyes onto a tranquil landscape peopled by hermits, one can discern, at the most, a pair of wading birds and three swans.

What has become of the birds that according to Vasari once studded his canvases, so much so as to earn him his nickname of Uccello? Who has scared them away? Most certainly it is the soldiers, who render the highways of the air impassable with their spears, and with the clash of weaponry silence trillings and chirrupings.

Fled from the colored surfaces, the birds are hiding or fluttering invisibly outside the borders of the paintings. They are waiting for the right moment to make a comeback and occupy the canvas. Following the Vasari tradition, Giovanni Pascoli in a narrative poem and Marcel Schwob in one of his *Vies imaginaires* have depicted the aged painter surrounded by birds born of his brush. But what we ourselves can testify to is exactly the opposite. In Paolo's most famous surviving works what catches the attention is the absence of birds, an absence that lies heavy on the air, alarming, menacing and ominous.

The most frequently depicted scenes of Paolo Uccello that are still to be seen today presuppose others, which he may have painted but which have since been lost: scenes that precede the above—a world all trillings and peckings and beating wings, taken by surprise and scattered to the winds by the invasion of the warriors—and other scenes that follow them: the counteroffensive of the birds, who swoop down in serried flocks and perch on helmets, shoulder plates and elbow guards.

Are crows and vultures there at the end of the battle? Not at all. It has already been observed that in all Paolo Uccello's battle scenes we see only one dead man on the ground; and even he might only have fainted. Every man on the field is still alive when the sky darkens and the air is troubled by a great beating of wings. The horses become restive, uttering neighs of terror.

The battle between the two armies is transformed into a battle against the birds, the swords raise eddies of feathers, the lances are shaken to rid them of grasping talons, while the blows of beaks rain down on shields. To put a horse out of action is the work of a moment: a magpie steals its glittering studded blinkers, a kestrel rips off its girth, ringdoves remove the saddlecloth. So you find yourself on foot, with a crow's wings wedged twixt sallet and chin strap, a capercaillie pecking off your throat-piece, a hoopoe perched on your crest. Your mouth fills up with jay's feathers, and by now you no longer know how much of you is armor, is man, is bird.

You holler for help. Here comes another warrior, no matter whether friend or foe: we are all allies now against the birds. The warrior lifts his vizor and out pop the beak and two round eyes of an owl. You cast around for a shield to protect yourself and find yourself grasping a wing with feathers spread. A sword is raised to protect you—but no, it is wielded by the talon of a bird of prey, and down it crashes on you.

Pointed or fan-shaped tails sprout under your flanchards, your greaves encompass slender shanks, while breastplates put forth feathers and the trumpets emit shrill bird cries, twitterings and chirrupings. There follows a chain-reaction metamorphosis of man into bird and bird into man. Or rather, on closer consideration, and seeing that men have already transformed themselves into crustaceans by donning their armor, it is between crustaceans and birds that the metamorphosis takes place; an exchange in which you do not know where—and if— man still exists.

PRESIDENT BILL CLINTON

Notebook

January 13, 1987
This is a day for decision. Our problems are clear: the collapse of agriculture; high rural unemployment except in areas immune to international pressures (we have worked to overcome the loss of factory jobs to overseas competition); increasing numbers of poor children with uncertain futures; too many unskilled workers.

What may not be so clear is our opportunity, indeed our obligation, to continue to prepare our people for and move our state toward the twenty-first century.

We have put off progress in favor of survival.

Survival *requires* progress.

May 16, 1987
When John Kennedy was running for president in 1960, we all divided up and fought our own campaign at my junior high school. Kennedy made a deep impression on me with his call for an Alliance for Progress with Latin America. The message I got, as I remember it today, is that there were millions of poor people down there suffering. Their kids have a right to a future. We're a big, rich, strong country, and this is something that we ought to do because it's the right thing to do. The message we should be preaching today is that we need to do something about this Latin American debt crisis, and the growth rate of the Latin American economy, not just for all those people, the people who nearly three decades ago tacked little pictures of John Kennedy up on the mud walls of their houses, but for ourselves too.

June 21, 1987
I think what you should insist on from every politician in this country, without regard to party, is that you want hardheaded problem-solving which recognizes the legitimacy of the needs of the cities.

July 15, 1987

For thirteen years the people of this state have made it possible for me to be in the public life, but they have not made it *easy* for me to be in the public life. I have been in fifteen separate election contests—as far as I know, more than any other state officeholder in the United States—subject to more rigorous scrutiny and tougher campaigns, more brutal battles than anyone else that I can think of.

The only thing I or any other candidate has to offer in running for President is what's inside. That's what sets people on fire and gets their confidence and their votes, whether they live in Arkansas or Wisconsin or Montana or New York. That part of my life needs renewal.

The other, even more important reason for my decision is the certain impact that this campaign would have had on our daughter. If I had been gone six or seven days a week, think of the impact on an only child. I made a promise to myself that if I was ever lucky enough to have a child, she would never grow up wondering who her father was. And to be perfectly selfish, the thought of missing all those softball games, soccer games, plays at the school, and consultations with teachers mortified me.

When I came home from New Hampshire I was happy, flying like a kite, because of the reception I'd gotten. I really believed that if I could have entered the race right then, within three or four weeks I could have been in second place in New Hampshire. But I could not bring myself to make those phone calls. I made more calls yesterday to tell people I wasn't going to run for President than I had made on any single day since I had been looking at this. I couldn't bring myself to close the deal.

August 19, 1987

One of the reasons I lost in 1980 was that I was responsible for a highway-improvement program which was very controversial. We built a lot of good roads and then people drove over those roads to find the polling places to vote against me. I became the youngest former governor in the history of the republic!

I was driving down one of those improved roads and I stopped at a little country gas station. I walked in and saw an old fellow in overalls.

He looked at me and said, "Aren't you Bill Clinton?"

I said, "Yes, sir."

"Do you know, fellow," he said, "I got eleven folks to vote against you in the last election, and I just loved it."

I asked him why.

He said, "I had to, Governor. You raised my car license fee."

"Now listen," I explained, "this county you live in had the worst roads in the state. We had to send emergency vehicles down here to pull cars out the mud! We had to fix those roads."

He told me he didn't care—that he didn't want to pay for it.

I decided to try a positive approach: "Well, that's water under the bridge. Let me ask you this: would you ever consider voting for me again?"

He looked at me and grinned, "You know I would, because we're even now."

I was so excited that I found a pay phone, called my wife, and said, "We're running!"

Near the end of the election about a year later, I walked into a little country store in north Arkansas where the owner had a reputation of knowing what was going on. There was one man in the store drinking coffee, and he said, "Well, son, I voted against you last time, but I'm going to vote for you this time."

I was pleased and told him so, and I asked him why he voted against me last time.

He looked at me matter-of-factly and said, "I had to. You raised my car license fee."

"Well, why are you going to vote for me this time?" I asked.

He said, "Because you raised my car license fee."

I said, "Sir, I certainly don't want to insult you, but it doesn't make any sense to me for you to vote for me this time for the very reason you voted against me before."

He patiently explained, "Oh, son, it makes all the sense in the world. You may be a lot of things, Bill, but you aren't stupid. You're the very least likely one to ever raise that car license fee again. So I'm for you."

October 16, 1987

To me it's clear what's at stake in this presidential election. We are all going to the polls conscious for the first time as a country of the fact that the post–World War II era is over. A majority of us know that America does not dominate the world and will not dominate the world again, at least in the lifetime of anyone in this room.

*   *   *

People complain about the Japanese all the time, but every study that's been done—three in the last two years—on the Japanese system of trade says that if we tore down all of their trade barriers, last year's trade deficit would have been reduced by about 5 percent.

If growth rates in Latin America in 1986 had been what they were in 1978, our trade deficit would have been reduced by 20 percent—four times as much. By permitting Latin America to grow again, we ourselves can grow.

Everybody complains about the Japanese because we had a $60 billion trade deficit with them last year. That's true. We did, but do you know how much money the Japanese invested in this country last year? $100 billion. Without outside money, we are going to have to lower our standard of living today and tomorrow. We'll have to shift spending from consumption and investment to debt service.

I am not pessimistic about the future but I'm telling you we have run out this present string about as long as we can run it. This old dog won't hunt anymore.

I had a course in western civilization with a remarkable man, the late Carroll Quigley. Half the people at Georgetown thought he was a bit crazy and the other half thought he was a genius. They were both right. He said something I'll never forget. He said, "You've got to understand the essence of western civilization. The thing that got you all to this classroom today is the belief in the future. The belief that the future can be better than the present and that people will and should sacrifice in the present to get to that better future. That has taken man out of the chaos and deprivation that has been the condition of most human beings for most of human history. The one thing which will kill our civilization and our way of life is when people no longer have the will to undergo the pain required to prefer the future to the present. That's what got your parents to pay the expensive tuition to get you into this class. That's what got your country through two world wars in this century and a depression in between. That's what produced such unparalleled prosperity. That's what got you here today." Future preference. He said don't you ever forget that.

November 17, 1987

We have been experimenting with a program I'm very excited about, called HIPPY, which is an acronym for Home Instruction Program for Preschool Youngsters. The program was developed in Israel to help immigrant families, most of them poor, uneducated people coming into a highly educated society. Almost twenty years ago now, the Israelis developed a way to teach the mothers of three- and four-year-old kids to teach their children how to speak, think, and reason, to prepare them for kindergarten. They taught even illiterate mothers to do it.

Last February, 49 out of the 50 governors voted for a welfare reform policy which calls for changing the whole system of welfare from an income maintenance system to an education, training, and independence system. Welfare, as it exists today, was developed over fifty years ago for a society that no longer exists. Unfortunately, the problems which bring the parents to welfare are not addressed at all by the system which provides the check.

The real disincentive to work is not benefits, which have gone down 20 percent in real terms since 1973, but instead is the cost of child care and the loss of medical coverage for children if the job taken is a minimum wage job without health insurance.

This proposed package offers mothers a chance to become contributing citizens without being bad mothers. It offers them a chance to break the cycle of dependency.

January 19, 1988

Internationally, the governor's role is more important. Not long ago, you would be criticized at home if you went to Japan. Now you are criticized if you don't go.

In the only partisan fight we have had in years, the Democratic governors got mad because the President had sent out a fundraising letter on behalf of the Republican governors, while the Republicans were all anti-tax like Reagan. In fact, a higher percentage of Republican governors had raised taxes than Democratic governors! Our bipartisan fight arose because the President's letter ignored the decline in partisanship among the governors on the tax issue.

January 29, 1988
The longer I stay in this business, the more I think we should evaluate ourselves not in terms of what others are doing, but in terms of whether we're really making progress on the problems we have.

You read all the estimates on the number of adult illiterates. We need to know who these people are and where they are. Where do they live and how old are they? Are they in the work force or are they idle? Are they people who could do better if they learned to read? Are they people who could get a job for the first time if they learned to read?

February 9, 1988
I was asked last Sunday to go by and talk to a singles Sunday school class in my church. Most of the members are between twenty-three and thirty-eight, most of them business or professional people. The Sunday school lesson I gave them was about the conflict between the idea of progress and the certainty of death. Now, I don't want to get into the theological implications of it, but the basic point is that sometimes it's hard to keep going when you know that the sand's running out of the hourglass. Yet you still have a moral obligation to try to make tomorrow better than today. For a politician the equivalent of that dilemma arises as your term runs out.

HART CRANE

Ten Poems

I

Dust now is the old-fashioned house
Where Jacob dreamed his climb,—
Thankfully fed both hog and mouse
And danced a ladder dance of rhyme.

Dust now is the old-fashioned house
Where Jacob dreamed his ladder climb,—
Thankfully fed both hog and mouse
And mounted rung on rung of rhyme.

ca. 1920

II

There are the local orchard boughs
With apples—August boughs
Their unspilled spines
Inter-wrenched and flocking with
gold spousal wine
like hummocks
drifting in the autumn shine.

ca. 1920

III

You are that frail decision that devised
Their lowest common multiple of human need,
And on that bleak assumption risked the prize
Forgetfulness of all you bait for greed . . .

ca. 1923–1926

IV

Her eyes had the blue of desperate days,
Freezingly bright; I saw her hair unfurl,
Unsanctioned, finally, by anything left her to know
She had learned that Paradise is not a question of eggs
If anything, it was her privilege to undress
Quietly in a glass she had guarded
Always with correcting states before.

It was this, when I asked her how she died,
That asked me why her final happy cry
Should not have found an echo somewhere, and I stand
Before her finally, as beside a wall, listening as though
I heard the breath of Holofernes toast
Judith's cold bosom through her righteous years.

ca. May 1925

V

All this—and the housekeeper—
Written on a blotter, Hartford, Bridgeport—
The weekend at Holyoke
His daughters act like kings
Pauline and I, the Harvard game
—A brand new platform
Way on Stutzing up to Spring
Not a cent, not a cent, wish we'd known
Beforehand.

And the last of the Romanoffs
Translated the International Code
Tea and toast across radios
Swung into lullabyes.
His father gave him the store outright
—All sorts of money, Standard Oil
And his two sons, their fourth or fifth cousins
How well he carries himself
And a stick all the time.

ca. March 1926

VI

I have that sure enclitic to my act
Which thou insure no dissonance to fact
Then Agememnon's locks grow to shape
Without my forebear's priceless model of the ape . . .
Gorillas die—and so do humanists—who keep
Comparisons clear for evolution's non-escape
And man the deathless target, derivational,
Sure of his own weak sheep . . .

ca. 1926–1929

VII

I rob my breast to reach those altitudes—
Abstractions to meet the meaningless concussion of
Pure heights—Infinity resides below . . .
The obelisk of plain infinity founders below
My vision is a grandiose dilemma.*

Place de la Concorde! Across that crowded plain—
I fought to see the stricken bones, the noble
Carcass of a general, dead Foch, proceed
To the defunct pit of Napoleon—in honor
Defender, not usurper.

My countrymen—give form and edict—
To the marrow. You shall know
The harvest as you had known the spring.

ca. 1928–1930

VIII
To Conquer Variety

I have seen my ghost broken
My body blessed
And Eden

In the original text, "near-sight" was an alternative to "dilemma."

Scraped from my mother's breast
When the charge was spoken
Love dispossessed
And the seal broken . . .

ca. 1931–1932

IX

Did one look at what one saw
Or did one see what one looked at?

X

They were there falling;
And they fell. And their habitat
Left them. And they fell.
And what they remembered was—
Dismembered. But they fell.
And now they dispell
Those wonders that posterity constructs,
By such a mystery as time obstructs;
And all the missions and votaries
And old maids with their chronic coteries
Dispense in the old, old lorgnette views
What should have kept them straight in pews
But, doesn't confuse

Doesn't confuse
These Indians, who scan more news
On the hind end of their flocks each day
Than all the tourists bring their way.

ca. March–April 1932

GERALD EARLY

Life with Daughters: An Essay on Proportionality

Of all kinds of knowledge that we can ever obtain,
the knowledge of God, and the knowledge of ourselves,
are the most important.

—JONATHAN EDWARDS,
The Freedom of the Will

I awake in Nashville every morning at 6:45. First, I turn on the radio to WFSK, the Fisk University station, and hear black gospel music, for that is what's played all morning, every morning, on that station. I recline on my narrow mattress on the floor and am not soothed or comforted by this music. I do not wish to be. I am in fact jolted, irritated, slightly unnerved by its emphatic holiness, by its unwavering confidence in the conceit of its own faith, by the self-absorption of its own artifice. Nothing makes me more sick of Christianity, if we come to the root of it, than the blithe expectation that one can actually believe it and be in good cheer. That one can actually believe it at all is another matter, just as the question of whether belief of any sort matters in this world.

I pull the covers up, for the apartment is cold; the heat is so low it never came on during the night. The room is dark, so effectively do the tacky red drapes cover the only window that I cannot tell if it is cloudy or sunny. I do not hear rain. And I think about my children. Did Rosalind finish her homework? Will she remember all of her books for school this morning? Do either of them have colds? Are their colds coming along? Are either of them constipated? Are they eating some fruit every day, drinking enough fluids? Is Linnet seeing the tutor regularly? Is my wife Ida able to help her with her work or is she too tired from her own work—meetings, cooking dinner, cleaning house, and so forth? Are Linnet and Rosalind dressing for the weather? It has been cold in St.

Louis, much colder than in Nashville, and I know how they like to wear light little jackets instead of their coats and scarves. Now that Rosalind has started her period, is she cleaning up behind herself? And how is that room of hers, such a pigpen! Every morning it is the same: ten minutes or more given over to this activity, this mother-hen-like clucking at the walls, the cluttered room, the dark.

Finally I kick off the covers, take off my clothes for my morning toilet, and another day in Nashville, studying Fisk University, begins. I do not think about Ida and the girls much during the day, for I am busy with other things. But upon awakening, and sometimes when I cannot sleep, I think of them, and it is difficult, thinking about them in these moments. I am not sure why I think about this. I am not sentimental about my children. I can go a good deal of time, even in their presence, when I do not think of them at all. One can never be sure, in the cell of loneliness, what any of one's actions mean; for, there, separated and overly sensitive to the idea of absence, one acquires, like a vertigo, a lack of perspective. There is at times an acute loss of proportionality, as if all relations were both equally absurd and equally concrete, equally dramatic and equally mundane, as if kindly cut by an unkind tool. Parenting, to borrow a phase Ty Cobb used for baseball, "ain't no pink tea." And it sure ain't for mollycoddles, Teddy Rossevelt's term. It is a tough, demanding business. I feel guilty, sometimes deeply so, when I am not pulling my share of the load. For having a family is a great deal like facing a disaster that is always impending and is something of a relief when it happens. "Your family must be a great comfort to you," many have said to me, and sometimes I have simply, almost stupidly, as if I did not understand the language, replied, "Oh." And it is right at these moments that I think, imperially, that, after all, I ought not to be pulling the same weight as Ida. I feel secretly a sense that I should be indulged as the more, let me say, cunning parent.

"Well, how's it going?" I asked Ida during one of our phone conversations. It must have been a particularly hard day, judging from her response.

"How do you think it's been?" she fired back, annoyed, I suppose, by my easygoing manner. "While you have been at Fisk, playing Mr. Researcher all day, I've been walking the dog, feeding the dog, getting the kids up for school, getting them to school, going to work, coming home, fixing dinner real quick, going out to a meeting, coming home to help somebody with homework, walking the dog. All that kind of stuff. It's been lovely, day in and day out stuff."

"You sound stressed," I said, concerned.

"Wouldn't you be if you were in my place? I don't have a job where I can go gallivanting around, taking time off, sitting in libraries writing books."

"Listen, Ida," I said, trying to measure my voice in the most diplomatic way, "you make it sound as though my job is my fault. You know what I have to do. We talked this all out before."

She was not relenting at all and probably thought my reason was nothing more than a whine of privilege. "It's just been a rough day, that's all. Linnet's having trouble at school again. Some of the girls there are picking on her, riding her, giving her a hard time. And she's becoming impossible here at home. I can't say a thing to her without her going off the deep end, blowing up, storming out of the room. That girl, at times, just gets on my last nerve."

"She's a teenager. They act like that when they're teenagers. I'm sure you were a whole box of tricks when you were a teenager. Everybody was," I said.

"I guess so. But I've just lost patience. Maybe you can talk with her. I just give up. She always liked you better anyway."

I had my doubts about the truth of that. Linnet and I had a certain closeness when she was younger but it eroded, for many reasons, as she matured. Linnet became a popular baby-sitter, so much of her free time on the weekends is now claimed by her jobs. She also has her own money, a good deal of it, as she is a fairly frugal kid. Moreover, she just tends, nowadays, to want to be by herself. I wind up spending a good deal more time with Rosalind, who does not baby-sit, still needs me for recreational income, and has not quite hit puberty yet.

Linnet is a worrier. She is worried about going to high school, about whether she can do the work in a Biology or a French class. She desperately wants to do well in school, but a learning disability, which has made school such a struggle all her life, looms over her like a lowering sky, beyond her like a wall without a door, beneath her like a turbulent sea in which she fears drowning. In part, she desires academic brilliance because she wants to go to college; in part, she wants the respect and admiration of her friends, whom she considers smarter and better-looking. But there is another reason as well.

"She wants to please you," Ida said to me once. "She has a father who is a college professor. All the adults she knows have enormous respect for your intellect. They hold you in a kind of awe. And she feels that."

"I have never pressured her to go to college or follow the path that I took," I interjected self-defensively. "She knows I will be happy with whatever she does in life as long as she is happy."

"I know that. But that's not the point. She wants to be worthy of having a father like you. She hears it from her teachers, from the adults at church and in the neighborhood. 'Your father is a famous writer.' 'I heard your father on NPR.' 'I read a piece your father wrote in *Harper's*.' Blah, blah, blah. She wants you to be proud of her in the way other people are proud of you. That's why so much of her self-esteem is at stake with the academics. If you were a bus driver, a minister, or a mailman, she would feel differently about how she would have to please you."

"Well, if she feels that way," I replied, slightly distressed, "she shouldn't. She has no right to. My life is mine. She should live her own. This is putting a lot of pressure on me that I don't want and I don't deserve. And a lot of guilt too for trying to be something worthy of self-respect. I want to make my kids proud of me. But I don't think I should be made to feel guilty of making them neurotics." I lapsed into silence, dropping that topic of conversation entirely, as nothing that was being said was helpful.

"Nobody's trying to make you feel guilty," Ida said, finally.

II

Whatever happens. Whatever
what is is is what
I want. Only that. But that.
—GALWAY KINNELL,
"Prayer"

I came to Fisk to write a book about the place. I had no desire to write such a book. Someone asked me. I had never given Fisk a thought. I had some relatives, aunts, who had gone to a black college, but it was not Fisk. I remember a young man my sister was dating when I was in junior high school told me once that Fisk was a great school and that W. E. B. Du Bois went there. "Oh," I said. I did not want to ask who was this W. E. B. Du Bois and where was this Fisk that was so great.

I think others, when they heard of my doing the Fisk book, thought this rather unusual intellectual act to be my rapprochement with black folk. After years in the white wilderness, I had come home, so to speak. Black folk these days are a bit awash in and simultaneously "burnt over" by sentimental race feelings. (This is understandable in a country where people seem capable of understanding themselves and their experience only if it is glazed over with sentimentality, spiked with trauma, and resembles nothing so much as a Hollywood film about family happiness of which precious little exists or has ever existed in the real world.) I felt no such sentimentality being at Fisk. It was just another school, except only black students attended it. I experienced no magical transformation being there, I came to no particular insights about black people—I did not expect to. I did not go there with the thought that I would have a détente with my blackness—would, in effect, apologize for having spent my college and professional life at white schools. What I felt when I walked across the Fisk campus of an afternoon was the same detachment I felt as a child as I walked in my neighborhood, mixed with Italians and blacks. What I felt was a densely deep intellectual wonderment, as if black people were a dazzling collection of possibilities of human consciousness. And I, amazingly, was one of these. I knew I had never earned their love or even their interest. I wonder if I had ever wanted either. I could walk across the Fisk campus and imagine myself walking across the campus of Washington University, lonely, shy, yet almost arrogantly untouched by anything around me. I was as unintegrated, as apart from the community here as I was at the white English department where I work largely as a politically useful appendage. "I never belonged to the white world," I said to myself, "and never belonged to the world of blacks, either. I have been, for better or worse, only and always myself." But it was while walking through the Fisk campus that I felt more importunately than ever that I was not happy. And I knew there was a major difference between my life at Washington University and my life at Fisk: I never have truly known how the whites I work with feel about anything or why they feel the way they do. On Fisk's campus, I knew how these people felt and why. Going to Fisk, on my part, was no expression of a wish to go home; it was more an acknowledgment of the impossibility of escaping one's fate or the unerring compass of one's will.

Late on a February Saturday evening, about five or six o'clock, my mother called me in Nashville and told me that my grandfather, her father, had died earlier that day. I think I was watching a video at the time, a 1950s film called *Plunder Road*. This has no significance except that I like to remember what I was doing when I receive important, epochal news. My grandfather was a very old man, ninety-three years of age, at the time of his death. He had been a very resilient man during his lifetime, very strong, in his way, and very black. He had no serious health problems in his life, nothing life-threatening. He had had a pacemaker inserted recently, but he did not have a bad heart. In fact, just a week earlier my mother had told me that he was doing well. He seemed healthier than ever. So I was a bit surprised to hear that he simply died on an airplane on the way to the Bahamas—the old country, as it were, at least for portions of my family—ironically, to bury his brother George.

My grandfather had the blackest skin of any man I knew and he always sounded like a Bahamian to me, although he had lived in this country since he was twenty years old. He worked until he was sixty-two as a laborer for the gas company in Philadelphia. My mother resembles him closely and has very black skin too. I think she would have been a good Bahamian, a perfect likeness of the Islands, if she had been born and reared there. Sometimes, as I grew older, I liked to imagine my mother a Bahamian, unAmericanized. But like all of us black folk, like my grandfather, who was very American (he loved baseball and "The Lone Ranger" television series), very Episcopalian (after he retired, he attended church every Sunday), and very Bahamian (he went back to the old country nearly every summer after his retirement), she was too much of a paradox, a mixture, to satisfy any fantasy about roots.

I did not go to the funeral. I had to go back to St. Louis to watch the children that weekend because Ida was going out of town. I sent flowers. That was not a good excuse. I should have dropped everything and gone home. But, of course, Philadelphia is not my home and will never be my home again, unless I might be led to think of it as a monument to a set of peculiar, rich, and often unsatisfying memories. My mother does not live in the home in which I grew up. My grandfather sold his home last year, when my grandmother died. I know nothing in Philadelphia as home. I was surprised that my grandfather died so soon after the death of his wife, their relationship having been a fractious expression of bitterly mutual contempt. When Linnet and Rosalind last met my grandparents several years ago, they were bewildered that they sat in the same room and carried on entirely different and rudely competitive conversations with me. I sat on a sofa between them, each blatantly and theatrically oblivious of the other, partly embarrassed and partly amused.

"Perhaps your grandfather died because he missed his home and what went on in it," a friend suggested.

"If that's the case," I said, a bit annoyed, "then I guess it's possible to miss anything, absolutely anything. If that's the case, any misery is a fondness we don't appreciate."

"Why didn't you just take your children with you to the funeral?" another friend asked me.

"Oh, well," I said, truly surprised by the question, thinking what a ridiculous question, "I couldn't have done that. That would have made the funeral an ordeal. I would have had to sweat through it." This person did not understand that it is not so easy for me to go back to the old country.

III

While through a throttling dark we others hear
The little lifting helplessness, the queer
Whimper-whine; whose unridiculous
Lost softness softly makes a trap for us.
And makes a curse. And makes a sugar of
The malocclusions, the inconditions of love.

—GWENDOLYN BROOKS,
"the children of the poor"

Perhaps if I had a special rapport with Linnet, as Ida believes, it would be because I can so thoroughly identify with her. I can so completely, at times intensely, see myself in her, picture her childhood life, her joys, her sorrows, as my own, that I sense myself reliving my childhood through her. But yet we were so different as children: I was not nearly so desperate, never felt so weak, was never so alienated from my peers. But I was so unable to care for others as Linnet does, never so capable of being given the burden of a trust. But a girl—as Linnet so unerringly knows—must be appealing to her friends of both sexes in a way that a boy does not. A girl must be appealing to adults of both sexes in ways that a boy does not. To be the weaker sex, one must be stronger. I was, in fact, for a good part of my childhood considered an academically gifted child—and yet, never have I felt as inadequate as I did as a child, such a fake (my sisters were so much smarter, so much more talented), so disappointing to those who believed in me. I was so undistinguished, a lazy mimic, self-pitying, badly educated, and unworthy of every privilege ever bestowed upon me. I was a poor boy who showed a little interest in the life of the mind. And that, and that alone, made all the difference. I have told Linnet countless stories of my childhood, but she still does not know, does not understand what it is, alas, that I am trying to say. "Be your own father," said the crazy vet in Ralph Ellison's *Invisible Man*. "Be your own father," says the father to his daughter.

Being away from the kids for a few weeks at a stretch means falling out of our domestic rhythm. There is always a sense of desperation in my trying to catch up on the weekends I am home. And I am never quite able to, never quite able to pick up the signals of the dance, my eyes never quite adjusting to the quality and sources of light that are there. I am, these days, always faltering, like a partner trying to learn to dance on a dance floor with a bunch of other couples and bumping into others helplessly yet straining to retain his good nature.

One recent weekend, I had Linnet and Rosalind to myself, as Ida had to go to New York for a meeting. Linnet was pretty sulky most of the time, as skittish and temperamental as a thoroughbred. If I would say the least critical remark, she would blow up, walk away. For instance, when I asked her to prepare some tea water for me, she burned up the kettle because she neglected to see if it contained any water. After many minutes, the kitchen was suffused with the smell of burning metal, the kettle was aglow like an overworked car engine.

"That," I said, obviously annoyed, "was not a very smart thing to do. I would think that it might occur to you to at least check the kettle for water before putting a light under it."

She hung her head. Her eyes almost immediately welled with tears of both self-pity and anger. "Well, I didn't, all right? Is it a crime? Or does it show I'm a moron? You never burned a pot before? Probably not, since you're Mr. Perfect. And you don't have to be sarcastic about things."

"Linnet," I said, trying to take a more soothing tack, "it's not that big a deal, but I do think it was a bit negligent on your part. All I'm saying is that you ought to be more careful in the future."

"Okay, okay," she said, bristling, "don't start preaching. I'll pay for the thing if you want."

"That's not necessary," I said, "and you know it."

We said virtually nothing to each other for the rest of the evening. I felt as though I was doing a poor job of it as a parent on this particular day. I am aware, of course, of how sensitive she is to criticism that impugns her intelligence. I should have broached the business of the burned kettle in another way. But, on the other hand, she must be reminded of her mistakes if she is ever to profit from them. She, naturally, feels that her life has been one unending reminder of her mistakes, the memoranda having, as it were, profited her little, as she sees the matter. This, coupled with the natural overwrought sensitivity of the teenager, makes dealing with Linnet at times the equivalent of walking across a field of landmines.

The weekend did not go well. I suppose I walked on more than my fair share of landmines, more than anyone has a right to bury in any one psyche. At least, I felt that way at the time. I thought I was not only going to give Ida a spell that weekend but that I would come to rescue, so to speak, as Ida had been having a hard time with Linnet. Daddy will come and make everything all right again, make rough passages plain, as he did when Linnet was a little girl. But she is a little girl no longer and she seems more than a little distracted, as I do myself—the complexities of our lives have gotten in the way of our lives. Both of us were living a pressurized existence that neither could help living and neither could help the other live. I was away writing a book. "My dad's always writing something or giving a lecture or something," I overheard her say to a friend. "He doesn't pay much attention to us anymore, not like he did when we were younger." She was growing up. "I would spend more time with her," I said to Ida once, "but I don't think she wants me to. She has a life of her own now. I can't interfere as freely as I once did."

By Saturday night, things were frayed between Linnet and me, a lot of minor collisions, angry eruptions, hurt feelings. She finally slammed the door of her mother's study to watch television alone. I went to my study to write. And there is where relations stood, as they had for several months: I in one room writing, she in another watching television or reading or playing music—as if we were strangers living in an apartment house. It's a normal phase parents and children go through, I thought and let it go at that.

On Sunday morning I awoke and for a moment I thought I was in Nashville. I could not quite understand fully that I was in St. Louis, that I was not sleeping on the floor, and there was no radio beside the bed. There was no moment of thinking about the children and what they were doing and how Ida was making out, just a kind of blankness. Where am I? Oh goodness, I've got to walk the dog, I thought. It was early, about 6:30. Perhaps I felt so disoriented that morning because I wished that I were in Nashville; perhaps I was wishing to be alone. There comes a time for every parent where *thinking about* your children is a great deal more rewarding and easier, a great deal more wished for, than *being with* them.

I walked across the bedroom and found an envelope had been thrust under the door. It was addressed "To Daddy" with the drawing of a heart. I recognized Linnet's writing. Her note read:

> *Dear Daddy,*
> *I am really sorry I've been such a pain but sometimes I get really mad at the wrong person. Please don't be mad at me for keeps. I'm really sorry and I hope that next time you come to visit we can have a lot of fun!*
> *Love,*
> *Linnet*

For an instant I held the card as if I could not quite recognize it in the dim light, as if it were written by someone I did not know for someone else. Then I shuddered, convulsed as if I were having a spasm of some sort. "Oh," I said. Then again, "Oh." I thought of some black folk singing and it hit me like a revelation; that's why they play so much gospel music at Fisk. Because of the Jubilee Singers and the founding of the school. It was on that rock that the school was built. God, what an idiot I have been not to have seen such an obvious thing. The gospel is in homage, a daily, unrelenting homage, to those singing black students who saved that school back in the 1870s. How I Got Over, Mahalia Jackson sang, and the race itself can sing, How I Got Over. I could hear some black folk singing, "God came down and my dungeon shook." Angels overhead, transformed in the dim light from niggers to saints in the singing, cauterized by the light.

When I went into Linnet's room later that morning she was sitting up in bed, blowing her nose, coughing, looking a bit under the weather.

"Well, daughter," I said, "you're looking a good deal peaked this morning," remembering how she always likes it when I call her "daughter."

"I just got a cold, Daddy. I'll be all right," she said.

"Better take it easy today. You know, such a gorgeous kid like you ought not even to be sick," I said.

She grinned at that.

"I remember when you used to say that to us all the time, Daddy, when we were little, me and Ros. You would say, 'What's such a gorgeous kid like you doing being sad?' or something like that. I liked it a lot when you used that expression. It made me like the word 'gorgeous.' It sounded so nice and rich. Like a wonderful thing to call somebody: gorgeous."

Yes, I thought, where did I get that? Perhaps from a movie I saw as a teenager. I used it as a pet phrase for a time when my kids were younger. But Linnet was still talking. I had missed something.

". . . that day when we went to the zoo and it was like zero degrees outside. We were little then, I think I was five or something and Ros was three. We should have gone to the baby-sitter, and you should have gone to work, but we went to the zoo that day instead. You never went to work that day."

"Yes," I said vaguely, distractedly. "Yes, I remember."

"And we were all bundled up, and you said, 'Let's go to the zoo today because nobody goes on a cold day like this.' And you said, 'I want to go to the zoo with such gorgeous kids like these.' And everyone was laughing about going to the zoo. And you were right. The place was empty. 'Nobody here but us fools and polo bears,' you said. Just like Bill 'Bojangles' Robinson said it in that Shirley Temple movie we saw, where he said 'polo bears' instead of polar bears. And it was kinda icy, and Ros slipped once and fell on her rump, but she had so many clothes on she didn't feel it, and she couldn't get back up because she was so bundled up, and everybody just laughed. And that was when you had to take us to the Men's Room when we had to go to the bathroom, remember? Because we were too young to go to the bathroom by ourselves."

"Yes," I said, but I was not quite focused on any of this. I could only remember it very faintly.

"And we went all over the zoo that day. Most of the animals weren't even out. It was so cold. Then we went to McDonald's for lunch and Ros got ketchup all over her snowsuit and sucked on her french fries like they were candy. And we went home that afternoon and looked at cartoons and you read *The Wind in the Willows* to us and said it was your favorite book when you were a boy. And then Mommy came home and she was real mad at you 'cause you took us to the zoo in such cold weather. And we were just messing around instead of being at the baby-sitter's and we were going to have to pay for that day at the baby-sitter's even though we didn't show up. And you were just laughing about it and you said something like, 'What's it matter? We're all gonna die anyway.' You were just like a boy that day. I'll never forget that day, that was one of the best days of my life." She said this so earnestly that it was as if someone had awakened me, gently but insistently, from a light but tenacious sleep.

"Yes," I said. "Yes, that's right."

She hung fire for a bit. Then she looked up at me.

"You can't be like that anymore, can you, Daddy?"

"No," I said, softly, "I can't be like that much anymore."

"And it does matter, doesn't it? Even though we are gonna die," she asked anxiously.

"Yes," I said, resigned, "it does matter. Things matter, even though we are going to die."

I rose from her bed, tucked the rose and white blankets snugly about her red-pajamaed body, grinned.

"Nothing ever stays the same, does it, Daddy?" she asked as I reached for the doorknob.

"No," I said, "nothing ever stays the same. But that doesn't mean that things have to go from good to bad or from bad to worse. Things can change between people but still be good. People don't really ever change. How they are forced to live may make them seem different."

"Yes, I know," she said.

"Take care of yourself, daughter," I said and quietly shut the door.

WILLIAM H. GASS

Finding a Form

The writer, by choosing to write, rather than ride Beckett's bike, or Don Quixote's nag, is choosing to relate to the world through words. This is as true of an historian or a philosopher as it is of a poet. In my case, at least, the choice was an illusory one, for early on in my life I felt overwhelmed by the world (which, for anyone young, is not likely to have borders far beyond the family). It was a world which was certainly no worse than average, not much better either, so it was not one inherently overwhelming, one which would do the strongest of characters in. No. It found in me a weak respondent, a poor player. I was the sort of actor who specialized in exits.

I had a lot of models to follow: first, a father who railed at the world while he listened to it on the radio, who blamed the wops for his discomfort, the bohunks, the spicks, the kikes, the niggers he had to try to teach in the industrial high school where he was a warden more than tutor, who took no risks, resisted advancement, remained satisfied to be safely a nobody who nevertheless would mutter under his breath about it; and then a mother who invested all her savings in bad stock—me—a woman of useless sensitivity and fruitless talent whom my father cowed and bullied, although he offered her (as he offered me) only verbal abuse. Still, it was abuse which never tired him, which could be continuous, proving to me what words could do, how words could empower the powerless. As a consequence of these repeated though bruiseless blows, and of the fact that for women then there was nothing to do but keep house and suffer hubby and raise kids (which meant that I—an only child—grew up and inevitably drew away as well), she was left marooned in her kitchen and breakfast nook where bottles of gin washed ashore as though a whole fleet full of spirits had foundered; and she took those bottles in as though they were meant for her womb—children to replace a kid—and that's how she bore her death to its term, for she was drunk more than a dozen years before the blood vessels in her throat burst and she drowned by drinking her own blood.

I had a maiden aunt, too, who had brought Grandma to visit,

moving this elderly woman about from relative to relative so each would have an equal share of the burden, and who stayed on after her charge died, discreetly, gradually, stubbornly, secretively, surely, taking over the management of the house, the helpless world of women, from my mother.

Passivity, self-mortification, substitute gratification, impotent bitching, drink: these were the ways of life set before me. Now, when considering the insides of a writer, pondering the psychology of the occupation, I always look first for the weakness which led them to it; because, make no mistake, writing puts the writer in illusory command of the world, empowers someone otherwise powerless, but with a power no more pointed than a pencil.

So it was in my own situation, where I was taught to deflect my desires from their real object onto another, safer, simpler one; where, when confronted with a problem, like a good Stoic, I strove to alter myself rather than the world, since my self seemed more in my power, and because my aim was usually to relinquish instead of conquer. During this character-creating time, I found I had one facility: I had, on my side, a little language. We do what we can do, and I could do that. Reading and writing aren't arithmetic. I read to escape my condition, I wrote to remedy it—both perilous passivities—and there is scarcely a significant character in my work who is not a failure in the practice of ordinary existence, who does not lead a deflected life. Often, though not always, they live inside a language, and try to protect themselves from every danger with a phrase.

All the world may be a stage, for those who can act in it; and it may, instead, be a game, for those who have the skill and can play; it may be reduced to a square of canvas, redone as a screen full of images; it may be replaced by the sheer shimmer of beautifully related sounds; but for me the world became a page. That, I said, with Stoical acceptance, was the way I wanted it; it was what I would have chosen. It is natural to speak of your own weaknesses so winsomely they will seem strengths, as if everyone else is inadequate if they do not have your inadequacies. We also contemplate what we cannot control. I contemplate the world through words.

The window, in this way, became a central symbol in my work, assuming more and more importance as that work went on. But if it were literally true that I saw the world through a window, I would merely be the street spy, peering out on the alley to see what I could see, and making sure nothing went by without my notice, nothing went on without my approval. But when a character of mine looks out through a window, or occasionally peeks in through one, it is the word 'window' he is really looking through, it's the word 'pane' which preoccupies, it's the idea of 'glass,' of separated seeing, of the distortions of the medium, its breakage, its discoloration, its framing, which dominates and determines the eye; it is, therefore, the fragility of knowledge which gets stressed, the importance and limitation of point of view, the ambiguity of "in" and "out" which it provides, the range of its examples, the fact that windows are display cases, places where wash is dried, pies are cooled, caged love birds hang, potted plants sit, souvenirs rest from ancient trips, and where light enters only to become a pale patch of warmth for the cat. But above all, it is a place which waits for that light, endures the darkness, receives each scene and then, through both the word and its phenomena, provokes reflection. But above all, it demonstrates how 'pane' permits me to say I am separated from the world by a transparent sheet of cruelty, as though its plane were a piece of paper, as though each word were itself a window, through which I could see other words, other windows, as well as myself: always observant, always passive, patient, speculative, so when an action is at last taken, as my narrator does in my novel *The Tunnel,* he throws a brick, as others did on *Kristallnacht,* but through a Nordic shop window by mistake. He's guilty all the same, of course, but now, by implication, he is guilty of the lesser (though larger) crime of hating the whole of mankind.

Consider the difference between an ordinary fact of experience—a woman's face reflected in what remains of a broken window—and the resonance of the simplest sentence when we listen to the vibration of the words: "Virginia's face was reflected in the broken pane."

It is during these early days of life too that the many motives one might have for doing anything are combined and given their priorities. The successful execution of any long and difficult project, especially one done alone and without the support of any social structure, requires the cooperation of every significant desire one has—the theft of their energy if you like—in order that more determination can be found for the task than its own allure might generate.

Freud's oft-quoted wisecrack that men write for money, glory, and the love of women might bestir a banker to his business, but will not suffice to account for the composing of poetry and the writing of fiction—fundamentally unfunded, unwanted, and unappreciated enterprises. Of course, writers want glory; they want money; they want to be loved, to be sexually pleased and politically empowered. They also want to play the sage, the moralist, the philosopher, and tell the world where to go. They dream of crowds rushing off at the insistence of their voice to pull down the statues of their rivals. Oh yes, indeed, they desire to impose their will. But it is a mistake to suppose that the speaking of this or that truth, the display of this or that moral stance, the advocacy of this or that point of view, is, or even ought to be, the principal aim of the artist. That is not to say these values and opinions will be absent. Who can set aside their beliefs, their angers, their greatest fears, as if un-feared at all? Who can fail to praise whatever has given them the most satisfaction, the deepest love? Why walk on one's hands when one needs to run?

What is critical to the artist is not the fact that he has many mo-tives (let us hope so), or that their presence should never be felt in his canvases or found in the narrative nature of his novels or heard amid the tumult of his dissonances. In the first place, our other aims won't lend their assistance without reward, and they will want, as we say, a piece of the action. No, the question is which of our intentions will be al-lowed to rule and regulate and direct the others: that is what is critical. It is a matter of the politics of desire, or, as Plato put it when he asked this question of the moral agent, what faculty of the soul is in control of the will.

I believe that the artist's fundamental loyalty must be to form, and his energy employed in the activity of making. Every other diddly de-sire can find expression; every crackpot idea or local obsession, every bias and graciousness and mark of malice may have an hour; but it must never be allowed to carry the day. If, of course, you want to be a publicist for something; if you believe you are a philosopher first, and Nietzsche second; if you think the gift of prophecy has been given you; then, by all means, write your bad poems, your insufferable fictions, en-joy the fame which easy ideas often offer, ride the flatulent winds of change, fly like the latest fad to the nearest dead tree; but do not try to count the seasons of your oblivion.

The poet—every artist—is a maker, a maker whose aim is to make something supremely worthwhile, to make something inherently valu-able in itself. I am happy this is an old-fashioned view. I am happy it is Greek. One decent ideal can turn a rabble of small-minded and nar-rowly self-interested needs into an army. I cannot help adding that, in my opinion, one of the most petty of human desires is the desire to be believed, on the one hand, and the will to belief, on the other. Disbelief is healthier, is a better exercise for the mind, and I admire it even when I see someone's disbelief busy disbelieving me.

To see the world through words means more than merely grasping it through gossipacious talk or amiable description. Language, unlike any other medium, I think, is the very instrument and organ of the mind. It is not the representation of thought, as Plato believed, and hence only an inadequate copy; it is thought itself. Certainly we can picture things to ourselves, but we picture them in order to consider their features, to analyze them, to judge their qualities. Even the painter talks to himself as he plans his vacation, he does not draw to himself; the lover speaks of his desire, he does not draw his penis on the bed sheets; even the musician says things to the grocer, he does not hum. The rationalist philosophers were not right when they supposed that the structure of language mirrored the structure of reality (language and reality bear little resemblance and come from different families); but they were right when they identified it with thinking itself. Words may refer to the world (though any finger can point to Paris), but words are also what we think with when we point our finger at Paris and say, "Paris." Literature is mostly made of mind; and unless that is understood about it, little is understood about it.

A sentence, any sentence, is consequently a passage of thought. Dare I give you, as an example, one of mine? A housewife has begun to discover, when she comes downstairs in the morning, the bodies of cockroaches on her carpet, bugs which have probably been killed by her cat.

> Never alive, they came with punctures, their bodies formed from little whorls of copperish dust which in the downstairs darkness I couldn't possibly have seen; and they were dead and upside down when they materialized, for it was in that moment that our cat, herself darkly invisible, leaped and brought her paws together on the true soul of the roach; a soul so static and intense, so immortally arranged, I felt, while I lay shell-like in our bed, turned inside out, driving my mind away, it was the same as the dark soul of the world itself—and it was this beautiful and terrifying feeling that took possession of me finally, stiffened me like a rod beside my husband, played Caesar to my dreams.

There is, in the first place, the movement of the character's mind, which thinks of the roaches as, in a sense, born with the punctures which killed them, in as much as she never sees them any other way. Nearby the bodies are little patches of body dust, probably from the punctures themselves, and she thinks, next, of their creation in traditional Christian terms. Her mind returns to the fact that they must have been dead and upside down when born. Next the cat is given a role in their conception. She puts the punctures in. Body becomes soul, and because the bony structure of the roach is on the outside, it is the true interior, in a sense immortal because it is bone. It will not decay. Furthermore, its composition is formally beautiful.

These thoughts are part factual, part conjectural, part playful. Their playful nature disappears when the point of the piece comes in view. The housewife thinks of herself as, like them, lying in darkness, and, like them, turned inside out, her bones becoming her being. The Pythagorean (later neo-Platonic) phrase "dark soul of the world" completes her odd epiphany. Beneath the traditional Pythagorean triangle of light, given over to the tyranny of the One, the Straight, the Male, is the dark triangle of the Crooked, the Many, and the Female. But now that triangle has been tipped over. Its elements are in plain view. Free. As most wives and mothers, lying beside their sleeping husbands, punctured themselves, are not. When she overcomes her fear of roaches and begins to appreciate the beauty of the bug; when she sees beneath the socially correct order of things (for which, we have to remember, she has no small responsibility herself), its hidden inner order, and can appreciate that interior beauty of which she should be the proper mistress, instead of her kids' health or the household laundry; then she will share the point of view of a god—that is, an artist, and therefore a god whose name is spelled with a very small 'g' indeed.

Well, the fiction from which I took this paragraph is a sort of feminist piece. That movement of the housewife's mind, however, which the passage at least elliptically presents, is not the same as the movement of the words themselves, and hence is not identical, either, to the passage of the reader's eye and understanding, which begins with 'Never,' proceeds to 'alive,' unifies these, continues immediately to 'they' ("they were never alive") and subsequently attributes this absence of life to every previous appearance of them whether actual or symbolic. After all, roaches wear their skeletons like children for Halloween. Soon the reader's attention is spirited away to theology, and to philosophy as well if he's alert to the reference, but only to select what seems needful from these realms, before returning from creation's little whorls of copperish dust to modify these few phrases once again (never alive, forever dust). In short, reading (any reading) is recursive and usually parabolic. While the eye and its attention is shuttling back and forth, the order of the language never entirely disappears, but continuously reforms the final amalgamation.

So far, the statically presented structure of the sentence has put two other minds in motion: that of the character, whose thoughts are being described, and that of a hypothetical Reader. The former is an active, fictive movement of thought, the latter is a devoted process of attention. An additional mind which the sentence must make us aware of is that of the capitalized Author, the constructor, for it is certainly worth realizing that, although the character feels, in that sentence, insightful, there is no reason to suppose she feels lyrical. She may feel frightened, moved, unsettled; but the author's mind is in a poetic mode, calm, measured, allusive. The author never thought these phrases in their printed order. The author never thought the sentence the way one might think, What time's lunch? The author did think a great many other things while in the so-called throes of composition. He wrote many more versions, tried numerous combinations, flopped about as awkwardly as a boated fish, said the words to himself time after time in a displeased mumble, but hoped they sang nevertheless, since the sentences he wants to make are like these roaches, firm, immobile, shaped, with their shell the same as their soul—that's what he, the writer, is thinking while he writes—and they are also like a residue the reader will find in the morning; for every sentence allowed to remain upon the page will resemble the dazed survivors of a battle, after the dead and wounded have been carried away, when the alternatives have been rejected and erased, to leave some words still standing on the field, but standing as markers over graves.

Of course, in the case of this particular sentence, written in the first person but in the past tense, the movement of the narrator's mind is itself multiple. There is what she thought at the time—that is suggested—and there is how she has chosen to think about it later, how she now describes it (which might be as lyrically as the author does, but also might not).

In any event, and after many years of scribble and erasure, I came finally to the belief that sentences were containers of consciousness; that they were certainly thought itself, which is one thing which goes on in consciousness, but they were other things as well, in more devious, indirect ways. In so far as the words referred to something, they involved—through those designations—our perceptions. Thus a good sentence had to see and hear and smell and touch or taste whatever it was supposed to see and hear and smell and touch or taste; that acuity and accuracy of sensation was, in those sentences which invoked it, essential. Even in sentences which describe a thought instead of a perception, the thought has to be well seen.

The narrator is writing about the legs of the roach. Both kinds, she says,

> had legs that looked under a glass like the canes of a rose, and the nymph's were sufficiently transparent in a good light you thought you saw its nerves merge and run like a jagged crack to each ultimate claw.

The author has to be sufficiently accurate about the world to preserve his authority, but what is crucial is not testability; it is rather the precision and clarity of the construction, because what the author is doing is creating a perception his character is supposed to have, and since the story is about "eye-openers," then the sentence had better seem open-eyed.

In reading what the character sees, the reader sees; but what the reader sees, of course, is not the thing but a construction. Since we know that we are witnessing a perception, we are, in effect, seeing an act of seeing, not merely an object, which might be seen in a number of ways, because in the text there are no more ways than are written. There is no more object than the object which is made by its description. Jack Hawkes is the American master of the sentence that sees. When his prose perceives a horse, that horse becomes visual as though for the first time. But what makes Hawkes' horse so magical is not merely the way it is made of precise visual detail—any vet might equal that—but the sense of responsiveness and appreciation, relish, worship, in the eye's sight.

The sentence is a literal line of thought, then, but also an apprehension, sometimes of a thought, often of some sensation. It is also aimed. It has energy, drive, direction, purpose. Now we are dealing, in our artificial consciousness, with the element of desire. Some sentences seem to seep, others to be propelled by their own metrical feet. Some sentences are ponderous, tentative, timid, others are quick, burly, full of beans. Consciousness is equally flaccid or energized, or, in more complex cases, some aspects are nearly asleep, others wholly on the *qui vive*. The short declarative fragment, brisk and assured as it is, can also, with its calm assurance and its confident closure, reduce the sense of urgency in the sentence, even introduce a feeling of unsleepy repleteness. For instance, in this brief list of the properties of a place:

> The shade is ample, the grass is good, the sky a glorious fall violet; the apple trees are heavy and red, the roads are calm and empty; corn has sifted from the chains of tractored wagons to speckle the streets with gold and with russet fragments of the cob, and a man would be a fool who wanted, blessed with this, to live anywhere else in the world.

Desire, thought, perception . . . next, passion: each inhabit the sentence they are made from. Feeling infuses the thought, is pleased or confounded by what is heard or touched or seen, is made despondent by what it expects, or eagerly awaits the fulfillment of its needs. Repetition, diction, the way the language is caressed, spat out, or whispered by the writer—every element, as always, combines to create for the sentence its feeling. I think of it as a kind of conceptual climate. Gertrude Stein believed that emotions were the property of paragraphs, not of sentences by themselves, though a sentence might often act as uppity as a paragraph. Here is another sample of my own method of mood management.

> For we're always out of luck here. That's just how it is—for instance in the winter. The sides of the buildings, the roofs, the limbs of the trees are gray. Streets, sidewalks, faces, feelings—they are gray. Speech is gray, and the grass where it shows. Every flank and front, each top is gray. Everything is gray: hair, eyes, window glass, the hawkers' bills and touters' posters, lips, teeth, poles and metal signs—they're gray, quite gray. Cars are gray. Boots, shoes, suits, hats, gloves are gray. Horses, sheep, and cows, cats killed in the road, squirrels in the same way, sparrows, doves, and pigeons, all are gray, everything is gray, and everyone is out of luck who lives here.

Above all, I believe, consciousness is the residence and nurturing place of the imagination. Without impudent comparisons, without freewheeling fancy, without dreams, without invention, without the transformations of metaphor, without the burglaries of meaning which symbols commit: without such aeration, prose deflates; our tires turn on air, flat, they will only leave their rubber on the highway. But, above all, the other elements of the good sentence—desire, feeling, sensation, thought—require the imagination for their construction. Let us go back a moment to the bugs, whose armatures are their armor, for a comparison of their state with our own.

> I suspect if we were as familiar with our bones as with our skin, we'd never bury dead but shrine them in their rooms, arranged as we might like to find them on a visit; and our enemies, if we could steal their bodies from the battle sites, would be museumed as they died, the steel still eloquent in their sides, their metal hats askew, the protective toes of their shoes unworn, and friend and enemy would be so wondrously historical that in a hundred years we'd find the jaws still hung for the same speech and all the parts we spent our life with tilted as they always were—rib cage, collar, skull—still repetitious, still defiant, angel light, still worthy of memorial and affection.

The finest writing is for the voice. There are several good, not to say decisive, reasons for this. No word is a word by itself. Every word is multiple, and not simply because there are homonyms and homophones hanging around, pretending to be friends. A word is made of sounds. A word is made of marks. A word is made of the little muscle movements in the throat which accompany our interior speech—that invisible, inaudible, yet clearly heard interior talk of which Samuel Beckett made himself the master. So there are two spoken tongues to set against the one we write. And if we let the written word stand for the spoken one, and silent speech to precede both, then the written word works in three realms at once, not just one.

The mouth is our sustainer: with it our body is fed and our soul made articulate. Moreover, orality as a developmental stage is as early as any, near to our deepest, and often our most desperate, feelings. The spoken language is learned at the point at, and in the manner in, which we learned to live: when we heard love, anger, anxiety, expectation in the tones of the parental voice, and later when we began to find the words we had heard forming in our own mouths as if the ear had borne their seed. Moreover, we still communicate at the daily and most personal level by speaking, not by writing, to one another. If the telephone suggests physical closeness at the price of spiritual distance, E-mail promotes that impersonal intimacy sometimes experienced by strangers. Writing has even lost the kinetic character the hand once gave it, or the portable conveyed through its worn fonts and pounded keys. Prefab letters pop onto a screen in full anonymity now, as if the mind alone had made them, our fingers dancing along over the keyboard as unnoticed as breathing until something breaks or the error beep sounds. As Plato feared, the written word can be stolen, counterfeited, bought, released from the responsibility of its writer, sailed into the world as unsigned as a ship unnamed, or under borrowed registry. Suppose politicians were required to compose their own lies, using their own poor words, instead of having their opinions catered—how brief would be their hold on our beliefs, how soon would their souls be seen to be as soiled as their socks.

The sentence—its shape, its sound, the space it makes, its importance to consciousness, its manifestation of the mind/body problem (meaning and thing fastened to the same inscription)—is it in my obsession with the ontology of the word that I find the ground for my own practice? Is that why I emphasize the music of the language, alliterate with the passionate persistence of old poems, wallow in assonance, clutter the otherwise open space of concepts with the clatter and click of dentals and other consonants? Are these the reasons I want the reader's mouth to move as if reading were being in that moment mastered and the breath were full of chewable food? No. The reason is I cannot seem to write in any other way; because sound sometimes rushes ahead of sense, and forces such sense, gasping and panting, to catch up. I often think, overhearing myself at work, that I do not write, I mumble, I whisper, I declaim, I inveigh. My study is full of static when it is full of me.

Harmonium, Wallace Stevens called one of his books. Harmonica, I'd like to call mine—rude mouth music. That's because every mark on the page, apart from its inherent visual interest, is playing its part in the construction of a verbal consciousness, and that means that commas become concepts, pauses need to be performed, even the margins need to be sung, the lips rounded as widely as the widest vowel, round as the edges of the world. **O** as in Oral.

For that's where every good idea should be found, melting like a chocolate in the curl of the tongue, against the roof of the mouth.

If we insist we write to be spoken (though no one shall speak us, neither time nor training nor custom inclining our rare reader to it), then a concept crucial to the understanding of literature and its effects is "voice." Even when we write in the first person, and construct a voice for our invented narrator to speak in, there is always an overvoice, in which our character finds a place—the author's voice, the style of which tells us that, whoever is speaking—Lear or Hamlet or Juliet—it is Shakespeare, nevertheless, in whose verbal stream they are swimming. Or we hear the unmistakable tones of Henry James, of Flaubert or

Faulkner in each red-necked, red-earthed farmer, in every bumbling bourgeois or bewildered American lady.

Who better than Thoreau to speak of the sound around one, for he chose the quietest of woods to inhabit.

> I kept neither dog, cat, cow, pig, nor hens, so that you would have said there was a deficiency of domestic sounds; neither the churn, nor the spinning-wheel, nor even the singing of the kettle, nor the hissing of the urn, nor children crying, to comfort one. An old-fashioned man would have lost his senses or died of ennui before this. Not even rats in the wall, for they were starved out, or rather were never baited in,—only squirrels on the roof and under the floor, a whippoorwill on the ridge pole, a blue-jay screaming beneath the window, a hare or woodchuck under the house, a screech-owl or a cat-owl behind it, a flock of wild geese or a laughing loon on the pond, and a fox to bark in the night. Not even a lark or an oriole, those mild plantation birds, ever visited my clearing. No cockerels to crow nor hens to cackle in the yard. No yard! but unfenced Nature reaching up to your very sills. A young forest growing up under your windows, and wild sumachs and blackberry vines breaking through into your cellar; sturdy pitch-pines rubbing and creaking against the shingles for want of room, their roots reaching quite under the house. Instead of a scuttle or a blind blown off in the gale,—a pine tree snapped off or torn up by the roots behind your house for fuel. Instead of no path to the front-yard gate in the Great Snow,—no gate—no front-yard,—and no path to the civilized world!

Even so, even when we hear the unmistakable voice of our friend in the next room, find the cadences of Colette on the page (as, once again, Plato warned us), we cannot be certain what part of the soul is speaking (the spoken language, like the soul, is triply tiered); because when desire, or *praxis*, says 'love,' it is *eros* who is invoked; when the spirited part of the soul, or *doxa*, says 'love,' it is *philia*, or friendship, which is suggested; and when reason, the *logos*, says 'love,' it is *agape* which is meant.

Of course, every philosophical catastrophe is a literary opportunity. Gertrude Stein finally concluded that the "I" who writes masterpieces had to be the "I" of the transcendental ego, the universal "I," making the text timeless and transcultural. But I am greedy. I like best the "I" which speaks for every layer of the self, sometimes harmoniously, sometimes in discord, as the occasion and the project require. I like ideas best, as I've said, when they are most concrete, when, when you think them, you fry them like eggs, when, when you eat them, the yolk is runny with the softest of dreams.

If words find comfort in the sentence's syntactical handclasp, and sentences find their proper place like pieces of furniture in the rhetorical space of the paragraph, what shall control each scene as it develops, form the fiction finally as a whole?

Well, the old answer was always: plot. It's a terrible word in English, unless one is thinking of some second-rate conspiracy, a meaning it serves very well. Otherwise, it stands for an error for which there's no longer an excuse. There's bird drop, horse plop, and novel plot. Story is what can be taken out of the fiction and made into a movie. Story is what you tell people when they embarrass you by asking what your novel is about. Story is what you do to clean up life and make God into a good burger who manages the world like a business. History is often written as a story so that it can seem to have a purpose, to be on its way somewhere; because stories deny that life is no more than an endlessly muddled middle; they beg each length of it to have a beginning and end like a ballgame or a banquet. Stories are sneaky justifications. You can buy stories at the store where they are a dime a dozen. Stories are interesting only when they are floors in buildings. Stories are a bore. What one wants to do with stories is screw them up. Stories ought to be in pictures. They're wonderful to see.

Still, a little story gets into everything. Thank the Ghost of Fictions Past for that.

My stories are malevolently antinarrative, and my essays are maliciously antiexpository, but the ideology of my opposition arrived long after my antagonism had become a trait of character. Like most kids, I loved the nineteenth-century novel with its wealth of colorful detail, its heroes and villains, its sympathy for the common and the ordinary, its smarmy coziness, its clear-cut characters, its unambiguous values (I was born bourgeois); I lapped up its sweet sentimentality; I allowed to beat in my chest its vulgar material heart. Implicit in much of the novel's melodrama, and explicit in the critics and readers who praised it and made it popular, was the idea that its value rested not on its language, its artifice, its drama, but on its representation of reality. I have no problem with Martin Chuzzlewit as a creature caught in a myth. I can believe in the triumph of the orphan and the importance of "doing good," at least for as many pages as it takes to complete the text.

Early on I learned that life was meaningless, since life was not a sign; but that novels were meaningful, however, because signs were the very materials of their composition. I learned that suffering served no purpose, that the good guys didn't win, that most explanations offered me to make the mess I was in less a mess were self-serving lies. Life wasn't clear, it was ambiguous; motives were many and mixed; values were complex, opposed, poisoned by hypocrisy, without any reasonable ground; most of passion's pageants were frauds and human feelings had been faked for so long, no one knew what the genuine was; furthermore, many of the things I found most satisfactory for myself were everywhere libelously characterized or their very existence suppressed; and much of adult society, its institutions and its advertised dreams, were simply superstitions which served a small set of people well while keeping the remainder in miserable ignorance.

Above all, I was struck by the traditional novel's vanity on behalf of man. When I looked at man I did not see a piece of noble work, a species whose every member was automatically of infinite worth and the pinnacle of Nature's efforts. Nor did history, as I read it, support such grandiose claims. Throughout human time, men had been murdering men with an ease which suggested they took a profound pleasure in it, and, like the most voracious insect, the entire tribe was, even as I watched, even as I participated, eating its host like a parasite whose foresight did not exceed its greed. Hate, fear, and hunger were its heroes. In Trollope and Thackery, as skillful as their satire was, flaws became foibles, wickedness the result of poor upbringing, too much port, and bad digestion. Flaubert saw how things were and told the truth, as if that mattered.

So I, like many others in every art, rejected a realism which wasn't real and tried to work in a less traditional, less compromised way. I organized my fictions around symbolic centers instead of plotting them out on graph paper; I assigned the exfoliation of these centers to a voice and limited my use of narration, while treating the style and characteristic structure of the sentences which filled the novel, row on row, as microcosmic models for the organization of the whole. I do not pretend to be in the possession of any secrets; I have no cause I espouse; I do not presume to reform my readers or attempt to flatter their egos either. My loyalty (and I have a few) is to my text, for that is what I am composing, and if I change the world, it will be because I've added this or that little reality to it; and if I alter any reader's consciousness, it will be because I have constructed a consciousness of which others may wish to become aware, or even, for a short time, share. The reader's freedom is a holy thing.

My views are what is popularly pictured as "off the wall," but it has seemed to me, for a long time, that fiction's principal problem, apart from its allegiance to the middle class, was not to be solved by finding a fascinating or outré subject, by maintaining a narrative suspense which was meaningless if you hoped to be reread, or by being blessed by your possession of the right beliefs; its problem was how to achieve any lasting excellence (in philosophy, mathematics, art, and science, always the same); that is, it was the problem of form. Writers had once looked everywhere to find the necessary regulating schemes. The novel began by imitating nonfictional genres: histories, biographies, collections of letters, diaries, accounts of travel, records of adventure. Later, novelists looked to other arts for suggestions: they pretended to paint portraits of young men and ladies; they composed pastoral symphonies and other metaphorical musicales; or they used their prose to steal from poetry many of its epical methods and effects, and grandly said (as I once muttered) that the strategies of fiction were the same as the strategies of the long poem.

In every case, wonderful stories, great novels were written, although against the grain, in forms not fashioned for fiction in the first place, with techniques not meant for the novel; but with methods its middle-class audience saw as comfortingly familiar, factual, realistic, acceptably hypocritical. All the while, like the purloined letter, a possible solution to the problem lay in full view, and had likely been in operation all along: first, the solution was apparent in the actual operations of the prose sentence itself; second, it was readily available in scholarly texts, through the nearly forgotten techniques of rhetoric and oratory, in those quaintly out-of-date but meticulously catalogued lists of tropes, schemes, arguments, illustrations, and outlines, which are contained in those countless unconsulted volumes on eloquence and public address from Aristotle, Longinus, Cicero, and Quintilian through Priestley, Adam Smith, and De Quincey to Emerson, Hugh Blair, and Edward Channing; and third, in the efforts of linguists and logicians to discover the secrets of syntax and to explain its regulating power.

George Saintsbury's admirable *History of English Prose Rhythm* told me more about the art of writing than a hundred literary critics, each eager to light like a fly on the latest fad and soon, predictably, to be abuzz with the energy so secondarily received.

That is, if we understand how prose is put together, not only logically or grammatically, but rhetorically and esthetically as well, then we might understand how an entire tale could be uniformly wagged, or how a whole novel could be unified. Moreover, philosophers have frequently ascribed metaphysical significance to propositional forms, and considered them to be the structural essentials of any conceived world.

This is not the place to dwell upon the course of development of my idiosyncrasies, but it is perhaps appropriate for me to conclude these remarks by looking at some of the reasons why such interests are so rarely shared. There are four dimensions to the writer's realm, and few occupy all axes equally. If a Realist were lucky enough to begin a piece: "When Gregor Samsa awoke one morning from an uneasy sleep, he found himself transformed into a gigantic insect," he would be distressed indeed if we disbelieved him and thought he was deconstructing *The Fairie Queen*. He would be calculating as he wrote the line the matter-of-fact effect such an event would have on the other characters Gregor Samsa would be plotted to encounter, on the consciousness of Gregor himself, and even on the mattress and the springs of the bed. The Idealist would immediately wonder what the event meant, and would be concerned to render it in such a way that it resonated as the writer wished. The night before, as Gregor's head hit his pillow, he was merely being treated like a bug, living and acting and feeling like one (as the Idealist might interpret his behavior), but now, this a.m., he was a bug, and the Realist had taken over.

Nothing prevents Kafka from being both, as he undoubtedly is. *Moby Dick* presents us with a similar tension. Every paragraph of data about the whale—its hunting, its capture, its cutting up—insists on the solidity and importance of daily life, its traumas and its tasks. A whale is a whale here, white or not, and a big bug in a bed is a bother, especially if it's your brother. What'll you feed him? What will friends think? How will the family fare without the funds the brother/bug brought home? The Realist pours over the world like a lover, and learns to render its qualities to a tee. When the Realist's "I" perceives, what matters is what the ego sees. The Idealist will insist that this story is not "about" Gregor Samsa and his family, but about sibling rivalry, for if Gregor is transformed into a bug in the beginning, Grete becomes a butterfly at the end. Let the Realist worry about bedbugs and their bite;

the Idealist will study Jewish family relations, and he will see that the name 'Samsa' contains 'sam,' that is, seed, or the cock's roach.

Meanwhile, the Romantic will have understood the sentence to be really about the author's own condition, for isn't he the put-upon person who has to work like a menial when his spirit would be free? Kafka writes about Kafka principally, and only secondarily about Gregor Samsa and his plight, or, if you insist on some theoretical intent, also about the anxieties inherent in the human condition. But of course I have gone too far. *The Metamorphosis* does not reveal Kafka; rather it delivers to us the consciousness presupposed by its creation. This consciousness is a construction, it must be admitted, and its distance from its swearing, sweating, farting namesake is substantial. This distance— this difference—is also the reason why we often admire an author whom, as a citizen or biographical subject, we can scarcely endure; or, to point to the problem from its opposite end, why we occasionally wish some dear, sweet friend were a better writer, even at the expense of their sweetness, and even if the friendship were to bend.

A fully felt fictional world must be at least three-dimensional, and bounded by the Real, the Ideal, and the Romantic. But there is, as we know, a fourth dimension, and I tend to emphasize it, not only because of its neglect, but also because it is the country to which I have fled, and that is the medium itself. There, if we are a Methodologist (my term for my type), we shall have found the other dimensions in miniature already, since the word rests nowhere but on the pedestal of its referent (Gregor Samsa, the bedded bug person); there it measures its mass by the number and nature of its range of meanings (all the definitions of 'metamorphosis,' for instance: the scientific, the poetic, the philosophical, the religious); nor is any word spoken without a speaker, or written without a writer (at least it has a human source). Consequently, every utterance has a cause, and, one presumes, a reason as well, so if we are content to explain the nature of any particular part of a text by appealing to the rest, we nevertheless have to turn to the author for the answer: Why did you write *The Metamorphosis* when you could have been engaged in something harmless like a game of golf?

A Methodologist (for whom the medium is the muse) will reformulate traditional esthetic problems in terms of language. Crudely put: in this milieu, point of view has to do with the deployment of pronouns; character with the establishment of linguistic centers, to which, and from which, meanings flow; themes are built with universals, and their enrichment depends upon the significance of a text beyond its surface sense; perceptions will appear to be fresh and precise if denotation is managed well; energy is expressed by verbal beat, through sentence length, and Anglo-Saxon or Latin vocabulary choice; feeling arises particularly from such things as rhythm and alliteration, although every element of language plays a role; thought is constructed out of concepts and their interconnections; imagination involves the management of metaphor at every level; narrative reliability rises or falls with the influence of modal operators; form can be found in the logic of the language —its grammar, scansion, symmetries, rhetorical schema, and methods of variation; and each of the qualities I have just listed, along with many others, can be used to give to a text its desirable complement of four dimensions.

So even if you hope to find some lasting security inside language, and believe that your powers are at their peak there (if nowhere else) despair and disappointment will dog you still; for neither you nor your weaknesses, nor the world and its villains, will have been banished just because, now, it is in syllables and sentences where they hide. Because, oddly enough, while you can confront and denounce a colleague or a spouse, run from an angry dog, or jump bail and flee your country, you can't argue with an image. A badly made sentence is a judgment pronounced upon its perpetrator, and even one poor paragraph indelibly stains the soul. The unpleasant consequence of every such botch is that your life, as you register your writing, looks back at you as from a dirty mirror, and there you perceive a record of ineptitude, compromise, and failure.

EDWARD GOREY

Serious Life: A Locket

The Fibleys
christened
their baby
Amelia Emily.

They had her
name engraved
on a locket and
put snapshots
of themselves
inside it.

The next week
she vanished
from her cradle.

Neither the
police, nor
anyone else
for that matter,
could find her.

After a few
months they
had her
baptismal
photograph
enlarged in
oils and hung
it over the
mantel.

A neighbour
brought them
a dog wearing
the locket in
which he had
recognized the
snapshots.

386 / Edward Gorey

Several days later Amelia Emily had puppies.

The Fibleys' declining years were spent with Amelia Emily, her great great grand-daughter.

ERNEST HEMINGWAY

The Unpublished Opening of
The Sun Also Rises

BOOK I

Chapter I

This is a novel about a lady. Her name is Lady Ashley and when the story begins she is living in Paris and it is Spring. That should be a good setting for a romantic but highly moral story. As every one knows, Paris is a very romantic place. Spring in Paris is a very happy and romantic time. Autumn in Paris, although very beautiful, might give a note of sadness or melancholy that we shall try to keep out of this story.

Lady Ashley was born Elizabeth Brett Murray. Her title came from her second husband. She had divorced one husband for something or other, mutual consent; not until after he had put one of those notices in the papers stating that after this date he would not be responsible for any debt, etc. He was a Scotchman and found Brett much too expensive, especially as she had only married him to get rid of him and to get away from home. At present she had a legal separation from her second husband, who had the title, because he was a dipsomaniac, he having learned it in the North Sea commanding a mine-sweeper, Brett said. When he had gotten to be a proper thoroughgoing dipsomaniac and found that Brett did not love him he tried to kill her, and between times slept on the floor and was never sober and had great spells of crying. Brett always declared that it had been one of the really great mistakes of her life to have married a sailor. She should have known better, she said, but she had sent the one man she had wanted to marry off to Mesopotamia so he would last out the war, and he had died of some very unromantic form of dysentery and she certainly could not marry Jake Barnes, so when she had to marry she had married Lord Robert Ashley, who proceeded to become a dipsomaniac as before stated.

They had a son and Ashley would not divorce, and would not give grounds for divorce, but there was a separation and Brett went off with

Mike Campbell to the Continent one afternoon, she having offered to at lunch because Mike was lonely and sick and very companionable, and, as she said, "obviously one of us." They arranged the whole business before the Folkestone-Boulogne train left London at 9:30 that night. Brett was always very proud of that. The speed with which they got passports and raised funds. They came to Paris on their way to the Riviera, and stayed the night in a hotel which had only one room free and that with a double bed. "We'd no idea of anything of that sort," Brett said. "Mike said we should go on and look up another hotel, but I said no, to stop where we were. What's the odds." That was how they happened to be living together.

Mike at that time was ill. It was all he had brought back with him from the two years he had spent in business in Spain, after he had left the army, except the beautifully engraved shares of the company which had absorbed all of the fifteen thousand pounds that had come to him from his father's estate. He was also an undischarged bankrupt, which is quite a serious thing in England, and had various habits that Brett felt sorry for, did not think a man should have, and cured by constant watchfulness and the exercise of her then very strong will.

Mike was a charming companion, one of the most charming. He was nice and he was weak and he had a certain very hard gentleness in him that could not be touched and that never disappeared until the liquor dissolved him entirely. Mike sober was nice, Mike a little drunk was even nicer, Mike quite drunk began to be objectionable, and Mike very drunk was embarrassing.

It was the boredom and the uncertainty of their position that made Brett drink as she did. There was nothing of the alcoholic about her. Not, at least, for a long time. They spent their time sleeping as late as possible and then drinking. That is a simple way of stating a very complicated process, and waiting for Mike's weekly allowance, which was always late, and therefore always spent and borrowed into a week or more in advance. There was nothing to do but to drink. The drinking was not done alone in their rooms. It was all at cafés and parties, and each day became a replica of the day before. There were very few differences. You had been to bed late or gone to bed early. You felt good or you felt bad. You felt like eating a little something or you couldn't face the thought of food. It had been a good party the night before or it had been a bore. Michael had behaved abominably or Michael had been a model of admirable behavior. But usually it had been a good party because alcohol, either brandy and soda, or whiskey and soda, had a tendency to make everything much better, and for a time quite all right.

If Michael had behaved well it was probably a good party, and Michael had a strong tendency to behave well. In fact you could always count on him to behave absolutely as he should until the alcoholic process had taken place, which always seemed rather like that old grammar school experiment in which a bone is dissolved in vinegar to prove it has something or other in it. Anyway the vinegar quite changed the bone and made it very unlike itself, and you could bend it back and forth, and if it were a long enough bone and you had used enough vinegar, you could even tie it into a knot.

Brett was very different from Mike about drinking. Brett had a certain grand vitality. She had her looks too. She was not supposed to be beautiful, but in a room with women who were supposed to be beautiful she killed their looks entirely. Men thought she was lovely looking, and women called her striking looking. Painters were always asking her to sit for them and that flattered her, because she herself considered that her looks were not much, and so she spent much of her waking time sitting for portraits, none of which she ever liked. She did not seem to mind how bad the painters were. The worse they were the more it amused her. It was the being asked to sit for her portrait that she liked. One painter was as good as another. Of course the best portrait painters had done her a long time before.

Brett drank much more than Mike liked, but it never dissolved her in any way. She was always clear run, generous, and her lines were always as clear. But when she had been drunk she always spoke of it as having been blind. "Weren't we blind last night, though?" It was short for blind drunk, and the curious part was that she really became, in a way, blind. Drinking, and this does not mean the odd drink, or two or three cocktails before dinner and wine at the meal, but real drinking of that sort that kills off the good drinkers because they are the only ones who can do it, affected Brett in three successive stages. Drinking, say, whiskey and sodas from four o'clock in the afternoon until two o'clock in the morning Brett first lost her power of speech and just sat and listened, then she lost her sight and saw nothing that went on, and finally she ceased to hear. And all the time any one coming into the café would never know she had been drinking. To any one greeting her she would respond automatically, "Hullo, *I* say I am blind," or something of the sort.

In sleeping and in drinking, playing bridge in the afternoon, usually having her portrait painted by some socially climbing artist who knew the value of a title on a portrait, a party somewhere every night, Brett and Mike passed the time in Paris. They were rather happy. Brett was a very happy person. Then Mike had to go to England, to London to see a lawyer about something connected with the divorce Brett was trying to get, and then to Scotland to visit his people and prove by residence that he was a dutiful son, in order that, among other things, they should not stop his allowance. Brett was left alone in Paris. She had never been very good at being alone.

Chapter II

I did not want to tell this story in the first person but I find that I must. I wanted to stay well outside of the story so that I would not be touched by it in any way, and handle all the people in it with that irony and pity that are so essential to good writing. I even thought I might be amused by all the things that are going to happen to Lady Brett Ashley and Mr. Robert Cohn and Michael Campbell, Esq., and Mr. Jake Barnes. But I made the unfortunate mistake, for a writer, of first having been Mr. Jake Barnes. So it is not going to be splendid and cool and detached after all. "What a pity!" as Brett used to say.

"What a pity!" was a little joke we all had. Brett was having her portrait painted by a very rich American from Philadelphia, who sent his motor-car around each afternoon to bring her from her hotel in Montparnasse up to his Montmartre studio. Along about the third sitting Brett stopped posing for a little while to have tea, and the portrait-painter asked her: "And when you get your divorce, Lady Ashley, what will you do then?"

"Marry Mike Campbell," Brett answered.

"And what will your name be then?"

"Mrs. Campbell, of course!"

"What a pity," the portrait-painter said. "What a pity!"

So my name is Jacob Barnes and I am writing the story, not as I believe is usual in these cases, from a desire for confession, because being a Roman Catholic I am spared that Protestant urge to literary production, nor to set things all out the way they happened for the good of some future generation, nor any other of the usual highly moral urges, but because I believe it is a good story.

I am a newspaper man living in Paris. I used to think Paris was the most wonderful place in the world. I have lived in it now for six years, or however long it is since 1920, and I still see its good points. Anyway, it is the only city I want to live in. They say New York is very fine but I do not care for night life. I want to live quietly and with a certain measure of luxury, and a job that I do not want to worry about. Paris provides all these things. Paris is also a lovely town to live in once you get an apartment and give up various American fetiches such as all the year round B.V.D.s and too much exercise.

In 1916 I was invalided home from a British hospital and got a job on *The Mail* in New York. I quit to start the Continental Press Association with Robert Graham, who was then just getting his reputation as Washington correspondent. We started the Continental in one room on the basis of syndicating Bob Graham's Washington dispatches. I ran the business end and the first year wrote a special war-expert service. By 1920 the Continental was the third largest feature service in the States. I told Bob Graham that rather than stay and get rich with him the Continental could give me a job in Paris. So I made the job, and I have some stock, but not as much as I ought to have, and I do not try to run the salary up too high because if it ever got up past a certain amount there would be too many people shooting at my job as European Director of the Continental Press Association. When you have a title like that, translated into French on the letter-heads, and only have to work about four or five hours a day and all the salary you want you are pretty well fixed. I write political dispatches under my own name, and feature stuff under a couple of different names, and all the trained-seal stuff is filed through our office. It is a nice job. I want to hang on to it. Like all newspaper men I have always wanted to write a novel, and I suppose, now that I am doing it, the novel will have that awful taking-the-pen-in-hand quality that afflicts newspaper men when they start to write on their own hook.

I never hung about the Quarter much in Paris until Brett and Mike showed up. I always felt about the Quarter that I could sort of take it or leave it alone. You went into it once in a while to sort of see the animals and say hello to Harold Stearns, and on hot nights in the spring when the tables were spread out over the sidewalks it was rather pleasant. But for a place to hang around it always seemed awfully dull. I have to put it in, though, because Robert Cohn, who is one of the non-Nordic heroes of this book, had spent two years there.

The Quarter is sort of more a state of mind than a geographical area. Perfectly good Quarterites live outside the actual boundaries of Montparnasse. They can live anywhere, I suppose, as long as they come to the Quarter to think. Or whatever you call it. To have the

Quarter state of mind is probably the best way of putting it. This state of mind is principally contempt. Those who work have the greatest contempt for those who don't. The loafers are leading their own lives and it is bad form to mention work. Young painters have contempt for old painters, and that works both ways too. There are contemptuous critics and contemptuous writers. Everybody seems to dislike everybody else. The only happy people are the drunks, and they, after flaming for a period of days or weeks, eventually become depressed. The Germans, too, seem happy, but perhaps that is because they can only get two-week visas to visit Paris, and so they make a party of it. The frail young men who go about together and seem to be always present, but who really leave in periodical flights for Brussels, Berlin, or the Basque coast, to return again like the birds, even more like the birds, are not gay either. They twitter a good deal, but they are not gay. The Scandinavians are the regular, hard-working residents. They are not very gay either, although they seem to have worked out a certain pleasant way of life. The only really gay person during the time I frequented the Quarter was a splendid sort of two-hundred-pound meteoric glad girl called Flossie, who had what is known as a "heart of gold," lovely skin and hair and appetite, and an invulnerability to hang-overs. She was going to be a singer, but the drink took away her voice, and she did not seem to mind particularly. This store of gladness made her the heroine of the Quarter. Anyhow, the Quarter is much too sad and dull a place to write about, and I would not put it in except that Robert Cohn had spent two years in it. That accounts for a great many things.

During these two years Robert Cohn had lived with a lady who lived on gossip, and so he had lived in an atmosphere of abortions and rumors of abortions, doubts and speculations as to past and prospective infidelities of friends, dirty rumors, dirtier reports and dirtier suspicions, and a constant fear and dread by his lady companion that he was seeing other women and was on the point of leaving her. Somehow during this time Robert Cohn wrote a novel, a first and last novel. He was the hero of it, but it was not too badly done and it was accepted by a New York publisher. There was a great deal of fantasy in it.

At that time Robert Cohn had only two friends, an English writer named Braddocks, and myself, with whom he played tennis. He beat me regularly at tennis and was very nice about it. Cohn gave the novel to Braddocks to read and Braddocks, who was very busy on something of his own and who, as the years went on, found it increasingly difficult to read the works of writers other than himself, did not read the novel, but returned it to Cohn with the remark that this was excellent stuff, some excellent stuff, but there was a part, just a small part, he wanted to talk over with Cohn some time. Cohn asked Braddocks what the part was, and Braddocks replied that it was a matter of organization, a very slight but important matter of organization. Cohn, eager to learn and with an un-Nordic willingness to accept useful criticism, pressed to know what it was. "I'm much too busy now to go into it, Cohn. Come around to tea some time next week and we'll talk it over." Cohn insisted Braddocks keep the manuscript until they should have a chance to discuss it.

That night after dinner Braddocks called at my flat. He drank a brandy. "I say, Barnes," he said, "do me a favor. That's a good chap. Read this thing of Cohn's and tell me if it's any good. Mind you, I don't think it can be any good. But be a good chap and run through it and let me know what it's all about."

The next evening I was sitting on the terrace of the Closerie des Lilas watching it get dark. There was a waiter at the Lilas named Anton who used to give two whiskeys for the price of one whiskey owing to a dislike he had for his boss. This waiter raised potatoes in a garden outside of Paris, beyond Montrouge, and as I sat at the table with someone else, Alec Muhr I think it was, we watched the people going by in the dusk on the sidewalk, and the great slow horses going by in the dusk on the Boulevard, and the people going home from work, and the girls starting their evening's work, and the light coming out of the *bistro* next door where the chauffeurs from the taxi line were drinking, and we asked the waiter about his potato crop, and the waiter asked about the franc, and we read the *Paris-Soir* and *l'Intransigeant*. It was very nice, and then along came Braddocks. Braddocks came along, breathing heavily and wearing a wide black hat.

"Who's that?" Alec asked.

"Braddocks," said I, "the writer."

"Good God," said Alec, who thereafter took no further part in the conversation, and does not again appear in the story.

"Hullo," said Braddocks. "May I join you?" So he joined us.

"Did you have a look at that thing of Cohn's?"

"Yes," I said. "It's a fantasy. Lot of dreams in it."

"Just as I thought," Braddocks said. "Thanks awfully."

We looked out on the Boulevard. Two girls went by.

"Pretty good-looking girls," I said.

"Do you think so?" asked Braddocks. "My word.'

We looked at the Boulevard again. The waiter came and went. Braddocks was haughty with him, speaking literary French through his moustache. Along the sidewalk came a tall, gray, lantern-jawed man, walking with a tall woman wearing a blue Italian infantry cape. They looked at our table as they passed, saw no one they knew, and went on. They seemed to be looking for some one. Braddocks clapped me on the knee.

"I say, did you see me cut him? Did you see me cut him? Can't I cut people though!"

"Who is he?"

"Belloc. Hasn't a friend in the world. I say. Did you see me cut him?"

"Hilaire Belloc?"

"Belloc. Of course. He's absolutely done for. Absolutely through."

"What did you row with him about?"

"There was no row. Simply a matter of religious intolerance. Not a review in England will touch him, I tell you."

I was very impressed by this. I can see Braddocks' face, his moustache, his face in the light from the Lilas window. I did not know that the literary life could become so intense. Also I had a valuable piece of information and gossip.

The next afternoon I was sitting with several people at the Café de la Paix having coffee after lunch. Along the Boulevard des Capucines came the tall, gray-looking man and the woman wearing the blue Italian infantry cape.

"There's Hilaire Belloc," I said to the people at the table. "'He hasn't a friend in the world.'"

"Where?" asked several people eagerly.

"There," I nodded, "standing with the woman in the blue cape."

"You mean that man in the gray suit?"

"Yes," I said. "There's not a review in England who will publish him."

"Hell. That's not Belloc," the man on my right said. "That's Allister Crowley."

So I have never felt quite the same about Braddocks since, and I should avoid as far as possible putting him into this story except that he was a great friend of Robert Cohn, and Cohn is the hero.

(The novel begins here.)

F. SCOTT FITZGERALD

Letter to Ernest Hemingway
on The Sun Also Rises

Dear Ernest: Nowdays when almost everyone is a genius, at least for awhile, the temptation for the bogus to profit is no greater than the temptation for the good man to relax (in one mysterious way or another)—not realizing the transitory quality of his glory because he forgets that it rests on the frail shoulders of professional enthusiasts. This should frighten all of us into a lust for anything honest that people have to say about our work. I've taken what proved to be excellent advice (On The B. + Damned) from Bunny Wilson who never wrote a novel, (on Gatsby—change of many thousand wds) from Max Perkins who never considered writing one, and on T. S. of Paradise from Katherine Tighe (you don't know her) who had probably never read a novel before.

[This is beginning to sound like my own current work which resolves itself into laborious + sententious preliminaries].

Anyhow I think parts of *Sun Also* are careless + ineffectual. As I said yestiday (and, as I recollect, in trying to get you to cut the 1st part of 50 Grand) I find in you the same tendency to envelope or (and as it usually turns out) to *embalm* in mere wordiness an anecdote or joke thats casually appealed to you, that I find in myself in trying to preserve a piece of "fine writing." Your first chapter contains about 10 such things and it gives a feeling of condescending *casuallness*.

P.1. "highly moral story"
  "Brett said" (O.Henry stuff)
  "much too expensive"
  "something or other" (if you don't want to tell, why waste 3 wds. saying it. See P.23—"*9 or 14*" and "or how many years it was since 19XX" when it would take two words to say That's what youd kid in anyone else as mere "style"—mere horseshit I can't find this latter but anyhow you've not only got to write well yourself but you've also got to NOT-DO what anyone can do and I think that there are about 24 sneers,

superiorities, and nose-thumbings-at-nothing that mar the whole narrative up to P. 29 where (after a false start on the introduction of Cohn) it really gets going. And to preserve these perverse and willfull nonessentials you've done a lot of writing that *honestly* reminded me of Michael Arlen.

[You know the very fact that people have committed themselves to you will make them watch you like a cat. + if they don't like it creap away like one]

For example.

Pps. 1 + 2. Snobbish (not in itself but because the history of English Aristocrats in the war, set down so verbosely so uncritically, so exteriorly and yet so obviously inspired from within, is *shopworn*.) You had the same problem that I had with my Rich Boy, previously debauched by Chambers ect. Either bring more thot to it with the realization that that ground has already raised its wheat + weeds or cut it down to seven sentences. It hasn't even your rythym and the fact that may be "true" is utterly immaterial.

That biography from you, who allways believed in the superiority (the preferability) of the *imagined* to the *seen not to say to the merely recounted.*

P.3.   "Beautifully engraved shares" (Beautifully engraved 1886 irony) All this is O.K. but so glib *when* its glib + *so* profuse.

P.5.   Painters are no longer *real* in prose. They must be minimized. [This is not done by making them schlptors, backhouse wall-experts or miniature painters]

P.8.   "highly moral urges" "because I believe its a good story" If this paragraph isn't maladroit then I'm a rewrite man for Dr. Cadman.

P.9.   Somehow its not good. I can't quite put my hand on it—it has a ring of "This is a true story ect."

P.10.   "Quarter being a state of mind ect." This is in all guide books. I havn't read Basil Swoon's but I have fifty francs to lose.

[About this time I can hear you say "Jesus this guy thinks I'm lousy, + he can stick it up his ass for all I give a Gd Dm for his 'criticism'." But remember this is a new departure for you, and that I think your stuff is great. You were the first American I wanted to meet in Europe—and the last. (This latter clause is simply to balance the sentence. It doesn't seem to make sense tho I have pawed at it for several minutes. Its like the age of the French women.

P.14. (+ thereabout) as I said yesterday I think this anecdote is flat
as hell without naming Ford which would be cheap.

It's flat because you end with mention of Allister Crowly. If he's
nobody its nothing. If he's somebody, its cheap. This is a novel. Also I'd
cut out mention of H. Stearns earlier.

Why not cut the inessentials in Cohens biography? His first marriage is of no importance. When so many people can write well + the
competition is so heavy I can't imagine how you could have done these
first 20 pps. so casually. You can't *play* with peoples attention—a good
man who has the power of arresting attention at will must be especially
careful.

From here Or rather from p. 30 I began to like the novel but Ernest
I can't tell you the sense of disappointment that beginning with its ele-
phantine facetiousness gave me. Please do what you can about it in
proof. Its 7500 words—you could reduce it to 5000. And my advice is
not to do it by mere pareing but to take out the worst of the *scenes*.

I've decided not to pick at anything else, because I wasn't at all inspired to pick when reading it. I was much too excited. Besides This is
probably a heavy dose. The novel's damn good. The centrol theme is
marred somewhere but hell! unless you're writing your life history
where you have an inevitable pendulum to swing you true (Harding
metaphor), who can bring it entirely off? And what critic can trace
whether the fault lies in a possible insufficient thinking out, in the bite-
ing off of more than you eventually cared to chew in the impotent theme
or in the elusiveness of the lady character herself. My theory always was
that she dramatized herself in terms of Arlen's dramatization of somebody's dramatizatatg of Stephen McKenna's dramatization of Diana
Manner's dramatization of the last girl in Well's *Tono Bungay*—who's
original probably liked more things about Beatrix Esmond than about
Jane Austin's Elizibeth (to whom we owe the manners of so many of our
wives.)

Appropos of your foreward about the Latin Quarter—suppose you
had begun your stories with phrases like: "Spain is a peculiar place—
ect" or "Michigan is interesting to two classes—the fisherman + the
drummer."

Pps 64 + 65 with a bit of work should tell all that need be known
about *Brett's* past.

(Small point) "Dysemtry" instead of "killed" is a clichês to avoid a
clichê. It stands out. I suppose it can't be helped. I suppose all the

75,000000 Europeans who died between 1914–1918 will always be among the 10,000,000 who were killed in the war.

God! The bottom of p. 77 Jusque the top p. 78 are wonderful, I go crazy when people aren't always at their best. This isn't picked out—I just happened on it.

The heart of my critisim beats somewhere apon p. 87. I think you can't change it, though. I felt the lack of some crazy torturing tentativeness or security—horror, all at once, that she'd feel—and he'd feel—maybe I'm crazy. He isn't *like an impotent man. He's like a man in a sort of moral chastity belt.*

Oh, well. It's fine, from Chap V on, anyhow, in spite of that—which fact is merely a proof of its brilliance.

Station Z.W.X. square says good night. Good night all.

(1931)

HELEN VENDLER

A Reviewer's Beginnings

I was thirty-three, teaching English at Smith College, bringing up a five-year-old son, when the *Massachusetts Review* asked me to do an omnibus notice of the year's work in poetry. I would get a boxful of poetry books, could choose the ones to write on, and would be paid $100. The books were more of a lure than the fee; I had never had money enough to buy new books. (It was not until later that I learned that it was my Smith colleague Frank Murphy, who had been a fellow student with me in graduate school at Harvard, who had suggested me to the *Review.*) I disappeared into the box of books and wrote the piece that summer. Then I moved away, to teach at Boston University, and thought no more about reviewing.

Two years later, Walter Clemons, the poetry subeditor of the *New York Times Book Review,* was leaving the *Times.* But before he left, he was asking friends' advice about poetry reviewers who weren't poets, in the belief that not only poets should review poets. The editor Robert Stewart mentioned me to Clemons, and I was asked to send on samples of reviews I had written. I had precisely one—the omnibus piece written at Smith—and I sent it on, just before I left for Bordeaux to be a Fulbright Professor.

In Bordeaux, my son David and I lived on the top floor of a house owned by a Madame Hézard, a seventy-eight-year-old widow who still quoted prices running to the millions in prewar francs. The arrangement I had with her was that I could use the first-floor telephone in her bedroom at (urgent) need. The urgent need turned out to be the *Times* asking me to write about John Berryman's continuation of the *Dream Songs, His Toy, His Dream, His Rest*—full, then as now, of mysterious, odd, and exhilarating poems, only half of which I suppose I understood at the time. Though daunted, I was glad of the task, since it had turned out that the University of Bordeaux, because of the disruptive events of the previous June 1968, was delaying its opening, and I had, temporarily, no job, no students, no office, no library, and no colleagues. Every night, my son came home from his long French schoolday cross, tired, and near to tears, and I was always near to tears from prolonged loneliness. As I recall, the tears on both sides broke out often enough to resemble the steady rain that washed out the 1968 vintage and prohibited seeing the countryside on weekends. Berryman's despairing and exalted verses were a tonic to my mind, and I wrote about them with intense joy at their arrival in my bleak life. Even so, I was taken aback to see my words, surrounding a photograph of Berryman, appear on the front page of the *Book Review*. It seemed unwarranted. Who was I to occupy people's Sunday morning attention? Still, the extra money was another bright spot in the dreary autumn; and then the *Times* asked me to do another, and another.

I found I liked reviewing. It was so much like teaching that it seemed natural. (I came from a family of teachers, all stemming from our Union veteran great-grandfather, a public scribe in Boston who wrote letters for the illiterate; his daughter, my grandmother, was famous in the parish for her letters of condolence; and my teacher-mother, his granddaughter, wrote poems, too.) Besides, I thought— and still think—that all people would like poetry if they were only brought up with it and shown how easily it is entered into and what enormous solace it has to offer. In my thirties, I believed that a few words could open the door of poetry to everyone. Now I know, with a sinking heart, that most people need more; they need to have nursery rhymes and poems read to them at home, they need a genuine daily poem in every grade, daily choral recitation, daily choral singing, a good poem learned by heart every week. After twelve years of this, they would be poetry readers forever. None of this now happens. Still, there are libraries, and readings, and a few still find their way alone to poetry. It is an art that nobody, once possessing it, ever willingly relinquishes.

In my youthful evangelism, I longed to tell the world about the modern poets, and felt glad when I could. It was a very different feeling that came over me when the *Times* asked me to review Mary McCarthy's *Birds of America*. I was not at home in novels as I was in poems; but then I was not rich enough, or so I told myself, to pass up the fee. The book seemed to me trivial and ungripping, and I (politely) said so, but I was haunted by having reviewed at a level of less-than-competence, and told the *Times* no more novels. I've kept to that vow ever since. I've reviewed nonfiction and biographies, but never, never another novel— those peculiar works so furnished with salaries and elections, chairs and tables, diseases and engagements, moors and factories, bills and indentures. As though one had not enough of these things cluttering up one's own life—or so I still feel.

Voices, though—voices in rhythms—are another thing. "What if this present were the world's last night?" says a voice, and I am all ears. "In this blue light I can take you there," says another, and I am yearning itself, ready to go. When John Leonard left the *Times,* and Harvey Shapiro came in, he began to request from me reviews of books on various subjects by or about women; a wall had come down between me and poetry. I pointed out that my subject was not women and their lives, but poets and their poetry, but all in vain. I was dropped from the *Times*.

At about this time—1975 or so—Robert Silvers called to ask me to review for the *New York Review of Books*—but alas, it was a group of books on Pound he wanted written about. "I can't," I said, "I don't like Pound." Mr. Silvers, somewhat bemused, said he'd call me another time; he generously did, and I've been reviewing for him ever since. I enjoyed that lavish space after the tighter confines of the *Times,* which was sometimes offering only 800 words for two books of poetry when I last wrote for them.

In 1978, I was at work at Boston University when a call came in for me:

Mrs. Vendler?
Yes?
This is William Shawn.
Oh, yes.
Of *The New Yorker.*
Yes, of course.
Do you think you would like to review poetry for us?
Oh, yes.
Well, we'll be in touch.
Yes, thanks.

And that was that. Five yeses. It was easy to work for Mr. Shawn, who edited me very little, but it began badly: he gave me a book to review, I reviewed it, and he did a "pay-and-kill" because he thought the widow of the poet might be grieved at the review. "It's a *very* good review," Mr. Shawn said in his soft voice, "and it's *just* the sort of writing I'm glad to have, but in this case. . . ." That never happened again.

Little by little, the reviews mounted up, and the fees helped put my son successively through Putney, Santa Cruz, and Harvard. Along the way, the Harvard Press asked me to collect my essays and reviews, first once, then again. I was astonished that they added up to so many hundreds of pages each time, since each review by itself had seemed a brief task.

The irony to me of my work of the left hand, contemporary reviewing—done hastily, in spare hours, during terms when I was often teaching four different courses—is that it made me better known in the world than my "real" writing, the much harder work of thinking through the whole career of a poet like George Herbert and explaining it to myself over two or three hundred pages. Still, my books, I think, benefited from the practice reviewing gave me in explaining a fairly esoteric subject to a general audience.

I had had exceptionally gifted teachers of poetry—Sister Marie Barry at Emmanuel, Morton Berman at Boston University, I.A. Richards, John Kelleher, Rosemond Tuve, and Reuben Brower at Harvard—yet poetry seemed to tax me beyond what I had been taught. When I tried to "get inside" a poet and to get the poet, entire, inside me, I felt like the Little Prince's boa constrictor trying to swallow an elephant; I could sense within me a large, unwieldy shape called "Wallace Stevens" that I had to digest down to his very DNA. A Smith student once found me in tears at my library desk late one night; she apologized for the intrusion, thinking, I suppose, that my heart was broken, but I stammered that I just *couldn't* understand *what* Stevens meant in one stanza. No review has ever reduced me so, because reviews come only one volume at a time, and the labor is curtailed. To see Yeats or George Herbert whole is another kind of effort altogether, comparable, in my experience, only to the equally immense and even infinite task of trying to know one's parent or child.

Sometimes I was impatient of the financial need that pushed me into reviewing; I used to think that without that need I would have been happy to put in all my time writing books of more depth and substance. Now I wonder. Without reviewing, I would never have known contemporary poetry so well; journalism has been for me a continuing self-seminar in the work of my own century. Left to myself, I might have stayed with the incomparably beautiful past, with its rich familiarity from childhood. But I would have missed the new—not *reading* the new, since I took to the modern poets in high school, but *thinking* about the new.

The painfulness of reviewing books that seemed inept or ludicrous or mediocre is something I could not avoid when I needed the money.

But I found it almost impossible to say anything interesting: "This book has no compelling rhythms; this book has no volatility, no depth"—it was a catalogue of zeros. There is everything in the world to be said about the most minor bit of originality—a phrase from a letter of Keats, or a parenthesis in Pope—but the inexhaustibility of the good, so inviting to thought, has no counterpart in the bad. I often felt, before a bad book, like a talent scout for new opera singers, saying of a candidate, "No—no breath control, no phrasing, no interpretation, no tone color, no stage presence, no. . . ." It is not a gratifying sort of writing to do. And mediocre poetry literally offers nothing for the mind to investigate, to grapple with, to respond to. I avoid, now, reviewing verse I don't like. With an inept book of criticism, there are things to say— about information, logic, interpretation—but confronted with inept lines, I fall silent.

What I remember best about the experience of reviewing is the sharp tang of individual style tasted for the first time. There is no experience like it; new fashions are trivial beside it, new music has less charm for my untrained hearing, and new people are, on the whole, less individual in their being than new poets. I can't explain the power of these "bolts of melody" to stun, but it must have something to do with the hard-wiring of the brain. The older poets were always already known to me from long quotation by my mother; but when I was fifteen the first murmur of Eliot, the first lilt of Thomas, the first beat of Hopkins became my adolescent definition of shocking pleasure. The nearest I come to recapturing that fifteenth year is when I review a new poet. I'm not, by far, the best reader for many poets, and I've learned the limits of my taste; but there are other reviewers giving, I hope, other poets their due. My interests in poetry are aesthetic, linguistic, stylistic, and psychological. I have no head for either philosophy or history, and I actively dislike the tedious moralizing or ideological puffery that goes by the name of commentary on poetry. A commentary that leaves out style and structure leaves out everything worth talking about. The lack of interest in poetry on the part of American intellectuals leaves a vacuum in public discourse that some, I know, think I have attempted to fill too often. I would myself prefer that there be a chorus of reviewing voices "burdening every bough"—but until our culture values poetry, especially its own poetry, more, non-poet reviewers will be relatively thin on the literary ground. It's odd that my youthful keeping of the wolf from the door should be an ultimate cause for too much visibility (and, some say, too much power as a result).

Single motherhood made me a reviewer, and I'm oddly grateful; if I had had a husband to support me, or if I had not had a child, I might still be a quiet scholar curled up with Shakespeare's sonnets. As it is, I have Shakespeare and (at the moment) Charles Simic too. What I regret, now, is the books I wanted to write about but had to let go by for lack of time. I still feel guilty about those, and apologetic to their authors.

PAUL BOWLES

An Open Letter

(To Those Interested in Surviving the Coming Decade)

We are aware that this message is addressed to a tiny minority of people who, for one reason or another, prefer to continue their existence during the nineteen eighties. The democratic ideal, upon which the civilization of the twentieth century is widely believed to rest, demands that any minority, however small, be taken into consideration. The following suggestions are proffered with the aim of preventing unnecessary suffering.

For those who have already applied to Humanity International for their VQ Tabs (personal cyanide pellets) there is no problem, save perhaps for some who live in the rural areas of the more remote countries. Deliveries are being speeded up, however, and by April it is predicted that every citizen of every country which recognizes our organization can be provided with his own tablet, to be used at his discretion.

A word of warning (which is by no means a digression) is in order at this point. Recently the market has been flooded with a spate of inferior and dangerous brands of cyanide. (Zoffo, Suremort, Hallelujah, Adios and others). These products are definitely not approved by Humanity International, and we cannot advise too strongly against their use. Death has been known to take a full half-hour in the case of Adios, according to a report issued by the research laboratories at the Attu Branch of Humanity International in November 1979. Those interested in the ideal escape will not find a product equal to our approved VQ Tabs; they are buffered, with added salidehydrocyanurodesoxycholic acid. The only safe pellet, the only one guaranteeing instant relief. No coma, no pain. Our service is absolutely gratis, as we constantly attempt to make clear in our thousands of broadcasts carried out in sixty-three languages. Unfortunately, human nature being what it is, suspicion is always aroused by the distribution of gifts; people feel that something paid for must be superior to something handed out free of charge, and this suspicion has been exploited by several unscrupulous pharmaceutical companies eager to profit by the present popularity of cyanide.

Humanity International does *not*, as has been charged, "recommend" the use of its VQ Tabs; it simply supplies them to those who ask for them. The worldwide response to our offers speaks for itself. In order partially to offset the accusations that have been leveled at the organization, we seize this occasion to address ourselves to the minority, to those hardy individuals who have decided to make the attempt to get through the entire decade without medical assistance.

First let us consider sustenance. It goes without saying that luxuries such as meat, fish, poultry, milk, eggs, butter, sugar, fruit and vegetables will soon be unobtainable. The recently developed protein substitutes such as Protoproxy should be used in quantity. An entirely new attitude toward food must be adopted. The concepts of "edible" and "inedible" must be abandoned. Both are conditioned by preconceived ideas which are no longer applicable to reality. It has been proven, for instance, that cats, dogs and rats will not only sustain life indefinitely if eaten in sufficient quantity, but that truly excellent dishes can be prepared with them by the efficient housewife. With an eye to preserving the gourmet tradition during the coming years, Humanity International has issued three useful handbooks: *Fifty Tasty Kitty Recipes, Man's Best Friend and How to Cook Him* (with list of breeds and the culinary treatment appropriate to each breed) and *The Rat Comes Into Its Own* (with a special chapter on the preparation of mice). For the first time in history these readily available sources of food, formerly used only in extreme situations and totally without scientific supervision, have been studied assiduously by top-flight dieticians and chefs, whose expertise is now within reach of anyone who wishes to profit by it.

The kind of foodstuffs we enjoy today will be in increasingly short supply, due to lack of fuel for delivery. We must learn the science of harvesting and preserving all edible plants. Each year billions of tons of weeds go to waste and disintegrate into the soil, only to produce more unused weeds. This great natural reserve must be exploited. It is true that citizens of tropical countries will be likely to have greater access to food, but this advantage will be outweighed by the incidence of disease.

Money will not be a problem, since it will be entirely without purchasing power. In addition, the list of purchasable commodities will rapidly shrink to zero.

Living space, on the other hand, will present intolerable difficulties to those accustomed to personal privacy. Because of the geometric progression in population increase and the impossibility of constructing new dwellings or even repairing old ones, requisitioning of floor space will shortly be instituted. The target of fifteen cubic meters minimum to be allocated to each adult is admittedly utopian, at least during the coming decade. For the foreseeable future the figure will remain in the vicinity of ten cubic meters. Since people who previously enjoyed the use of an entire house or apartment will now be restricted to one corner of one room, a certain amount of dissatisfaction, even of confusion, can result. A few practical hints here may be useful.

There are ways of making your corner comfortable, even attractive. Cut out a large triangle of thick foam rubber (if you are unable to find any, bags of straw or shavings will do) and fit it into the corner of the floor. On top of that you can pile attractive rags and stuffed sacks. The walls behind can be covered with artistically chosen magazine covers or tasteful advertisements, varnished over. If you have time, you can cut them up first and make personalized collages. A screen to provide a modicum of privacy can be constructed out of old crates, and perhaps covered with wrapping paper to give it that soigné look demanded by today's housewife.

The idea that fresh air is essential to healthy sleep was discarded by medical experts fifty years ago. It has been proven that, on the contrary, the instinct of the human species is to burrow deep into a relatively airless spot when sleep is desired. Apart from the possibility of contagious diseases, it is just as healthy to sleep shut into a room with several others as it was to sleep in your own room with the window open. Actually this enforced communal living can prove to be a blessing. It serves as a deterrent to mass attacks on living quarters by bands of starving teenagers.

Survival in the eighties will require enormous adaptability to adverse physical circumstances. A new, functional life-style is waiting to be created, one which will take into account the future as well as the present rapid deterioration of the situation. This requires a high order of talent, but there will be those who will rise to the occasion. Reduced circumstances need not, and indeed, must not be allowed to result in shabbiness, which comes from a morbid clinging to concepts of style no longer realizable. We must learn that the only consideration of any importance in the matter of clothing is that it should provide the warmth essential to normal human functioning. As the seasons change, the number of garments will vary, and from this simple phenomenon we can evolve a style that will be the very essence of sartorial elegance.

Instead of the three sweaters, blanket and mittens of winter, we find that when spring comes, we may have only two sweaters and no blanket at all. It is from such small things that we create the poetry of a truly functional life-style. The greatest pleasure comes from the close inspection of ordinary objects, according to the poets. Those who choose to brave it out can reap spiritual profit, if they will, from this unique opportunity.

Your corner need not be in total darkness every night. You can make your own lamps out of rags soaked in vegetable oil, squeezed into interesting shapes and placed in oil-filled saucers. They give a dull, romantic glow. A welcome addition to gala occasions is a set of small alcohol burners to be used as hand-warmers. (Stock all the burning alcohol you can now; during a cold spell it has been known to make the difference between life and death.) The ideal garment for winter corner-sitting is a large woolen blanket with a slit in the center for the head. Your corner can be made cozy, and you can be comfortable in it. It is up to you to decide whether you want to make the effort.

We at Humanity International believe firmly that if it is worth-while living at all (and a few of those who read this will be of the opinion that it is), then it is also worthwhile to spend the effort necessary to transform what could otherwise be a humdrum existence into a meaningful life, a life of joy, created, not in spite of hardships, but thanks to them. This is Humanity International's New Year message to the courageous.

Remember: VQ Tabs are always yours for the asking.

Paul Bowles
Director of Public Relations
Humanity International

ED KOREN

Airborne Antæus

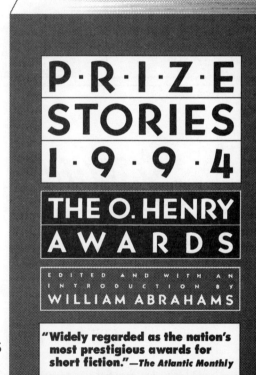

THE
NATIONAL
POETRY SERIES

ANNOUNCING THE 1995 COMPETITION
BOOK PUBLICATION & 1,000 AWARDS

T he National Poetry Series was established in 1978 to recognize and promote excellence in contemporary poetry by ensuring the publiction of five books of poetry each year through a series of participating publishers. This year, five distinguished poets will each select one winning manuscript for publication from entries to the Open Competition. Each winner will also receive a $1,000 Award.

Recent Judges: Charles Simic, C.K. Williams, W.S. Merwin, Denise Levertov, Sharon Olds, Margaret Atwood, James Merrill, Seamus Heaney, Louise Glück, Carolyn Forche, Robert Hass, Mary Oliver, Ann Lauterbach, Hayden Carruth, and Barbara Guest.

Entry Period: January 1 - February 15, 1995

Entry Requirements: Previously unpublished book-length manuscripts of poetry accompanied by a $25.00 entrance fee. You must be an American citizen to participate. Due to the large volume of submissions received, manuscripts cannot be returned.

FOR A COPY OF THE COMPLETE GUIDELINES,

PLEASE SEND A STAMPED, SELF-ADDRESSED ENVELOPE TO:

THE NATIONAL POETRY SERIES
P.O. BOX G
HOPEWELL, N.J. 08525

Unterberg Poetry Center
OF THE 92ND STREET Y

E. L. Doctorow

Yusef Komunyakaa

Nadine Gordimer

Since its founding in 1939, The Unterberg Poetry Center's mission has been to present the best contemporary literature in all of its many voices and forms. We invite you to join us as we continue this mission in our fifty-sixth season. Readings are followed by a wine reception and book-signing.

Authors reading this season include (in order of appearance) --

AMERICAN WRITERS

E.L. Doctorow, Sam Shepard, Mary Jo Salter, Mark Strand, Garrison Keillor, Edward Albee, Linda Gregg, William H. Gass, William Gaddis, Cyrus Cassells, Martín Espada, Marilyn Hacker, Tony Kushner, Elizabeth Tallent, James Welch, Yusef Komunyakaa, William Matthews, Sandra Cisneros, Grace Paley, E. Annie Proulx, Jane Smiley, Anne Waldman, Jay Wright, Carolyn Kizer, Ursula K. LeGuin

INTERNATIONAL WRITERS

Alice Munro,Carol Shields, Sir Stephen Spender, Doris Lessing, Nadine Gordimer, Hugo Claus, Cees Nooteboom, Caryl Churchill, Robertson Davies, Pawel Huelle, Ivan Klíma, Octavio Paz

SPECIAL PROGRAMS

History and Fiction with Daniel Aaron, Russell Banks, Shelby Foote, George Garrett, Allan Gurganus, Charles Johnson, Thomas Keneally, Patrick O'Brian, Marilynne Robinson, Simon Schama, Mary Lee Settle and Madison Smartt Bell

Women in Mind: New Musical Melodramas with Claire Bloom and Brian Zeger

After Ovid: New *Metamorphoses* with Eavan Boland, Amy Clampitt, Alice Fulton, Jorie Graham, Kenneth Koch, Michael Longley, Derek Mahon, Paul Muldoon, Robert Pinsky, C.K. Williams and others

A Martin Luther King Day Gathering of Poets

At $125, a Poetry Center Membership entitles you to attend all these events, running October through May, and much more, including a 20% discount on authors' books, a 25% discount on one single ticket per event, and a subscription to The Poetry Center's Newsletter. The Unterberg Poetry Center also offers an extensive Writing Program and a Sunday lecture series, "Biographers and Brunch."

Call **996-1100** for a brochure or to order your tickets.   P57

92Y St

CELEBRATING
LIFE AT
120

The Unterberg Poetry Center of the 92nd Street Y • 1395 Lexington Ave NYC 10128 • An agency of UJA-Federation.